THE
BLEEDING
Stories of Bengal Partition
BORDER

THE BLEEDING BORDER
Stories of Bengal Partition

Edited by
Joyjit Ghosh and Mir Ahammad Ali

NIYOGI BOOKS

Primarily translated from *Deshbhager Galpa: Rakta, Bedona O Smritir Alekhya*, originally published in Bengali by Gangchil, Kolkata, in 2016.

Published by
NIYOGI BOOKS
Block D, Building No. 77,
Okhla Industrial Area, Phase-I,
New Delhi-110 020, INDIA
Tel: 91-11-26816301, 26818960
Email: niyogibooks@gmail.com
Website: www.niyogibooksindia.com

Text & translation © Joyjit Ghosh & Mir Ahammad Ali

Editor: Arkaprabha Biswas
Design: Nadeem Ahmed
Cover Design: Pinaki De

ISBN: 978-93-91125-01-1
Publication: 2022

This is a work of fiction. The names, characters and incidents portrayed in it are the work of the author's imagination. Any resemblance to actual persons, living or dead, events or localities, is entirely coincidental.

All rights are reserved. No part of this publication may be reproduced or transmitted in any form or by any means, electronic or mechanical, including photocopying, recording or by any information storage and retrieval system without prior written permission and consent of the Publisher.

Printed at: Niyogi Offset Pvt. Ltd., New Delhi, India

❝The European holocaust in the 1940s was followed by a huge mass of research by psychologists, psychiatrists and psychoanalysts studying the killers, victims and survivors. This research not only influenced research on other genocides, but also enriched literary works on the subject. The genocide that accompanied the partitioning of British India did not trigger such research, despite the presence of well-trained psychologists, psychiatrists and psychoanalysts in the region. For some reason, they maintained an unnatural silence. The few who touched the subject, did so coyly. That silence was only broken by a few gifted, feisty writers who documented the psychopathic nature of the violence bypassing the professional psychologists. Two generations later, in the 1990s, a new group of young researchers, mostly women, once again smudged the border between social research and literature and, simultaneously, challenged the tyranny of the political borders dividing the intellectual and literary cultures of South Asia. This collection of Partition stories is an excellent byproduct of that movement. It will remain one of finest reminders of the psychopathic violence of which we are capable.

—Ashis Nandy, Political Psychologist and Social Theorist

Contents

Editors' Note — 9

Introduction — 13

STORIES

Acharya Kripalani Colony — 29
Bibhutibhusan Bandyopadhyay

The Public Hero — 40
Satinath Bhaduri

The Tale of a Tulsi Plant — 72
Syed Waliullah

When the River Rebukes — 82
Satyapriya Ghosh

The Guardian Deity — 93
Dinesh Chandra Ray

Jatayu — 114
Dipendranath Bandyopadhyay

Batashi: The Wild Breeze — 130
Atin Bandyopadhyay

The Bait of a Dice — 150
Jyotsnamoy Ghosh

The Refugee — 176
Debesh Ray

Homeland — 202
Asish Sanyal

The Exile — 211
Hasan Azizul Huq

Hearth and Home *Jiban Sarkar*	229
The Lady and the Red Rose *Sadhan Chattopadhyay*	243
Ends of a Broken Bridge *Jatin Bala*	299
Homecoming *Sailen Sarkar*	318
Border *Devi Prasad Sinha*	338
Photograph *Adhir Biswas*	358
The Other Jews *Kapil Krishna Thakur*	370
Soil *Anil Ghosh*	387
Address *Goutam Aalee*	406
One Land *Amit Mukhopadhyay*	412
Between the Borders *Sohrab Hossain*	420
Therefore, a Border Tale *Niharul Islam*	446
A Mother Divided *Ahana Biswas*	456
Authors	*484*
Glossary	*492*
Acknowledgements	*501*

Editors' Note

The idea of an anthology of Bengal Partition stories in English translation was conceived in a conversation with Sri Sadhan Chattopadhyay, the editor of *Deshbhager Galpa: Rakta, Bedona O Smritir Alekhya*, over a cup of tea in an international seminar on Partition and the Bangladesh Liberation War in Kolkata in 2018.

Immediately after the seminar, we started searching for the existing volumes of partition stories from the two sides of Bengal, available in English translation, and found a couple of collections to our profit and pleasure. In a way, they are milestones too. But the absence of representation of writings from the margins in these volumes fairly surprised us. We at once decided that our anthology would include stories by the mainstream as well as the marginal authors. By including the stories written by the marginal/Dalit authors, we like to bring home the point that partition literature can never be monolithic and there is always a space for an alternative discourse. Therefore, the canonical partition stories like 'Acharya Kripalani Colony', 'The Public Hero', 'The Tale of a Tulsi Plant', respectively by Bibhutibhusan Bandyopadhyay, Satinath Bhaduri and Syed Waliullah, find their place in this anthology along with the lesser-known but poignant stories like 'Ends of a Broken Bridge, by Jatin Bala, 'Address' by Goutam Aalee and 'Therefore, a Border Tale' by Niharul Islam. There is also a representative partition story from the north-east titled 'Border' by Devi Prasad Sinha. In fine, the present anthology takes a humble attempt to be eclectic in its approach and reach out to those who are keen on exploring the tragedy of Partition through the prism of Bengali fiction in English translation. We would also like to point out that most of the stories included in this volume have, for the first time, been translated into English.

Translating a text from the source language into the target language is always a challenging task. But there is a scope for happiness associated with the act of translation. At this point, one may recall the words of Paul Ricoeur: 'The happiness associated with translating is a gain when, tied to the loss of the linguistic absolute, it acknowledges the difference between adequacy and equivalence, equivalence without adequacy'. The translators of the present volume acknowledge this 'difference' but they have tried their best to remain as close as possible to the texts in the original. The titles of certain stories like 'Kulapati', 'Janmabhumi', 'Nadir Bhortsona', 'Parabasi' among others, with their socio-cultural connotations in the source-language texts, initially posed a challenge to the translators; however, our translators have resisted the temptation of making a literal rendering of the same and tried to reach out to the target audience by providing titles with which the non-native readers can identify. Thus, 'Kulapati' has been translated as 'The Guardian Deity' and 'Parabasi' as 'The Exile'. The culture-specific terms and intertextual references have in most cases been italicised in the body of a text along with English rendering within the parenthesis. Apart from that, a glossary is appended at the end; it contains notes on partition-related incidents, mythological allusions, ritualistic practices and very regional terms. The bio-notes of the authors at the end of the volume are indeed brief, but let us hope, they will interest the readers across South Asia and beyond.

Introduction

It was a thinking day. We were reading Sujata Bhatt, our eternal favourite, and enjoying the magic of her poetry where the real and the surreal often marvelously blend. All on a sudden, her poem titled 'Partition' drew our notice. We read the poem time and again, particularly its concluding lines, 'How could they/have let a man/who knew nothing/about geography/divide a country?'.[1] The question continued to haunt us, and we believe, it haunts many like us even today, after more than seventy years of the Partition. The irony is, the 'man'—Cyril Radcliffe—whose fateful line of demarcation divided the Indian territory into a 'Hindu' India and a 'Muslim' Pakistan, had never before been to India[2], nor had he the necessary skills for drawing a decisive border[3]. But it was he who emerged as the *destiny* in the history of Partition that involved gruesome sectarian violence, persecution of minorities and wide-scale migration whose legacies (unfortunately) are visible even to this day. People coming from socio-economically disadvantaged background in particular had to face the heterogeneous forms of atrocities that included arson, murder, child abuse, rape, pillage and uprooting. The history of Partition, in fact, is not only huge but immensely complicated as well. But there is no scope to dwell on this history at this point. Our prime objective here is to explore how the partition narratives deal with the discontents of Bengal Partition and represent the trauma of countless masses who lost their homes and became rootless when the Bengal borderland was created with suddenness.[4]

The Bengal border, to borrow a poignant expression from Bashabi Frazer's poem 'This Border', indeed 'cuts like a knife/Through the waters of our life',[5] and it bleeds still. Its wounds are hidden in the nerve cells of those victims who are alive, and its pain is often transferred from one generation to another—gradually establishing a redefined map. The Partition in 1947, therefore, is not an isolated incident. It surpasses a fixed temporal frame and speaks of a conscious present that continues to plague people on both sides of the border.

It is often said that Bengal Partition in comparison with that on the western border of India has not received much literary attention. Some even go to the extent of saying that celebrated Bengali writers more or less remained 'silent' regarding this cataclysmic issue. Thus, 'Partition Literature' has become almost synonymous with the writings of Saadat Hasan Manto, Krishan Chander, Bhisham Sahni, Ismat Chughtai, Intizar Hussain, Joginder Paul and others, and we often tend to ignore the contribution of the authors from the eastern and north-eastern parts of the country and Bangladesh.[6]

This obviously speaks of a politics in the formation of canon particularly when it is evident that Bengal Partition fiction is no less powerful and appealing than its western counterpart. One may think of short stories and novels by the authors like Jyotirmoyee Devi, Pratibha Basu, Ramesh Chandra Sen, Satinath Bhaduri, Manik Bandyopadhyay, Narendranath Mitra, Sunil Gangopadhyay, Atin Bandyopadhyay, Shirshendu Mukhopadhyay, Prafulla Roy, Debesh Ray, Sadhan Chattopadhyay, Amar Mitra, among others, from this side of Bengal, and Syed Waliuallah, Hasan Azizul Huq, Rizia Rahman, Selina Hossain, Akhteruzzaman Elias from that side, which is Bangladesh. The list of authors of Bengal Partition literature is not only huge in its corpus but immensely relevant in the socio-political context of the present day.

The stories of the present anthology include some of the most striking and dominant themes of the Bengal Partition and its aftermath. One major theme is obviously the ceaseless movement of rootless masses in search of safe shelter in an ambience of generalised violence. Dinesh Chandra Ray's 'The Guardian Deity' depicts the journey of refugees (on the road, through the forests and even crossing the river) in the direction of Hindustan when communal riots began. The protagonist of the story thus narrates her own experience: 'There was a journey of three days and three nights ahead of me... There were robbers at the street-corners hiding in darkness. Yet I was taking myself forward safely; there was some sort of a valour in it.' The experience of the narrator is therefore represented in a positive light because once she is on her way, she is free from her past which was almost synonymous to the strict rules imposed on her by her father-in-law in the name of the service of the deity. But this kind of depiction of a journey is very rare in partition stories. Border-crossing is almost always portrayed as a terribly painful and wearisome experience in these narratives. One may remember the agonised experience of Rajab Ali, the central character of Devi Prasad Sinha's 'Border': '…that is the border. So impossibly long, impenetrable has become this little path—as if someone is pulling a piece of rubber continuously from both the ends—no matter how much he runs, the path goes for eternity.' This represents 'the territorial and human consequences of a border', to echo the words of William Van Schendel.[7]

Thus, the Bengal border, as depicted in partition stories, is often huge as well as 'impossibly long'. But there is an ironic dimension to the border as well: the border is porous[8] and fragile—fragile like the body of Fazila in Sohrab Hossain's 'Between the Borders', who knows that women like her have to yield now and then to the ugly desires of professional touts or the BSF, or the BDR: 'They had come to accept these professional hazards for the sake of livelihood, and to keep base life afloat for their children. They knew that it was necessary to extend such favours if their bundles were to cross borders.' A woman's body at the border is therefore cheap like her knapsacks.

In their Introduction to *The Trauma and the Triumph: Gender and Partition in Eastern India*, Jashodhara Bagchi and Subhoranjan Dasgupta observe that in both the divided states of Punjab and Bengal, 'women (minors included) were targeted as the prime object of persecution. Along with the loss of home, native land and dear ones, the women, in particular, were subjected to defilement (rape) before death, or defilement and abandonment, or defilement and compulsion that followed to raise a new home with a new man belonging to the oppressor-community.'[9] This statement is based on historical truth. Urvashi Butalia's *The Other Side of Silence: Voices from the Partition of India* (2000) and Joya Chatterje's *The Spoils of Partition: Bengal and India 1947-1967* (2007) bear testimony to it. Regarding the fictional representation of the 'spoils of partition' we would like to refer to two stories: Hasan Azizul Huq's 'The Exile' and Ahana Biswas's 'A Mother Divided' . In the first story, the portrayal of violence is gruesome. The reader may remember that section of the narrative where Bashir wildly runs to rescue his near and dear ones from the clutches of the criminals but to no avail:

The house has already been gutted to nothingness. They are gone. Bashir's seven-year-old son, pierced and stuck to the earth by a spear and the body of a twenty-six-year-old woman, looking like a black, burnt piece of wood, were there in the ruined gutted house. The air was heavy with the foul smell of raw flesh burning.

So, the story shows that the perpetrators of violence targeted mainly women and children, although old fellows like Wazddi could not escape from their bloody grip either. The portrayal of communal violence in the narrative sends a chill down our spine.

'A Mother Divided' is a cruel story of 'defilement' of a Hindu woman at the hands of ruffians in the backdrop of Noakhali riot followed by the 'abandonment' of the woman by her husband. The story, however, goes beyond the set pattern and shows that a man 'belonging to the oppressor-community' rescues the woman when she is on the verge of committing suicide. The new man gives the woman shelter and protection. But the scar of trauma is not healed up. It surfaces when she sees her son and daughter-in-law after a long while. She cries out, 'I feel scared... I am terribly frightened of menfolk'.

Bengal Partition stories sometimes represent the horrible aspect of gendered violence. A clear example is 'Jatayu' where Durga, a victim of communal riot, narrates her traumatic experience through a kind of stream of consciousness technique: 'And when the sky was smitten with the sound of azan they took me out in the field, laid me there on the ground in the light of the burning house. My mother was laid by my side. And a hand started to squeeze my breasts.' This 'hand' becomes an unidentifiable source of fear and continues to haunt the psyche of this woman and makes her restless. While speaking of different forms of violence that accompanied Partition, Meghna Guha Thakurta writes, 'What is crucial to note is that violence also typifies a state where a sense of fear is generated and perpetrated in such a way as to make it systematic, pervasive and inevitable.'[10] This is exactly what happens here because the 'hand' leaves no moment of peace for Durga. She feels, ...'there is no escape for me. Slowly a hand will raise its finger, point at me and tell she is here; it is that woman.'

Violence, however, is not a major dimension of the human experiences in Bengal Partition stories as it is in the stories from Punjab. Stories from Bengal are 'relatively free from violence in its crude form'.[11] But these stories, on the other hand, articulate the idiom of 'a loss of a world'[12]—a world in which Hindus and Muslims lived in amity and harmony over generations. Partition shattered the fabric of peace and unity overnight, 'signifying the death of the social', to use a telling expression of Dipesh Chakrabarty. It is just 'inexplicable' and bewildering how 'neighbours turned against neighbours, friends took up arms against friends'.[13] Jyotsnamoy Ghosh's 'The Bait of a Dice' poignantly portrays this 'inexplicable' situation involving the sudden breakdown of communal harmony. But the story is open-ended and its ending seems to contain a positive note. Bula, the victim of 'Partitioned Bengal' (to echo the original title of the story), does not lose self-confidence when she is deserted by her parents. She writes to her mother from a spot 'where the borders of the two countries have merged', that she has 'an invitation from a loving heart'—from Firoj—to go back to him when she has none to look forward to, and she believes that she will have 'the strength to respond to that invitation someday'. Bula, therefore, attempts to triumph over her trauma by her resilience.

But the partition victims, as the narratives from Bengal unfold, sometimes fail to keep their resilience intact when they are subjected to 'uprooting'. Jayanti Basu describes this 'uprooting' as 'soft violence', distinct from 'raw violence' including 'bloodshed, abduction, arson and looting' which was 'more rampant on the western frontier of the country'.[14] She states that 'the study of soft violence holds a special place in the complete understanding of politically induced trauma.[15] There is no denying that the partition victims often suffered from this 'politically induced' trauma when they were placed overnight on the wrong side of the border. They became 'refugees'; they became the 'other'. Kapil Krishna Thakur's 'The Other Jews' is a classic case in point. Bishtucharan, who was respected as a 'pandit' in his village in East Bengal, had to leave his own place along with his young daughter Runu when his elder daughter Jhunu was raped and killed one night by the ruffians. He started selling food items on the local trains and Runu engaged herself in stitching sleeves onto blouses along with the sister of Braja who gave him shelter. But their struggle for survival was brought to an ignoble end when one night all the young girls including Runu were picked up by the criminals. Thus, the portrayal of the border line between 'soft violence' and 'raw violence' in the narrative becomes thin. The ending of the story is almost cathartic as Bishtucharan's agonised question 'Which is my land?' echoes the uncertainty of hundreds and thousands of 'refugees' and migrants whose fate was shaped by the illogical cartographic boundaries drawn during the Partition.

The search for 'land', for *desh* (motherland), as signified by the titles of some stories included in the present volume ('Soil', 'Homeland', 'Hearth and Home'), takes various forms. The story entitled 'Soil', for example, shows how desperate the uprooted people are in preserving the memory of the village which they had left long ago by requesting others to send a photograph of their birthplace! Adhir Biswas's 'Photograph' is another powerful story that may come to one's mind in this context:

> I very clearly remember: mother was seated in a chair in front of the space where the husking-pedal was kept. Mother wore a katki sari and had a deep red vermilion dot on her forehead. The mild winter sun made mother blink. Chhorda and I were holding a cloth, hiding bundles of jute plank stalls, sacks containing cow-dung cakes and heaps of leaves of bamboo-plants and jackfruit trees. Nabakumar kept his camera on a stand and shouted 'one, two, three' from under a cloth-cover.

This photograph is an object of 'material memory'[16] associated with the place of birth, the village that the narrator left long ago. The past cannot be retrieved; it can only be recalled. The photograph helps in the act of remembrance. Partition as such is not directly referred to in the story but a sensitive reader will certainly feel the pain of partition hidden in the deeper layers of the text.

In 'The Partition of Bengal and of Assam', Debjani Sengupta draws our attention to an interesting aspect of

Bengal Partition stories. The argument of Sengupta is that even when the reference to Partition is 'indirect', the stories 'explore the "close link between the narrative form and historical knowledge."'[17] The observation is indeed insightful. And it is well borne out by an analysis of the story by Sadhan Chattopadhyay 'The Lady and the Red Rose'. The story, to a great extent, fits into the form of a bildungsroman and charts out a journey of the protagonist's self through the history of the fateful partition. The 'historical knowledge' that the story draws our attention to is 'the failure of the Cabinet Mission' which, along with other crucial socio-political factors, made the partition inevitable. And the story towards its end raises a debate whether this 'failure' has anything to do with the 'relation' between Nehru and Lady Mountbatten.[18] Interestingly, the story does not force any rigid conclusion nor does it explain any happening which might have its historical significance. Rather it keeps its ending open to further debate and discussion in this regard. One may be reminded of Dipesh Chakrabarty's remark, 'What cannot be explained belongs to the marginalia of history—accidents, coincidences, and concurrences that, while important to the narrative, can never replace the structure of causes for which the historian searches'.[19] Thus, 'The Lady and the Red Rose' is not just a historical narrative but its appeal lies in its wonderful engagement with the 'marginalia of history'.

The interface between 'history' and 'memory' is another engaging theme of Bengal Partition literature. There is a debate revolving around the issue whether one should attach much importance to memory in connection with the history of Partition because memory is often selective. But it is argued on the other hand that memory is an archive.[20] While speaking on historical criticism, Ranabir Samaddar in his essay titled 'The Historiographical Operation: Memory and History' states that it 'produces actions, which transgresses limits produced by memory and creates new "present" times and conditions', and adds that it 'offers us new insights into what Pierre Nora calls the "strange places of memory".' In this context, one may remember Satyapriya Ghosh's 'When the River Rebukes', where a river tries to revive all the memories of a partition victim who visits Banaripara, his ancestral village, after a long time. Banaripara becomes a focal point in the narrative. And the river, in the role of a chronicler of socio-political history, narrates how the village bears witness to some of the most significant historical moments including the mass resistance to the Partition of Bengal in 1905. Obviously, recollection plays an important role in the narration. The river exhorts the son of the soil to 'recollect' everything associated with the history of the place including the recovery of her name after it was 'written in the map of Barishal district.' In other words, the river, with the help of 'historical criticism', offers 'new insights' into Banaripara. Following Samaddar one may ask: Is Banaripara merely 'a locality'? Is it 'an archive built in mind'? Is it the 'nation'?[21] These unavoidable questions defy definite answers but they engage the readers of partition literature in a meaningful dialogue between history and memory.

The stories included in the present anthology are representative of Bengal Partition fiction in their reflection of the unmitigated tension and anxiety at the border between West Bengal and Bangladesh; the exodus of the 'refugees' (particularly the Hindus of East Pakistan) at different points of time and their struggle for survival in different spaces, particularly Calcutta (Kolkata) and its surrounding areas; the travails of uprooted people caught in a 'no man's land' before they reach their destination; the 'communal riots' or 'inter-community violence'[22] from time to time; and the nostalgia for the soil, among other things. The stories under concern are not a part of the grand narrative of Partition, rather they constitute micro-narratives of agony and affliction of millions of people belonging to underprivileged classes of society, who, like the protagonist of Goutam Aalee's 'Address', are victims of a cruel and irresponsible political decision when the partition of the country was thrust upon them all on a sudden. But these narratives are not entirely tragic in tone; sometimes they passionately affirm that the 'country may have been partitioned but earth, air, water and mind—these cannot be partitioned'.[23] This very affirmation adds a positive edge to the Bengal Partition stories.

One may in this context speak of another interesting dimension of these stories: they voice a longing that may remind a reader of a few poignant lines in Matthew Arnold's 'To Marguerite': 'For surely once, they feel, we were / Parts of a single continent! / Now round us spreads the watery plain–/ Oh might our marges meet again!'[24] These lines throw an interesting light on the concluding section of Amit Mukhopadhyay's 'One Bengal' that mirrors the desire of people for uniting the two parts of Bengal through writings, movies and songs. The story thus addresses the theme of cultural exchange between two countries that may help us triumph over fundamentalist and other divisive forces.

Bengal Partition literature, therefore, offers more than a stereotypical discourse. It has a tremendous sense of contemporaneity and it addresses various issues with which the readers of the present day may immediately identify. We will consider our efforts fruitful if readers across generations could relate to these stories whether in their private sphere or in the realm of a collective consciousness.

Endnotes

1. See the poem in *Sujata Bhatt: Collected Poems*. Manchester: Carcanet, 2013, p.315.

2. Jenni Ramone, *Postcolonial Theories*. Palgrave Macmillan, 2017. P. 59.

3. Yasmin Khan, *The Great Partition: The Making of India and Pakistan*, New Haven and London: Yale UP, 2007, p. 105.

4. William van Schendel, *The Bengal Borderland: Beyond State and Nation in South Asia*, London: Anthem Press, 2005, p. 2.

5. The poem is included in *Bengal Partition Stories: An Unclosed Chapter*, ed. Bashabi Frazer, London & New York: Anthem Press, 2008, pp. 593–94.

6. One may this connection refer to the section on 'Partition in literature' in *Postcolonial Theories* by Jenni Ramone, Palgrave, Macmillan, 2011; there is not a single reference to Bengal fiction in this section. pp. 61–66.

7. *In The Bengal Borderland: Beyond State and Nation in South Asia* (2005) Schendel writes that the border separating India, East Pakistan (Bengaldesh from 1971) and Burma was 'a huge territorial gash of over 4,000 kilometres' p. 2.

8. Sadhan Chattopadhyay in his well-informed Introduction ('Notun Juger Bhore') to *Deshbhager Galpa: Rakta, Bedona O Smritir Alekhya*, (Kolkata: Gangchil, 2016)

draws our attention to the fact that the border of West Bengal is still alive, porous and mysterious, and partition literature is being written on this border even today across generations (p.14).

9. See the Introduction to *The Trauma and the Triumph: Gender and Partition in Eastern India*, ed. Jashodhara Bagchi and Subhoranjan Dasgupta, p. 3.

10. Meghna Guha Thakurta, 'Uprooted and Divided', in *The Trauma and the Triumph: Gender and Partition in Eastern India*, ed. Jashodhara Bagchi and Subhoranjan Dasgupta, p. 99.

11. Bidyut Chakrabarty, *The Partition of Bengal and Assam, 1932-1947: The Contour of Freedom*, London: Routledge Curzon, 2004, pp. 226-31.

12. Debjani Sengupta in 'The Partition of Bengal and of Assam (1947)' writes, Madness is not a 'trope' in the Bengal stories ... Instead of a pathological experience, partition is seen as a cosmological occurrence, a loss of a world rather than a loss related to prestige. See *Partition Literature: An Anthology*, ed. Debjani Sengupta, New Delhi: Worldview Publications, 2018, p.175.

13. Dipesh Chakrabarty, 'Memories of Displacement: The Poetry and Prejudice of Dwelling', *Habitations of Modernity: Essays* in the *Wake of Subaltern Studies*, with a Foreword by Homi K. Bhabha, Delhi: permanent black, 2002, p.117.

14. Jayanti Basu, *Reconstructing the Bengal Partition: The Psyche under a different violence*, Kolkata: Samya, 2013, p. 4.

15. Jayanti Basu, Reconstructing the Bengal Partition, p. 208.

16. The expression 'material memory' is borrowed from the title of Aanchal Malhotra's *Remnants of a Separation: A History of the Partition Through Material Memory*, Noida: Harper Collins, 2017.

17. Debjani Sengupta, 'The Partition of Bengal and of Assam (1947)', p.175.

18. The relationship between Nehru and Edwina Mountbatten has been a matter of much controversy and recently with the publication of the book, *Daughter of Empire: My Life as a Mountbatten* (Simon & Schuster, 2013) by Mountbattens' youngest daughter, Pamela Hicks, the controversy surfaces once again: 'In later years, reading Panditji's inner thoughts and feelings in his letters to my mother, I came to realise how deeply he and my mother loved and respected each other. I had been curious as to whether or not their affair had been sexual in nature; having read the letters, I was utterly convinced it hadn't been. Quite apart from the fact that neither my mother nor Panditji had time to indulge in a physical affair, they

were rarely alone. They were always surrounded by staff, police, and other people, and as my father's ADC, Freddie Burnaby Atkins, told me later, it would have been impossible for them to have been having an affair, such was the very public nature of their lives'. (Chapter 13, p. 160).

One may also visit https://www.tribuneindia.com/2010/20100410/saturday/main1.htm.

19. Dipesh Chakrabarty, 'Memories of Displacement: The Poetry and Prejudice of Dwelling', p.117.

20. This refers to an interview by Dipesh Chakrabarty. It is quoted and discussed in the essay titled 'Itihaase Parigraha: Deshbhager Smritikatha' by Biswajit Roy in *Deshbhag: Smriti Aar Sbodhota*, ed. Semanti Ghosh, (Kolkata: Gangchil, 2008), pp. 232-33.

21. See the essay in the *Economic and Political Weekly*, Vol. 41, No. 22 (June 3-9, 2006), pp. 2236-2240. Stable URL: http:///www. jstor.org/stable/4418297. Accessed on 23.03.20.

22. Priyambada Gopal, *The Indian English Novel: Nation, History and Narration*, Oxford UP, 2009, p.69.

23. This is a quotation from the story 'Soil' (*Mati*) by Anil Ghosh.

24. The poem is available in *The Golden Treasury of the Best Songs and Lyrical poems in the English Language*, selected and arranged by Francis Turner Palgrave with an Introduction and additional poems selected and arranged by C. Day Lewis, London: Collins, 1987, pp. 405-06.

Acharya Kripalani Colony

Bibhutibhusan Bandyopadhyay

My wife was nagging me relentlessly. Our home was in East Bengal. If we didn't buy a piece of land in West Bengal right off, would one be available later on? We didn't have the money to buy a house or a land in proper Calcutta but after 15 August, would we at all get a piece of land in the close vicinity of the city either? Whatever was to be done had to be done right away.

As a result, I started my land-hunting in every direction—Dum Dum, Ichhapur, Kashipur, Khardaha, Dhakuria and the like. The daily newspaper was full of advertisements of plots being bought and sold. House and land owners had lost no time in grabbing the opportunity of taking advantage of the helpless and bewildered state of the terrified Hindus who came away from East Bengal. A piece of land that would not sell for Rs 50 a *bigha* was being sold at the rate of Rs 700–800 per *katha*.

I was gradually growing exasperated in this never-ending scouting.

The price of land, close to Calcutta, had shot incredibly up; and we could not afford buying land at those places either. And even if we had the money, where were the plots of our choice?

Meanwhile, my wife brought a paper to me and said, 'You don't seem to like any of the plots. You are very choosy! If you want it right, do it yourself. What if there's no scenery? You don't like this, you don't like that! Will you ever be able to buy a plot at all? Get going and see this plot. Looks like it's very good, just what you're looking for. Read it.'

Whatever my wife might think, I was not sitting idle. I was searching in earnest, with heart and soul. And none would be happier than me if I could clinch something truly nice.

I asked, 'Where did you get this paper from?'

'I went to Beena's place. They are also in search of a plot. Many of their distant relatives too are migrating to this place, in the close vicinity of Calcutta. They collected it from somewhere.'

I started reading:

ACHARYA KRIPALANI COLONY

Come today! Get your name registered!!!

Only a few miles away from Calcutta, close to the station on a vast area, this mighty township is developing. Beautiful natural landscape. The bottom of the colony is washed by the sacred waves of the crystal-watered Ganga. 50 ft-wide thoroughfare, electric light, tap water, school, library and all the pleasures and amenities of urban life are available here. Send only Rs 50 to get your name registered.

The name of the place suggested it to be close to Calcutta indeed.

My wife said, 'Have you read it? Doesn't it sound good?'

'At a glance, looks good. Has Beena's uncle bought a plot here?'

'No, but he will. He's already got his name registered. Talk to him and send Rs 50. You'll have to send Rs 50 per *katha*. Send the money first, you can see the plot later. Even he hasn't seen it yet.'

'Shouldn't I see the land first? Alright, let me talk to him.'

Beena's uncle was Chintaharan Chakraborty. He had always been in service away from home, never built a house anywhere and therefore, was highly interested in landed property. Earlier he thought of building a house in Calcutta, but recently forsook that hope.

Chintahran *Babu* said, 'Please come. Did you see the pamphlet? It appears to be good.'

'Don't you think it's a little too far?'

'Where will you get anything closer than that?'

'That's true. It is supposedly close to the station, on the bank of the Ganga.'

'It's still cheap, but won't be even so after a few days. Electric light, water connection, 50 ft-wide road—'

'Did you send the money?'

'Of course! Got the receipt too. If you decide to buy it, send the money.'

'Even without seeing the land?'

'Look here! Get your name registered now, you'll lose

the chance later. The address is—New National Land Trust, Rajibnagar.'

My wife was happy to see the receipt in my name. She said, 'It's Rs 50 per *katha*; how much did you send, only for two *kathas*?'

'Yes, for the time being. Let 15 August pass by. Let the decision of the Boundary Commission come out. Can arrange something afterwards.'

The long-awaited 15 August passed by. The verdict of the Boundary Commission did not come out. My wife said, 'Why don't you go and see that plot? Take Beena's uncle along—people are pouring in from Mymensingh, Pabna, Noakhali. The flats of our neighbouring building are overcrowded. Three to four families are taking shelter in each family home.'

'But why? There's no trouble anywhere.'

'How should I know? And who shall I ask? Even at Beena's place, her cousin and her grandfather's younger brother have arrived with their children.'

It was not a bad idea. As I got my name registered, it was a sure investment. I should visit the colony now before deciding whether to buy a few more *kathas* or not.

Beena's uncle stormed into my room in the evening. I said, 'What is it? Why are you in such a tearing hurry?'

'Buy it, buy it. Not even a little bit of land will be available later. Thousands of refugees are pouring in from East Bengal. My house is already full. Whatever land you want to buy, you should buy it now.'

'What are you saying!'

'I'm speaking the truth. Let's go tomorrow and visit the colony. Afterwards buy some more plots there. They haven't as yet disclosed the rate of the plots. We will ask that too—'

'And their office?'

'Rajibnagar, near Konnagar.'

But the next day, I had to go alone. Beena's uncle could not come with me, as two more families arrived at his place the next day and he fell busy with them.

As I got down at Konnagar station and started going towards Rajibnagar, I felt utterly disheartened. It was nowhere close to the station. On the contrary, full two and a half miles away. Unmetalled road, full of muck. Shrubs and bushes infested with mosquitoes.

After some search I found a local doctor to be the owner of the land. In a tin-roofed room he was examining patients, whose number, however, was not enviable. Looking at me he asked, 'Who do you want?' Politely I answered, 'You must be Manindra Ghatak. I am coming from Jessore. You gave an advertisement in the newspaper…'

'I see,' the doctor said rather indifferently and turned his attention to his patients again.

I reached there with a lot of hope. It was a piece of land adjacent to the station, just 9 miles away from Calcutta. It would be useful to buy the land for various reasons. But why is the owner so indifferent? Has he changed his mind about selling the land?

About ten minutes passed. I was standing all along, nobody asked me to sit.

Mustering courage I said again, 'Actually I wanted to take the return train again...'

Raising his eyes the doctor said, 'What is it?'

'The land—'

'Which land?'

'You advertised in the newspaper—close to the station—Kripalani Colony—'

'Oh!'

His attention reverted to his patients. I also did not venture again to disturb the owner of the highly lucrative landed property.

Another ten minutes passed.

At last the doctor spoke, 'Well, sit down.' I gave a sigh of relief being permitted to sit at last. I was standing for quite some time. After a couple of minutes, I ventured again, 'Well...er...the land...'

The doctor raised his face, 'Yes?'

'I was talking about that piece of land. Actually, I wanted to have a look at it. And it's getting late also, so I thought –'

'You want to see the land? Hey Kartik, Kartik! Go and show the land to this gentleman.'

I was somewhat bemused to find that the next room to this doctor's chamber has 'New National Land Trust' written on it in bold letters in English. The colony will develop on a large area on the bank of the Ganga. But Rajibnagar itself was two and a half miles away from the station. But it was also possible that the office of the trust was here whereas the land was in close vicinity of the Ganga.

Being called by the doctor that man named Kartik came.

'Which land, *Babu*?'

'The one on the west side of the *boroj*—'

'Land?'

'What a nuisance! Don't stand there like a buffoon! Yes, land. Idiot!'

The servant appeared to be a simpleton; otherwise, shouldn't he know about the highly precious well-advertised land of his master?

Coming out on the road I said, 'Let's go.'

As the man started walking to the west I said, 'Where are you going? The land close to the station, Kripalani Colony—'

'But there is no land close to the station, *Babu*.'

'Of course there is one! You know nothing.'

'No *Babu*. There is no land that side.'

'Look, close to the station—the advertisement was published in the papers. Rs 50 was charged for registering the name. I got my name registered and the receipt is still in my pocket.'

'Why didn't you say all that back there, at the chamber, *Babu*? I know nothing about any other piece of land. Yesterday another gentleman came; he also got his name registered.'

'Didn't he see the land?'

'No. The doctor said, come and see the land next Sunday.'

'All right. Take me there—'

'*Babu*—'

'What now?'

'You want to see the land?'

'What rubbish! What else should I do?'

'You wait here. I'll go and ask.'

Somewhat annoyed, I went back to the doctor myself and said, 'Your servant has no idea where to take me.'

This time I saw the doctor talking to another gentleman. He, too, appeared to have come for the land. For he took money out of his pocket to get his name registered. The doctor gave him a receipt. I did not know what else transpired between the two, the man took the receipt paying Rs 2 and left.

The doctor now said, 'You want to see the land? All right, I'll come with you.'

Afterwards, he took me along—skirting stinking gutters, wild taro shrubbery, broken thatched huts, he led me to some indefinite mystery.

Once I tried to put up an irresolute protest—perhaps he forgot that the advertisement read, the land was very close, 'adjacent' to the station—

The doctor turned an angry gaze on me and said, 'What an idea! Do you think adjacent to the station means right beside the ticket counter of Konnagar station?'

I could have questioned whether 'adjacent' meant 2 miles away either, but decided to keep quiet. I was a hapless Hindu of East Bengal; it was useless to quarrel with the owner of a land here. I need to have a foothold here. He might even refuse to sell his land to me if I annoy him this way.

Politely I asked, 'How far is the colony?'

'It's about a mile away.'

Astonished, I blurted out, 'What do you say! Then it's altogether three and a half miles away from the station. Is this adjacent? Never heard of anything of the sort—'

The doctor stopped dead on the path and said, 'If you have never heard of anything of the sort what can I do? I'm telling you, not an inch of the colony land will be left unsold. The plots are all getting registered against individual names. Don't buy if you don't want to. Do you still want to see the plot?'

'Let's go.'

Taking out a bunch of letters from his pocket and waving it under my nose the doctor said, 'Look here. Money orders are coming to the office and we're receiving a bunch of letters every day. See for yourself. Visit the colony or you'll regret later. Nevertheless, none will force it on you if you don't want to buy—'

The road was extremely slimy. We were walking through a locality of dairy people; cattle-sheds on all sides. The air was heavy with the stench, the area mosquito-infested. Not far was a non-Bengali coolie slum—dirty and congested. After that again, shrubs and bushes, bamboo groves and ponds.

About a mile further on, by the side of the forest, beside the road was a tin signboard. On it was written in large letters—'Acharya Kripalani Colony.'

Reaching the place, the doctor stopped. Pointing towards the front he said, 'Here it is.'

Surveying all the directions I stood dumbstruck. I even forgot to be astonished. This is called 'Acharya Kripalani

Colony!' Is this the much-advertised piece of land? Where is the Ganga washing the foot of this land? Where is the beautiful scenery? I tried my best to fit this area of dark bamboo groves, wild taro shrubs and mosquito-infested ponds into my cherished image of 50 ft-wide road, electric light and tap water. I tried to rationalise to a great extent. What was Rashbihari Avenue a few years back? What were other places? But I couldn't sustain it for long. And where was high and dry land here? The whole area was a marshy land and here and there rose taro root bushes from the swamp.

But there was no point in saying all that.

The doctor spoke with pride, 'Rs 650 per *katha*, selling like hot cakes. All the plots have already been registered against individual names.'

But 'plot' meant a piece of land. But here was no land, only wetland. The sacred, clear-watered Ganga did not appear to be anywhere in the vicinity of the area.

I asked, 'How far is the Ganga from here?'

'Not far off—a mile or a little more than that—'

How was that possible? It couldn't be less than 4 miles from here.

Anyway, I didn't wish to start an argument here. And I returned thoroughly disheartened. Maybe even this marsh with the dense undergrowth of taro plants would become scarce later on.

As I returned home my wife asked anxiously, 'How was it—good?'

I said, 'Wonderful!'

'Tell me, what is it like— close to the Ganga?'

'It can be called adjacent.'

'The road is very wide?'

'Yes, quite.'

I did not say anything to Beena's uncle that day. Rs 50 was a sheer wastage, but I was much relieved now. East Bengal was just fine. I decided not to search for land again.

The next day the Radcliffe Commission's verdict was published. My hometown had fallen under the jurisdiction of West Bengal.

ॐ

Translated by Baisali Hui

Baisali Hui is Professor of English at the University of Kalyani. She did her doctoral research on Indian Partition Writing.

The Public Hero

Satinath Bhaduri

River Nagar borders the Gopalpur Police Station of Purniya district and the Sripur Police Station of Dinajpur district. The river, freakish in the hills, is sober here. So, ignoring with some sort of a rude indifference the profuse caress of its flow, a ramshackle bridge can still stand unbroken. The bridge comes in the way of the path formerly used for the purpose of sending troops from North Bengal to North Bihar. On either side of the bridge, the path is intact although it has way passed its former glory days. Of course, due to the war-time uncertainty, the Aruakhoya market that comes under Gopalpur Police Station has emerged as a smuggling centre of Bihar and Bengal in the last few years. The market is located on the western side of the bridge. Close to the market lies another road that runs from the Malda district to Siliguri through Purniya and Jalpaiguri. Hundreds of loaded bullock carts carry merchandise from three sides of Malda, Dinajpur and Jalpaiguri up to the bridge point. Last year the motor car of the S.D.O. got stranded here when he came to collect an undertaking from the leaseholder of the market for maintaining peace during the Bakrid. So the potholes of the road were subsequently repaired.

Sudhani station, as far as 16 miles from this place, is its only link with the outside world. From the smuggling centre of Aruakhoya market, cows, buffalos, sugar and ghee are smuggled out to Bangladesh across the bridge as rice and unhusked rice grain are smuggled in by the same route from Bangladesh to India.

The area has a mixed population of Hindus and Muslims. Most of the Hindus are of Rajbanshi community. Last year (1946) many news, mostly distorted half-truths, of Calcutta, Noakhali and Bihar had no doubt deeply shaken the minds of the people, but within a few days their riven minds got healed. In the changeless struggle for existence their patched life was continuing in its hackneyed fashion; but all of a sudden, the old wound reopened. The *munim* (rent-collector) of Jahurmal Dokaniya of Sudhani Storehouse was going towards Aruakhoya market on a Saturday night in his cart. The cart was loaded with sugar sacks, covered with tarpaulin sheets. Starting after dinner, one would reach Aruakhoya the next morning. Having taken his last puff of the bidi, he handed over the butt end to the cart-driver. Bilot, the cart-driver, felt obliged.

'Spread your towel on the sacks and go to sleep, Munimji; you will wake up in Aruakhoya. Since it is a night journey, let's keep an hour extra in hand. But, don't worry. Even then you can reach early in the morning and brush your teeth'.

Munimji is very happy these days for his gradually rising importance. Nowadays in the market, people ask him questions about the recent developments of the country. Whoever meets him on the way, including the school master of Consi L. P. School, try to get a news or two from him. On one hand he is the rent-collector of so big a storehouse; on the other, there is an 'electric' communication system in the house of his master. Even the Governor talks to Dokaniyaji through that system; many others use it for sending news; so many professional female singers-cum-dancers perform to please him. So Munimji is respected as a source of authentic news.

'Take care. If anybody asks you what is being carried, say it is only potato. Is the potato sack placed in the front?', said Munimji.

'Yes,' replied the cart-driver.

'Let me lie back on the sugar sack. If the sugar sacks could be kept in the front to lie on, I would have suffered fewer jerks during the journey'

The driver agreed.

'Be alert when you pass through Mirpur. The secretary of the village advisory committee there is a naughty fellow. Haven't you noticed that everyone is a secretary these days? If anybody asks you anything there, wake me up. While crossing the village, sing loudly; if you pass silently, you fan up everybody's suspicion. Sheer waste of money! On an average, a village secretary can be appeased by a bribe of ten rupees. But the secretary of Mirpur never accepts less than fifty. So be alert'.

'Relax, sir, you need not remind me of that. Avoiding pits and pots, I'll drive with care,' responded the driver.

Munimji could hardly sleep as he lay on the sacks. The news he was carrying today would take the whole market by surprise. No such big news stirred the heart of the people of this area in the recent past. What nonsense! These ants of the sugar sacks would not let him sleep. That stupid driver Bilot certainly did not shake the ants off properly before loading the cart with sacks.

'Hey Bilot, are you drowsing?' he asked.

'No, sir. Only the eyelids are heavy with sleepiness.' Munimji knew that now Bilot would hesitantly ask for a bidi to ward off his slumber. What else would the poor fellow do? He would have to remain awake all through the night. Bilot must not share the floating news with the passers-by.

'Here Bilot, take it and the matchbox too. Don't divulge to anybody what you heard today in Sudhani.' Till then Bilot had not given any thought to it. Hearing the words of Munimji he tried to recall the precise news.

'No, sir, you need not alert me. I have been serving you for so long. Have you ever seen me betray your trust? We are poor small fry. What will we do with big news?'

He gladly accepted the bidi and the matchbox. Then with recharged enthusiasm, he twisted the tails of the bullocks and hurled abusive interjections to make them haste forward.

The cart reached the shop of Mushar Sao at about 10 a.m.

'Ram Ram, Munimji '

'Joy Gopal, Joy Gopal'.

Mushar Sao and his son promptly unloaded the sugar sacks and carried them indoors, to avoid the inquisitive notice of other people.

'Just four sacks?'

'You don't know the risk involved. Have to face a lot of trouble to carry that. Times have changed. Now the mill-branded sacks must be re-sacked to avoid getting detected'.

After unloading the potato sack Saoji said to Munim, 'Now tell me, what's the news over there'.

Munimji became serious. Without answering the question directly, he asked for a twig to use it as a toothbrush. Saoji guessed that the news must be very serious. By this time, more people, mostly shopkeepers, crowded in. Of course, a few people were from far-off villages who have come to the market with rice carts. Hundreds of 'Ram-Ram' greetings of these people were exchanged with silent gestures by Munimji, still brushing his teeth, as if he was vexed with life. Everyone was eagerly waiting for him to brush his teeth, dry his face with a towel and open his mouth. There was also a ripple of anxiety in their heart as to whether Munimji would now ask for body oil to finish his bath before he speaks.

On other mornings Saoji himself would have raised the issue of morning-bath; but this time, out of curiosity for the latest news, he won't remind Munimji of that. Munimji gave Bilot money for arranging their breakfast with curd and *chira*: 'Buy some molasses as well, for since the formation of the congress ministry, you find it hard to collect even a pinch of sugar'. He then put the remaining coins in his cloth-fold and addressed the gathering without looking at them. 'What to do, Dinajpur district goes to Pakistan'. It seemed that it was not great news at all, for regularly many districts go to Pakistan. At last he found time to look at the people who had assembled there. His manner of talking was expressive of self-confidence, as if a world-famous leader was attending a press conference.

Immediately the whole gathering became silent. The news dropped like a bolt from the blue on the head of Darpan Singh, a Rajbanshi from Sripur. Others waited with a throbbing heart, not sure about the state of their districts. They waited for what Munimji would say about their villages. Saoji's face became pale in fear—what would happen to his shop, his wife, children, his family? He somehow gathered the courage to ask ,'What about Aruakhoya?'

'Aruakhoya comes under Purniya district and it is in Hindustan. It is not Bengal, it is Bihar. Here they have no scope of bargaining'.

The shop owners of the market heaved a sigh of relief. Munimji never divulged all news in one breath—he used to drop it slowly. So many people were staring anxiously at him; like the air-talk of the Governor, each syllable of his words was valuable to them. This period of curiosity had to be lengthened as much as possible, so that Munimji could relish the pleasure to the full.

Sellers from distant places come to the market with carts of rice much before others. Many of them had gathered there.

One such villager Achhimaddi asked, 'Master, could you please tell us where goes Mirpur?'

'Which district does Mirpur belong to?'

Puzzled, almost in tears, Achhimaddi muttered, 'It falls under Harishchandrapur Police Station;

Saoji clarified, 'It is in Malda district only'.

'Malda district has gone to Pakistan,' Munimji replied curtly. On hearing this, Achhimaddi got so much overwhelmed with the infinite grace of Allah that he could hardly find any word to express his surging emotion Poragosain of Bajargaon now managed to come forward through the crowd. By profession he was the priest of the Rajbanshi community. He had many clients in this area. Saoji stood up to vacate a space on the cot for his sitting. But he hardly noticed it. Moving closer to Munimji he asked, 'What about Bajargaon? It comes under Titlia Police Station of Jalpaiguri district.'

'Father, you need not worry about Jalpaiguri district. By the grace of Lord Rama, it is in Hindustan.'

'Can it be otherwise? We have been living here for two-three generations. How can our village go to Pakistan? Can the land of Lord Jalpeswar, the state of Lord Mahakal, go to Pakistan? The Governor is a man of profound understanding,' remarked Poragosain, as he kept on invoking Lord Narayana.

While bowing before his Lord, he angrily looked at Achhimaddi. Due to the surging curiosity and anxiety, others did not notice him till now. Now all pairs of inquisitive eyes fell upon him and he was embarrassed. Except Kasem, everyone looked upon him as an offender. Certainly Asgar Ali, the leaseholder of his village, pulled the strings to attach his village to Pakistan—he thought.

His only offence was that he was pleased by the news. He could well guess that his presence was not particularly appreciated there. He held the hand of Kasem and took him out of the crowd. Coming near his cart, parked at a distance, he remarked with a smile: 'Asgar Ali, the leaseholder, is the chip of the old block. He has kept his word. Let's sell our rice quickly without bothering about the price we get and move homewards. Returning home, I must meet Asgar Ali and congratulate him.'

Kasem said, 'Let's proceed right now. My heart sinks in the company of these people in the market.'

'If you take back the rice without selling it, how would you buy medicine? While coming here you had to grease the palm of the rice-police of two districts with as much as two rupees per maund. If you take back the rice you'll have to spend as much. We don't have any other source of income. We need not fear anybody as reverend Haji is the leaseholder of the market. If anybody interferes, he will send his clubmen to lynch the miscreants into silence.'

Kasem gathered the courage to visit the office of the leaseholder—after all, he was a Muslim. Before this time, Kasem would not have guts to visit him. But ever since last year's Bihar incident, all Muslims are comfortable in the company of a Muslim. Kasem found many others sitting there. Everyone was threatening the leaseholder who tried to pacify them. He advised the people from distant villages to go back immediately: 'There are Hindu houses all around. Be careful. Keep watch by turns all night long. Can Kishanganj sub-division be allowed to be acceded to Hindustan? I will take up the matter to find a remedy. The news is not yet confirmed. Why should we trust Munim?'

Kasem and Achhimaddi were shocked to hear the last words. Together they protested against it. The other people present there looked at them angrily. They requested the leaseholder of the market to buy their sacks without any delay—whatever be the offer price. As if not interested to buy yet eager to bail out the community members from a serious crisis, the leaseholder commanded his men to buy the whole quantity of unhusked rice grain: 'Masum, settle properly the price of each sack.' Masum was his man with a long experience. He correctly interpreted the suggestive words of his master.

Now the leaseholder tried to convince the folk, 'Don't worry, even the order of the Governor can be revoked if you can exert strong force. I am going to the district headquarters tonight. The leaders there who collected Rs 500 as donation for the District Pakistan Conference gave us clear assurance. How can the district now be included into Hindustan? To prevent it we'll have to cough up a few more bucks. That's it.'

The spirit of the *haat* got damp for the day. Everyone was interested in listening to national news from Munimji's own mouth. He remained busy answering their various queries. The Hindu tradesmen from Dinajpur and Malda thronged round him to take his advice. Munimji instructed Saoji to clear the unknown faces off, lest there should be a Muslim hiding in the crowd. For long he conversed privately with the Hindus from Malda and Dinajpur. They gathered a mental boost in this crisis from his spontaneous sympathy. Staying in that country was no longer safe; they must arrange for shifting families from their ancestral home. So without waiting for long, they became eager to return home before business gains momentum in the market. In a soaked voice Munimji advised them not to waste a single moment. As if at their insistence he bought all their rice,—at a price of Rs 16 per sack. At the last market-session, the price was Rs 19 per sack and yesterday, at Sudhani market, it was Rs 22.

After some time, the sepoy of the leaseholder called on Munimji to inform him that the leaseholder wanted to meet him. As soon as Munimji reached his place, he took him to a separate room. After some discussion about radio news the leaseholder said, 'This market will no longer be my area of operation. What to do? What is destined cannot be blotted. Such changes will not come to an end overnight. Let's talk business. How many sacks of sugar have you brought today?'

'I have managed to collect four sacks. One sack is to be given to Saoji. I can give you three sacks at the most. This time you'll have to pay Rs 70 per maund'.

'What a wonder! Till the other day, the price was Rs 60; how can you raise it to 70 all of a sudden? Keep half a sack for Saoji and give me three and a half. Last time the sugar was not dry at all.'

'Saoji's share is just one sack and now you are staking Pakistani claim even for that. This can't be done. He must get one full sack. I can't break my promise. How will the sugar get wet when the sacks are covered with tarpaulin? And the two jute sacks that you get gratis, don't these have any cost? Am I to pay for them? I won't accept the blame that the sugar was wet. Now that Malda and Dinajpur go to Pakistan, people will arrange a party to celebrate the occasion. The holy Eid is also round the corner. So people will try to collect sugar from here. You will easily get Rs 2.5 for each kilogram.' The flood of words of Munim carried off the arguments of the leaseholder. Failing to defend his stand, he softly protested, 'You are not right Munimji; where is money in the account of a Musselman?'

'Okay, then pay Rs 2 less per sack. By the way, I want your help in the matter of arranging a few bullock carts to carry my rice sacks to Sudhani Storehouse. I don't have adequate space here to store so much rice. It's anyway monsoon and the sacks are lying outside the shed. You have so many cart-drivers at your command'.

'Don't worry, I'll arrange. Carts will move at early dawn'.

Suddenly Masum dropped in and informed that the Hindus in the market have become excited. They started storming into the office building. They wanted Munimji to be back, for they feared that the leaseholder would not let him go back alive.

One could hear the great uproar outside. 'Are they mad?'—the leaseholder's face became pale in fear.

Together they came out of the room. Seeing the leaseholder, the owners of the permanent shops pushed him to the group of market-men, for he was, after all, their zamindar. Munimji came forward to pacify the excited crowd. In a hushed tone he remarked, 'Dare they do any harm to me? Are you still not back home? In these turbulent days the more you stay at home, the better. You know everything. What shall I advise? Consult your village head-man and decide what is best for you. The security of women should be your priority. We could not take the risk of keeping women even in Sudhani market area. So we took them all to the safer place of Rajputana this month. You cannot always bank on mechanical instruments or the official announcement that is brought by them. If the Governor had just mentioned Purniya to be in Pakistan, everything would have been spoilt. So beware.'

The narrow eyes of the Rajbanshi listeners dilated in fear. The 'Polia' women started wailing.

'What's the use of buying salt now?'

'Hello, Bachchidai, where have you fled? Come sharp; rise up, you prince. Will you ruminate still?'

'Munimji, please take this money as my deposit—I have hardly any self-confidence to keep it with me.'

Tension weakened even the sound mind. The market became silent after a brief period of brisk activity.

The colour of Aruakhoya market started changing from the next day. In the past, a weekday was fixed for business in the market. Now day and night it is the dejected meeting place of anxious people. Crossing the bridge, carts are coming from Sripur one after another. Large groups of boys, girls, cattle, goats move on foot. Even a little child carries a load on its small head. The skeletal figure of a victim of black fever marches forward gaspingly, with a cat in lap. An old asthmatic woman coughs as she trips on—she is about to lose her life in her desperate effort to escape from Pakistan. Until very recently their world was small enough. Having the night for rest in the market, many of them will pace aimlessly forward like a chased deer. Some will hang around, expecting some earning from farm works. Food is no great problem for the walkers, this being a season of ripe palm fruits.

Neither the district board of Purniya nor that of Dinajpur takes the financial liability for the maintenance of the bridge on the Nagar river. These days the ramshackle bridge knows no rest. People have camped on both sides of the bridge. Munimji has persuaded a Calcutta-based relief society to run a service camp for the refugees in Aruakhoya. With the help of a physician hired through the local board, he provides medical service to them. Munimji's help is there in every arrangement.

So many people visit Munimji to share with him the stories of their distress. He consoles some of them, advises some to pray to Lord Rama and asks many of them not to lose their patience. Occasionally he blames the Congress government for the weakness of its policy.

He concentrated on issuing relief-slips for food. 'How many members are there in your family? Pay Rs 5. Get the slip stamped from that flagged tent and go to Saoji's stall. Everything will be okay.' Gratitude oozed from the eyes of the refugees. Very few people in the world would talk to you so sweetly in times of your crisis, they thought.

The green-coloured crescent and star flag of the Muslim League was raised upon the railing of the far side of the bridge; the tricolour of the Congress party was flying on this side. On that side, groups of people continued to shout 'We have divided Hindustan', 'We have created Pakistan.' At high pitch '*Bande Mataram*', '*Jai Hind*' slogans were being raised from this side.

In days like these, it does not take much time for minds to get poisoned. Tension kept on rising to the flashing point. Someone spread the rumour that the bridge would be burnt so that no one can cross the river to come to this side with their belongings. The angry crowd on this side took no time to meet it with a rejoinder: 'We won't let a single cow or buffalo cross the bridge from this side. We would torch the bridge first.' If Munimji pacified the mob on this side, the leaseholder tried to restrain his people on the other. If the bridge is destroyed, they won't have the thriving business in the market.

Munimji persuaded them, 'Wait for a couple of days. Let's see what happens. Will Mahatma Gandhi sit idle without interfering? He has constituted the "Commission" headed by the Governor—not a small fry but one of true royal blood.'

Immediately the news spread. Everywhere people started talking about the 'Commission'.

Chuyalal Rajbanshi of Sripur is well known for his wits, Munimji did not share all the news he had in his stock. So Chuyalal was sent to Sudhani station to collect the latest information about the Commission. Chuyalal was not a lily-livered chap. He went straight to the pointsman of the station and asked him about it. Confusing it with pay commission, he told Chuyalal that the report regarding pay hike had come out. People of Sripur cannot make a head or tail of what is meant.

'Commission'—the circulation of the word crossed the bridge. Izrael, the long-serving sepoy of the leaseholder, struck the ground with the staff and remarked, 'Commission at first stage is collected from the jute sellers as *dharmaday* or faith-tariff. Henceforth no Muslim is going to pay it. We will see how they are going to collect this commission from us. We'll resist by all means the inclusion of Aruakhoya into Hindustan.'

The father of Darpan Singh, very old, patted his own thigh and said, 'Don't pay any commission for business in this market to any Muslim leaseholder. It is not for nothing that we left behind all our possessions in Pakistan. We heard that they won't let any Hindu live with his wife or daughter in Pakistan. Will they dictate terms even in Hindustan? Are we to pay levy to a Muslim leaseholder?'

He wanted to say something more but his mother stopped him and took him away thinking it unwise to antagonise wicked people.

Payment of commission for business in the market stopped from that very day.

Munimji told Saoji, 'Have you noticed that the leaseholder no more stays on this side at night? Is it he who bears all expenses for those relief camps on the other side of the bridge?'

'No, he collects donations for that purpose. He has also raised money from the people in the name of bribing the Commission staff of Calcutta so that Gopalpur Police Station may go to Pakistan.'

Munimji's eyes sparkled, whether out of envy or respect, was not very clear.

Saoji further said, 'Munimji, we can also collect some amount from the market in the name of stopping the inclusion of Gopalpur into Pakistan. The leaseholder is a cunning fellow—he may manage the Commission staff by greasing their palm. If you just try, you can protect our interest, and also that of the whole district of Purniya'.

Munimji had been silently making this very calculation so far. His calculation never failed. He balanced the expected profit against the enormous risk involved in it. He hit upon a plan. It is better to do nothing after raising the donation. If the place goes to Pakistan, you can refund the money saying that the magistrate could not be bribed. And if it remains with Hindustan, you can appropriate the collection and say that the money was spent to bribe the Commission. But that may also lead you into trouble. Better drop the idea—grasp all, lose all.

He broke the silence and said, 'No, Saoji, I don't want to get into trouble. The Congress government is there, Mahatma ji is there, and my master is there to take care of it. Just advise me how to make the movement of goods from either side of the bridge hassle-free. The river is full of current due to the rains. Some alternatives could be explored if it were not the rainy season!'

'The rice-police on both sides have recently started assuming honest airs as if they are the offspring of Yudhisthira. Today they refused their due of Rs 150 for allowing buffaloes of equal number to be carried from Muzaffarpur to Mymansingh. The rice-officer on that side also has refused to take any amount. The market is to be closed if nobody entertains any bribe. It is not for nothing that the leaseholder has stopped passing nights in the market.'

'Perhaps in fear of complaints to the magistrates, they won't accept any bribe. But things will become normal in a few days. Don't be upset. Why are you so anxious? The relief service is being controlled from your office. We are businessmen, we will surely make profit by some means,' he said. Saoji agreed but his face revealed an absence of confidence. Munimji was to be paid his share of one fourth of every rupee of profit upon sale of relief articles—how little would be left for you then!

The jute plants were as high as a man. My obstinate son-in-law refused to come; my daughter will be in distress. Did not think of leaving my village in the year when diarrhoea spread like epidemic and took a toll of so many lives—the language, the voice may be new but each tale harps on the same chord of agony and affliction.

Darpan Singh consoled his father, 'The land may be lost, but at least the honour of the women has somehow been saved'.

The old man bursted into tears, 'My own servant Irfan will get all sixty *bighas* of my land. Is it divine justice?'

The tricolour fluttered on the top of the office building of the leaseholder in the market—as if to fan up by its three colours the venom of disappointment, hatred and terror. He identified himself with the green flag fluttering on the other side of the bridge. The distance between the two flags was so little but the difference implied was unbridgeable. One flag he could call his own. It signified peace, happiness, pure joy, security under the image of the crescent. But if out of fear of these Rajbanshis, you left the space under your command, would you be able to raise a single farthing from the market? Nobody could predict the judgement of the Commission—it was the decree of *Khoda*, the Lord.

Saoji's mother met the wife of Darpan Singh to ask endless questions and collect every bit of information about the culture of Pakistan. 'You were there for so many days after the creation of Pakistan. Is the air there heavy with the fetid stink of garlic? Strictly non-vegetarian, did they allow you that night to cook and eat spinach and plant-stalk? Did they try to disturb you?'

Darpan's wife felt at a loss before the volley of questions and could not come out with the right answers. She muttered on, 'I could not cut off for my own eating a single soft tendril of the pumpkin in the yard. At the time of leaving home, I chopped off its root. The pair of oxen also got panicked, for they turned away from the pumpkin tendril given as fodder. So nicely I maintained my fireplace so far! I myself smashed it with logs—how can the oven be left intact for uncle Irfan's cooking, that too of foods that are forbidden? The problem was with the idol of God. I was anxious about it. God's grace is infinite, we stupid people think of God's safety. Now I can carry my idol with me. Let me consult the priest about the rules and rites of purification. Here in this crowd of mixed castes, it is impossible to follow the strict rules of purity in religious offerings.'

Uttering these words as she tried to raise her hands in supplication, Darpan's wife felt the pressure of the hands of Saoji's wife. Brushing aside business-mindedness, she had subconsciously touched her hands in sympathy. Darpan's wife relished the affectionate touch and resisted the desire of raising her hand to pray to her Lord. Their familiarity was only three days old. Saoji's wife is from a distant land—Balia. Yet, placing her head on her chest, Darpan's wife could unburden her feelings through tears.

The sudden blow of destiny pulling strings from afar confounded people for a few days. Gradually as they were trying to adjust to the topsy-turvy, anxiety lost its initial sharpness. Cart fare and price of food that got doubled came down. The rice-police reverted to the known habit of dishonesty. Cart-load of rice continued to be smuggled to this side of the bridge as thousands of smuggled cattle were taken across the bridge to the other side.

Amidst these regular activities people retained their curiosity about the Commission. Munimji regularly sent Sudhani dozens of bullock carts, all loaded with rice bought cheap from growers at the time of distress sale. He had much command over the cart-drivers—so he had to pay less than usual fare. He had so much influence over the people that if they could serve him without charging any fare, they felt obliged. Saoji defended him: 'Munimji is no cheat. He is a true Hindu, not the fish-eating type of this side. He is from Rajasthan—the land of heroes, of kings and merchants who did not bow their head before the Muslims for a single day. He will not hire your carts for free; the leaseholder may exploit you in that way. He will always pay you the exact fare.'

'We know that very well. When will the report of the Commission come out?'

'God knows. But it is likely to come out within a couple of days. Munimji has come to know that the Muslims have claimed a share even in it.'

'Saoji, let me carry today the letter of Munimji.'

'Sukdeb, you carried it the day before yesterday. Hand it over to me today.'

All the cart-drivers remained eager to carry the letter Munimji sent every day to Sudhani Storehouse. They considered themselves to be lucky to be chosen as the bearer.

Sirilal asks Saoji, 'Do they record in the huge register all the government messages that are received through the communication system installed at Sudhani storehouse? The letter of Munimji that was taken there the other day was, however, recorded in the register. Then having consulted the record book, the register-keeper wrote a reply to Munim ji's letter.'

'Maybe. That's a big deal, beyond the knowledge of small fry like us. By the grace of God and by serving you, I earn a small amount to keep my family. Mishrilal will carry the letter today. Sirilal, tomorrow Munimji himself will go to Sudhani. Can't you set a shed on your cart for this purpose? Okay, I will find it for you. The leaseholder will consider himself lucky if he can arrange one of his carts for Munimji. But Munimji is a man of principle—he will not entertain such an offer. A trusted cart-driver is required tomorrow. Some amount of money deposited to Munimji remains unspent even after procuring rice. The money belongs to others, so it must be kept in the secure place of the storehouse. It is unwise to keep the money in the market full of thieves and cheats. When peace is restored, he will refund the entire amount without deducting a single *paisa*. Dokaniya ji's is not just an ordinary storehouse; even the Governor has information about it.'

'Munimji', 'Munimji'—wherever you go, you hear this name. He had no time to have his bath or take his food in time. He had been, as if, fretting himself sick round the clock to provide some relief to the refugees.

He had promised Darpan Singh's father an advance which the old man needed to snub Irfan for wanting to marry a Rajbanshi girl. Ignoring all risks Munim had promised to buy all the sixty bighas of land of Darpan only to teach Irfan a lesson. And he also promised to concede to Darpan fifteen bighas of land near the storehouse for cultivation, of course after the publication of the final report of the Commission.

The government employees of both Bengal and Bihar were satisfied with Munimji's performance; the Relief Society of Calcutta was all praise for him. The Hindus were grateful to him; even the Muslims were not disgruntled.

Munimji informed all the shop owners, 'The country will become independent on 15 August.'

'What about Pakistan?'

'Pakistan will also be independent on that day,' replied Munimji.

Hundreds of voices in the crowd wanted to ask, 'Can't that be forestalled by any means?'

As if forced to address this silent question, Munimji remarked, 'If you can't be happy without Pakistan, be off with it.' In the show of broadness towards the Muslims, the words 'You will feel the prick within a few days' got stuck in his mouth.

The panic-stricken faces of the refugees from Dinajpur and Malda darkened with the shadow of anxiety. In one voice all of them asked, 'What about the judgment of the Commission?'

'It will be declared within a few days. But it is settled that Purniya district, that includes this market of Aruakhoya, will not go to Pakistan. The people of Purniya, especially those in the Aruakhoya market area, started shouting, 'Three cheers for Gandhiji.' Wooden slippers, umbrellas, towels were hurled upwards in an expression of joy. Jadu the *panwala* started dancing and scattering his entire stock of betel leaves.

Many from Malda and Dinajpur reminded Munimji of his promise of distributing a share of land in Purniya district.

This part of Purniya was notorious for black fever and malaria. Acres of land lay untilled in absence of farmers and, worse still, in want of money required for the purpose of cultivation.

So many growers! In addition, prospects of huge profit from collection of the landlord's fee. The major part of the land was farmland for cultivation. The luck was favourable, or else why should the ministry take steps for the abolition of landlordism? Munimji's eyes glittered as he visualised his bright prospect. Without making any verbal reply he pretended as if he had no interest—it's up to them to decide whether or not to take the land.

'By the by, we will find time to discuss the issue of land distribution. What is important now is that the refugees have come here with their cows and buffaloes which are grazing here and there. Why will the landowners allow that? I can arrange pastures on payment of cheap monthly instalments but it must be paid in cash.'

People thronged around him to get a ready solution. They started jostling each other to get priority.

The cheers on this side crossed the bridge and stirred up sensation there: 'What's the matter? Certainly, something happened. Don't be upset.'

Iqbal shouted through his tin-speaker, '*Nare takbir*', others join voices '*Allah Ho Akbar*'.

'Are you dead? Can't you shout louder? We must drown their voices.'

Hanif, Iqbal and others dispersed to find out the cause of jubilation on the other side of the bridge.

'You should continue to shout till we come back.'

'Here you have the son-in-law and the daughter of Darpan Singh of Sripur'.

'Search their cart, maybe they are escaping from Pakistan with valuables'. In no time Irfan came to the spot. 'Who are here—dear sister and brother-in-law? Let them go. Why are you escaping? What's the fear as long as we are here? Let me meet your kid. He is afraid of me. Sister, don't be panicky. Meet your parents and come back. Dear brother-in-law, I thought you're truly a man. Why then are you escaping?'

The person spoken to could not reply with confidence. Irfan offered a paper flag of the League to the child. 'Is it not nice, my dear?'

Then he himself went with the cart as escort and ensured its safe crossing of the bridge. At the time of farewell, he threw a humorous comment at Darpan's son-in-law: 'The king is on foot, the subject in the cart.'

The moment the news spread, all Muslims of Purniya district, who were with Iqbal, became furious with the leaseholder. 'He has certainly taken the money collected as subscription. Today he must be taught a lesson. Maybe he is in Aruakhoya office now. He must be busy collecting money from the Hindus to influence the judgement in favour of them. Let him come to this side tonight.'

The news of Munimji stirred up ripples of excitement on both sides of the bridge. Even the old father of Darpan Singh attempted a forced smile—for how many days can one sustain the hope of inclusion of Sripur into Hindustan? Hard days were ahead—right from the moment of crossing the bridge, misfortune was being felt. The carefree life of comfort and happiness did exist now only in memory. Was it possible to start a new life at this ripe old age, and that too in this country? All through life the western side of the River Nagar has been looked upon as a land of fever. How can he now dance in joy in its praise shouting 'Long live Hindustan, the land of gold'! The incongruity involved in the idea pricked his seasoned mind. Why at all this happened cannot be figured out by him.

Last time when Nagar flooded the land, they had to live for days in makeshift camps pitched on the road. Even then he could not think of crossing to this side. After sometime, as he recalled the name of Irfan, all his arguments get lost in the web of unexpressed grudge.

Amidst this tumultuous excitement, people forgot to ask what articles Munimji had brought in six loaded carts.

Munimji ordered to stop the quarrel between crowds on both sides of the bridge. On 15 August, brushing aside the recent happenings, both the sides must celebrate the occasion of national independence.

Unsolicited, Munimji moved to conciliate the people on the other side of the bridge. Till date he would walk up to the middle of the bridge, treated as no man's land, now he moved to the camp on the other side. Everybody whispered, 'He is certainly a man of great guts.'

Munimji mediated in making a pact not to use the '*Murdabad*' slogan targeting each other. 'Have you collected the new flag of Pakistan? No, no, not this one. It is the flag of the League. Have you no information about the new flag? If you want that, I can supply it. I have with me flags of different prices.'

Munimji then acquainted the people of this side with the new flag of Hindustan.

'Where can we find it now?'

'Have I not arranged that? You will get flags of different prices'.

Now it was clear why people were crazy about Munimji. Then and there he could supply everything one needs.

The relief camp was in a festive mood. The brother of Bilot, the cart-driver, used to work in a jute mill. It was feared that riot would break out there on 15 August. So he had fled the place with his ten-year-old son. He and his son have been working in Relief Society camps for the past two days. The young man with a promising exposure in Calcutta has projected himself as the captain of the innocent group of village rustics. He taught them a new 'ghost-game'—learnt, of course, from the babus of the relief camp. A group played the role of Hindu ghost—*Brahmadtti*, the other of Muslim ghost—*Mamdo*. One side is called bel-tree, inhabited by *Brahmadatti*. The other side is grave-side, inhabited by *Mamdo*. There is a thin stick-drawn line of demarcation. If you die in Noakhali you become *Brahmadatti*, if you die in Bihar you become *Mamdo*. As soon as a new player joins the grave-side team, the *Mamdos* greet him in nasal intonation: 'One more has come from Bihar'; if one joins the bel-tree side team, everyone asks, 'From Noakhali?' The player is required to reply, 'No, from Chitpur.'

The boys distorted the place names in pronunciation; the elders watched the funny game and burst in laughter.

Munimji came and chased all, 'What nonsense going on? Will you again fan up a feud? You imps—be off. If I find you again playing the game, I'll throw all of you into the river from the bridge'.

Then he admonished the babus of the relief camp: 'I expected you to be more responsible'. They felt embarrassed.

Within two days all flags got sold at high price. Afraid of people of his own community, the leaseholder disappeared—according to many, he was at Patna.

On 15 August people celebrated the independence with endless energy and enthusiasm. The tricolour of Hindustan flew on this side of the bridge as the flag of Pakistan on the other. Amidst *aarti* and spill of flowers the bridge seemed unreal—part of it in Pakistan, part in Hindustan and part hanging above the ground. Darpan Singh could not forget about the bridge even when he participated in the festivity. Though physically in Aruakhoya, his mind went somewhere to his farmland in Sripur. The bridge, as if, was a link between his body and mind. Without the bridge, he could not possibly make a timely escape to this side. If God favours, he will use the bridge to cross to his own land again. No, it is not God but the Commission that must favour him. Is the Commission greater than God? With the consent of the people assembled on both sides, the babus of the relief camp staged a show at the middle point of the bridge. A group of boys, their bodies covered with the dead imperial flags, left the stage in tears singing *matum*. Then two other groups carrying flags of Hindustan and Pakistan embraced each other. The dejected mind of Darpan's father cheered up a bit.

When everyone except the refugees had almost forgotten the issue of the Commission, Munimji all of a sudden announced, 'The verdict of the Commission has been declared'. No wonder that all rushed to him to know the result.

'Sripur has fallen on the Bengal side.'

Darpan Singh hugged Munimji with affection. His mother, unable to figure out the outcome, started wailing. His father saluted the divine invisible as well as the Commission. At last the Commission has smiled upon them.

'The Haripur Police Station comes under Pakistan'.

'What about Malda?'

'Sukdeb, your side has come under Hindustan. Great victory, isn't it?'

With a tilak on his forehead, Poragosain came in a hurry. He cracked a joke, 'Just arrived. Getting down from the cart I found "KAPSTAN" painted on the wall of the shop of Siri Sao. Got shocked—thinking that 'KAP' is 'PAK', thus written following the reversed order in Urdu style of writing. Then I thought that Aruakhoya must have gone to Pakistan. Later I discovered that 'KAPSTAN' (CAPSTAN) is just the advertisement of a cigar brand. Munimji, now tell me our state of things.'

Munimji won't give an answer on purpose. The Rajbanshi community became surprised that their guru was deliberately ignored by Munimji.

At last, Munimji, as if unwillingly, opened his mouth to drop the ill news: 'Titlia Police Station of Jalpaiguri district has gone to Pakistan.'

'Who decides? How can that be?'

Saying this, bending on his staff, he slowly slipped down on the cot. '*What have you done, God?* Is it my fate that after my death my body would be buried, not cremated? I will have no temple in the locality to visit for my worship? Was it written as my lot?'

Most of the refugees felt relieved at last. The old scenes got repeated. The refugee camp broke up in a day. Carts, people, cattle from distant places started returning to places where they came from. The tricolour flag fluttered on the carts, some people in large processions were carrying it, the brightness of victory writ large on their faces. The women folk were happy to escape from the mouth of the predators.

Life flows on very fast. Even those who have past experience could not imagine such a fast rhythm of life. In the past, nobody would dare trifle with the minds of such a multitude—Iqbal mulled over all these as he un-hoisted the flag of Pakistan from the bridge-top. What for was this short show? Why should the food platter be removed after tantalising the hungry? It took two hundred years to remove the Union Jack, and his flag has to be furled in less than three days. Agony and shock apart, the insult was unbearable. Hundreds of people on the bridge, the huge procession of crowd on the pathway, the large gathering in the market were watching him. His mortification knew no bounds. He thought of jumping into the river to commit suicide. With how much enthusiasm he hoisted the flag! 'The three-day kingship of a water-carrier is over'—this taunting remark of Ramji Sao cut him to the quick. They would soon hang the flag of Hindustan here. Was it for this, under the flag of Pakistan, he cracked his voice to shout the slogan 'Long Live Pakistan'? Maybe tomorrow on this bridge the boys of Sripur will start playing the game of 'Dead Flag Ghost' with it. Who must he blame when the whole world was against him?

Without looking at anybody, Iqbal un-hoisted the flag and carrying it on his shoulder moved towards the north where the flag would be honoured. Hanif was smoking a bidi to wear a face of indifference. Before his departure, he left the butt-end on the bridge wishing it to catch fire and get destroyed. Only then Sripur would get separated from Aruakhoya. But he knew for certain that it was impossible for the small bidi-fire to set the huge wooden structure ablaze. Yet the very thought pleased him. Munimji occupied the camp of the leaseholder located on the other side of the bridge.

His henchmen came to him with a captive family, hiding in the sugar-cane field. Whether they had any intention of torching anything was not clear.

'Hey Achhimaddi, if I am not mistaken'.

Achhimaddi broke down in tears. He fell on the feet of Munim and explained: 'Escaping from my village I was going towards Haripur. I heard that Mirpur has been included into Hindustan. It is said people will force you there to offer namaz facing the east. You won't be allowed to cull a chicken in the Muslim way. So I left the village without any belonging. I thought of hiding in the sugar-cane field during the day and start walking at the fall of evening.' He clasped the feet of Munimji while wailing.

'Free him now. I know this family'—Munim ordered.

'The master is mercy incarnate'.

Triumphant outcry glorifying Munimji in the same breath with Mahatmaji filled the sky.

Munimji instructed the gathering on the other side of the bridge: 'Don't keep a single flag of Pakistan with you. Return them to me. I will send them to the government. Keeping Pakistani flag in Hindustan is prohibited'.

The flags of Pakistan which he himself sold come back to him.

He made his calculation—these flags are to be carried to Titlia. He would shelter in the vacant house of Poragosain to make a survey of his lands. These Pakistani flags would sell like hot cakes there. He must also collect all useless flags of Hindustan from that place to sell those in Hindustan. He would profit a lot from selling the same item twice to two different communities. He also calculated the margin of his profit. The Commission has given many things to many as it has robbed hundreds of everything. But he got his commission from this verdict of the Commission. None of his shrewd calculations misfired.

Sound of 'Long live Munimji' poured into the room from outside. Only one lapse in his game plan pricked his mind. He should have ordered for a khaddar cap—that would have given him a greater mileage. He might then have had a more advantageous position. Anyway, one must not cry over the spilt milk. What he has harvested by the grace of Lord Rama is enough and hence, he must be satisfied. Munimji opened his pocket-notebook to enter all accounts in cryptic business diction.

ଔ

Translated by Sukriti Ghosal

Sukriti Ghosal was awarded PhD in 1993 for his thesis on the literary criticism of Oscar Wilde. He had retired as the Principal of M U C Women's College, Burdwan, in 2020.

The Tale of a Tulsi Plant

Syed Waliullah

The house was some hundred yards away from the bow-shaped brick-and-mortar bridge, a big two-storey structure looming up right above the road. Pavements were unheard of in that part of the country and so the house did not have any space left, even for courtesy's sake, in front of it. The backyard, however, was pretty large. Besides a lavatory, a bathroom and a kitchen that occupied the large open space at its centre, it contained a nearly impenetrable cluster of fruit trees, its damp floor covered with thick grasses and its air laden with a thick smell. The place remained dimly lit even on the brightest of days.

They wondered why no one had thought of having a garden in front of the house. Matin thought, had there been some open space, in default of a garden, they might have created one, with some seasonal flowers along with *bokul*, *gondhoraj*, *hasnuhana*, and perhaps, roses. After hard work at office, they would have sat around on cane chairs or easy chairs with canvas seats, which they might well have bought, and gossiped together. Amjad had a habit of smoking hookah. A fancy hubble-bubble could have been bought in honour of the garden. Kader was a great teller of tales. A gentle evening breeze would have made him wax eloquent, his tales sweetened by the aroma of night jasmines, just bloomed. Or they might just as well have done without stories on moonlit nights. Wretched thoughts like this came pouring in even more bitterly when at the end of a long day they climbed up the stairs rising almost directly from the street to reach their rooms upstairs.

They had taken possession of the house. Of course, they did not have to fight over it nor did anyone acquiesce out of fear of their martial prowess. They had been looking, day in and day out, for shelter of some kind since their arrival in the town amidst the turmoil of Partition. One day they ran into this house, big and empty, for want of inmates. The initial shock of surprise was soon followed by great excitement as they broke the lock open and roared into the house. They were like small children gathering mangoes after a heavy storm. It never occurred to them that they were behaving like dacoits. They were too full of laughter to feel any prick of conscience.

When the news began to spread towards afternoon, some people, wholly unwelcome, began to pour in. Soon, others started coming in large numbers in the hope of having some roof over their heads. Then they fought back. Would you take it by force? They kept their cool with some effort of will and said, 'Sorry. There is no room. All the rooms are full. Look, Sir, we have four beddings in this dark little room already. With four 6/3' bedsteads, about six chairs and a table that are yet to come, there will be hardly any space left.' One of them feigned sympathy, 'We can well understand your difficulty. We too suffered a lot. Had you come four hours before, or even two, you might have possessed the small corner-room downstairs which is now occupied by a fat man of the accounts office. Not a bad one, I would say, although it stands directly on the road. You might have enjoyed the benefit of streetlight for nothing!'

There was indeed a great upheaval in the country but no part of it was entirely lawless. Later on, police came to supervise over this illegal work.

It was not the fugitive landlord who had approached the police to get back his property. In fact, it was really doubtful, whether he would have done anything of this sort, had he known about this forcible occupation. It would be too much to expect this of a man who had, for dear life, spirited his entire family away within two days. The police were informed by those who were too busy looking for opportunities to loot properties elsewhere to come four or at least two hours earlier. Sheer bad luck. But here they argued that their luck could be bad as well. To protect the fruits of fortune, even mealy-mouthed men could sometimes be formidable fighters. Inwardly ready to fight it out, they managed to convince the police inspector in such a fashion that he left with his party without much ado. He submitted the report so intricately worded that his superior preferred to keep it confined to the official file. At any rate, it made little sense to sympathise with the fugitives or bother oneself unless the absconding landowner showed up to make a complaint. Moreover, although these men were petty clerks, they after all came of genteel families, did no harm to the house nor did they smuggle away its beams, doors and windows.

Overnight, the house was abuzz with activity. The majority of them had to pass their time in Calcutta variously, in the company of dock labourers at Blockman Street, tobacco traders at Syed Saleh Lane or in the squalor of Chamru Khansama Lane. The big rooms, large windows in the fashion of *neelkuthi*, the large courtyard, and the cluster of fruit trees at the back of it had filled their minds with unspeakable delight. They might not have been living like lords, having a room each, but the free circulation of air and the abundant sunrays made them feel happy. Now they would live independently, drink in pure air, have a taste of healthy life, enjoy the glow of well-being and keep out the germs of malaria and *kala-azar*.

Yunus, for instance, lived at Macleod Street. In spite of its foreign name, parts of the lane remained littered with the morning refuse like a dustbin. There he shared an upper-storey room with some leather dealers in a ramshackle wooden house. Someone had told him once that the smell of leather killed the germs of tuberculosis. But its obnoxious smell would drown the stench of the drains below and could even overpower the putrid smell of the decomposed carcasses of cats and rats. Yunus would derive comfort from its alleged power to kill germs. A frail man with weak constitution, he shuddered as he lay in bright sunlight near the broad window in the large southern room thinking of his life at Macleod Street. He wondered whether the damage was already done. He would have seen a doctor if he could afford to.

In the courtyard, on the left side of the kitchen, there was a low square brick-platform with a tulsi plant. One morning, while leisurely brushing his teeth with a neem twig, Modabber noticed the plant. Habitually given to raising hell at the drop of a hat, he brought everyone down to see if something, indeed, had happened. 'Look at this plant. This must be weeded out. I don't want to see any trace of *Hinduism* now that we are around'. All looked at the plant. The deep green leaves were turning brown and wilting. Lying uncared for, the plant was surrounded by grasses at its root. They were surprised to find that no one had noticed it before. It somehow managed to hide itself.

They all fell silent. The house that appeared so empty, so derelict despite some letters scrawled with a childish hand on its wall beside the staircase, suddenly looked so different. The plant, as if caught red-handed, seemed to speak up stories overlooked. Noticing their silence, Modabber roared again. 'What do you think? Not another word. Weed it out'.

They were not very well aware of the Hindu rituals. Yet they had heard somewhere that in a Hindu household the lady of the house puts a lamp near a tulsi plant in the dusk and drapes the *anchal* round her neck before bowing down to it. Someone, to be sure, used to put an earthen lamp every evening before this plant too, now overgrown with grasses.

When the bright pole star, with its lone splendour, stood still in a corner of the evening sky, in that all-swallowing silhouette, a small bright lamp may have burnt for many years with a quiet tinge of the blood-red of the vermilion. The practice must have gone on over the years, despite many storms in the family or even deaths.

Where is the lady now? Where had she gone? And why? Matin who, at one time worked in the railways, thought that she might have been living in the house of a relative in Calcutta or Asansol or Baidyabati or Howrah. Or may be, at Liluah. The red-fringed sari hanging from the line on the roof of a black two-storied house near the large railyard might be hers. But wherever she might be, she would surely think every evening of this plant and perhaps, secretly shed her tears.

Yunus had caught cold. He was the first to speak.

'Let it be. We are not going to worship it anyway. Rather, it is good to have a tulsi plant around. The juice of its leaves helps you get rid of cold and cough.'

Modabber looked around. Everyone seemed to be of the same mind. Even Enayet, who was more a fundamentalist, wore a beard, prayed five times a day, was silent. Was he also thinking of the tear-filled eyes of the homeless lady?

The tulsi plant lived on, unharmed.

The atmosphere of the house was good. The languid mood of the Calcutta days seemed to be over. The gossip, as a result, became lively, sometimes leading to heated debates on all kinds of issues—social, political, economic. The issue of communalism, too, sometimes popped up.

'They were at the root of it all,' said Sabir, 'The meanness and the orthodoxy of the Hindus is responsible for the Partition'. He cited many examples of their tyranny and injustice. Blood boiled in their veins. Maqsud *Miyan*, known in the group for his leftist views, sometimes tried to object: 'Let us not overstate the case. We are not much behind'. Modabber showed teeth. The needle of the compass of the leftist wavered. He gave up. Just as we complained against them, they might just as well complain against us. The matter was far too complicated. He thought perhaps these were right. They should know. The needle vacillated a little in doubt and then finally tilted right. He had earned the bad name of a leftist because of the needle which sometimes tilted left without rhyme or reason.

One could see the tulsi plant near the kitchen on one's way to the lavatory. Someone had removed the weeds. The brownish leaves were turning green again. The plant was being watered by someone, albeit surreptitiously. Who was not afraid of reprovals from many corners, after all!

Yunus had thought that he would never have to return to the squalid quarters of Macleod Street and hoped to spend the rest of his life here in open air and bright sunlight. But he was mistaken. Not only Yunus but all of them believed that if they could not afford to buy good food or remit money to their families in those hard days, they might at least continue to enjoy the comforts of independent existence. They all were mistaken. Thank God, the house did not have open space before it. Otherwise, they might have felt tempted to make a garden and at least try to grow marigolds in that time of the year. That would have been a terrible mistake.

Modabber came in rushing one day to announce the arrival of police. Why? Maybe, some pilferer had taken shelter in some corner of the house. But they were thinking like poor rabbits that, chased by the hunters, shut their eyes to believe that none could see them. They were thieves themselves, not hiding but blinking at the truth.

The sub-inspector of police held an old hat under his armpit and was wiping the wrinkled forehead with a handkerchief. He looked innocent. The two armed constables standing behind looked just as meek, their large pairs of moustaches notwithstanding. They were looking at the beams overhead. They might as well have been looking at the two pigeons, one white and the other grey, sheltered near the ventilators. They held guns after all.

Motin asked politely, 'Who do you want to see?'

'All of you. You have possessed this house illegally. You have to vacate the house within twenty-four hours.'

They were shown a copy of the official order. This meant that the owner of the house had returned, and lodged the complaint at the police station. Afjal craned his neck to see if he accompanied the police team but could see none other than the two constables.

Has the house-owner made a complaint?

The government has requisitioned the house.

They stood still for a moment. Then Motin blurted out, 'We are none but the people of the government.'

How foolishly sometimes one would talk! Even the two silent constables lowered their eyes and looked at them. Their contemplative eyes were suddenly eloquent.

A shadow descended over the house. There was no end of worries. Where would they go? Someone among them flared up, 'Not going anywhere. We shall stay put. Let us see who can remove us. They must tread over our corpses to enter'. They recalled, somewhere a house was occupied by a group of students and even the highest officials were having a tough time of it, trying to vacate the place. Their blood started boiling. No, they would not budge by any means. Anyone trying to come should know that they would fight to the last man.

The blood boiled for a few days. They could not concentrate on work or enjoy their food. There were only words, acerbic ones, dipped in gall. Then the words became less and less. It did not take long for the blood to cool off.

They were not students, after all. Didn't they tell the police proudly about themselves? Didn't they say, after a moment's resentment on hearing about the requisition of the house, that they were people of the government?

One day they left in a body. They had stormed into the house and then left the house, just like a storm. Scattered in the room lay pieces of old newspapers, a weak portion of a string for holding clothes, butts of bidi or cigarette, discarded sole of an old shoe. The doors and windows of the large mansion-like house looked blank. But the days were not far when they would be hung with colourful curtains.

The tulsi plant behind the kitchen was fading away. Its leaves were turning brownish again. No one watered the plant since the police came with the order. Didn't they ever think even of those tear-filled eyes of the lady, not to speak of the plant itself?

The tulsi plant alone knew why they did not. For a tulsi plant could live or die, depending on whether the human beings wished to destroy it or let it survive. It did not have the power to either live or thrive on its own.

ଔ

Translated by Tirthankar Das Purkayastha

Tirthankar Das Purkayastha has retired as a Professor of English at Vidyasagar University, West Bengal. His English translations of the poems of Sunil Gangopadhyay have been published in *South Asian Review: Creative Writing Issue* (University of Pittsburgh) and *Indian Literature*, A Sahitya Akademi Journal.

When the River Rebukes

Satyapriya Ghosh

What happened? Seems, you can't recognise my voice? After a long time you are here again. Do you remember that even after the Partition, you could not help returning? Even back in 1948, during the *Durgapuja*, first, you came running to me, sat here by the bank, leaning your face upon the knees. On that day, too, I was anxious whether the lad had been weeping. Later, when I looked closely, I understood that you were only trying to cry, but there was not a single drop of tear in your eyes. It got all dried up through frantic searches for homeland in a foreign country.

Are you surprised at my archaic Bengali? What to do? You have severed the attachment with your village; now you are in West Bengal living as a refugee, and with the help of a border-slip you've got the citizenship of India. Hope, by the accumulated virtue of your ancestors, you can understand some of the implications of this archaic usage.

You write so much on the 'love for motherland'. Then cramming some foreign poems in a grave tone, you buy and sell your 'patriotism'. The country was torn in twain on 15 August 1947 in the midnight, by firing cannon. You became crazy with boiling nationalism. But amidst all those patriotic activities, have you been able to feel the pain in your conscience? Have you been able to sense the awful anxiety and anguish that your grandparents and your old servant Kunja felt sitting by the lamp-stand at this village home in the dead of that night in the all-enveloping darkness? Then, by any chance, at least for once, did I come to your mind? Do you know that when you were busy with the celebration of your new-found independence by lighting crackers and flying paper-lanterns at your side of Bengal, this insignificant bank of mine and your dear 'dreamland' were resounding with the inspiring songs of the well-known jatra, *Matripuja* by Mukunda Das? Do you at all remember the jatra was made as a protest against the evil intentions of the Simon Commission of 1928? Riding on my waves on sampans and canoes you sang: *Ore mayer name bhasano tari jedin dube jabere vabey, jedin dube jabe,/ Sedin Rabi-Chandra-Graha-Tara tarao dube jabe re vabey, tarao dube jabe re* (Oh! My countrymen! When the floating sampan dedicated to Mother would sink/ On that day the sun, moon, planets and the stars will all set in this universe). And we indeed sank in the fountain of your mirth and merriment!

Now, after all this time on this waning dusk of summer, what do you expect of me? Do you want to know whether I can recognise you? It seems, you have no hesitation at all to come here to forge an international connection with me.

Why didn't you sing a Tagore song today on 25 *Baishakh* in your beloved dreamland? Is it because, this canal side, your 'dreamland'—all are under the siege of the fundamentalist Jamaat e Islami? Neither there was any observance of *Rabindra Jayanti* in the village library premises this year nor did any of the school children sing the anthem *Sonar Bangla*. But my miserable heart finds some solace as you paid homage to everybody's favourite Kumada by clearing the outgrown weeds around the grassy cenotaph of the late revolutionary Kumudbandhu Guha Thakurata in the library premises, and also by lighting candles all around the place.

Do you remember how much all of you were astonished to see your grandfather making the old single-storey building to a double-storey one when you had come here for the *Durgapuja* in 1948? All of you tried frantically to convince the aged and elderly couple that it would not be possible to stay back in this village. All the agricultural and landed property, the house and habitations required to be sold, and the need of the hour was to move and settle on the other side of the border. It was not Bangla any more, it had become East Pakistan. The entire property could be put for an exchange, if not properly sold.

You might recollect how the old man got enraged at those wicked words of politics. But he took enough care to cater to your recent taste. He, on his own, planted a variety of flower-plants from the corridor to this bank. You were so glad to see the flowers in their autumnal bloom that you sang so many songs in your outhouse, and your *Sundarkaku*, with an ardent enthusiasm, organised a lively performance of his favourite play, *Chand Saodagar,* with a new group of actors. Well! Has your ancestral household become headless only because it is now in Pakistan? Had your grandparents become Pakistani because they refused to leave their homestead and declined to accompany you to that side of the border? Have you become severed from the Ghosh family of Banaripara, which had been residing by my side for nine consecutive generations? Did not you remain the descendents of Ramjiban Ghosh anymore? Truly, you are the real glorifiers of the family!

Alas! Did I also cease to be a part of your 'dreamland' with that?

Has this been your empty dream? Then, why have you come here after such a long time? Why are you sitting in despair? What have you been searching around before coming here? There is nothing out there except the plinth. The pandal, the outhouse, the large two-storey wooden building—so many things are gone! Why are you so stupefied at the sight of the ricemill in place of the age-old brick-kiln on the other bank of the pond?

Came to know that Dr Jekyll and Mr Hyde had become a double-faced personality, having suffered from a mental disease called dissociative reaction. What about the nature of your malady?

At last, you contrived to take your grandmother over to that side of Bengal. And eventually alienating your helpless grandfather along with the aged Kunja from their native household with the help of a false telegram, took them to Calcutta where the old man had undergone a slow agonising death. What was your idea? You would shift the entire household, your long-wished 'dreamland' the other side of the border! And now, are you brooding over whether I have shrunk to a trickle from your absence?

Listen! Still, sampan and pinnace boats, along with aimless water hyacinths, float on my waves. Though the kettle-drumming stage boats are not seen these days, small straw-covered boats do ride on my waves and the boatmen sing even today: *E kul bhange o kul gare ei to nadir khela* (The river breaks one shore and makes another at whim).

Mind it, still now I surround this Banaripara, the ancestral village of yours. As in the past, I still carry forward all your muck and litter to the River Kaleejira. She takes them to the River Keertankhola who, ultimately, hands them over to the sea-like river, Meghna.

Do you remember in your boyhood days how Satish Sil from Chandrahar used to come during the days of Durga Puja and train you to handle the scull boat properly and to push it with a bamboo-stick? You have always been lean and feeble. I used to tease you and call you a pea-pod and you would become so annoyed. At the wee hours during those puja days, with a hurricane lantern, you came to pluck so many flowers at the *Bainyabari—shefali, tagar, jaba*. But, to satisfy your temptation to have land lilies, you used to escape through a boat with Satish towards the temple premises of the Roy family of Narottampur. Are you thinking whether they bloom even today or not?

Look! A few canoes are afloat. Let's board on them and go back to the place where those trees used to be and see how they are now. Let's see, how from your absence, the temple has lost its lustre—its plasters exposing the brickskeleton from within.

Listen! You do have your own fast-paced life, and leaving me, your life is afloat on a different stream. But I have not dried up yet. Still, I keep vigil over Banaripara, your ancestral village, from all directions, like a baby in my lap.

Let's move! I will show you all today. You are constantly gazing at the Mahishpota village in the far north. But first, let's move towards the market in the West, from the market towards Chhagalkanda, then towards Najirpur, Jambudwip, Swarupkathi, and upto Sohagdal. A tributary flows from Nazirpur to Vandaria. If fortune favours, you might chance upon a steamer in Baleswar, my own tributary. Steamer, you see! Now they are called ships, launches, ferries, sea-trucks, casters, barges, tankers—so many things! Now, it is a different mechanism—the ups and downs of the piston along the crankshaft fuelled by coals in a steamer has changed radically. No coal, only diesel.

Then we would move towards the south. En route Baisari, Kundahar, Iluhar, Muninag, Kaukhali, Sharshina, Alankarkathi, Machhrang. When we head for the eastern stream, you will again find Narayanpur, Varukathi, Ghuthia, Ghorakandi, Bamna, Ponabalia, Gava, Keertipasha, Narattampur under the jurisdiction of Jhalkhathi Police Station.

Oh! You seem to have become a little disconcerted just listening to the names.

Though, by mistake, you turned up here after such a long time and as you suffered so much, I will not deceive you; neither will I behave like a stepmother. I will show you all. Lastly, we go to the North—en route Ujirpur, Habibpur, Bamrail, Chakhar. Don't feel jealous to see the present affluence and popularity of the college in the memory of Fazlul Saheb Haq at Chakhar! The village Machhrang is still there, but the great professional actors of the village are no more. One of the greatest children of this side of Bengal, Kshirod Natta, left the country in 1950s, with only the tom-tom, a gift from his mentor Yajneshwar. Sheer misfortune that he had to find shelter at the refugee camp at Dhubulia on the other side of the border! Then, the dagger of communalism brandished again. During early 1950s, all the member-artists of the Baikuntha Sangeet Samaj fled the country in single clothing with all their tom-toms and shehnais. What can I do? Narattompur is still there, the weekly market established by Nanda Roy still assembles on Wednesdays and Saturdays; the village fair commemorating new year is still organised at Goluia. But there are no Roys and no Ghoshs. Now don't start shedding tears at the sight of the derelict condition of the temple and monastery dedicated to *Paramhangsadev*. But the hanging bridge which the Jeshop Company had built in 1855 by combining the wooden tablets with iron bars like a glorious necklace on my chest has not broken down yet in your absence. Even the concretised JBD bridge in memory of Jagabandhu Banik is still there. I will also show you that.

In June 1950, your younger uncle came and took away your grandfather. Steamer service was closed then. He boarded the boat on me from this place, but remained insensate and motionless up to Khulna. How long had you been able to detain him? He, along with the old Kunja, returned to my dock again. But in 1951, your younger uncle took forcibly those two old people once again. I have heard that in December 1952, he left this earthly abode, and with his death, the relationship between you and this village, you and me, got severed for good.

Four decades after that episode you have come again. Why on earth are you showing affectations sitting over there, now? Why?

You did not know my name even. Do you recollect what happened in 1905? At the time of the movement relating to the Partition of Bengal and Foreign Goods Boycott Movement, the boys of Banaripara, inspired by patriotic ideals, took a bath in my water, tied yellow-coloured threads on their arms and gave a clarion call to forsake foreign dresses, sugar and salt, and started picketing at the market since dawn, causing much embarrassment to the bloody-eyed administration. Do you remember the names of those great sons of the soil? That movement was headed by people like Rajanikanta Guhathakurata, the headmaster of the village school, Barada Ganguli, assistant teacher of the school, Sashthicharan Das, the head pandit from Narottampur, Hemanta Kumar Basu, the student leader, Debendranath Basu, Prafulla Kar. Being heavily disturbed by that fiery agitation at Banaripara, the then district magistrate, Statefield not only had deployed punitive police in this Hindu-populated village but also had started collecting punitive tax from the people. Consequently, the spirited boys pelted bricks and stones at his boat while he was leaving. Perhaps, being enraged by that, he had forbidden my name. You just came to know my name Sandhya only when Bangladesh got liberation from the clutches of Pakistan and those people wrote my name in the map of Barishal district. The so-long nameless river got her name. Shame! Shame!

Let me stop here. Please don't mind my harsh and bitter words. You have come here after such a long time. Look at Swasti, your sister! Look how she is sitting stupefied to discover the television set of your Muslim usurper under the bed of the middle room close to the corridor, where your grandmother's metal tray used to contain betel leaves. The great wheel of time!

I can understand how deeply all of you love me. It is not possible that a Barishal-bred boy would fail to grasp the inner feelings of rivers, canals and other water bodies!

We are the sharers of your fortune, after all. Listen what happened once—

An unfortunate incident took place in your family when your aunt's marriage got fixed. Thanks to the wrong treatment of two doctors from Barishal, Bina, the youngest child of your grandparents, died only when she was eight and a half years old! All were coming home by two boats with loads of wedding goods and articles from Barishal. But no one was glad of the event. The boat was moving upstream past Kashipur. The boatman was driving the boat along the canal side and your father, leaving the boat, was walking with him. Before the boat fell into the Kaleejira river, your father stopped the boat by the bank in between Karhapur and Madhabpasha, and brought down your aunt and Ranga *Kaku*. And said to them that he would be teaching them a new Tagore song. He began singing: *Padaprante rakho sebake, Shantisadana sadhanadhana deva deva hey/ Sarbalokparamasharana, sakalmohakalushahrana, dukhhata pabighnatarana, shokashantasnighdhacharana* (O God, keep your devotee at your feet and allow us to sit us in the abode of peace/ We are all disciples to you/ You cleanse the sin of impurity and illusion/ You help us overcome misery and grief, /and bring solace to the bereaved.) In this way, the twenty-four-year-old man was trying to fill in the void created by the death of the youngest member of the family. He was trying to find consolation in Tagore's song, walking along the canal banks under the shade of coconut and betel nut trees with his two other younger siblings. But did it mellow down the heat of the summer or soothe the despair?

No. I am not going to make you distressed by narrating only the sad memories. There are memories of happiness, too.

After one year or so of your aunt's marriage, all were going to attend another wedding ceremony. Two boatloads of people from Dehergati to Lata village. Your father himself wrote a poem almost imitating Tagore to commemorate the occasion: *Etadin je bosechhilem path cheye aar kaal gune/ Dyakha pelem Shravane*)(I waited for you for long and vividly counted hours./ And at last met you in the monsoon). Two pinnace boats were moving through the billowy waves of the river. You know, a boat trip is meaningless without a song. The harmonium was there and your *Ranga Kaku* was playing the harmonium to the tune.

Do you know how everybody was delighted by that spirited song while moving on the swollen river? The real essence of such pleasure could only be understood by those who are born and brought up amidst the rivers and rivulets.

Memories of bygone days. Some people forget, some don't. I came to your mind after such a long time—you have been sitting by my side since then.

But you come to show your love and affection only at the time of leisure, but our love for you is timeless.

The river is your mother, after all!

ଙ

Translated by Bisweswar Chakraborty

Bisweswar Chakraborty works as an Assistant Professor in the Department of English, Government General Degree College, West Bengal. His area of interest includes Indian English Literature and Translation Studies.

The Guardian Deity

Dinesh Chandra Ray

I came to this house as a newly married bride. Just a year before my wedding, my mother-in-law had passed away. And soon after the wedding reception, the whole household was ready to bestow all its responsibilities on me and even did not mind taking orders from me either. So much hope, expectations, complaints, requests grew around me. Yet I was so new here that I had not even seen all the rooms in the house; had not gone around the entire house. One night I asked my husband, 'Dear, do I have to look after everything in this huge household?' My husband smiled mischievously and didn't say anything; hence it became even more mysterious. Two days after the wedding, I went to my parents' home for *Dwiragaman*; I thought that I would think about these responsibilities once I returned.

A few days after I returned, my father-in-law sent for me; he was a grave person—very tall, of fair complexion, completely bald. When he walked, it seemed like the earth beneath him shook. With a trembling heart I entered his room and saw him sitting silently on his bed. I couldn't discern whether he was sleeping or awake. As I stood there for a couple of minutes, he opened his eyes, gently smiled and asked, '*Ma*, how are you? Do you miss your home? This is your home now, *Ma*, check everything aright.' Then he fell silent, stretched his *poite*, scratched his back, and again started talking, 'In the temple, our Kalachand is a very *jagrata* deity. There's no end to his miracles. We have been worshipping our house deity for four generations now. This house, wealth, guards, everything belongs to Kalachand. As worshippers we are only using these.' My father-in-law scratched his ears with his right index finger and continued, 'Your mother-in-law passed away a year ago, now you are our *lakshmi*, you will see to it that there is no ignorance in the offerings and worship of Kalachand. Otherwise, we will have a disaster. You are the new bride of this house; you will have to bear the responsibilities of this household; hence tomorrow morning you will be welcomed in front of Kalachand. Tomorrow you will cook the *bhog* for Kalachand; that is the custom of this house.'

The next day, a maid came and tied my hair. I wore a Benarasi sari, adorned myself with ornaments and went to the temple. My husband and I sat beside each other, facing the idol. After a prolonged ritual, I was either anointed as Kalachand's *sevika*—his prime servant—or I was re-wedded to Kalachand, though I could not understand which. But I understood that my existence was now divided between my husband and Kalachand.

I forgot to mention that there was a huge pipal tree in the space between the inner quarters of the house and the temple. The tree was even older than my father-in-law. Its shade was so immense that it felt as if in a river of sunshine; it was a piece of newly formed sand bed of shade. Whenever I came here, it felt that my feet were getting muddied in the cool soft silt of the sand bed.

For about four generations Kalachand owns a huge property. Actually, Kalachand was not established but received as an order in a dream. He is like a *gharjamai*—a son-in-law who stays at his in-laws. But after staying in this house for long and enjoying a son-in-law-like hospitality, a dispute cropped up one day. Just after my husband was born, certain relatives demanded that they were the real worshippers of Kalachand. They filed a case in the court and in this dispute, the whole extended family got divided into two groups, some in my father-in-law's favour, others in that of the opposite party's. The state appointed a receiver to take care of Kalachand. Both the parties were asked not to enter within hundred yards of the temple.

Kalachand is a serene, flute-holding idol of Lord Krishna, made of touchstone. The eyes are set with diamonds. The whole body is adorned with gold ornaments. Even the flute in his hand is of gold. The crown is bejewelled with precious stones. Next to the room of worship is the bedchamber of the deity. There is a milk-white bed and mosquito net with frills on it. There is also a hubble-bubble made of silver with a pipe rolled with a lavishly decorated piece of cloth.

On the door of the third room there are thick metal bars, and a huge strong lock. Inside that room, the jewellery belonging to the idol is kept in three black metal safes. In two wooden safes, the clothes of the idol are kept. The idol is dressed according to the seasons and festivals.

The opposing party of my father-in-law argued that so many invaluable ornaments and crockery were not safe inside the house. Hence the court ordered armed guards to be posted here. They removed their leather belts and shoes and started guarding the temple—something that became more a hindrance than a help in Kalachand's service. It was, as if, a preparation of some would-be war. It continued for four years. A shadow of paucity loomed over the household. We had to let go of the servants. My mother-in-law's jewellery was pawned out and my father-in-law started borrowing money on high interest rates in exchange of promissory notes. The prayer, worship, everything stopped; my father-in-law had to rush to the court frequently like a crazy gambler in the racecourse. At last, one fine morning he came down from the palanquin and announced that we had won the case.

Since then, there has been no lack of attention to our *gharjamai*. Throughout the month of *Baisakh* (mid-April to mid-May), one has to give *jharna* to the deity. In the afternoons, an offering of fruits like snap melon, saffron and watermelon is made; and at night three kinds of sweets are offered to the idol, along with *paramanna* and *luchi*. This continues till the month of *Ashaad* (June–July), when ripe mangoes, ripe bananas and condensed milk are offered. From Durga Puja to the month of *Phalgun* (February–March), every day, ghee and rice and seven other dishes are prepared for the deity. And throughout *Chaitra* (March–April), *luchi* and a pumpkin dish are offered.

On Jamai-Sasthi, *Hari-nam* is sung for a day and night along with the mela, and other festivities. On Janmashtami, a hundred Bramhins are fed and given a farewell. On Dol-Jatra, we play with colours all day long, followed by smoking tobacco in the evening and finally return home in a palanquin borne by seven bearers. The first fruit of a tree, along with the milk from a cow that has given birth to its calf just twenty-one days prior, and the new rice must be offered to Kalachand. Kalachand is a man of many moods, a crazy son-in-low, he might get annoyed at the slightest irregularities.

It has been a year since my wedding. I gaze at the idol with its diamond-set eyes, playing the flute, wearing the golden crown like a king, in the land of babus; and I think to myself that this emperor is the owner of all our property. We all survive at his mercy, as this almighty lord is the provider of our food.

I still clearly remember the day of my first *Dol Jatra* in this house. Very early in the morning, Kalachand, adorned in princely robes, was placed in his silver swing fixed on the dol-*mancha*. Throughout the day, innumerable worshippers played with festive colours along with flowers of the coral tree. Towards late evening, Kalachand was given a bath and dressed in silk and a new set of jewellery. Kalachand had a meal of fruits that day; then he rested till five in the evening.

Later that evening, there were even more elaborate rituals. Kalachand was again dressed in his princely attire after his meal, and as the evening descended, a huge crowd of curious people gathered in front of the temple; it's only on this day that Kalachand sits on his throne and smokes his silver hookah. They say they can see smoke coming out of Kalachand's mouth. A sweet smell pervades the air. People sing praises of the deity while they gorge on this sight. A brass pitcher full of money from the offerings is brought inside the house.

After smoking, Kalachand goes out on a stroll. In the first row, there are seven torch-bearers, in the second there are *lathiyals* (guards with clubs), and in the third row are my father-in-law and husband, wearing silk; and at last, the whole crowd. My husband reminds me of the morning glory drenched in fresh water. Well, my husband anyway looks good. He is tall and well-built, with thick black hair, fair complexion and beautiful facial features. He has a dimpled chin. Whenever I look at him, it seems that he has just woken up from sleep. If face shows a sign of the self, his demeanour never reveals any desperation to confront anything. I have some observations about a man's physique: the moment they cross adolescence, they begin to look like warriors. When young men of mid-twenties smirk and pop their pimples beside the nose, they look very carefree. Their hair flowing in the wind, unbuttoned shirts, their sleeves rolled up above their wrists; and when they chew something, their jawbones undulate; they also have a manly odour to their bodies—I find all this pretty manly. But my husband seems to be helpless like a nestling. The summer heat doesn't tan him, the monsoon showers do not darken him, he doesn't want to be a conqueror in autumn, nor does he want to be disorderly in winter. Often, I compare my husband with Kalachand nowadays—there is so much strength and glory in Kalachand. I am a slave to the deity, my father-in-law is his servant as well. Hence, in the afternoons, I feel like a lonely shipwrecked woman under the shade of the massive trees, waiting for a man on horseback to pull me by my hair and take me. But who would take me? Who? My docile husband? No. Our sole sustainer Kalachand?—I am sitting forlorn in the shadows—where is my man on horseback? Where?

The sound of my father-in-law walking in his wooden shoes reminds me of a racing horse. He walks and sits straight. He sits on a white carpet with sacred thread hanging and looks over the zamindari documents. The expenditure of the family is in my hands. And no matter how I spend, more or less, he does not ever interfere. But his calculations remain intact and the daily expenses are always duly recorded in his notebooks. On the first ten days of every month, my father-in-law visits the estate; he keeps exact records of the income, money yet to be received, the last dates of submissions and even the amount pocketed by his employees. He keeps a track of all our cows, he releases the minnows in the pond. He keeps a record of all our yield from the fruit-bearing trees and the ripening fruits just with feline fierceness; he looks over the entire property like an old cat protecting its kittens. When it comes to the property, he does not give any leeway to anyone, not even to his son.

Meanwhile, one day a strange thing happened. I had not been to the temple for the last three to four days. It was forbidden to go anywhere near the temple during *those days*. So, I stayed in my room instead and tried to keep a track of everything from there only. But on the fourth day of my absence, I had a rather uncanny dream, where I saw Kalachand complaining '*Notunbou*, when you are not here these people do not take proper care of me. Today they offered me one dish less than my usual meal'. I informed my father-in-law the very next morning. He smiled a little, as if he understood everything. In the afternoon when he came back for his lunch, he said, '*Ma*, Kalachand did tell you the truth in your dream. I got to know that they actually offered him one fries less than the usual offering.'

That winter there was a bone-chilling cold. As the evening set in, everyone would quickly go underneath the blankets. We would have meals earlier than usual. Only the servants warmed their hands by making a fire in front of the cowshed. Even in this cold I would wrap myself with a grey thick blanket, bought from abroad, and go to the terrace. The whole house was silent as a log. I felt every pang of the biting cold despite the thick blanket; the tip of my nose became cold as ice.

I do not find a moment to rest throughout the day. In the severe cold, I take a bath early in the morning, and go to the temple. By the time we are done with the cutting and chopping, the offering of *bhog* and worship, it is usually two in the afternoon. I feel famished by then. And by the time my father-in-law and husband finish their lunch, my eyes feel heavy with sleep. But lazing is not something I have ever been destined for. By late afternoon I have to start the preparations for the evening rituals and worship. Then I come back to my room to tie my hair, wash my hands and face with soap, apply some powder. I wrap a blanket around myself tightly and go to the terrace. I stand on the roof of my prison, under the stars; and there I feel like a queen, even in the biting cold. The dogs bark and let me know that all the prisoners are intact in number. The foxes start howling. My husband returns home after a game of cards. He comes to the terrace wrapping a muffler around himself. We talk in hushed tones, like prisoners talk to each other. Usually none of what we talk about makes any sense, as if it's only confused noises that surround the two of us.

'I don't like this at all. I don't see you even once throughout the entire day'

'What can I do? I am juggling the tasks of the temple and the household'

'I cannot stand this anymore'

'What will you do?'

'I will get a small job in Calcutta. I will take you there with me. On holidays we shall roam around all day, have peanuts, watch circus.' One day we will speak up. We will definitely do. We will, we will.'

A youthful announcement of revolt on the roof of a silent prison, in the hope of an escape—where my husband would be that victorious horse-rider and I shall sit in front of him with my flowing hair, and we would fly away! I became happy. I felt strong. As the stars shine upon my muffler-wrapped husband, he looks like a Bedouin. I embrace him. Like an illusory wolf the blanket drops from my body.

The magistrate who was supposed to look over the properties belonging to deities came for his yearly round to the Kalachand Estate. Such a pandemonium in the entire house! The areas around the temple were quickly cleaned up. My father-in-law started getting all the documents of the estate in order. The magistrate would come and see these —it wasn't a minor issue, hence Kalachand wore his princely robes. I didn't go to the temple that day, rather I spent the entire day managing the kitchen of our inner quarters. My husband tried to appease the sahibs all day long. The next day, the magistrates had *luchi*, took a huge sum of money and left. I went to see Kalachand in the afternoon. He was looking magnificent in the princely dress. I stuck out my tongue at him—the way newly wed brides tease their husbands, when they are alone.

Two days after the magistrates had left, something happened out of the blue. Early in the morning when the priest opened the door, he found that Kalachand's throne was empty. He searched everywhere in vain. I had just come out of the bathroom after taking my bath, when I heard the commotion. The priest was crying aloud on the steps of the temple. A crowd had gathered in the meantime. My father-in-law was looking tense. When the chaos subsided, he looked at me and said, 'I came here last night to pay obeisance, there was no one here. I locked the door and gave the keys to the gatekeepers myself. The gatekeepers guarded the door all night; where could Kalachand go?'

As the day rolled, the news of the deity's disappearance spread everywhere. The villagers came in a throng to search for Kalachand. Some took vows, while some started crying. But no matter how much they searched, Kalachand was nowhere to be found. Food in the name of the deity was offered in the afternoon, a bath was prepared, the evening prayers were offered as usual, and the ritual of putting the deity to sleep also took place—all without the idol. Afternoon onwards, my father-in-law started doing his chants and vowed not to drink water until Kalachand was found.

In the evening, I went up to the roof, wrapped in my grey blanket again. The fact that Kalachand was not there made me a little happy in fact. I spent my childhood at my maternal aunt's house. She was extremely strict. I was so afraid of her that I would get startled and wake up even in sleep at the thought of her presence. My aunt died after suffering from fever for two days. I mourned like everyone else, but I was a little glad inside. That day, after the mysterious disappearance of the idol, the whole village was in mourning, yet I felt glad. I felt happy that I got released from my burden. If Kalachand was not found, there would be a missing report in the newspaper—'Kalachand come back, your slave has stopped eating and drinking.' His photograph would be stuck to the walls in railway stations. A report would be filed with the

Police: 'Such eyes, such face, pitch-black complexion, name: Kalachand, missing from the house.'

I laughed to myself. Who shall be worshipped in the ownerless property of the deity? It would be wonderful if the pipal tree gets worshipped. It is a strong tree, even stronger than my father-in-law.

The next morning, I went to the temple after taking my bath, and heard that my father-in-law received an order in his dreams the previous night. Yesterday the gardener had cut a bunch of bananas. Usually, the first yield from all trees is offered to Kalachand with *khir,* but somehow everyone had forgotten that. Hence, Kalachand was angry and was lying amongst the banana trees. As soon as my father-in-law received the orders in his dream, he got the idol from there and placed it back on its throne.

In the year 1946, the only son-in-law of the house fell severely ill. As soon as my husband received the news, he left; and seeing the condition of the patient, decided to take him to Calcutta for treatment. From the treatment of Dr Bidhan Roy to Ayurvedic practitioners, homeopathy, herbs, sorcery—nothing could cure him. At last, my husband returned with his sister and brother-in-law. The moment she entered the house she slumped down on the stairs of the temple, even before she could eat or freshen up. '*Jamai*, we have tried every doctor and every possible treatment, and now, you are our only hope. Please protect us, protect my *shankha-sindoor*, the holy symbol of my marriage, I will give you a flute set with diamonds, and offer a meal of 10 tonne rice for seven days. You are our son-in-law for three generations, and we have served you diligently; please save us, save my husband.'

My sister-in-law started cooking the *bhog* daily. She would clean the wooden slippers of the deity with her own hair. She cleaned the portico of our temple like a servant. My father-in-law started chanting with meditation beads in a corner of the temple.

Towards the middle of the month of *Baisakh*, my brother-in-law's health improved. The village doctor would visit him twice a day. The doctor was very experienced and also orthodox. Till the other day he used to leave with a long face; but now the doctor would leave smiling, occasionally cracking a joke or two. The whole house heaved a sigh of relief. Everyone sang praises of Kalachand. My sister-in-law made sweets of *khir* and offered *harir looth*. I witnessed how a nearly dead man came back to life by the grace of the household deity. All the impurities of my mind were washed off and I felt blissfully happy.

In the end of *Jaistha*, there was a terrible thunderstorm; we finished off all our works and meals earlier than usual and went to bed. In the middle of the night, I was woken up by a loud scream. I quickly got out of bed and rushed to my sister-in-law's room and saw that my father-in-law was already present there—my brother-in-law was dying. 'Are you Kalachand or a rascal! For three generations you are being served by us, but do you see anything with your gold-plated eyes? I will throw sand in your eyes. I have worshipped you, chanted your name for nights, wiped your feet with my hair, but you are stone-hearted. You do not have compassion for us. I will never see your face again', cried my sister-in-law.

In early 1947, relationship between the Hindus and the Muslims heated up. News of violence started pouring in from various parts of the area—news enough to send a chill down one's spine. In the nearby town, our relative's house was burnt down by Muslims. They tried to loot the Kali temple there, but the old-fashioned door was so heavy that they couldn't break it open, and hence they made the place unholy and left. Our police station was at a little distance from our village. The area was Hindu majority. Peer Sahib's mausoleum was considered a very holy place there. Both the Hindus and Muslims would make offerings of sweets in the name of the saint and take vows. But now the Hindus performed unholy activities there and even murdered the current Peer Sahib. In our first estate, the people of lower castes set fire to hundreds of Muslim houses. They even killed a few Muslims. And all this reached its peak when the Muslim labourers refused to work at our place.

My father-in-law went to the headquarters and requested for guards to protect Kalachand. But at that point there was unrest in every corner of the country, and no one had time to spare a thought about some idol's jewellery in an obscure village. Since we didn't get any police protection, we had to get *lathiyals* from among the people of lower castes from our estates. They would stay in the portico of the office and throughout the night they would guard the house and make a lot of noise. On waking up in the middle of the night, I could hear their conversations.

All around there was an air of dread. My father-in-law sent his people to villages and towns to know about the current state of all the other home-deities—'Baaleshwar' of the Majumdars in Bolamara, 'Radhamadhav' of the Chowdhurys in Nalkhola, 'Kali' of the Bhaduris in Porjonya, 'Narayanshila' of the Pakrashis in Sthal, 'Baalkrishna' of the Kayasthas of Raksab, 'Jamaigopal' of the Basaks in Kalukhali and 'Tarasundari' of the Sahas in Tarapur. He wanted to be sure of what the worshippers of these deities were planning to do in this hour of turmoil. But it was soon clear to us that we couldn't solely depend on the Namashudra (lower-caste) *lathiyals* and keep living in this Muslim-dominated village.

In the meantime, we heard that the Majumdars of Boramara had fled leaving back their Baaleshwar and their house. The strong winds were lashing against the doors and windows of their homestead. Baaleshwar was sitting quietly on his throne. In Nalkhola, the Chowdhury's Radhamadhav was missing; the temple and the house had been reduced to ashes. No one knew if Radhamadhav had also been burnt in that fire. It's impossible to move the huge idol of Kali of the Bhaduris in Porjonya, so they left it back to be worshipped by an old priest, on assurance of the Muslims of the locality. The Pakrashis of Sthal had immersed their Narayanshila in the river before leaving their house. Raksa's Baalkrishna, Kalikhuli's Jamaigopal and Tarapur's Tarasundari had been removed to a place of worship in Nabadweep, Hindustan, where they would be worshipped with many other deities in exchange of some monthly allowance.

The moment there was a declaration of Hindustan-Pakistan, the complexion of the whole situation changed abruptly. The Namashudra *lathiyals* refused to stay any longer. The situation deteriorated quickly. Kalachand's temple was attacked twice in a single night. The local police inspector, who was a Muslim, helped stop the attack. But one day the inspector informed us that there was so much trouble everywhere that it would not be possible to protect Kalachand each time.

Once I had watched a play in the village: I remember how during a scene of battle the two gas lamps suddenly went off. The entire audience was submerged in darkness. On looking towards the stage, I found that the dead soldiers of the battlefield were crawling towards the stage-wings. Today all of us are crawling in darkness like those dead soldiers.

That night the air became like a distant shepherd—calling his cattle from a faraway land. I tapped on the windows of all the rooms, I was wrong, not three, but four people. We sprinkled a lot of *gangajal* (holy water of the Ganges) on Kalachand before wrapping him in a towel. Before wrapping up the idol, we had stripped off all its fineries; without the crown, diamond eyes, fine clothes, the idol looked like a little toy. I almost felt pity for it. In the brief spell of my life, I have seen time and again that no matter how degraded, impoverished or defeated you are, there will always be someone who will love you. I hid the toy-like figure inside my blouse. In between my breasts, in the darkness, Kalachand remained safely like my baby. My breasts were looking heavier, so I covered myself with a shawl.

We walked all night, and when the cock crew at dawn, we reached a place which was a Muslim-majority village. There was a forest beside the village, and a river ran through it. As decided earlier, we entered the forest, crossing narrow streams, and intended to wait there for the day before commencing on our journey at night. There was a journey of three days and three nights ahead of us.

We consciously avoided looking at each other. My father-in-law looked shabby like a storm-tossed crow, even with his stature and personality. Yet I felt no pity for him. Even if he died at that very moment, I might not have felt sad. But my husband? Dishevelled hair, wrapped in a shawl over a vest, tired eyes, bare feet. This disaster hit him badly, and created a new person altogether. I knew when we reach Hindustan, my husband would get the position of a general in the army. I could breathe properly. There were robbers at the street-corners hiding in darkness. Yet I was taking myself forward safely; there was some sort of a valour in it. The life henceforth was uncertain, yet I could build it independently. In the village, I was nothing more than a slave girl serving Kalachand for sustenance; I had no regrets about leaving that life behind. The prison term of my whole life was as though remitted all of a sudden.

On the very second night, we faced perils. We reached a village, which, according to our knowledge, was a Hindu majority. Hence, we started looking for food and shelter here. Suddenly, a group of men emerged from darkness with torches in their hands, and surrounded us. What we did not know is that all the Hindus of this village had fled. The Muslims had taken over all the houses and were robbing and killing the Hindu refugees who were fleeing to Hindustan.

After being surrounded by the torches I could clearly discern that I would get looted. We stood in the centre of a circle lit by torches; outside the circle it was pitch-black darkness. Bearded men, with gleaming eyes and a vicious smile writ large on their faces, stared at me. My husband tried to resist but was struck by a club and fell down. I hunched down in that ominous light to see him bleeding, but could discern the wound wasn't too critical. But he kept lying, cleverly pretending to have lost consciousness. I don't know how my father-in-law struck a deal with them at last. We handed over everything to the torch-bearing dacoits. My injured husband held my hand, in front of my father-in-law, and started walking in darkness. Behind us was light from the torches, the tired shadow of my father-in-law, and ahead of them my husband and I holding hands. That was the first time we broke our prison walls.

After last night's incident, we made a detour. The dangers on this route were lesser but we had to go through dense forests. We were pushed back by seven days and seven nights. Even amidst all this affliction I felt liberated. One day we reached a place very early in the morning; and we were fortunate enough to get an earthen pot and some rice, grains and lentils from another group. We took turns in carrying these things.

When we sat down to eat *khichudi*, we weren't looking at each other. There was plenty of food but we were famished. None of us was asking for more food, and when I was offering to them more, both my husband and my father-in-law refused. Anyway, I was becoming very generous. Inside the dense forest, in a clean space, the birds were chirping, the leaves formed a maze, and it was tranquil. We were relieved at getting food after starving for days. Suddenly my father-in-law exclaimed, '*Bouma*, what have you done? Such a huge blunder! Our Kalachand is starving, and we relished our food without offering the deity a morsel! Such blasphemy!' I was resting behind a tree trunk then; beside me Kalachand lay wrapped in a small bundle.

Within a couple of days, we shall reach Hindustan. Meanwhile, another incident took place. With all other refugees, we reached the banks of a river. Once we cross it there would be no more problems. If there are no further mishaps, we'll cross the border safely. But in the evening, we heard that the Ansar forces have got an inkling that many refugees are fleeing to Hindustan via this detour, taking with them precious jewellery. They have set up camps on the other side of the river to catch us. And hence we must not cross the river now. Perhaps, people become more patient when their much-awaited destination comes near after a long road of thorns. So we did not become too anxious either. We somehow accepted that we must stay back on this side of the bank for a few more days. Food started appearing from all hidden places. We cooked behind the trees and had our meal together. I took a bath in the river and cleaned myself after a long time. It felt like we were on a picnic. We had completely forgotten that we would have to go across the river, face the devilish Ansar forces waiting on the other side, and the uncertainty on the way to Hindustan.

Beside the river lies the forest and then, across that a clear field. In the field there are huge shawl trees, then again there's the forest. The field feels like *Tapovan*. I wonder how this slice of land full of shawl trees is surviving in the midst of this ever-closing-in wild forest. In the cold night, everyone fell asleep wherever one could. I was lying a little further away, behind the trunk of a tree. My husband and father-in-law were sleeping. In the middle of the night many birds started chirping. I heard the ceaseless sound of crickets and the cry of unknown insects. Sleep evaded me. After bathing and eating to our hearts' content, this peaceful night suddenly turned me into a perfect housewife. With folded hands I prayed for more blessings from the night.

A little later I realised my husband was awake as well and somehow, just beside me. We wanted to disappear into the darkness like reptiles. Suddenly my husband shrieked as if something hurt him. I thought, it's probably a snake in the forest, but soon the matter became clear to me. I pulled the cloth-wrapped heavy bundle from my blouse and flung it into the deep dark night.

We woke up to the shouts when it was still dark. The Ansar forces had moved to another village nearby because of some fresh complications; this was our chance to cross the river and we did so very quickly. When we reached the other side, I felt the burden on the chest was no more.

So many people were crossing the border. They were distressed with hunger, soiled from the journey, parched from thirst. Some welfare volunteers, who seemed like ascetics, gave us *khichudi*. Quite a few times, on the way, my father-in-law wanted to ask something but instead said, 'Let it be'. Later we were put inside one of the many white tents that were put up on a huge field. Once inside the tent, I fell into a deep, deep slumber.

ଔ

Translated by Sneha Pan

Sneha Pan currently teaches at Gokhale Memorial Girls' College. She has completed her MPhil at the University of Calcutta. Her area of interest includes Holocaust studies and Trauma studies.

Jatayu

Dipendranath Bandyopadhyay

The sound of the departing train was gradually getting feebler until it was lost in the chirping of crickets. Darkness engulfed the surroundings again. Some murky trees covered with soot and blackness were standing here and there between the earth and the sky.

There were even no fireflies tonight. It is said that not even a firefly comes out on the new moon night. Darkness all around looked like a thick and sticky layer of mud. Everything was covered in the all-absorbing mire; so even and abysmal it was that all distinction between light and darkness was lost. It was a December night. Darkness was dripping like winter frost.

Amidst that outlandish surrounding, the small stage looked more unreal in the light of a few petromaxes. There was a small canopy of gunny bags only over the image of the goddess. Dasharathi has made the idol this year as well—deep-blue body verging on the glowing black with big eyes and an outstretched scarlet tongue. There was a garland of severed heads around the neck, one or two in the hands. It seemed as if these have been cut off just now.

All arrangements for the *Sondhi Puja* have been made neatly. Sitting on the sacred seat of *Kush* the old priest was looking at the deity as if in a state of trance, muttering the mantras like a sleepy storyteller. Giving out deep sighs intermittently he was crying out in a shattered voice—'*Ma, Ma!*' The sound gets carried away and lost with the fluttering of the bats' wings. There were four drum-beaters sitting on the pandal. The small boy was there to beat the gong; now pepping himself up with puffs of ganja. A little later he would have to play on the gong with Nityacharan's dance. Then there would be an animal-sacrifice followed by the final puja.

The place for the dance was fixed in front of the deity. Eight to ten yards of square land had been dug to a depth of about six inches, and then sufficient water is poured on it to make the soil quite slippery. It becomes difficult to walk on this ground. But Nityacharan would be dancing on it like a bird flying over it. He will carry a brass tumbler on his head and hold another with his teeth. The tumbler would be filled with fire. Holding these Nityacharan would keep his balance on his feet and dance marvellously, twisting and tossing his whole body. He would be dancing in the midst of burning fire. He would dance while carrying fire in his body. Nityacharan would become a ball of fire.

A bunch of eager boys were running helter-skelter to fix up small things. But in that strange atmosphere everything seemed meaningless; the last-minute hurry, the scattered cries of the organisers seemed to carry no sense. Someone, for no rhyme or reason, put down a heap of jackfruit leaves in front of the sacrificial goat. People sensing the heat of the fire even before it was lit, moved a little back to clear the place for Nityacharan to start his dance. Women sat separately at one side. The temple was just by the side of the burning ghat of the village. So there was no noise of the children shouting or playing. But the stray dogs of the village were right there in time—moving here and there smelling the soil.

Durga drew her veil a little closely so as to remain unnoticed. She sat almost at the edge of the row of women. Darkness cast a different shadow at this side. Formerly, on this very night she used to occupy the place of prominence in the front row; used to feel the slight heat of the fire close by. She could very clearly see every twist of Nityacharan's torso and every movement of his eyes was palpable to her. Looking at the muddy patch of soil, Durga tried to think absent-mindedly how she was many, many days ago, what she was…and suddenly came to realise that she could no longer think coherently.

Indifferently she could see that even other women, whether married or unmarried, looked at her with a sense of difference. They still had a respect for her as Nitya's wife. Astonished, she felt that she was not yet past the stage to get regards on account of her identity as Nitya's woman. Instantly she felt a burning sensation between her thighs. With bated breath she closed her eyes and sat helplessly. She felt that the fear, that stubborn fear has overtaken her once again. Her heart was pulsating with bouts of fear; her hands and feet were getting numb.

While returning from work at the close of the day, she saw the man in the crowd at the station. He looked at her, squinted his left eye a little and smiled. Durga turned away, walked very fast and got into the ladies' compartment of the train. Thereafter, all the way she trembled like a dried-up bamboo leaf. *Who was the man? Why did he look at me in such a manner? Why smiled? Were there specs on his eyes? Narrow line of moustache? Did he wear a dhoti or a trouser? Couldn't remember, couldn't recognise...no, no, can't recognise really. Why did he smile? Does he know me? Which station will he get down? Or was he just following without any definite reason?*

She was trying to find out the man in every station with a keen gaze, though often unmindful. Then at the time of getting down, she saw a young man lighting a matchstick standing by the railing of the station. But as soon as his eyes fell on Durga, he forgot to light his bidi. Durga immediately turned towards the paddy fields without looking at anything. *Was this the same man? But the youngman did not have a moustache, he was also wearing pyjamas. Then why did he look at me? Was he the same man or someone else?*

She tried to recollect the faces one by one. But no figure stood out clearly. She could not remember anyone particularly. Only a vague figure seemed to be floating hazily before her eyes. Durga tried to match the figure with the face but all in vain. She started gasping and panting in desperation. But only a hand, a hairy hand, squeezed her breasts hastily. Then it tried to throttle her.

There was a huge crowd on the narrow alley of the paddy field. Everybody was going to see the puja and the dance on that occasion. On her way, Durga heard the name Nityacharan uttered by many. Along with that, many words, both facts and rumours. Those who knew her, talked with and smiled at her. Those who did not know, looked at her in wonder and started to whisper among themselves. And Durga, with a suppressed excitement and suspicion, walked fast as if goaded by an unknown fear, but she was all ears to whatever people said.

I can no longer stand any crowd. Don't like it; I feel shaky with an unknown fright inside. If someone looks at me, I feel like fleeing from the place. I have a suspicion about any stranger. Even when someone known talks to an unknown person, my whole body trembles in an indefinite fear. I can't stand any crowd, no, I don't like any crowd. My trust has been shattered and I always apprehend a conspiracy going around me. I feel its tentacles being spread even here. It spreads the net slowly and I shall get into it. I know, I feel there is no escape for me. Slowly a hand will raise its finger, point at me and tell, she is here; she is here. The hand will not titillate me on the belly, neither will it press the nails on my throat. Still, I shall die, die and go, God knows where. There was peace in the house; we were spending our days hiding in our own room like thieves. Even the braves were spending the time hiding like thieves. Everyone took pity on us. We were almost at the verge of being erased from the conscious memory. But the man came out again today. Drew me out. I can't stand the crowd, can't withstand the gazes of so many. For us, always, the worst may turn out today, this very moment! I shall remain a witness to it with bated breath and anxious eyes. What shall I do then? Then me, that man—oh! that hand! Will it dance? I shall watch the dance.

He was looking like a hero. He was wearing a tight underwear. The oil-smeared bare body looked glowing and greasy. Only a loincloth was hanging from the waist like a drop of oil on water.

Nitya had dressed up well today. He must have applied a lot of soap on his hair, making it fluffy. His forehead was red with vermillion. On the arm and the neck were hanging garlands of false stones that looked like blackberries. The broad chest was pumped up into two distinct halves. Black manly hair sprouted on the thigh and the legs. The whole body looked muscular with the veins clearly visible. It was a spectacle to see. Nitya was in a state of intoxication with an indifferent smile of an obstinate man.

Then suddenly the fire flared up and it spread rapidly to form a circle around Nitya. He was within the circle of fire but had no hands—down the elbows there was nothing. Gradually with the third attempt, the circle would get narrower and narrower. Nitya was dancing with a brass container of fire on the head and holding another with his teeth. He was careful with his steps on the slippery soil.

Suddenly the drums started beating. With a taut cover of hide, it was very loud and exciting. The feathery decoration on the *dhaak* seemed to hold a sort of ceremonial umbrella over a dancing non-Aryan statue. The gong was continuously giving out a simple yet intense ring. The old priest cried out—'*Ma, Ma*.' The sacrificial goat also bleated out once out of fear but then started munching the jackfruit leaves lying in front. And all the dogs started barking and scratching the wet soil with the paws.

Durga sat silently with an intent gaze at the fire. Fire coming out of the ground, fire breaking out of the darkness. There were whirlpools of hundred colours in the fire and smoke. Darkness was trembling and with that, fire and smoke were quivering, coupled with the relentless beats of the *dhaak*.

I have not seen so much fire for a long time. Dance was there in Nityacharan's blood. Nobody thought that he would dance this time. Always a little hesitant, preoccupied with somewhat a sense of humiliation and foolishness, he now spends his days with a head bowed down for living on the income of his wife! Today again, he has stood out with his head upright and chest expanded just like the former days. Everyone was enchanted but how ugly the whole spectacle appeared to me. I had a feeling of nausea as I could clearly identify every stitch in his mutilated elbows in the light of the fire. Oh! Why doesn't he feel ashamed? He must have devised a plan. I don't believe him. What does he want? Oh, what more do you want? Why does he come down to dance, making me sit like a joke in the middle of the crowd? Does he suspect anything? Suspicion! Will he suspect? I was there that day—that day in the fire! Fire, a bigger fire that burnt down the whole house. They threw my father in that fire. My father was running from one room to another with fire catching his hair and beard. He dragged and dragged and put off the dhoti. All his life my poor father sang and performed the myths from village to village. But no hero from the mythology came running like the wind to save my innocent father. They did not allow him to come out of the house. The sweet singing voice of my father turned into a devilish cry of pain! That cry got mixed up with the sound of the bursting bamboo poles of the house. And when the sky was smitten with the sound of azan they took me out in the field, laid me there on the ground in the light of the burning house. My mother was laid by my side. And a hand started to squeeze my breasts. The ashes from the burnt house came flying in the wind to drop down on my eyes. I was feeling terribly hot and yet shivering bitterly in the cold!

'Ma, Ma'—the old priest cried out again!

Startled with that cry Durga looked at him. How long have I not addressed anybody as 'mother'! She vaguely remembered everything sitting here by the burning ghat on the other side of the river. My mother was gone, father was gone, even the motherland was gone. There was no one to do the final rites after my mother's death. No ritual, even no cremation for mother! I haven't called out anybody as 'mother' for such a long time! What is the old priest crying out for? Who will respond? Does anybody respond? Ever? Then why such a thing happened to me? Why? Why? Fleeing from the country while I was living by the station, I got married to

Nityacharan. Then they gave us a piece of land by clearing the jungle there. We erected our small hut, set up our home. The indifferent but dominating man used to move around with his head held high and chest expanded without worrying for anything. Didn't feel afraid of anything or anybody even on this side of the river. But I was constantly in a fear, a vague fear for the unknown even living with him and sleeping by his side. I was always afraid of that hand. I could visualise it clearly when alone. A rough and rugged hand with blackish nails and swollen veins like a centipede. That hand still tries to destroy my new house, my cozy shelter. Tries to make me stand like a convict in front of those simple and trusting eyes. That hand plays with me and squeezes my breasts. Many a time in sleep I instinctively cried out in agony clasping the hand of Nityacharan. He tried to console and calm me down, gently patting on my head. Told me obstinately that we will get everything back, everything on this side of the river. He used to console me like a mother. Oh, how long have I not called out anybody as *mother*!

'Ma, Ma'—the old priest cried out again. And suddenly the sound of the *dhaak* became lighter. Then someone from outside threw a bundle of jute sticks. With a superhuman skill, Nitya caught hold of the bundle and fired the second fence around him. The fire spread out with a great vigour. Two fences of fire were burning brightly in a circle and in the middle was Nityacharan, dancing in a trance. The sound of the *dhaak* was gradually getting louder and faster with the gong ringing in right unison. The sacrificial goat got frightened and started bleating out loudly. The shadow of the fire was quivering in the eyes of the goat. And in that darkness the image of the goddess Kali, the sound of the *dhaak*, the appearances of some shadowy figures and the ghostly dance of Nityacharan within the fence of magical fire with the incessant bleating of the goat created, as if, a beastly trap for me.

Who is crying out in whispers to my ear? The man had a penchant for beating on his chest when emotionally charged. *Who is crying out in whispers?* Listen, *Bou*, I can't move out on the streets, with both my hands cut off. Nityacharan could not beat his chest that day. *Bou*, how will you survive? What will you eat? *Bou*, I stay indoors and you go out earning! He could not beat his chest. *Bou*, there will be nobody to call you a mother. He could not beat the chest. *Bou*, what do you do outside so late at night? *Bou*, why have you reddened your lips munching betel leaves? *Bou*, how do you get new sarees? *Bou*, I do not know anybody but you. *Who is crying out in whispers?*

The sound became clearer gradually. It was a goods train. It had just crossed the distant bridge creating that sound. Only the flashlight in the front, with fire in the engine room, and a few men were visible. They bent over to see what was happening on this side. While dancing, Nityacharan seemed to look at the train with an inscrutable wonder in his eyes. Unknowingly his feet started moving faster, the beating of the drum became faster with the sound getting louder and louder. Unknowingly, everyone cried with the old priest in unison—'*Ma, Ma*'. Durga was awestruck to see that the brass container fell down from Nitya's head, as if he was disgusted with carrying that extra load and shed it off. The bleating of the goat was drowned by the collective barking of the dogs. The sound of the train became clearer and seemed so near as if Durga could touch it by stretching out her hand. She could visualise the black pebbles, old wooden planks and the shining railway track. The wheel was on the move, the nut-bolts were clanging loudly and the two lines were shaking rapidly. The train was moving fast. Two or three bundles of areca nuts were tied to the belly, chest and the back. It was rumoured that the train would be stopped near the bridge to make a thorough search for all contraband goods. So all the goods were tied below the compartment of the running train. The two tracks were trembling dangerously; even the pebbles and stone chips were shaking. The wheel of the train, the nuts and bolts were producing an uncanny clanging sound. And suddenly, absolutely unexpectedly, Nityacharan slipped and fell down between the two lines. So he did not die. But out of fear or obstinacy he tried to stop the train by pulling it with his might. The iron wheel bit off one arm completely and the other from the wrist. *Who is again crying in a whisper behind my ears*? Why it happened, *Bou*, tell me why? Whose sin was it? What sin did I commit? Who is crying, *Bou, o Bou*, oh why? Then the sound of the *dhaak* swallowed the sound of the train. It disappeared like the sound of a sigh. Everybody present groaned as if in a violent yet fearful way—'*Ma, Ma.*'

Nityacharan was then dancing in the ring of two fire fences. Occasionally he became invisible, covered by the fire and smoke. With a body full of drops of sweat, he was putting his steps on the sticky mud. A few moments ago, he appeared to be a hero but now to look at him I feel terribly shaken, my whole breath seems to have been drained out. A while back the eyes were reddened and there was that indifferent, impudent smile on his face. When I looked at that dominating, naked body with two barren arms dangling without anything from the elbows, it seemed to me that a mythical man had come down to the earth. There was a fire chariot ready before him. And the Goddess Kali felt ashamed with her outstretched tongue to see that spectacle.

Somebody again threw out the bundle of jute sticks. Nityacharan puts the fire on the third fence of the ring. Now the fire burnt within the mud. He had now only two to three yards of space to dance. It seemed, as if, the fire was burning out of his body itself. Some people groaned out in fear, the rest stood up in excitement. The old priest cried out again—'*Ma, Ma*'. This time nobody accompanied him. The goat was desperately trying to tear off the rope. Its dried-up tongue came out in desperation and the dogs were giving out a low monotonous cry. Even the dogs got frightened, they also wept.

Someone caught the neck tightly. The youngest daughter-in-law of the neighbouring house raised her eyes in a state of trance. She could not realise that Durga's neck was in a very tight grip. Someone whispered in her ears 'Demon'. Durga turned her head slowly, as if waking up from a dream and saw that no one was there. Yet she could hear a whisper—'It's your sin'. Someone said—'She shall die'. Durga stretched out both her hands to catch the two legs of a man. But both her hands lay inert on her lap like two dead leaves.

The drum-beaters also started dancing in excitement. Drops of sweat trickled down their rock-hard bodies. The old priest, too, was dancing in front of the image of the deity. The man from the other village sitting in the front row had been looking at her for a long time. It seemed he was also moving his waist and dancing towards this side. Durga saw that suddenly all the men and women had begun dancing. And the fire was dancing in a circular way in three rows. Red, yellow and violet in colour. Smoke was dancing—ash, brown and black. The smoke overpowered the fire and got swollen and huge in shape and size. Became grey in colour. The curtain in the hotel room swelled up and became grey. The door of the cabin was closed from inside with two chairs. The fan was moving overhead. Yet she felt terribly hot and strangely she was also shivering in the cold. She saw the house burning in front of her eyes, saw father running from this room to that but failing to come out. Heard the sound of azan and felt burnt ashes over her eyes. Then the sound of the train, the wheel moving on the track, nut-bolts clanging violently, and he tried to stop the train by pulling it with all the power of his two hands. Burnt ashes drew her attention. Radio was playing in the counter of the hotel and then that rough hand with rings on the fingers titillated her on the throat. Durga tried to shout with all her might but got choked.

No one responded. Within a second a train ran off with a terrible sound, casting a ghostly shadow in the tracks behind in the dim light—as if the great deviser of machine was being chased away by something. And fire was dancing in the three fences of the ring. Nityacharan was dancing. All the men and women were dancing. The drumbeats were dancing.

Someone seemed to shout from the fence '*Bou*'?

'What do you say?'

'Let's go to die.'

'No dear, I am very afraid of death.'

'What shall we do then?'

'You tell me.'

'Should I live like this?'

'Oh yes, at least you will be living.'

'Will you live like this?'

'Do not know.'

'Should we live like this?'

'Oh yes, we will survive at least.'

'Bou, do you want to live like this?'

'I can't, really, I can't.'

'What do you say then?'

'I can no longer continue like this!'

'Let's come to die.'

'I can't do like this.'

Durga was muttering inaudibly: *I cannot, cannot, cannot, I cannot*. Again, someone seemed to whisper in the ears—'You, evil spirit'. Someone seemed to tell—'It is because of your sin.'—The old priest cried out again. In a trembling, feeble voice, many shared that cry in a whirlpool of fear, reverence and elation. And Nityacharan's both eyes then looked like the outstretched tongue of the Goddess Kali. Sweat seemed to burst out of the whole body. Uneven steps were moving in the thick mud. Any moment he might collapse. He let the tumbler of fire fall from his teeth. The fire of the last fence was burning very close to his body. Fire was inside the mud; fire was burning on the chest of the soil. Fire was burning bright, burning and dancing; dancing and burning. With uneven steps he was dancing. Any moment he might lose his balance and fall flat on the fire in the mud. The severed elbows looked strange and uncanny. As if a tired, supernatural soul was somehow fluttering its wings. And all the stray dogs were crying in unison with the sacrificial goat.

Durga saw the fire advancing like a snake—slithering through the ground. The three fences now rolled into one. The three domains of creation rolled into one. It seemed, as if, someone stood out churning the wave of fire and declared in a high-pitched voice—'I have come. I know everything. You could not cheat me'. Durga knelt down in a state of magical spell. Nityacharan was no longer visible. Their colony caught fire and then the fire chariot ran towards Calcutta. The curtains of the cabin in the hotel where she works caught fire and burnt to ashes. Like a cruel ruler the fire began to destroy everything around. A small boy with a doll in hand ran away and the fire spread. All people ran towards the river with sighs and groans. The river had dried up to a desert. River Padma has turned into a desert. The whole country has turned into a desert. The world has become a desert. The fire was running fast. Where shall I hide? Burnt-out ashes came flying and fell on her eyes. Durga felt the scorching heat, yet she was shivering in cold. She almost whispered inaudibly—'Who has given me such a huge burden?' She said, 'I do not want you to die. Never wanted so, never, never. Had so much love for life, dear.'

Then Durga clearly saw that her destiny had come out of the fire-fence to stand in front of her. The enemy, whom she could never clearly recognise and yet in whose fear she would always tremble, had come out in the form of Nityacharan with his two broken wings. He held out the broken wings to draw Durga's attention and said—'It is here, it is here.'

ଔ

Translated by Sankar Prasad Singha

Sankar Prasad Singha is retired Professor of English, Vidyasagar University. A former Commonwealth Fellow at King's College, London, Prof. Singha served also as the Dean of the Faculty of Arts and Commerce at Vidyasagar University. He has co-edited and translated several volumes like *Survival and Other Stories: Bangla Dalit Fiction in Translation.*

Note

In the *Ramayana*, Jatayu is represented as a divine bird who tried to rescue Sita from the clutches of Ravana while he was taking her to Lanka. Jatayu was mortally wounded with both the wings severed by Ravana and he succumbed to death. In the present story, Nityacharan is the Jatayu figure. His two hands were severed in a train accident although he did not die. The story narrates his valiant struggle for survival.

Batashi: The Wild Breeze
Atin Bandyopadhyay

Batashi looked up, her eyes met a forest full of trees, beyond which lay a walking path. The early morning rays glimmered on the tree tops. It was the month of *Ashwin*. Dew drops sparkled on the blades of grass like fireflies, the branches and leaves spread a musty smell. Or perhaps, thought Batashi, the heavy air of household tales, of griefs and joys, was wearing off with the warmth of the morning sun. She pulled the baby in her arms still closer, then holding the hands of little Nibaran, started walking.

From far came the sounds of music, the offering of worship. These children loved to visit puja pandals. It being the month of *Ashwin*, thoughts of rivers and rivulets came flowing in her mind, as did those of the flower *kash*.

She lacked the courage to set out on the long walk. Her knees were giving in, she felt dreary. Her last and only place of shelter was lost. She had cried the whole night—her eyes swollen, with lines of sorrow visible beneath them. Batashi said, 'Nibaran, son, let's walk fast'. They began walking towards the pandal for *prasad*.

Yesterday Nibaran had cried the whole day, along with the child in her lap. Time and again, Batashi held God responsible for the scarcity of food and for her missing husband. Batashi was worn out with hunger and found it difficult to walk. An undefined restlessness was working within her. Little huts, big houses by the roadside, the puja pandal—every place seemed far off, and one had to trudge along. Batashi had hoped to get some sort of a job in a couple of days, then she would be relieved of the never-ending burden of anxiety about feeding two mouths. She kept on moving from one pandal to another for a plate full.

But it had only made her hungrier. Batashi could not decide what to do. She remembered her best shelter on earth, the place of her maternal uncle Mohanchandra. Uncle Mohanchandra Mondal had two *bighas* of land and a house. He told Batashi the other day, 'I am also a refugee like you, and I cannot give you food anymore. You have to fend for yourself, for the three of you.'

'Please wait for a few days, uncle. Let your nephew return,' said Batashi.

'Will he ever come?' Having said so, Mohanchandra got busy in tending his hookah. His ailing wife, while drinking water shouted, 'One's family is one's own'. She uttered a folk proverb that stung Batashi to the core.

Mohanchandra's children finished their meal, though he and his wife were still eating. Batashi and her children stood staring at them. Their eyes were brimming with tears with images of a morsel floating across their vision. Batashi even thought of committing suicide that night. She said to her uncle straight, 'What do you want me to do then?'

Her children were without even a morsel for the whole day; she could no longer endure it. She began crying, seeking an honest advice from her uncle, 'What will happen to me?'

Mohanchandra gave a very abrupt reply, 'What will happen? The one who has none, has God, has ten to help. She has ten doors to knock at'. So Batashi stood, looking at the path, for a long time. She had come a long way. If she crossed the scattered houses, she could take the road that led to the town. Batashi said to her son, 'Nibaran, son, when will you grow up? Where will I search for your father?'

Nibaran stood face to face with her.

'What will I do, son?'

'Your uncle says, they have killed father,' Nibaran said. Batashi put her hand on his mouth. She could not utter a word. Excruciating pain made it difficult for her to breathe. The sounds of *dhaak* and *shehnai* could be heard from afar. Nibaran kept on whining, '*Ma*, I am hungry'.

Batashi pushed her dry nipple into Tagor's mouth. They were crossing fields of vegetables. Nibaran got no reply from his mother. He kept looking around and said, '*Ma*, I am going to pluck an okra'.

The plants were full of them. In the last phase of their yield, they looked so old. And they were largely worm-eaten. Nibaran did not wait for his mother's permission; he rushed into the field and plucked a couple.

Seeing him eating, Batashi was a little relieved. The boy was no longer curious about his father. He was chewing and looking at the birds all around. Looking at him, Batashi saw the same feeling of safety and security in his eyes. While crossing the border he had asked her, 'My father has come away here, isn't it, *Ma*?'

While crossing the border, everything was so delightful, so pleasant. The same people ploughing, birds flying, no trace of sorrow anywhere—neither in the sunshine, nor in the fields and not even in the minds of the people. It was the time to sow seeds. On both sides of the border, it was the same bushes and copses, birds were flying from here to there, the same peepal tree welcoming one, or just another old man like Abbas, looking after everything. Abbas said, 'Hide inside the *dol*. Make your son wear a *tafan*.' And while crossing the border, Batashi thought, surely somewhere she would find old Abbas. So in search of a safe shelter and for her missing husband, Batashi, at times by boarding trains, sometimes like the commodities of the commoners, helped herself to cross the borderland.

Batashi walked along so many paths, went beyond so many local markets to reach the crowd from East Bengal in search of her husband. Sometimes it was the compassion of the government, at times physical labour, yet at other times the aid of the distant acquaintances helped her ward off the hunger. Keeping her own grief for her missing husband within herself, she would often hide her tears. She would say, 'Where are you? Your children only say, where has father gone? Where have you gone, leaving us behind?' Or perhaps all she wanted to mean is that such sorrow, such agony, such gloom—everything is a longing for Sadhucharan.

Batashi could not stand anymore. She could not think of anything. Her head was reeling. When the farmers were sowing seeds in the months of *Chaitra-Baishak* and the rivers were wailing for water, perhaps somewhere her husband Sadhucharan Mandal was sitting like a mendicant. She had imagined this thousands of times.

They went beyond the bamboo fence. Nibaran was walking alongside his mother holding the part of Batashi's sari. The little girl was all the while drawing in milk from her mother's breast. Batashi kept her sari rather slack, and with extreme neglect, she had carelessly wrapped the sari around her bare body.

The early morning fog was still lingering in the open spaces among the trees, like smoke.

The wind was blowing gently, and leaves of the plantain trees were fluttering. Nibaran tore a part of the plantain leaf and made a horn to blow into. His pants were torn, he was without a shirt and his nose was running. Batashi's gaze was almost blank.

A gentleman sitting in the verandah, with his legs up on a chair, was observing Batashi. She stupidly entered the courtyard. She did not speak anything. With a bewildered gaze she looked all around.

The man asked, 'What do you want here?' Batashi faltered and pulled her children closer, in fear. Then desperately she said, 'Oh master, please give my children something to eat'. Her words were indistinct. Batashi could not believe her own ears. Her face, her mouth started burning. She wanted to recite the same words again. But could not. The gentleman and his wife were a little aggrieved, so they were asking her several questions.

Batashi said, 'Then I had sat down to eat.' ...She wanted to give a detail of the riot, the sheer horror of it: they carried torches, they were running by the sandy land of Sitalakhha, and in the name of the Lord they were uttering awful, appalling names. The innocent could not eat in peace. Sitalakhha turned into a river of blood.

Batashi said, 'He did not return from work. People say, he, along with many others, had left for Hindustan. And, I along with the others, came here in search of him'.

Nibaran's face, like the magician's wand, came out from the folds of his mother's sari, and uttered, 'People say, they have cut and hewed father'. On knowing about the murder, the gentleman in an impassioned outburst asked his wife to give rice for the three, and some cash.

Then, on receiving some *muri* in her lap, Batashi broke down into tears. Nibaran, seeing his mother's tears, cried too. The baby looked at her mother's face, then began to suck again. The kind-hearted man could not endure this unfolding tragedy. Batashi, in search of a new shelter, set off towards the light house. The man could see as if this light house was just a beacon to serve as an aid to reach the sea. It did not signal a return to home nor did it help to anchor in a port. He said, 'Do not cry, what will you get by crying?' Perhaps he wanted to say, *sorrows make one noble*. Then he said, 'Till Sadhucharan does not return, you will have to wait'.

Batashi went away. Nibaran walked behind her. There were tears of sorrow in Nibaran's eyes, and so in the eyes of his mother. The disgrace of begging from door to door has brought her to this agony today.

'Nibaran, son,' Batashi called out.

'Rice is ready,' said Nibaran.

Tagor, his sister, was walking around. Crows were cawing in the main road. It was morning—*Ma* would eat, so would Tagor, and Nibaran will wait. Then, he would wash and clean everything.

Nibaran served and then called out to Batashi. She sat down to eat and said, 'Yesterday I brought two potatoes'.

'Yes, I have kept it,' Nibaran replied, 'if I get an eggplant, I will prepare a juicy dish'.

Batashi mixed boiled lentil with rice. That lady had given three green chillies. Batashi took them out from her bag with care. She smashed one into the rice and lentil, inhaled its odour, then with utmost care, picked up a handful of rice and ate it to her heart's content. She drank water from a jug.

Having pushed a betel leaf into her mouth, Batashi said, 'You know Nibaran, what Tagor said yesterday? She says, they have chopped up father. Exactly like you'.

Nibaran said, 'I could say that with a tune'.

Batashi said, 'Even Tagor will, after a few days'.

'Do you remember that man? You and I were crying. Tagor was also crying', said Nibaran.

'Yes, I go there,' said Batashi. 'But he does not give alms as before, his wife has passed away.' Batashi was chewing betel leaf, she pushed it into one side of her mouth, and her face lit up with a ray of happiness.

Nibaran said, '*Ma*, give me a bit of it'.

Batashi gave him a little of the chewed leaf. So even Tagor wished to taste it. She put out her hand, inarticulate words in her mouth. While giving her a little of the chewed leaf Batashi said with irritation, 'Today if you do not walk, see what I do to you'.

This brief hour of the morning is devoted to her family. She does not think about her husband Sadhucharan now. This little time is their very own. Batashi, Tagor and Nibaran try to take into account the things obtained by begging, and to survive thereby. There is happiness in life in having boiled rice and betel leaf. Young bottle gourds are hanging on the bamboo trellis right in front of them and the trees are all bedecked with flowers of spring.

A life exactly like this that she has left behind and for which there has always been a sense of deep attachment, is sprouting somewhere very slowly.

With her bundle of rags and other things, Batashi came out with Tagor. She was walking along the main road. It was springtime. The trees were covered with tender green leaves. The heat of the sun was gradually increasing. It was time to sow seeds again.

In front of them lay the road they are acquainted with. Buses were plying to the town. The creaky sound of the cattle-drawn carts and the chirping of the birds goaded Batashi forward. A longing for the town from the confines of her home, a craving for an entry to the nearby domestic dwellings kept her desperate, inconsolable. Batashi paused under a known *kamranga* tree. Once the tree had helped her with its withered branches, so once again Batashi looked wistfully if another such branch or a ripe *kamranga* was dangling above her. Or, still at some other time, while moving around in the District Board main road, to taste the mouth-watering *koyetbel* pickle; she gave the land surveyor a lot of edible spinach without his asking. Like the magician's wand, Tagor peeped from the folds of her sari and sweetly said, 'People say they have chopped off my father'. *As if a conjuring trick*! For begging, Batashi with Tagor's help, was showing this very magic to all. And to survive, such a trick is essential; for this, Batashi could sleep peacefully at night, she had no regrets, no remorse.

Today, Batashi would not go towards the town. She took a different road and reached the colony. The road being familiar, Tagor moved ahead of them and ran sometimes, as if she had got an invitation for a festival! Batashi knew that at this time, wide varieties of edible spinach and many wild flowers and fruits would be available. She collected all this in plenty. From the side of a bush, Tagor was calling out, '*Ma* just see, a lot of *gima*!'

Batashi got elated at having found this spinach at such hard times. She sat down to rest with Tagor. The primary school at a distance, the din and bustle of the children came floating in the air. Batashi said, 'Tagor, when you grow up, I will send you to school to study'. Batashi was plucking spinach carefully and talking to Tagor. Sometimes she was humming a song of joy.

The whole day was a struggle for existence. But there was an exceeding happiness in this struggle. She tapped the lap of her sari to find spinach in plenty. At some village, she would surely get something in return. A sense of business was working within her every moment. She moved from house to house with a tambourine in hand, singing songs: *E ki herilam nayane* (What is this that my eyes behold?). Tagor in a broken voice followed up. The aged women said, 'Sing one more'. Batashi sang: *Nadiay elen Shrihari* (To Nadia came Sri Hari). Then she would open her bag and call out to the aged mistress of the house. Being well acquainted with all the family members she would say, 'Where is your daughter-in-law? Cannot see her!' The moment rice was poured in her bag, she would mutter a few words that sounded like blessings. Everything is needed to survive. Batashi mastered it all well. Some families were close to her like her relatives. She put the spinach in one household and asked the daughter-in-law to take that. After that she drank water on the verandah. Batashi used to say, 'You know mother, at the Sarkars' pond a big otter was caught'.

She often told, 'We had then sat for our lunch. My husband was out at work'. When the early morning sun reached noon, Batashi would say, 'Mother, we belong to

Narayangunj. Have you heard the name? The port is on the other side of the river. My husband used to work at a guernsey factory. O mother, time does not remain the same forever'.

When the members of the family were busy and no one was listening to her, or perhaps asking her not to sing, then she would say, 'Heard of Nangal port? Your native place was quite near to it. All were burnt. Not a single blacksmith or a potter at Nangal port today'.

Then the members of that family would begin seeking information about their native place, about the land, the fields and fallows, and Batashi, like a *Kathak Thakur*, would keep on narrating. And in this way she would win her battles. Seeing her, one felt the urge to see those pictures of a land whose birds, fields and grains are more sublime than life itself.

Batashi used to say, 'O mother, I saw everything. My life in just one year is as old as a hundred years'. She wanted to describe the pictures of severed human heads left in the bushes month after month, the face of a naked young girl hidden in the leaves of *kalmi*, or narrate stories of unknown passengers moving away to places, no one knows where.

She had seen in just one lifetime so much! They plundered, they pillaged, they broke the leg of the *bhairabi* living at Nangol port. Her eyes dilated with fear as she would continue, 'Do you know one man hid his face under an earthen vessel in the water for five days! They came to the landing stage of the pond one day and cried, "Just see, the water is flowing, why isn't this vessel drifting down the current?" They gave one blow'. Tagor opened her mouth wide at this point, and after a pause, Batashi said, 'O God, the man's head broke into two'. After this, Batashi would take Tagor's hand and say, 'Well mother, I am off'. The family members would say, 'Wait, they would give two more handfuls of rice to her'. Looking at the field Batashi would say, 'Mother, the field is full of eggplants; give me one please. Nibaran wishes to prepare a thick soup with potatoes and eggplants'.

The sun had by then begun slanting. She entered into a few more houses, begging. At this time, far into the midday, people would say, she had no sense of time. Batashi had kept hidden the magic wand under the fringe of her sari. Her face was looking pale and her voice was touched with affectation. Tagor, in the meantime, would be peeping from the folds of her mother's sari to see around. The mistress of the family looked so terrible. Still, Tagor came out and said, 'People say they have cut up my father'. And this was Batashi's master stroke.

Looking up at the sky Batashi realised it was time to return. The farmers were plodding homeward. She was fatigued, having moved from door to door the whole day. She sat under the *shimul* tree keeping Tagor by her side. She took out a betel leaf from a small container and looked at the wide field in front of her. Whenever she saw such fields she remembered the faces of the dead, remembered darkness, light of the torches in far-off places, blood-curdling shouts in the name of God. Sadhucharan was as though walking towards her. Sadhucharan would never return. He was perhaps hacked and hewed by the people of the factory.

At night, when her hut is engulfed in loneliness, when bushes and thickets are lit up by the fireflies or the motorcar with a loud piercing horn rushes to the town, then as it were, the soft hushed voice of Sadhucharan is wafted across the air.

The atmosphere is stricken with extreme heat. Batashi feels drowsy. Tagor was lying, with her head on her mother's lap. There was no wind, from far came the sound of crows and the mynas. People are going to the town by bicycle. The sound of their cycle bell brings back memories of Sadhucharan's broken cycle with a bag full of rice, potato and eggplant by its side. So, there is no trouble, no pain now, only Sadhucharan's presence is earnestly desired. She can feed Sadhucharan now. The whole day passes in enthusiasm and excitement to stock the provisions. Hours pass too quickly. But nights are long. Batashi stays awake, alone, yearning for Sadhucharan. Tears well up in her eyes. She sobs.

Batashi had removed the sari from the upper part of her body because of the sharp rays of the sun or perhaps because the place was rather deserted. In the bushes one could hear the chirping of insects and worms. The uneven field lay in front of her. From the gaps between the trees the tin roofs and walls could be seen. With her day's collection, she sat under the shade of a tree with Tagor in her lap, humming a tune. The thought of walking through these paths, keeping the wood apple trees and bushes by her side or that of going to the town by rickshaw—everything seemed immensely exciting to her. It is for this that she wanted to survive, her desire was to live independently. And Batashi suddenly felt all have become the articles of her love. The image of Sadhucharan appeared awfully pale by the side of these birds, insects and wood apple trees.

When the rays of the sun mellowed down, when bullock carts from the town turned and went down towards the village, Batashi called out to Tagor, 'Wake up now, won't you go home?'

Batashi took a dip in the nearby pond. Then, in the late afternoon, with her hair unkempt, she moved homeward singing a song in praise of the Goddess Kali. She sang, *Shyama, boson por, bhushan por* (O Mother, put on raiments and wear ornaments); and she felt how the hidden desire for clothes and trinkets always haunted mankind. She said, 'Tagor, tomorrow we will go to the town for alms'. Having decided so, they turned homewards.

Their faces were looking forlorn, as if they were two pilgrims, who had just alighted from a fast-moving vehicle.

Batashi was asleep at night. The room was shrouded in darkness. In a corner, a frog was croaking from time to time. It was raining along with gusty winds and sounds of thunder on tree tops. Nibaran was fast asleep. Tagor once cried out in sleep while Batashi saw frightening dreams as though Sadhucharan was standing outside, calling out to her, to open the door. It seemed to be a dream because of the rain and the roll of thunder. By the side of the door Batashi remained alert. She heard a human voice: Mohanchandra was calling, 'Open the door, Sadhu is here'. She was stricken with a fear, as if she saw a ghost, her eyes dilated, and she had a terrible pain in the heart. Shuddering with dread, she went to open the door. From the little gap she could see the shadowy forms of two human beings. Nothing was clearly visible, so Batashi lit the lamp. Keeping it in one hand she asked, 'Who are you?'

'I am Mohan. I have brought Sadhu.'

Batashi opened the door and saw it was indeed Sadhu. She could not speak clearly as everything seemed mysterious to her. She stood nonplussed. Sadhucharan in front of her, with his soiled shirt, long beard and bright, glowing eyes! After Mohanchandra left, Batashi fell on Sadhu's chest. She touched him, and then broke down into tears knowing that it was really Sadhucharan. Batashi said, 'I did not let your children suffer'. Sadhucharan asked, 'Did you stay at Abbas's place?'

'Yes. But I felt Abbas won't be able to save us at night. So I wore Abbas's wife's *burkha*, put on a nose ring too, and clothed Nibaran in a piece of *tafan* and set out.'

Sadhucharan was about to begin his story, but Batashi intervened, 'Your tales of pain can wait, you change first'. She wiped his dishevelled hair. She said, 'I could not sleep at night for you. Your uncle says they have cut you in pieces'. She pushed her hands in his beard, and then moving closer to him said, 'I will not cause any more sorrow to you'. Sadhucharan said, 'Come close, don't stay far'. 'I am feeling shy', she said. Sadhucharan stood up. He pulled Batashi so close that she spoke out in alarm, 'Nibaran is a grown-up boy, Tagor is grown-up too. Blow out the lamp'. Sadhucharan did not do so. Rather, in the glow of the lamp, he gazed at Batashi's face, or perhaps he was breathing in the smell of her mouth. He wanted to see if the mouth had the odour of any incurable disease. Batashi spoke up, as if something she forgot came to her mind all of a sudden, 'What did you have in the afternoon?'

'Nothing.'

Batashi tore herself from his clasp and said, 'Let me boil some rice for you'.

It was raining outside. Nibaran and Tagor were still asleep. Batashi gathered dry leaves and twigs from a corner of the room to make a fire. Then she took rice, pumpkin in a bowl, washed it and set it to boil. The fire was burning in the oven. Sadhucharan sat next to it, speaking about joys and sorrows. The loin cloth wrapped around him, he was looking at Batashi's face. Such a grace in her face! It was looking enchanting in the fire of the hearth. He hugged her again beside it, and said, 'Batashi, your face is my God. I went to so many places looking around, if I could find a face like yours. People said I was mad. They beat me up'.

Batashi could not look at Sadhucharan. His long hair and beard, his sunken eyes made him look so helpless—helpless like a child. With a desire to caress him, she stretched her hands. She said, 'Those who beat you up, may their hands be severed'! She sat in the night cursing them. Sadhucharan continued, 'Back at Nawadip, I got the news from Santosh Pal that you had gone to uncle'.

Mohanchandra's name itself maddened Batashi. Her face became dreadfully gloomy. So great was her hatred that she could not look at the man, when he brought Sadhucharan. She sat, all the while, bewildered.

Sadhucharan looked around the room. Fence made of the stalk of jute plant, thatched roof. It was still raining. The sound of the moving trucks came floating in, frogs were croaking. And Sadhucharan, sitting by Batashi's side, felt that his life's journey had at last reached the final shrine. He took Batashi's face in his two hands and said, 'Will I be able to enjoy such happiness?' Saying that, he burst into tears.

Nestling close to Batashi later, he said, 'Batashi, uncle says, you beg?'

'Tell me then, what to do?'

Sadhucharan had no answer. The next day Batashi said, 'Since you are here, today I will not go out begging'. So the whole day Sadhucharan and Batashi spoke about their place, their village. Nibaran and Tagor remained with their father. The little desires of this family were floating in the soft air. Sadhucharan caught fish with a hook. And with coriander leaves, Batashi prepared a delicious dish. Sadhucharan called Nibaran and Tagor when he sat for lunch. They ate happily with their father and let out deep belches. It being a sunny day, moisture in the air was less. Batashi's sari was fluttering in the air. Then, at night, when the moonlight spilled on the soft earth, with the chirping of the insects, sound of the wheels of the bullock carts were fading away in the distance, Sadhucharan said, 'Batashi, I want to tell you something'.

'Okay.'

'You have to keep my word.'

'Say, what it is.'

'From tomorrow you will not go out begging'. Batashi did not reply. Sadhucharan asked, 'Why do you keep mum?'

'What can I do, other than keeping quiet?'

'Answer me.'

'I won't. If I give my word today, how will things run tomorrow?'

'Why? Why will things not get on?'

'First, get a job.'

So early the next morning, Sadhucharan set out towards the village with the hope of toiling as a daily wage-labourer. Batashi too, like other days, having explained everything to Nibaran, held Tagor's hand, and among the chirping of birds, walked down the shaded paths, so well known to her, and moved from one house to another. Singing her songs and narrating those stories, as if she were the steer man, Batashi traded like a skilled merchant. Returning home after the day's work, Sadhucharan said, 'Where is your mother, Nibaran dear'?

'*Ma* has gone for begging. Tagor is with her.'

Sadhucharan's face, marked with lines of bitterness, looked sad in the late afternoon. When Batashi returned after trading, Sadhucharan did not speak to her. He sat in the courtyard like a stranger, drawing deeply on his hookah.

Batashi walked straight inside. Giving her bags and other belongings to Nibaran, she came out. She said, 'Why are you sitting with a sulky look on your face? See what I brought for you'. She kept a small cucumber near his feet and said, 'Take it with a handful of *muri*'.

Sadhucharan looked indifferent, as though he had not heard anything. Then from the folds of his loincloth, tied at the waist, he brought out his day's earnings and said, 'Take this, tomorrow you will not go out to beg. You are my wife and I am Sadhucharan, a sando factory worker. If you remember this, you will never go out begging'.

Batashi smiled, 'Did you eat anything?'

'Yes'. Sadhucharan's voice still had traces of bitterness. So Batashi went and sat near his feet.

'Tell me, for whom do I do it? For you and for your children I beg. If you are annoyed, where will I go, tell me'.

Sadhuchran said, 'I am telling you again, don't go for begging'.

The evening was dying out. Sadhucharan did not go anywhere.

The two vividly waited for the moonlit night to sit close to each other. When the moonlight came down upon the courtyard, when the cool breeze started blowing and the body was no longer sweaty, Sadhucharan said, 'Tomorrow I'll go to town, if I can get a job at the factory'.

And one fine morning he indeed got a job at the sando factory. Returning in the late afternoon he said, 'Now I am telling—for the last time—you will not go begging anymore'.

Batashi bent down in sorrow. Like other days, she did not say a word. She crossed the drain and stood on the main road. All these paths take strange winding directions. The familiar trees, the birds are as though all alone.

Batashi stood for long, holding Tagor's hands in hers. No one would now listen to her narratives like that of a *Kathathakur*, no one would listen to her songs, praising Goddess Kali. Or while listening to the twittering of birds, if she got lost in the village paths, no one would find her woebegone. Begging almost became a pilgrimage for Batashi. She returned home like a boatman moving against the current. She sang songs of Shyama: '*Shayama, basan por, bhushan por*' (Deck yourself Shyama with raiment and ornaments). And then she sat down to mend her carrier bag and the accessories for her trade.

ଶ

Translated by Anuradha Sen

Anuradha Sen taught at Kharagpur South Side High School, West Bengal. She is a copious translator. *Anil Gharai: Stories of the Downtrodden* is one of her representative works of translation.

The Bait of a Dice

Jyotsnamoy Ghosh

Dear *Ma*, I—your ill-fated daughter, disgrace to your esteemed caste–religion–family—am writing you from a distant land. When my heart twists in pain, when my deep-stored prejudices mislead me constantly like a whirlpool of a labyrinth, when I can no longer find a solution to the sum of my life crafted by many hands, then, dear *Ma,* just then your face like that of a Durga idol flashes before my eyes. To whom but you should I confide in the chronicle of my disgrace, of my dishonour, of my twenty-two-year-old life burnt up by the epoch-ending fire of history! You're my *Ma,*—no caste, no religion, no pride of family, you're only my *Ma*; you're not the scripture-versed daughter of *Vedantabagis*, nor the wife of *Samkhya-Smrititirtha*, you're my *Ma*, this is your true identity; you held me once in the depth of your being, I'm a companion of that tree-self of yours; whom shall I share with a slice of the endless pain of my battered, bloody heart, except you...

The town in East Bengal where once I, sprouted from the seed of my devoutly religious father, was interwoven with this living world with a fine thread of unity, where my childhood, adolescence and budding youth were spent, where I came to know humans, flowers, plants, rivers, sky, creepers, shrubs, forests, where I trembled in the immense wonder of the vivid and delightful mystery of my becoming—there, in that very town, the lord of the earth etched the badge of misfortune on my forehead. I cannot forget that night. Even at the slightest recapitulation of that event, I still turn blue in fear—

From the afternoon it was gradually becoming clear that something would happen. And yet till noon everything seemed normal. The school was closed after a couple of periods, though we couldn't guess anything. The headmistress called us in her chamber and said to us, 'Don't loiter around and engage in any *adda* anywhere. Go home straight away. Remember, you have your qualifying test ahead. Don't go by the road through the market. You don't listen to me at all.' Coming out of her chamber, we all laughed covertly. We knew that Rabeya di had an unreasonable fear about the road through the market. As a matter of fact, the permanent address of the *adda* of the college students and the loitering young men at Bakultala crossing was then a spot of common dislike for all the guardians in the town, including Rabeya di. We knew that they daringly discussed politics, literature, sports and girls at the highest pitch of their voice, even occasionally fought too; seeing us they would become loquacious. We didn't particularly dislike them: they elicited a response from the deepest recesses of our being.

We went by that very road through the market. As soon as we reached Bakultala crossing, Poppy whispered to me,

'C.H.'—'C.H.' stood for Chandan. Chandan, Firoj, Maqbul and Anowar stood under the *bakul* tree. They all glanced at us for once and the next moment became engrossed among themselves. They appeared to be somewhat subdued and distracted. We thought they perhaps had a fight with someone. We knew very well that if Chandan and Firoj were together, any mishap might take place. As we walked along, we kept on gossiping on these. Poppy suddenly said, 'Why is Runa's heart a little heavy? My elder brother probably didn't look at her!' Firoj was Poppy's elder brother. Runa said in a ringing tone, 'Mind your own business. You needn't bother about me...'

I reached home with quite a light heart. But seeing me you were about to break into tears, *Ma*, and said, 'Oh! You're back!' As if you assumed that I wouldn't come back at all. I was amazed and said, 'What do you mean!' Then you couldn't withhold tears, your voice almost choked in terror, and you said, 'O, a disaster has fallen! The Bhattarcharyas of Kendua were all hacked to death last night. They'll attack this town tonight.' It took some time to sink in, then I grasped you. You slowly drew my head on your lap and said, 'Don't be afraid, my child. Why are you afraid? We are with you, aren't we?' Back in our childhood, when we would be afraid, you would often hearten us this very way. Then with anxiety in your voice, you said, 'Those two have gone out so early in the morning; there's no news of them at all since then. As if they need to lead in all affairs! And I've to face all misfortune!' The 'two' referred to Chandan and *Dada*—my elder brother.

I felt I couldn't possibly disclose to you, *Ma*, that I've seen Chandan with Firoj and his pals. You quite often repeated, 'I've to bear all the burden of danger for this boy from another family. His parents have sent him here to study, and only God knows how he's doing in the college. The fellow has grown wings after setting foot in the town. I won't be able to take the responsibility of this boy. Let everything pass peacefully, then I'll...'

The rumour spreading from mouth to mouth since the afternoon was gradually turning into a news. The nameless, shapeless clouds of horror were slowly coalescing under the clear sky of autumn. They were trickling together one by one in the big mosque. Chandan and my *Dada* used to go out frequently, they couldn't sit down quietly; their faces were gradually growing pale, the sheer sense of conviction was gradually melting down drop by drop through the chink of their closed fists—there was hoping against hope. Towards the onset of the evening, they took a round for the last time. I remained lying in my own room. They spoke with you in a hushed tone for a while in the big hall. Once Chandan came into my room, sat down by the cot, took up my palm and said, 'Don't be afraid Bula, I'm standing by you, can't you trust me?' Chandan, with his strong build, appeared like a hero from the myth: I sank my face into his arms. He was caressing my hair, his hot breath was falling on my neck, at the tip of my ears, on my tresses; my terror was gradually taking the shape of an untasted intense joy—my face was cupped inside his two hands, the fragrance of Chandan pervaded my whole body and the consciousness inside it. Chandan! Ah Chandan! Chandan was trembling, I was trembling, and the darkness in the four corners was also trembling...

'Chandan, Chandan, Shankar'—

No noise from outside then reached my ear distinctly. It seemed that someone from afar, and with much worry, called Chandan and my *Dada*. Chandan went out, stricken with fear, as if he knew that the call would come; all of you, including my *Dada*, were then on the courtyard. Perhaps you wanted to restrain them, *Ma*, for you said in a tone of warning, 'No one must open the front door.' Perhaps Chandan said, 'Aunti, Firoj is calling.' You said, 'Nobody I trust anymore.' Without paying heed to you, they opened the door and went out. The tinkling music of the ankle-bells of my heart had finally stopped, the shadow of fear surreptitiously thickened there—why weren't they coming back, Chandan and *Dada*, oh God, why weren't they? Chandan Chandan... Sinking my face in the pillow I said to myself, 'They may have murdered Chandan', the lizard didn't say 'tick tick'; I said to myself, 'Chandan is alive', the lizard didn't say 'tick tick' this time either. It seemed that the sound of opening the door vibrated the air-waves ages and ages ago. The fear inside was terrorising me; many different pictures of fear in their complex geometric shapes in the roomful of darkness kept staring at me without blinking, like the eyes of a bodiless female ghoul...

At last they returned. We all sat close together in the big hall. It was Chandan—his throat as dry as a piece of blotting paper, he was licking his lips with his tongue—who broke the silence, saying, 'Many people are going to Dayamayee House. There are armed guards and footmen, there are guns. It's better to spend the night there.' *Baba* uttered something for the first time and we knew that there was no difference between his comment and decision. He said, 'You're talking of safety, aren't you? Have faith in God. I can't just go away, leaving the idol of my family deity. I've a *duty* to protect the idol. Rather, you go.' *Ma*, you said, 'That can't be. If we have to die, it's better to die together.' So the idea of leaving home was abandoned. *Ma*, you thought of my father, father thought of the safety of his idol, the responsibility of maintaining the safety of God was invested on man that day; you thought of only death as the greatest calamity; that there could be an irresistible disaster other than death didn't at all appear in your mind, *Ma*; the arrow of calamity came from the opposite direction of your thought which was like the one-eyed deer. *Ma*, no thought about me specifically did cross your mind that day…

It was around midnight. Reducing the wicker of the kerosene lamp, the five of us sat like five shadows in the big hall. My elder brother and Chandan had two *lathis* on their laps. *Dada* said, 'The Muslim youths would resist the communal riots with their own lives. A few *goondas* who have come from Uttar Pradesh as refugees are as fierce as wounded tigers, and they are the cause of fear.' *Dada* had hardly finished his words when Chandan jumped and went outside, and from there called in a hushed tone, 'Shankar—'

The sky in the east was entirely red, the wind was full of the anguished cry of people. We were standing on the verandah of the big hall, the heat of the fire as if touched our body; I was desperately trying to prevent a terrible fit of trembling. Just at this moment the noise rose, shaking everything all around—'*Allah Ho Akbar*. I was falling down, grasped the pillar in front of me with both hands with all my strength; you sat down on the ground stiffly, *Baba* sat down on the steps of the puja room, shaking; Chandan and *Dada* loitered all over the courtyard aimlessly like soldiers without a captain. The noise stopped just after rising once, then came down a deathly hush; in that silence I almost gasped for breath, all my veins, arteries, nerves, organs, senses were loosening and the stream of consciousness was suspended; I couldn't bear that silence, *Ma*.

Then rose the waves of sound, the front door was struck, they began to drum up the name of God in beastly exultation. Chandan and *Dada* awoke, as if struck by something. Chandan called in a hushed tone, 'Auntie, Bula, please come down.' But we had no strength to go down; *Dada* dragged you, Chandan dragged me, and they took us into the forest at the back of the house, densely woven with bamboo, fig tree, cane, *jalpai, amloki, pitraj, haritaki* and many other plants and creepers and shrubs. Chandan called father, 'Uncle, come away.' Father said, 'My idol—', but without completing the sentence ran helter-skelter and entered into the forest; at that very moment our front door was crashed down with a bang.

After walking quite a while Chandan stopped, breathed heavily, leaning on the *jalpai* tree; he was sometimes massaging, as if examining, the muscle of his one hand with the other, just as the sacrificial animals are examined. I was lying at the feet of Chandan, like a *devdasi*. I very much wanted to have you, *Ma*, near me during that time. But you, *Baba* and *Dada* were separated from us; I wanted to stand up; I was shivering like a patient of tertian fever. There was liquid darkness all around us, the green moonlight of the full moon night was melting down the leaves of the trees. The howl of rioting, and the noise of breaking up things raised by the men drunk even without a single drop of alcohol were coming out from inside the house. Someone shouted loudly, 'The residents have all fled, ustad.' A command in a bass voice was heard, saying, 'Irfaan, try to find out Chandan, I want Chandan.' Chandan shivered under the immemorial darkness of the *jalpai* tree, and said in a heavy voice, 'Bula, the henchmen of Ramjan have come.'

Once Chandan severely thrashed the daredevil Ramjan, a refugee from U.P., at the Bakultala crossing, as the latter had made obscene advances to Shahid's sister, a friend of Chandan. Chandan was not at all afraid of Ramjan or his henchmen at that time or even after that event; he would say, 'Have we to live with the fear of a goonda?' But today Ramjan was not a goonda—he was a Muslim and Chandan, a Hindu; Chandan was afraid, *Ma*. He bent on me and said, 'Stand up Bula, we are not safe here.' I couldn't raise myself, my shuddering rather increased. I proffered a hand to Chandan, he made me stand up, I was faltering often, Chandan clasped me with his whole body, my face, my wood-apple like small round breasts, my abdomen, my shanks—my whole body was full of Chandan. My tongue dried up, and was gradually going inside, my body was cold; Chandan's strong arms, wide chest, abdomen, *sal*-tree-like thigh—everything had the cold sensation at the middle of the wintry month of *Magh*. Just at that instant, rose a yell convulsing the darkness, 'Who's there?'—and instantly pushing me back Chandan vanished like magic—darkness wobbled in front of my two eyes, I wanted to run, I wanted to go back to the secure shelter of your womb, *Ma*, catching the torn umbilical cord. But then the dice had already been cast by the hand of an invisible player:

Duhshasan caught her hair with a howl, the hair that was wet with the water sanctified by the mantra of Rajasuya yajna. Her body bent by the pull of Duhshasan, Draupadi said, 'Evil-witted non-Aryan, I'm wearing a single piece of cloth, menstruating, don't take me to the royal court.' Duhshasan said, 'Menstruating, wearing a single piece of cloth, or no cloth at all, whatever condition you may be in, you have become our slave, being won over in the dice game, you have to worship us...'

Duhshasan was about to take Draupadi away by pulling her cloth robustly. To rescue her from shame Draupadi began to invoke Krishna Vishnu Hari. Then Dharma Himself covered her in the form of a cloth. As Duhshasan was pulling her, hundreds of pieces of cloth, coloured in diverse dyes as well as white, began to appear.

I invoked your God with my entire being, *Ma*, but the length of my sari finished just after twelve cubits. I grasped a *pitraj* tree for life, that guy was pulling me behind, trying to make me fall down, often pressing me from behind like a mad animal, howling like a hyena; after a while he caught my legs and started pulling me towards the ground, my resistance gradually shrinking, my body lacked sensation, I was slowly tumbling down towards the ground, the skin on my hands, breasts and ribs was getting scratched and bruised; I collapsed on the ground with a thud. At that instant, shaking the darkness another voice rose, 'Beware!' Ramjan turned back, the man in front came forward cautiously; I could recognise Firoj in the thin darkness. Ramjan drew out the knife from his waist, and gnashing his teeth said, 'You dog of the Hindus, the lout has come here again.' Firoj was unruffled; the blade of his knife was shining brightly in the moonlight, just as the weapons in the hands of the idol of the Goddess Durga. Ramjan ran towards Firoj with a cry, Firoj took away his body slightly to the left, Ramjan couldn't keep his balance, and instantly Firoj's right hand moved towards his abdomen, Ramjan tumbled with face on the ground, shrieking intensely. Firoj stared at him for a while, and then put him on his back—o horror! Firoj came towards me with cautious steps, and coming close, felt embarrassed and helpless, started to look around for something, then ran towards the *pitraj* tree, took my sari from under it and threw it to me, went a little forward and turning his back towards me called out loudly, 'Maqbul, I'm on this side.' Many voices shouted out, 'Roj, have you found out Chandan and others?'

Looking at me, Ramjan's motionless, dead body and Firoj, they grasped the situation. Firoj came near me and asked, 'Chandan, Shankar, your parents'—I was trying to speak, but couldn't. Firoj understood my condition, said, 'Please calm down. You needn't worry at all.' I could talk only after a long time. As soon as I finished, they turned to different directions of the forest and shouted out, 'C-h-a-n-d-a-n, S-h-a-n-k-a-r, we're here, C-h-a-n-da-n'. No response came from either of you. They became exhausted and felt at a loss, shouting, and finally stopped. They closed in and discussed among themselves in a low voice; then Firoj came near me, thought for a while before he spoke, as if arranged the words in his mind and said, 'You're Poppy's batchmate, aren't you? Poppy is my sister, you may have to stay tonight with Poppy; we can't think of any other alternative. Please tell us if you have any idea of any other alternative arrangement.' Dear *Ma*, I couldn't possibly have told of any other alternative shelter that night, could I? Firoj said, 'So come along with us.' I couldn't stand up, despite all my efforts. It seemed that my limbs had become paralysed. Firoj extended his right hand—the hand with which he pierced the knife into Ramjan's abdomen a little while ago. I looked at Firoj's stretched hand for a long time, how could I make you understand the power of that hand, *Ma*; I'd never ever seen such a perfect, manly pair of hands of a man. I grasped Firoj's hand with infinite trust.

They managed to find a rickshaw from somewhere. Firoj said, 'Please get in.' I grasped Firoj firmly, reluctant to separate myself from him. Firoj looked at his friends with an embarrassed face. Maqbul said, 'Roj, you get in, too, she needs help.' Firoj sat on my left. Shahid lowered the hood of the rickshaw, saying, 'It's not proper to go in an uncovered rickshaw at a night like this.' Maqbul was on the seat of the driver, their friends were both on the front and back of the rickshaw. The main road was deserted and completely empty, the mystery of the chiaroscuro enveloped the houses and the shops and every other object all around. I was reclining, exhausted, with my head on Firoj's shoulder, my head was swinging, my every breath, shaking the ribs, was falling on Firoj's shoulder; he was frequently telling me, 'Your parents will be traced as soon as it is morning. There's nothing much to worry—'

Our rickshaw was moving slowly, sometimes in a zigzag way, sometimes straight, sometimes in a semicircle; the handle couldn't be controlled by Maqbul's hands. So they held the handle on both sides, Maqbul took off his legs from the paddle, and they began to push the rickshaw. Suddenly a jeep came from behind and halted with a screech on the left of our rickshaw. Putting his neck out someone asked, 'You?' Maqbul held the brakes on and said, 'Uncle, it's us.' Another voice was heard, saying, 'What's the matter!' They came out of the jeep—Haydar Mallick and Sams *Miyan*. Immediately

Mallick Saheb said, 'Who's inside the rickshaw?' Without waiting for the answer, he put his face under the hood and called out immediately, 'Sams!' and lowered the hood. Sams *Miyan*, as if stricken with fear, cried out, 'What have you done!' Mallick Saheb said as if lamenting, 'Look Sams, look at my golden boy's achievement! Rascal!'—and slapped Firoj furiously like a mad man. Firoj could not maintain his balance and bent on me, and said in a bewildered tone, '*Abbajan!*' Maqbul and all the others shouted out, 'Uncle!' Mallick Saheb raised his hand again; the pain struck me, covering his face with my hands and pressing it on my breast, I said, 'No, no...'

Amazed, Mallick Saheb withdrew his fist. Immediately, Maqbul narrated the entire happenings, and after hearing everything, Mallick Saheb gave out a sound from the depth of his heart, 'Ah! Ah!' Then putting his hand on his friend's shoulder he said, 'Look here, Sams!' Sams *Miyan* smiled. Mallick Saheb turned to them and said, 'Get into the jeep.' He said to me, 'Come *Ma*, come on!' Firoj drew his hands from my palms and said, offended, 'I'll walk.' Mallick Saheb felt amused, and turning to Sams *Miyan* said, 'My son's prestige has been hurt, Sams, he's become angry', and laughed out loudly, creating quivers in the heart of the solitude reigning all around.

They didn't get you, *Ma*. Spending the night at the shelter of Jaanik Sheikh, the next morning all of you set out by train for the other side of the border. You didn't think of me, my devoutly religious father forgot the idol of his family;

confronting death face-to-face, you all lost the rhythm of life on that day, *Ma*, all you wanted was security. When I read what you had told the journalists after crossing over Darshana, I cursed you in shame, chagrin and humiliation. It would have been even better for you to be killed by the knife of a goon like Ramjan. It was Firoj who brought the newspaper, and said with a dry smile, 'Please read it. It's called *honest journalism*.' Then he became serious, and with a heart full of anguish said, 'They'll never let the fire douse.' They used the banner headline: 'Hindu-*medh-yajna* (the ritualistic sacrifice of the Hindus at the hands of the rival community) in the Towns and Villages of East Pakistan' ...On the fifth page were your recounting and statement reported by the staff reporter:

The newly arrived family from the town huddled... at a secluded corner of the platform. Everyone knew Shri Tarakinkar Bhattarcharya throughout East Bengal. He had to leave behind this wealth of learning, too, along with all his movable and immovable property. And he had to leave his daughter. He said that he, along with the other members of his family, had concealed themselves in the forest behind his house. The brutish bloodthirsty raiders attacked even there and forcibly took away his only daughter in front of the very eyes of her parents. My devoutly religious father said that the entire Muslim community had become insane; they had lost all the humane values of life...

I couldn't look at Firoj, sitting at an arm's distance. My face and eyes had a burning sensation, the two veins on my forehead were throbbing in pain, there was unbearable pain in the cells of my brain; I crumpled the newspaper and threw it outside through the window. O *Ma*, how could you forget the elderly farmer Jaanik Sheikh, his wife Fatema *Bibi* of our Muslim neighbourhood! These people gave you shelter, these very people at the very early hours in the morning took you to the station along with four Muslim farmers guarding you, and it was they who gave you the money required for going to Calcutta; dear *Ma*, you didn't at all care to acknowledge the values of these human beings with so unsullied conscience! Maybe what Firoj says is true. He said, 'In human history sometimes the black clouds of evil times thicken; it is difficult to recognise the friend and the enemy amidst that darkness. So it's pointless to blame anybody for this.'

The family of Mallick Saheb was gradually facing social embarrassment in several corners about me. That night somehow passed. They started to think about the problem from the next dawn itself. Mallick Saheb, his wife and Poppy discussed the matter in secret for a long time. Then Firoj's mother said to me, 'Fruits do not cause any impurity; my darling, you may eat fruits for this half of the day. Your parents will surely be found out by that time. Besides, your relatives are there in Dayamoyee House. You may stay there, too. By the next half of the day, some arrangement will surely be made. Don't worry at all, my child.'

At noon when Firoj came back, it was known that you were no longer here. Mallick Saheb returned a little later; a pall of anxiety was cast over his whole face. He called me aside and said with the smile of a man in great danger,

'My darling daughter, please stay here. Can't you cook for yourself? I can't send you to some unknown place, after all, I've a responsibility.' Later I came to know, *Ma*, that my 'relatives' in Dayamoyee House didn't agree to give me shelter there; Chatterjee Uncle of Fulbere made a despicable hint involving Firoj and me.

I had no other alternative but to stay in the home of Mallick Saheb. Sin, virtue, purity, all of these, and the complex prejudices of the Hindu society nourished inside through all of you began to decay within me slowly since that very moment—a belief started to grow in me that you people infused in me some age-old prejudices just like those shrewd businessmen taking advantage of the ignorance of others in an attempt to pass off counterfeit currency. So after three days' stay, none of my blind beliefs got jolted when I ate the food cooked by Firoj's mother. The society that couldn't protect me, didn't help me reach an island of safety from the whirlwind of danger, didn't hesitate to paint my whole body with an indelible ink of disrepute, if I had to follow any blind custom of that society, I would have to take myself down to a new low, dear *Ma*.

As the situation normalised, the issue was raised in their society, too; even after the riot had stopped, why had Mallick Saheb let the young Hindu woman remain in his house? The question spread far and wide through many whispers. The day I heard the anxious discussion of Mallick Saheb and his wife, the very next day I told him that I wanted to go to Hindustan. Exactly after twenty-five days, Mallick

Saheb said, 'I've got your parents' address. The Nayeb of the zamindar of the one-third estate of Sherpur had come here to settle the exchange of property; I heard everything from him.'

And after three days they came together to get me on the train. They all were weeping, dear *Ma*, I was weeping, too; I bowed and touched the feet of Mallick Saheb and his wife disregarding their objections. One by one Sinjaani station, its staff quarters, the bungalow of PWI, the two gulmohar trees, Shankar Theatre, the town of my entire childhood gradually disappeared from the limits of my eyesight, and my heart with a deep emptiness burst into a prolonged wailing.

I boarded the train for this side of the border at Phulchari Ghat at about 8 p.m. that day. Firoj took tea, offered me too. He didn't speak a word throughout the journey, only kept reading a book with a sombre face. He had begun to keep distance from me since the day I had declared my decision to go to Hindustan. The train started to move, and after a time, the jetty steamer, the blurred inlet of River Jamuna, the hotel illumined by the light of the patromax gradually disappeared. Stretching his legs Firoj was reading the book a little away from me; his face wore the solemnity of a mask. Apart from the two of us there were two more passengers in the moderately lit compartment; as soon as the train started, covering himself under a wrapper one of them had fallen asleep, and the other opening a thick file was reading it and marking lines on the paper with a red pencil. The moving night outside was enveloped in a sleepy darkness of fog.

I kept watching Firoj without batting my eyelids; I felt suffocated at his unconcerned behaviour. After a while with pain in the eyes I asked, 'Won't you speak to me?' He listened to the question attentively, looked me in the eyes, closed the book noisily, then said in a light tone, 'Yes, please, what do you want to know?' Layers of agony piled up under my breast just then melted in a salty liquid tear, with a strong jolt. The slim night inside the compartment, the endlessly spread-out night outside, Firoj's black-and-white-striped full-sleeve pullover—all gradually started to become indistinct. Resting my face on the folded hand kept on the train window, I started weeping loudly like an illiterate rustic woman; the incessant metallic noise kept ringing along with Firoj's discomfited utterance, 'Oh, what happened, what?'—

The night was deep; we were moving forward touching the sights far and near—we were crossing over Nator of Ila Mitra, Firoj's hand in my hand; the cool breeze from outside was blowing over our faces and eyes, occasionally an uncannily thrilling sensation was pushing upwards through the backbones, the lips had turned into ice. Perhaps the moon rose somewhere in the far-off sky, the gloom was slowly fading.

On a moment like this Firoj spoke on, in the mode of a reciter of *Bratakatha*: During the dice-play when Draupadi was laid as a bet, she didn't know anything about it. But she couldn't escape the consequences of the temptations of her gambler husband. In a similar political gambling in our land, a few tired and exhausted leaders used us as a bet without our knowledge. The country was partitioned, and with it we were divided, too. I can remember one incident. My father, who has opposed the Muslim League for all his life, said to me after a few days of Partition, 'Munna, we can't afford to stay in this country anymore. Kader *Miyan* had called Sams and said to him, "Everybody is angry with you. If you want to be safe, accept the membership of the League; otherwise danger is almost knocking at your door. Tell this to Mallick Saheb, too"'. My father said, 'Maybe we have to leave this country.' Only a few days later, the riot started in Calcutta. Every day flicking through the newspaper, with pale eyes he would almost groan in pain and say, 'Munna, Gandhiji, Jawaharlal, Maulana are all being vanquished!' I've seen how a landslide took place in my father's unbroken world of confidence. My father, who was a lifelong fighter, forgot about struggle and resistance. There can't be a more heartening tragedy than this. Today we all are mere characters of a particular scene of a particular act of this great tragic play. I'll accompany you till Darshana station; you have to go to your own country, the country that you're not familiar with; you have not yet established any emotional bond with the people of that country, the sky-air-rivers-stars-plants-flowers of that country are all new to you, you don't know whether the paths of that country will at all be taking you to security; and yet an unknown young man of that country how easily may say to you at first sight, 'Bula, I love you'—

O dear *Ma*, all the strings of my body and mind were as if shredded and lay scattered into pieces.

With the last whistle blown, Firoj got down from the compartment, stood beside the window and said, 'Please take care. You aren't much accustomed to travelling alone. Hope you'll write letters, at least send the news that you have reached safely. It'll be a pleasure for those of us who are on this side of the border if no false assumption is indulged about them.' The train started to move, Firoj proceeded slowly along with the moving train, and said, 'I have some apprehensions about the prejudices of the Hindu community. If you don't find the space of dignity for you there, please remember the country you belong to, and us, please come back, please come back, please come...'

Firoj's voice in high pitch got suppressed under the noise of the train; he stopped at the middle of the platform, his body marked by signs of helplessness; raising his hand he shouted desperately and tried to say something, but it couldn't reach my ears; his stout well-built body took various shapes by turns within my two dilated eyes and at last vanished without a trace. The sound that was ringing so long, touching the strings of feelings of my body and mind, in a low key, like the *alaap* in a musical raga, instantly reverberated with the sound 'Roj, Roj, Roj'... rocking the sky and air of the three worlds.

The newly sprouted colony was at the far end of the town with its illuminated road, bright beautiful shops, lots of people and conveyances; the *rickshawala* got me down at this place and said, 'This is the new locality—Nutan Pallee. We don't dare go inside. These people wrangle too much over the fare, even thrash us in a group. Please go inside and ask about the address, you'll surely find out.'

The pathways of Nutan Pallee were dark, the air smelt of wetland, a lamp suspended from the top of a pole was burning in the sky close by. Walking a while I saw a tea stall; many voices were talking together there. Water was boiling with a bubbling noise on a portable earthen oven. The bunch of men there seemed to be worn out in the dim light of the kerosene lamp. Looking at me they fell silent, kept staring at me with boundless wonder. I proffered the piece of paper with the address written on it, and it began to be passed on from hand to hand, and their look kept roaming around me. At last one of them asked, 'Are you *Pandit Moshai*'s daughter?'

'...Ah. Coming from Pakistan?'

'...That means—'

'It is you that the *Moslas* kidnapped, isn't it? The bastards. If once I can get my hand on them'—

'How come those rogues freed you?'

'Ah, the "fun" was over, wasn't it? So... you understand?'

'Oh! What are you talking about?' Saying this someone came forward from inside. Coming close by, he said, 'Please come with me.'

'Look, I don't hesitate to speak out bluntly.'

'What happened? Please come,' he called me again.

My legs refused to move; the whole body was as heavy as rocks; the darkness around me was trembling. Numerous fireworks were burning and vanishing in the darkness...

He asked me to wait on the road, and himself went inside one of the houses. A little later your voice came out from there; then I could hear your whisperings in low voices; uneasiness, apprehension and the clouds of unknown horrors rumbled within my heart—with darkness in my eyes I was falling down under the *jiol* tree and somehow clutching the earth with both my hands, I sat down there. After some time came my *devoutly religious* father, stood there maintaining a distance; the white sacred thread enclosed the naked upper part of his body. *Ma*, I was afraid seeing *Baba* that night. He announced his decision in his bass voice, 'Here there is no room for you. None of us want you back; I can't accept you'. He went inside the house. The huge hairy body of darkness started to swing and dance before my eyes, and I felt tremors under my feet; the *akash-pradeep* lighted in memory of the ancestors stared at me with cold unmoving eyes like a one-eyed ghost. A suffocating emptiness encircled me, my conscious self was gradually becoming insubstantial and insupportable, and was fusing itself with that emptiness. At that very instant I could hear your hushed voice, 'Didn't you feel ashamed to come back! Why did you come back, Bula, O Bula, why did you come!'

Someone, as if, hurled me from the orbit of this earth towards the ever-revolving galaxy—turning and turning in the void and then passing into a deeper void, gyrating in the darkness and then entering into a further, deeper darkness I kept floating like a raft—then at one time I got completely lost like a straw in the face of a flood.

When I awoke on the damp floor of a room, there was a loud hullabaloo from a huge crowd gathered outside. The air inside the room was heavy with the smell of the rotten cow dung and the urine; the autumn air was blowing in freely through the chinks of the bamboo fence, and the room was full of the humming of mosquitos that swarmed on me from all four sides. The hushing of the crowd outside along with the noise of blowing the hookah began to enter into my ears: 'Yes, you're right on this point; if the society is to survive, its rules must be obeyed, even if these are very stringent, we're bound to obey these rules.'

'I want to say something. If it's a sitting for justice, then I must say clearly—my father can't be the judge of this trial session. Please ask him why he didn't sacrifice his life to save his daughter from the attack of the *Mussalman goondas*.'

'Shankar!'

'Not only my father, none of you have the eligibility to sit in judgment. Those who have run away in the darkness of night, giving up their ancestral homestead, their family gods, their lifelong beliefs—we do not accept any judgment delivered by such fugitives. Bula will reside here.'

'You bastard!'

My father probably slapped my brother, who went away. After that they sat silently for a long time, only the sound of blowing the hookah could be heard. Suddenly a wave of sound arose near my ear—*ma-a-w-w*. It swirled around for some time in this fetid, stinking room and the courtyard occupied by the crowd; then life came back again in the silent crowd, someone remarked in a full-throated voice, 'Even her mother Bhagabati does not want her daughter to live with them, and that boy threatens us saying "Bula will stay here." This is nothing but an indication that nothing of our faith, customs and practices will survive under the hands of these immature angry young men.'

'There's a lot to think on, understand? Yes, Shankar hasn't spoken well. But it's true that we've become rather mean and despicable in the eyes of those immature boys, we have been defeated. What do you say, *Gosainji*?'

'Humm!'

'Let me give a proposal. Arrange a ritual of expiation; donate some money to good Brahmins; ask your daughter to shave her hair, eat the *panchagabya*—the five articles derived from the cow—and purify the girl. Otherwise, where'll she go? Tarakinkar, what do you say?'

'I can't do that, uncle. I can never give shelter to the daughter who's been sinned by the touch of *yavan*. I must not send all my ancestors to hell. Please don't give me such advice.'

'Well, you're free to do whatever you think fit.'

After this everybody went to their home. From the dark courtyard your subdued cry could be heard, *Ma*; occasionally, father's bass tone was rising, '*Ma*, Mother of the World, o *Ma*'—

The two of you, companions for long thirty-five years, sat through the urban darkness like two islands; the night gradually deepened; my moments, made uneasy and fearful by the humming of the mosquitos, the exhalation of the sleeping cows and the smelly air, were passing away motionless. My father kept walking over the courtyard raising the sound of his wooden slippers, and said while walking, 'Shankar can no more be allowed to live in this house. It's better to let him know my order. You're listening, aren't you?'

You stopped crying, and took some time to let his words sip in; your tone revealed not affection for your child, but the fear of insecurity, 'If Shankar goes away, how will we survive? It's his job at the jute mill that we depend on. *Ma* Dayamoyee, so many people died, and you allowed this girl to live on, *Ma*! This girl set my house on fire. O God—'

I came away from your cosy home, *Ma*. It was quite late at night; the darkness was fading, slowly pushing the door I came out into the silence of the night, felt the touch of winter in the air, saw the doodles of numberless stars in the vast sky; the rows of houses of Nutan Pallee seemed to be wombs of barren women, your pathways were very narrow. I didn't waste even one drop of tear to desert you all, *Ma*; the weariness within me wasn't allowing my body to stand erect, my heart was constantly palpitating, I was almost falling down, I was crawling. Your cosy home, like a watchdog, was driving me away, *Ma*…

Still I haven't yet been able to reach the end of the road, *Ma*; in this hemisphere I've only one shelter—Firoj is waiting there with a throne of honour and a heart full of love. I haven't been able to reach there, my prejudices aren't allowing me to reach there—I'm a prisoner of my own will in the fort of prejudices. I want to break this fetter enmeshed in the coils of my blood stream, I'm being defeated by the self within me, *Ma*...

The place where I'm writing from is where the borders of the two countries have merged. If I walk just a few steps, I can go into my country and closer to Firoj. Through the vast green paddy field, the dense blue trees and plants, the endless sky on the other side—through all these, a loving heart always beckons me. Maybe someday, I'll have the strength to respond to that—I'm still alive with that faith, *Ma*.

Another epoch-ending wildfire of history will burn into ashes all our prejudices and narrowness, I'll take his hand into mine that day, and say, 'Roj Roj'; he'll take up my hand, and say, 'Bula, Bula, Bula'—

O dear *Ma*...

ଛ

Translated by Amzed Hossein

Amzed Hossein is Professor of English at Aliah University, Kolkata. He completed his PhD on the poetry of Ted Hughes at IIT Kharagpur in 1993.

Note

The *Mahabharata*: 'Sabhaparba', pp. 133–35, quoted in the original story from the Bengali translation of Rajshekhar Basu.

The Refugee

Debesh Ray

Sipping at a cup of bed tea is the first luxurious preamble to a day-long drudgery. Even though his wife does not nudge him out of bed, his own urge shoves him off, within 8 a.m. Morning rituals like washing hands and face, defecating, fetching essentials from the market run till 8:30 a.m. People advise to keep at least half an hour for several other things like buying coal, medicines or taking fresh clothes from the laundry, and so on. And eight hours follow thereafter—just as the whore sells herself for a couple of hours or so, he sells his own skills at writing letters in English or joining his daily job on time. And the rest twelve hours that the earth needs to revolve around its own axis are spent dozing off. When the question of priority between life and livelihood pushes one towards the edge, there remains not much reason to stay in bed even beyond 8 in the morning. At such a moment, one feels privileged enough to be repeatedly called, implored, coaxed and cajoled by his wife and daughter, with the teacup being held close to the lips! The money in the provident fund is more than enough for his last rites and *shraddha* ceremony, keeping aside the burden of the loan. Dust is the body, returning to dust in death makes the whole world stand straight like a tower of memories sans corpse, and the condolences (the man was well-organised, led his life methodically, and breathed his last at the right time) only bear the memories left behind. The children of the dead reminisce as to how the man's roots went deep and far, and how the man hardly cared to establish his roots anywhere else.

Satyabrata was having a good sleep that day, like a self-reliant rightful owner, beneath a cotton mosquito curtain worth rupees four-and-a-half only, on a bedstead made of kerosene wood. No doubt, it was his wife who came to wake him up from his sleep by calling him, 'Hey you, can you hear me, can you? Hey you, listen, hey!' Well-cared-for Satyabrata turned to the other side, needlessly. It seemed as if Anima's calls would slip through the upper aperture of his ears, and melt away smoothly inside. Anima said instead, 'There are a few people outside, looking for you.'

Hence, Satyabrata opened his eyes and asked, 'Who's there?'

'How can I say? I don't know. I asked them to be seated, but they are still standing there,' said Anima. As she was leaving the room, she added, 'Tea is ready, have it before going. Otherwise, it will get cold.'

By then, letting his legs hang loosely, by the edge of the bed, Satyabrata began to take stock of all the things around him that the young visitors might have expected to glance at in his house, and stopped thinking of himself as the owner, instead. He rolled his gaze around his room for a few seconds, as if his house was being taken for auction as per court order. And then throwing a glance at Anju, lying on the other bed, feeling much relieved, he looked at himself. He wore a two-rupee-four-anna *lungi* faded out, and as he was not in the wont of putting on underwear, the *lungi* draped him like the thin end of a sari. The vest lay beside the pillow, he took it up and slipped it on. And then, he imagined his looks— a fine *lungi*, tattered vest, just woken up from sleep—static! It seemed as if the two persons, waiting outside, had come to put up Satyabrata, and none else, for auction! Just a few minutes ago, the man who was sleeping in pride, for being an owner of everything around, just went out rubbing his face in both his palms, as though he decided to deny his own name.

Having said this much, Anima went to keep the teacup on the table, covered it with the saucer and kept nudging Anjana, 'Hey Anju, Anju, hey you, oh God, shall I slap you on your face?'

The two men stood with their bicycles beside them. Just stepping outside, Satyabrata welcomed them, 'Come in, please.'

'No need, we have come to deliver the news to you, and we will leave right now.'

From the smile on the man's face, Satyabrata tried to assume whether there was any possibility of getting an invitation from somewhere nearby.

'Why don't you come in to sit—'

'No. Look, you have to go to the police station, in a day or two, any time, to meet the Inspector. At your convenient hour...'

'Police station? Me?'

One of them rejoined, 'Yes!' The other one fished out a notebook from his pocket, turned a few pages to read, 'Yes, your name is Satyabrata Lahiri, right? Your father's name is Late Punyabrata Lahiri and your holding number is 230/A/6.' Then, slipping the notebook into his pocket, he said, 'Yes, it's you!'

The other man said while turning the cycle to a circle, 'Go at your convenient hour, no hurry. Any day would do—'

Both of them were almost about to leave. Satyabrata accosted them to stop short, 'Could you please tell me what for?' Both the men turned around from where they stood, and one of them rejoined, 'It's nothing, nothing at all. What can we say again? A government order has reached us, stating that, "In your place, a town in the border, to be precise, reside many such inhabitants, as our sources affirm, who are not the *real ones* as they feign to be".' And then, flashing a seemingly rehearsed smile, both the men said in an assuring tone to Satyabrata, 'What to say, Sir? According to the central government, those who inhabit this locale are not the "actual ones". Just think, what can we do? After all, we have to do our job. Okay, we are leaving now, please come one day, to introduce yourself.' As soon as they left, Satyabrata went inside hurriedly, as if in order to give the impression to them that he had gone inside before their departure. Again, Anima might have eavesdropped. He would not let Anima get a hint that he got scared of paying a visit to the police station; he kept standing there, at the verandah, for long.

However, Anima had not heard anything. Satyabrata lifted the cup from the table and took a sip. Just then, Anju came in nibbling at a piece of bread, with Anima at her heels. He laughed to himself thinking that Anima had spent all day with Anju in the kitchen. And then, he thought, why he was holding back everything from Anima, he was nabbed neither for pilfering nor for robbery!

'You know, I have to go to the police station to prove that we are "real" us, complying with an order issued by the government, to this effect.'

'Really? But why?'

'To prove that I am the "real me".'

'Why?'

'Because the government has said so.'

Then he kept the teacup on the table and in brisk steps went near the well. Freshening up, he would have to leave for the market.

Satyabrata made up his mind to walk up to the police station in half an hour, kept aside for accomplishing less important matters. For that, he hurriedly finished buying essentials from the market. But the men asked him to see them at his convenience. It would be most convenient for him if he could drop by, on his way of return from the office. But he was surprised to find himself in an awful hurry to be there, just on receiving the summons! Hurriedly he left the things he bought from the market, and left in no time. Anima tried to intervene, 'Why do you hurry? Late afternoon would have been the best time for a visit.' Even Anju was around, with a sum to be solved. Satyabrata went out scurrying and walked down towards the police station.

And when he returned, the sun had already set. Anima was all nerves, darting in and out of the room, pacing up and down the verandah since afternoon. After 10 a.m., not an adult soul could be seen hanging about, who could be sent to the police station to fetch the latest news. Waiting till late afternoon, she sent a man in search of him, and the youth assured her of Satyabrata's presence there. In her usual round in the locality, she came to know that each and everybody had been asked to pay a visit to the police station, at least for once, for the same reason—for final verification and for self-introduction, to prove that the man he was known to all was himself only and no one else. Bidding adieu to the land in which he had his roots, leaving the family of which he had been the part and parcel, he would have to be present before the cops, to prove his 'soul', today or tomorrow, he would require to prove his existence, that very day or the day after.

Satyabrata was walking with his legs stretched straight before him, dragging his feet along. His neck kept hanging loose, like a cock with a broken neck, his mane stood dishevelled like that of a water-soaked dog, his collarbones seemed to hold the chill of death in them, the fingers, a semblance of leather gloves, were just a replica of the five-finger-imprint! With no words on her lips, Anima kept tiptoeing behind him, right from the door outside. Once she kept her hand on his back, but later a sense of dispossession made her take it off, almost immediately after. Like a person, just back from the crematorium, she sat down on the stairs, at the crack of the dawn. A little later, she leaned back, closing her eyes. If no pillar was there behind her, she might stretch straight, lying supine. Anima skipped her bath, skipped her meals even. Groping for an answer in the whole being of Satya, she sat down with a thud which caused Satyabrata to hold his eyes wide open and roll his eyeballs around. It might be in quest of something unknown. At last, Anima broke the ice, 'Anju has gone to her friend's place.' Listening to her, Satyabrata fixed his gaze on Anima's face and just then, Anima delved deep into his glance and could get a glimpse of the 'real' Satyabrata, the man she knew so well! Satyabrata fished out a ream of papers from his pocket and handed those to Anima, and closed his eyes again. Darkness descended all round, thick and fast. Longing for a patch of light, Anima went out to stand beneath the glow of the sky.

Being circulated for the cognizance of the public:

The significant changes in history and geography of the earth, caused by the Second World War, spanning from 1939 to 1945, have not been recorded systematically. Hence, ascertaining the nation, race, language and family lineage of the residents of this world has run into difficulty. There is no definite yardstick to identify a person as a 'real' one. The ongoing documentation of facts has dawned the truth on us that lately, a horde of absconders and men with fake identities are around, on this planet. Especially, in nations like India, Pakistan, North and South Vietnam, North and South Korea, East and West Germany, so forth. Hence, on the basis of a charter of actions of the United Nations, we are carrying on a programme titled, 'In Search of the Real Man', in order to identify 'the man' as he is known to all. And we are requesting the people of the world to pay a visit to their nearest police stations to prove their own identity.

A case from Ballavpur Police Station:

One. Mr Satyabrata Lahiri, son of late Mr Punyabrata Lahiri, hails from East Pakistan and now is the resident of the address, on the holding no. 230/A/6. For the last twelve years he has been paying the municipal tax for this holding. On 10 June 1950, this holding was registered in the name of Mr Satyabrata Lahiri, on proper verification of the sale deed, as he bought the same from its previous owner, Mr Banabehari Mallik. But on special investigation, it has been found that, Sk Mansur Ali, son of late Kadam Seikh, resident of Halsakin, Raichar of Pabna district, is the lawful owner of this particular holding. In 1950, following the Hindu–Muslim riot, Kadam Seikh (now dead) left for East Pakistan, with his son, Mansur, daughter, Amina, and his wife, Noora. Before leaving, he left his house in the care of Mr Banabehari Mallik, a resident of that locality, for three generations. And in the same year, Mr Banabehari Mallik sold the holding to Mr Satyabrata Lahiri as its sole owner. The copy of the original deed, dated 13 December 1921, lies with Sk Mansur Ali, now a resident of Raichar of Pabna district.

Hence, Mr Satyabrata Lahiri cannot be the real owner of the holding no. 230/A/6 of Ballavpur municipality. Or the name of the owner of the aforesaid holding of Ballavpur municipality is not Mr Satyabrata Lahiri.

Two. After 1947, Mr Satyabrata Lahiri, the so-called son of Mr Punyabrata Lahiri, served as a school teacher or a clerk in government or non-governmental sectors at various corners of the Indian Union. In all these places, he introduced himself as Mr Satyabrata Lahiri, the son of Late Punyabrata Lahiri, a graduate from Dacca University in 1945.

After his work for certain days, when his diploma and BA certificates were asked for, he said that, he had to leave the riot-torn land without the original certificates after his examination, and it was not possible to retrieve those now, because of the partition. In a case or two, he had to relinquish his job, as he could not yield to the continual demand of the authority for the certificate.

Investigation unearthed the veracity of the fact that the person known as Satyabrata Lahiri had earned his BA degree from Dacca University, but just the following year, he died as a victim of a communal riot, on his way to Khulna by train.

And there is a possibility that the persons who camouflage themselves under the identity of late Satyabrata Lahiri at present, had been quite close to the dead person, and thus, employ the finest details pertaining to him to their advantage Thus, Satyabrata is still around as a living entity, though dead and gone. In fact, the living Satyabrata Lahiri is dead now.

A cousin of late Punyabrata Lahiri used to work in Calcutta, since long before Independence. While facing the Enquiry Commission, he reported knowing about ten cases in which the candidates tried for a job, appearing as Satyabrata Lahiri. Learning about the ten cases as stated by him, it was understood that in many other places too, such attempts have been made. Not just a job, many even tried to marry under that identity and one such union had been successfully consummated, as backed by proper evidence.

Referring to the gazette of Dacca University, it has been found that two individuals with the same name, Satyabrata Lahiri, had passed their BA from there in 1945. The second one proved to be the root of all complications. Otherwise, any person, producing the BA certificate of Dacca University of the year 1945, could have been taken to police custody, without a second thought.

According to the documents preserved in the offices of different district administrators, eighty-seven gentlemen bearing the name 'Satyabrata Lahiri' got married after 1947. However, it is not clear how many of them obtained BA degree from Dacca University in 1945.

As the other one, bearing the name, Satyabrata Lahiri, had passed his BA from Dacca University in the same year. But this cannot be properly ascertained whether he is the 'living' or the 'dead' Satyabrata. It is plausible that the 'dead' Satyabrata (alias, 'fake' Satyabrata) made use of the name of the father of the 'original' and dead Satyabrata or that of the 'original' and living Satyabrata as that of his own father according to his convenience.

A BA degree-holder from Dacca University in 1945—the fake Satyabrata uses this as the sole tool to switch over to another identity and hence, he never alters this, whatever the case may be. Thus, he does not invite disbelief as this is an undeniable fact that some Satyabrata Lahiri had obtained his BA degree in 1945. As the father's identity is not of much importance in case of the 'fake' Satyabrata Lahiri, it keeps changing. Hence, all these three facts are never seen to coexist in this case: a) the son of late Punyabrata Lahiri, b) a BA degree-holder from Dacca University in 1945, and c) a man bearing the name Mr Satyabrata Lahiri.

Moreover, uncertainty of the demise of the original Satyabrata Lahiri problematises the issue even more. It was reported that in early 1946, a band of ruffians had attacked a Khulna-bound train, causing the death of a large number of people. Satyabrata Lahiri's name was found in the list of those dead persons. It might be the printer's mistake! This Satyabrata Lahiri might have been a different man altogether! But, setting out for Khulna, Satybrata Lahiri, the son of Punyabrata Lahiri, had not come back again. Hence, he was taken to be a man, who was no more.

Therefore, problems line up as follows:

Primarily, is it illogical to consider that Satyabrata Lahiri, the son of late Punyabrata Lahiri, the BA degree-holder of

Dacca University, in 1945, killed in the Khulna train assault? So, is the original Satyabrata being taken as a dead man, though alive?

Secondly, if the real Satyabrata is no more, then who has/have usurped his identity?

These two queries may elicit a befitting reply from just one individual. Those who have become 'one', getting donned in the identity of 'Satyabrata'! Hence, this query is being driven door to door to those who married after 1947, have offspring and are into a family-life, supported by cushy jobs.

Until befitting replies to those couple of queries are not available, neither a Satyabrata Lahiri can consider himself to be so, without a doubt, nor any wife would be able to think her husband to be Satyabrata Lahiri, the son of dead Punyabrata Lahiri, without an iota of doubt! Again, no child would be free to think of their father as the original self, Satyabrata Lahiri!

Come, prove yourself to be the person, as the world knows you. Take your original and authentic identity proof to your nearest police station and prove that you are *Him*, truly the real Him! Thirdly, on 30 July 1952, Mr Satyabrata Lahiri married Ms Anima Sanyal, the second daughter of Mr Hemchandra Sanyal, observing Hindu rites like keeping the *salgram* stone and having the holy fire as witness. Late Bishwanath Bhattacharya and late Narendranath Chakraborty, both acted as priests in this wedding, and their signatures certainly prove that this union had been consummated with strict adherence to the scriptures. Both

Mr Satyabrata Lahiri and Mrs Anima Lahiri have been residing at the address, 230/A/6, under the jurisdiction of Ballavpur municiplaity, for the last ten years, as husband and wife. On 17 March 1953, Mrs Anima Sanyal gave birth to a girl child at the Ballavpur Sadar Hospital. This deserves special mention, that it was a case of normal delivery and though the baby was born after seven months of their marriage, it was full-grown, hale and hearty and quite normal. The documents of Ballavpur Sadar Hospital aver that, Anima Lahiri got discharged from the hospital in just five days. This baby girl, Miss Anjana Lahiri, happens to be the only child of Mrs Anima Lahiri and Mr Satyabrata Lahiri.

A spontaneous response from a citizen of East Pakistan, Enamul Haque Chowdhury, to the call of the worldwide operation titled 'In Search of the Real Man', apprises us of Anima's father, Mr Hemchandra Sanyal's residence in their locality. At the outbreak of the communal riot in East Bengal in 1950, Hemchandra Sanyal took refuge at Enamul Haque Chowdhury's place, along with his family. Enamul's father, Janab Mainul Chowdhury, was alive at that time. He and his son, Enamul, sheltered the family of Hemchandra Sanyal, with extraordinary firmness. In about fifteen–twenty days, Hemchandra moved into the Indian Union. His second daughter, Anima Sanyal, stayed back in East Pakistan, and under the name of 'Kumkum' she was wedded to Enamul Haque Chowdhury, the son of Mainul Haque Chowdhury on 5 February 1951. Along with such a statement, Janab Enamul Haque Chowdhury sent a photocopy of that marriage registration certificate. In that document, his wife's name was recorded as Kumkum, her father's name being Mr H.C. Sanyal.

In support of that statement, the following circumstantial evidence could be seen as valid.

When Hemchandra Sanyal came to the Indian Union, no soul had seen his second daughter, Anima, with him. Even after coming to the Mukhera village, Hemchandra told his neighbours that his second daughter, Anima, was with his older daughter, Anjali, at a tea garden in Assam. The older son-in-law used to work at a tea garden in Assam. But their witnesses revealed that Anima had never been there. Such witnesses, thus, indirectly support the fact that, in 1950, when Hemchandra Sanyal left Pakistan, Anima had not been there with him.

Was it then Anima, on appropriating the identity of Kumkum, really married to Enamul? But save the initials of the name, H.C. Sanyal, no proof surfaced to aver that Kumkum and Anima were the same individual!

If not so, then why did Anima stay back in Pakistan?

A couple of opinions are there in this regard.

Firstly, Janab Enamul Chowdhury and Anima were in love with each other since their childhood. Both of them were residents of the same locality. Till eight or nine years of age, they were in the same *paathshala*. Enamul used to address Anima's mother as '*Ma*'. Mainul Haque Chowdhury, Enamul's father, was quite an influential figure in that region. The bond between Enamul and Anima, and the sweet relationship the two families shared, stood as a solid reason for Hemchandra Sanyal's staying back in Pakistan even after 1947. Anima's father used to call for Enamul if he failed to visit the Sanyal residence for a couple of days. A set of utensils including cup-saucer-glass had been kept aside for Enamul's father.

At such a juncture, the communal riots broke out in 1950. Enamul then came to the Sanyal house, leaving his own residence behind. Janab Mainul Chowdhury, Enamul's father, was not at all willing to get involved in all these matters. But when his only son was in jeopardy, he could not remain detached any longer and welcomed Hemchandra along with his family to his own place and ensured the security and peace of that locality with the aid of the cops and the government.

Closing all the doors and windows, the Sanyal family kept itself confined to just a single room. Each noise beyond the door made them all ears in panic. When they sensed that Enamul had gone out, they could not even take a deep breath until they became certain of his return. Their only ray of hope was Enamul. He had been their sole centre of trust and with him towed his family, the family of the Haque Chowdhurys. They were served meals four times a day, following a push on the door. And there had been no separate arrangement of utensils for the Sanyals. All around, the shrieks of frenzy of the slayers could be heard, coupled with the cries of agony, the pain of the wounded and the yell of the people silently foreboding the lolling tongues of fire. The firm and conventional beliefs were being shattered to smithereens with each successive blow, just as a devastating earthquake would verify the permanence of an object on earth. And being encircled by death, all could feel that it was the love of Anima and Enamul which acted as a bark, needed to cross the sea of turbulence. If their love did not blossom, Sanyal family could not win shelter in this family; Enamul's father would not compel the state administration to maintain peace in this area and Enamul would not lead a peace league, with the help of a handful of friends, to douse the fire or rescue the wounded lot. This was proven as an axiom in mathematics that both the Sanyals and the Haque Chowdhurys were keen on saving the grace of this love, hand-in-hand, just as our nerves work, rather unconsciously, to save our eyeballs from smoke and dust. To these lives, which were escaping peril in each instant, this appeared to be transparent as daylight.

And this was best understood by Anima. During the peaceful days, Anima and Enamul though met up in seclusion, it was something next to impossible in the days of communal riot. Enamul would drop by, at the most for just three to four times in their room, irrespective of the time of the day.

The tender emotions like affection and love are difficult to be put forth as evidence for judiciary investigations. Yet whenever Enamul came back home, perspiring, weary, after roaming outside, Anima used to hand him the towel or the fan, on her own accord, lovingly. These things prove that their love had bloomed at this point of time. All prejudices were being blown off, and the throbbing hearts of so many members of the Sanyal family in such deadly, intimidating times were showing Anima straightaway, with all her senses intact, the power of Enamul's love for her. Why else then Anima would turn down the offer of going to the Indian Union with her family after Mainul Haque Chowdhury's incessant, arduous efforts for over ten–fifteen days to arrange everything for the journey?

Hemchandra Sanyal was surely reluctant to leave Anima behind, in Pakistan. But, his daughter's self-declaration, without any direct intervention of Enamul, perhaps intimidated them, or they might have thought that it was discourteous of them to express a note of dissent after what Enamul had done for them to save their lives. Whatever the case might have been, Anima stayed back in Pakistan.

When all went quiet after the melee and riots, Anima on her own accord, tied nuptial knot on 5 February 1953, with Janab Enamul Haque Chowdhury, assuming the name, 'Kumkum'. A registered deed to this effect is available. But why was the change of name necessary?

Perhaps both Enamul and Anima had thought that if the news spread like wildfire, it would pose problems for the Sanyal family, who had settled down in India with dignity and respect. Hence, the full name of her father had not been mentioned.

Secondly, Enamul had been attracted towards Anima even before the birth of Pakistan. After the formation of Pakistan, Enamul had written quite a number of letters to Anima. Failing to get any response from them, he tried to strike up a conversations with Anima on the road. Off and on, he used to drop in at Anima's residence and address Anima's mother as '*Ma*' and demanded for cups of tea and other savouries. Finally, he came out of a tea stall to threaten Anima to be his *bibi*, otherwise, he would chop up all the members of the Sanyal family into pieces. And right from that day, Anima was stopped from going out by any means.

Meanwhile, the riot broke out in 1950. At its outset, Enamul intruded into their residence with his force to announce blatantly that, if Anima had not been married off to him, each member of the Sanyal family would be brutally murdered. Being informed by Mr Sanyal, Enamul's father, Mainul Haque Chowdhury, in turn, let the police know that Enamul was out to maintain peace in the locality with his team. Naturally, the police did not visit the locality and Enamul stood as the sole ruler of the ghetto.

At about 10 p.m. one day, people suddenly started to pelt at the house. All the members of the Sanyal family sat behind closed doors and windows. In an hour, a mob besieged Sanyal residence, shouting '*Allah Ho Akbar*'! And they yelled from outside that if the door was not opened, they would set the house on fire. At that instant, Enamul came forward to say, 'Please open the door for once, and I shall make everything right.' They were compelled to unbolt the door. Enamul said that they would stand a probability of being spared if they would seek shelter as a family. Hapless Sanyals had no other option than moving on to Enamul's place. They had narrow escapes every moment, encountering death.

Every now and then, Enamul entered the room and asked Anima to fan him or wipe his sweat, in front of everyone. The sense of 'family' was no more there with the Sanyals; the sole question was that of self-defence—just as a devotee in a temple, chiefly concerned with his prayers being answered, and unmoved even by the blood of animal-sacrifice. Thus, Enamul's uncouth and indecent attitude towards Anima made each member of the Sanyal family feel at least relieved and protected. As though, if Anima had not been there as a protective shield, Enamul would turn into a devil of slaughter and misbehaviour. As though, the skin covering the exterior of Anima's body spared him no moment to concentrate on the blood flowing within her. If any attempt would have been made to save the skin, then blood would have to be sacrificed to compensate the effort.

In the case of legal investigation, enough importance has to be attached to passion, greed, torture, rape, so forth, which would naturally have a source and an aim, lest the veracity of the incident can hardly be ascertained. Without recognising Enamul's weakness for Anima's flesh, we cannot at all comprehend why the Sanyal family yielded to the offer of Enamul for arranging their journey to the Indian Union after ten–fifteen days of their stay at his residence in exchange of Anima's staying back with him. During the days of riot, the shriek of frenzy in the slaughter of humans for one and their shrill cry in fear of getting killed for the other, the collective voice of mankind silencing the flames of fire and fury—all kept smashing the conventions and beliefs to pieces.

Hemchandra had not at all readily agreed to leave Anima behind in Pakistan. But on permutation and combination of the loss of so many lives and Anima's loss of caste, he certainly had come to a profitable conclusion. And hence, he came to the Indian Union, leaving Anima back in Pakistan.

As the riots and turmoil came to a stop, Enamul Haque Chowdhury converted Anima to Islam and renamed her as 'Kumkum' to marry her through proper registration, on 5 February 1951. At that time, it was feared that after the turbulent times of riot and skirmish, investigations might begin on these issues. For that, Anima had to assume a new name and conceal her father's identity, by using only the initial letters of his name.

Apart from these two reasons, there remain no excuse for Anima's staying back in Pakistan. The statements of the eldest son-in-law of Hemchandra Sanyal, a neighbour of the Sanyals at Mukhera and now a resident of Assam, and those of his wife, Anjali, to the effect of Anima's not coming to settle in the Indian Union are proved in such a way, that, no logic would ever take Kumkum and Anima as different individuals. If any such opinion of different entities was held, problems would crop up too on this issue. One had to wait for untying the knot whether they were one entity or separate individuals. But since such doubts were not raised, it was indirectly accepted that they meant the same person.

If on 30 July 1952, Anima Sanyal got married to Satyabrata Lahiri at all, then why and when did Kumkum Haque Chowdhury come to the Indian Union, bidding adieu to Pakistan?

This issue is bolstered by two viewpoints.

Firstly, in the month of June, 1952, Anima was first detected pregnant. Nausea, giddiness, loss of appetite and other associated symptoms too surfaced in the meantime. A few days later, Mainul Haque Chowdhury, Enamul's father, breathed his last. His household suffered from a lack of educated and experienced women. Again, owing to weak physique, Anima lost her nerves and went on talking about her father, mother, brothers, sisters and so forth.

In this case, a certain thing has to be taken special note of. Enamul was so taken aback by Anima's decision of not accompanying her parents to India that he used to stay away from home for quite a long time, for coming to terms with an altered situation and allowing Anima to get accustomed to the changed system, following their wedding. Enamul was aware of the fact that, their thoughts and beliefs on belonging to separate religions were so firmly rooted in their minds that mere external pull would not suffice; it needed an extirpation from within instead. Besides, Enamul wanted to keep her at a respectable distance only because she chose to stay back in Pakistan, willingly, for him. He might have been too conscious of not exerting any sort of pressure on Anima, by any means. On the demise of Mainul Haque Chowdhury, Enamul had to be close to Anima and he then discovered that even Anima maintained a certain distance like him, thinking of Enamul's inconvenience. Later, they were blessed with a happy conjugal existence. And for this reason, in just a year, Anima had conceived.

Enamul made all arrangements for sending Anima to Mukhera, considering the fact that she would feel better to be with her parents in her present condition. Again, it would smoothen the relationship with the family of his in-laws. But he desisted from going himself, as it might cause a social problem for his father-in-law's household.

And because of Enamul's active will, encouragement and for her mental and physical comfort and peace, Anima had come to the Indian Union. On coming here, she wrote a letter to Enamul, stating her safe arrival and her happy stay at her father's place. It carried her name on it: Anima.

This was her only letter after leaving Pakistan. After that Enamul wrote her three letters at short intervals. He felt hurt when he got no response from her end and even stopped writing. But he wrote again and finally sent a telegram to her.

On the other end, no sooner had Anima reached Mukhera, Hemchandra made the news rife that Anima had come back from her elder sister's place, as her wedding had been fixed. Following this, Hemchandra confined pregnant Anima in a closed room, made sure of severing all ties with Enamul, stopping all communications with him, concealing all his letters. He launched a frantic search for a certain sect of Brahmin groom--*Barendra* Brahmin—belonging to some clan other than *Baatsya*, at any cost. The cash along with ornaments and furniture which he could manage to bring here with the aid of Mainul and Enamul Haque Chowdhury, helped him to win everything in the Indian Union—right from his residence at Mukhera village along with the land it stood on, his identity as a Brahmin and his religious consciousness, all intact, all compact. He was keen on wiping off the memories of a few days, in between.

And at last, on 30 July 1952, just within one-and-a-half month of Anima's return from Pakistan, Hemchandra married off her two-month-pregnant daughter, Anima, to Satyabrata Lahiri, the son of late Punyabrata Lahiri. And, just after seven months, on 17 March 1953, Anima gave birth to a full-grown, healthy baby at Ballavpur Hospital. This child came into Anima's womb, while she was the wife of Enamul Haque Chowdhury and was delivered, when Anima became the wife of Satyabrata Lahiri.

Second Viewpoint: Moving to the Indian Union, Hemchandra failed to keep any track of Anima for long, although he hoped for or apprehended Anima's return someday. Hence, he kept all in the vicinity, aware of his second daughter's existence and he also said that she was presently with her elder sister in a tea garden of Assam. At last, Anima came to Mukhera in a very sorry state, with a frail health. It was reported by herself that she made an escape from Enamul immediately after Hemchandra Sanyal's exit from Pakistan and following immense oppression and distress. Later, tapping a slew of sources, she managed to get the address of Hemchandra Sanyal.

Getting back his lost child, Hemchandra, at first, concentrated on getting her back to health. Naturally, she had to stay indoors mostly and did not have any chance to mingle with others outside. In about a month or so, she recovered and was back in spirits. And before the doctor's treatment was over, the proposal for matrimonial negotiation for Anima came up from Mr Satyabrata Lahiri, BA, the son of dead Punyabrata Lahiri. Driven by the responsibility towards his daughter and failing to depend much on his decaying health, Hemchandra gave his nod to this marriage. And on 30 July 1952, Anima got married to Satyabrata.

In about one or one-and-a-half months, as Anima came to her father's place, she was detected to be in the family way. This could be validated by the neighbours at Mukhera, as witnesses. Just after four months, Anima was sent to Ballavpur. And at the end of seven months, on 17 March 1953, Anima gave birth to her only child. This pregnancy happened after her union with Satyabrata and the sole father of this child was Satyabrata himself.

If Enamul had got an opportunity to exploit Anima, would she ever get a chance to escape? And, if she kept staying with that lascivious ruffian, would it take one long year for her to conceive?

Considering all opinions and viewpoints, these conclusions can be drawn:

—Did Anima love Enamul or was she detained by him, forcefully?

—Did Anima marry Enamul out of her own will or under compulsion?

—Did Anima marry Satyabrata, changing her clan, willingly or under duress?

—Who is the father of Anjana—Enamul or Satyabrata?

Right answer to these queries would decide the real identity of Anima and Anjana. These queries would take us closer to the fundamental queries related to humans, in general—too fast, too straight.

Till you come to know the true, straight answers to these four questions, the woman you know as your wife cannot be your 'wife'. The offspring you know as your own, may not be yours.

Hence, with your basic and original identity proofs, please approach the nearest police station to prove that you are the real YOU!

In the rear entrance, in the front one, on the staircase, at the nook where the tulsi-*mancha* stood, in the corners of the room, everywhere darkness reigned supreme. Like fast-spreading deluge, like life-threatening epidemics, stood the darkness. Anima and Satyabrata, the two refugees, the two beings without any self-identity, longed for getting lost in the darkness, taking it to be the ocean of hot, molten iron.

Just an instant ago, it was a 'household'; now it got transformed into hollow, lightless eye sockets. Sticking out false eyelids, those eye sockets fixed their steadfast gaze on Anima in the courtyard, and Satyabrata on the staircase. That very room, that house, that family itself and that happiness grew into a monster, with lately formed legs, engulfing Satyabrata and Anima with a dizzy confusion. And in the sky of enveloping darkness, a silent oracle thundered: 'Satyabrata, you are not real YOU, and you are not your real self, Anima.'

Two selves, absolutely unrelated to each other, lay with their faces down, waiting avidly to listen to the lone, tender, plaintive voice of Anju, *'Baba...Ma...'*, piercing like an arrow the stygian gloom, and offering peace and solace to their souls! They kept waiting…

ॐ

Translated by Ketaki Datta

Ketaki Datta is an Associate Professor of English at Bidhannagar College, Kolkata. Her translated stories have been published in *Indian Literature* and a few other anthologies, published by Sahitya Akademi and Visva Bharati.

Homeland

Asish Sanyal

Someswari. A little mountain river. Somewhat dozing in coldness in the month of *Poush*. One slit of water pierces through the chest of the sandbank as it rushes towards the ebb tide. On both the banks one can hear the chirping of many unknown birds. Immediately on crossing the river is a small concrete path. It zigzags forward. On going ahead a short distance is a huge tamarind tree. Keeping the tree to the right, on advancing a little further, one will arrive at their home's boundary.

Paritosh remembers clearly, the house was surrounded by paddy and vegetable fields. A pond lay in the north. On its banks were numerous *keya* trees. When the flowers bloomed, oh what an enthralling fragrance spread across the air. In the midst of all this were a few tin-roofed rooms. The large one was the bedroom. Exactly opposite to it was the kitchen. A little away the well-decorated room was meant as the drawing room. The cowshed was quite a distance off.

Alighting from the bus Paritosh stood there for a while. Cool breeze skimming over Someswari blew against his body. Ah! What a comfort! There's magic in this breeze. Paritosh drew a deep breath.

He moved towards Someswari. On breaking an ascent, he set his feet in the river. Knee-deep water. Maybe a little more in some places. Paritosh recalled those days when he sat drenching his feet in this water. He had spent so many nights gazing at the stars scattered over the clear sky, as he sat on this river's bank.

But this same little tame river would turn a monster in the monsoons. It would rush forward snorting like a wild boar, overflowing its banks. All means of communication between one bank and the other would be snapped. The sight would send shivers down the spine.

All of a sudden, the huge patch of watermelon vegetation on the riverbank drew his attention. A strange glee boiled somewhere in his chest. Does Ramashray still work in the filed here?

Paritosh still remembers, now and then they would play truant from school to come here to steal watermelons. Once they were caught red-handed! If Kali weren't with them, they'd be buried in this very sand bank. Paritosh even remembers the time. It was evening. The soft sunlight was gleaming on the banks. The environment was loud with the chirping of so many variously coloured birds.

That day there were six of them. Immediately on setting foot in the watermelon field, some men ran towards them with staves and surrounded them. Actually, they were the guards of the fields. Paritosh's legs were shuddering in fear.

But Kali suddenly advanced towards those men. As he stood before a hefty man with a moustache he asked—

'Has Mahboob *Chacha* come?'

'Which Mahboob *Chacha*?'

'Don't you know him? The Inspector of Police. Has he come here?'

'No.'

'When he comes, tell him that we left not finding him here.'

'Why will he come here?'

'No idea. He said, there is some sort of trouble here. He asked us to come here, to take us home on his way back.'

The men had become somewhat confused. And they too had slowly slipped away from that place. Paritosh laughed to himself. What days those were—the days that have long disappeared. But to his amazement, deep down in his mind, all these little fragments of memories began to spread an inexplicable pleasure.

Unknowingly he moved towards the watermelon fields. But everything appeared somewhat new to him. Completely new—as if he hadn't ever come here before. Paritosh stared in that direction with a helpless gaze.

Thereafter, with a different thought, he returned again. Crossing the river he went to the other bank. But where is that familiar concrete path? Putting the suitcase on one side he paused for a while. The very village whose soil, sky, water, path, river-steps were all so familiar to him, why does it appear so new to him? Yet it was here that he was born.

In this very village he spent his childhood and early youth. Why does his motherland seem terribly ruthless to him? There was a day when Paritosh would get the fragrance of his own mother in this soil and breeze of this village. That scent would take him to some unknown world.

But today? Everything has changed somehow. Nearly fifty years. Seems all has turned topsy turvy. Picking up his suitcase Paritosh moved forward. But where is that tamarind tree? Kaisul *Chacha*, Enamul, Haren, Kali, Sneha *Didi*, Parul and Haseena? Paritosh cannot find any of them. Perhaps, people get lost. But earth? The earth on which people are born, does it get lost too, like human beings?

Paritosh's father used to say, 'Don't go away, ever, leaving your soil behind. This soil is your mother. Don't neglect her. I'll never go away leaving her behind.'

He never ever did go. The country was partitioned. People in groups abandoned their villages and went away, perhaps forever. However, Paritosh's father couldn't snap his bond with the homeland. On a terrifying night his blood was soaked in this very soil. Yet he did not leave his dear land. That day had become a piece of blurred photograph to Paritosh now.

14 August 1947. Tearing apart India's bosom, Pakistan was born. The next day at midnight, the flag of independent India was hoisted in Delhi's Red Fort. However, the dream of a new morning that inspired thousands of people to sacrifice their lives was never realised. In his teary eyes Kaisul *Chacha* said to Paritosh's father, 'What did we get after all this? At the

end they managed to divide the whole country. They have created disputes between brothers.'

'Can just a new map create a split among the people?' Paritosh's father had said. Kaisul *Chacha* had said while wiping his tears, 'You'll understand. Let a few days pass.'

Within a few days everyone could realise the horrible tragedy that had happened in the life of the nation. Echoes of an ongoing catstrophe reached every rural corner of the country. The Hindus from this side were leaving behind their ancestral land to go over the border and the Muslims from across it were arriving here. Riot and ruckus were going on everywhere. On that evening, Kaisul *Chacha* arrived in a hurry. Paritosh's father asked, 'Have you read the newspaper today? Saw that people are leaving, band after band. The situation here is not good either.'

'Why? What has happened here?'

'What is happening everywhere! A group of men have begun plundering in their greed for land and property. I don't find the situation normal. You all stay alert.'

A little later sounds of commotion and crying were heard on all sides. Flames were seen in some houses at a distance. Surenda had come running to tell Paritosh's father, 'Run away!'

'Why? What happened?'

'Can't you hear?'

'But?—'

'What do you mean "But"? If you don't run away now, you'll not get another chance.'

Everyone at home had gathered in the outer room. There was a mark of panic in everybody's eyes.

Parotish's father had said in a helpless tone, 'You all run away right now. Go with Suren.'

'Where?'

'Across the border—to India.'

'Where will we put up there?' Paritosh's mother had queried.

'Heard that the government is providing with aid there. Hurry up and run away.'

'You?'

'I'll stay here. I'll never leave this land behind.'

'But?'

'No ifs and buts now. Save the children.'

Following Surenda in the dense darkness of the night, they had set off that day. That is one history. After a few days how that terrible news had reached them, now he doesn't remember. On hearing the news of his father's horrific death everyone had broken down in tears. Father had kept his word. He did not come over abandoning the land.

Paritosh is walking on. After many days, today, those words of his father are thudding in his heart. Has he come here, drawn by the love for the land? Does the land have this much power?

After moving a bit, Paritosh stood under a tamarind tree. Keeping the suitcase aside he sat for a while under the tree. This tree is a witness to numerous incidents of his childhood. Paritosh felt somewhat relieved on discovering that the tree had survived in the midst of many changes. It was just like seeing a familiar face in a crowd of strangers. Paritosh spoke out absently.

In the gentle wind the leaves of the tree made a somewhat jingling sound. Has the tree responded to his utterance? He feels, everything is unreal. But on rare occasions, even the unreal assumes the shape of the real. Paritosh remembered Haseena. It was his early youth then. And Haseena? The empress of the kingdom of his youth. Haseena's father used to work in their fields. She used to come here with his midday meal. A strange splendour was spread over Haseena's form. Paritosh would stare at her with his wide-open eyes. Her warm touches made his blood boil for so many occasions. Today, all that has become history. All the dreams of those bygone days shall not touch the present any more. Is this the ever-familiar village of his dream! Or has he arrived somewhere else by mistake? He cannot see anything familiar anymore.

A kind of restlessness was tormenting Paritosh. He sat up. He recalled, keeping this tree to the right, advancing just a short distance, was their house. Paritosh hurriedly moved forward in that direction. Advancing a little he stopped at one spot. But where is the wood-apple tree? Where is that pond? He stared blankly in that direction.

'Who's that? Why is he staring that way?'

Instead of giving a straight reply to the question, Paritosh enquired, 'Is this Kshetra Roy's house?'

'Kshetra Roy? What do you mean? This is Sujauddin's house.'

'No, I mean, was this Kshetra Roy's house in the past?'

This time the man almost rushed towards him. Everyone appeared to be staring at him with a strange look. An aged man advanced towards him. Asked him very politely. 'Where are you coming from?'

'From Calcutta.'

'You're Indian? I mean, is your home in Hindustan? So, what do you want here?'

'I have come to breathe in the air of my birthplace.'

No one could comprehend any of his words. Someone commented from the crowd, 'See, if he's an informer!'

'Do you have a passport? Visa?'

Paritosh nodded his head.

'Come, let's go to the police station.'

'Police station? Why?'

'We think you're a suspect. Do you have any second motive?'

Paritosh couldn't understand what he ought to say. He hadn't realised before that he'd find himself in this kind of a situation. He stood there speechless. Then, brooding on something he suddenly spoke out, 'Can you tell me the direction to Kaisul *Chacha*'s house?'

This time an aged man advanced towards him. He asked, 'Did you know him?'

'He was a close friend of my father Kshetra Roy.'

The aged man then looked into Paritosh's eyes. He said, 'You're Kenubabu's son? Who'll recognise if you say Kshetra Roy! Can you recognise me? I'm Nabi. Your Kaisul *Chacha*'s son. Come with me.'

Holding Nabi's hand Paritosh advanced through the paddy fields.

Paritosh is contemplating, the earth on which he was born, the air which reared him, why can't it be addressed as 'Mother'? Why is his motherland not his own country? He was gradually being immersed into the depths of a strange dream.

☙

Translated by Jolly Das

Jolly Das is an Associate Professor, Department of English, Vidyasagar University, West Bengal. Her area of interest includes works of T.S. Eliot Girish Karnad and Translation Studies.

The Exile

Hasan Azizul Huq

He tried to listen to something. Some sound, any noise. But nothing could be heard, neither the sound of the wind nor that of a leaf falling. Within this short time, the earth has become as cold as ice. The pale leaves, bathed in the chill of the silent dew, have become wet. It's the end of winter; a very strong northern wind has blown over the field the whole day, sucking away the last bit of warmth it had. Then the gust comes back again. But just before the evening, the gust of wind has fluttered its wing for the last time and shedding the dry leaves from the trees, has left this land for this year. And thereafter, a dead silence came over the vast fields, over the small pond with its slimy water, over the mound of yellowish wild unknown shrubs, creepers and thorny bushes. Save a few yards of space around it—fog, like the cough of a pneumonia patient, has settled all over the place. The stormy wind of the day has now been replaced by mist. The world around him suddenly became silent amid that mist and the pale corpse-like watery darkness.

He tried to hear something. Any sound. But nothing was heard. Sound of wind or of leaves falling, or at least of dewdrops falling on dry leaves or the sound of hurried footsteps of a small, wild animal. He could hear nothing. Wrapping himself well with the torn thick blanket he lifted his head high, placing the two elbows on the wet, straw-coloured grass on the rough, uneven ground and looked at the mist.

At present the world of sound, except his own heartbeat, might be lost to him entirely but the whole day, even after the evening, there was no pause in the countless sounds. Buses and trucks making furious noises had been plying to and fro on the distant black asphalt road. He also heard the sound of the small cars and even the sound of a train that rattled past making shrill whistling sounds. He was listening to all such sounds throughout the day. While he was lying inside the large bush in that lonesome field, all these sounds merged with his absurd incoherent thoughts. The moment evening descended, a flock of crows flew over his head. Herons fluttered away in pairs. Then came a white-breasted kite. At the end of all there were one or two lonely birds, flying all by themselves. Finally, an enormous bird, moving its huge wings slowly and with long pauses went away. Flapping its legs backward it flew parallel to the ground, moving its beautiful head to every direction. Making a whizzing sound, it had, with great serenity, gradually receded and then vanished through the eastern tip of the field. At one side of the field, amid the bamboo thickets, birds of all size and variety had started to chatter. However, with the passage of the evening, they could no more be seen. By that time, trembling in the chill, he had covered himself up completely with the wrapper and had also become almost naked trying to hide the big hole in the middle of the wrapper with his *lungi*. Even in a condition like this, he was feeling very hungry. He took out some coarse *chira* kept in a small shabby piece of cloth and chewed on absentmindedly. 'Good, they have all gone to sleep', he said to himself.

After that he didn't think of anything else for quite some time. Carefully avoiding the mud, he took water from a canal in his palm and drinking it, staggered forward. When the cold became too fierce, when his head became a heavy slab of ice, his legs became numb, like a wounded animal, he took shelter in a dry canal. Crouching himself tightly he got back some warmth and could think once more. He thought, 'It seems quite late at night. How long have I been walking? Don't even know where I have reached. And it is such biting cold!'

In the blunt head of the man squatting in this dreary cold of the dead harvested field, came his first thought of this winter. He heard as if someone was shouting, 'Hey Bachir, Bachir. You are sleeping idly. The master will surely punish you. Such sleep you have!' He heard the cry only once inside his head. After that it was all silence again.

It was indeed very cold this season. On one hand winter came quite early—as soon as the month of *Agrahayon*—and on the other, it is lingering too long. Even on these last days of the *Magha*, it is still bitterly cold. This time winter arrived much earlier, even before one could enjoy the charm of autumn. Like every other year, the old folks said, 'It is really cold; very cold indeed. This is what we call freezing cold. We have grown old and all our hair and beard have turned white and yet we have never seen such cold.'

Like every year, the young men of the village laughed at such words and said, 'You only imagine this. As we don't feel the cold now, you did the same when you were young. The cold is nothing; it's all about the strength in your blood.' Some of the old folks nodded in agreement. They said, 'While we were of your age, if necessary, we used to cut the crops till late at night in the month of *Poush*. We often went to the fields after watching the morning star. What you have said is true. What matters is the strength of blood.'

There were one or two old men who were of a different view. But this year everyone has to accept the opinion of these few old men. Indeed, it is a little too cold this year. Especially at midnight, chill seems to overflow from the sky over this plain flat land. From the very beginning of *Agrahayon*, unruly northern wind blowing throughout the day has brought about a layer of black frost over the land. And after dusk, when the wind is gone, the land becomes one solid piece of ice. This land of spotless white soil has turned black this year. A thin blackish slimy layer has covered it. By no means can the thick mossy cover be seen in the paddy fields during the months of autumn.

In this bitter cold the work of this year has started. What can winter do when one has jobs to finish? The cold might be freezing, the harvest might be very little, half of that little harvest might have to be given to the land-owner, but winter can do nothing. So, all the scythes of the village have become active. Wearing either a thick, torn wrapper or a soiled stinking *kantha*, these people had to face the winter. By the time it was the middle of *Poush*, the iron scythes, made with a little hint of steel, turned white as silver. Bundles of paddy, reaped and tied, were left in the field, like innumerable dead soldiers, for a few days. Washed in dew, the grains got the shining hue of gold. After this, the work with the scythes was over. With shapeless slippers, as hard as bone and made by the village cobbler, in their feet, they have started to pile these bundles of paddy in the shape of hillocks.

When all the traces of green were gone from this flat plain land, there was nothing but deep black mud in the canals. The long beaks of snipes had pricked the raw mud; the big cranes in their black and white feathers, standing on one leg, had started to perch there in long lines. Northern wind had gradually made the land smaller; the trees became absolutely bare and keeping with the vegetation of the land, the deep green grasshoppers had turned into the colour of mud. And this grey flat land got crisscrossed with the parallel lines made by the wheels of the bullock carts.

This entire winter season and the picture of this land, so severely affected by that winter, very faintly float in the illiterate, almost barbaric mind of his. The description given above might be very apt with its detailing but the picture in his mind is far more deep and warm by virtue of the liveliness of feelings. Therefore he might have missed some dry details but has added much and the picture became an ultimate truth for him. Even though he was losing consciousness in hunger, even though he was numb beneath the lonely horrifying night sky that poured chill, the moment he got the picture, leaning on his elbows, he turned back his head eagerly. The fog froze and put a curtain over his eyes. He saw nothing. The wide field remained still and unmoved. The canal in which he took shelter, instead of providing warmth, bit him with large wild teeth. Becoming almost a round bundle, he saw pictures in the eyes of his mind and to his ears clearly came the words, 'Bachir. Hey Bachir. You are sleeping idly. The master will surely punish you.'

The one who used to call him didn't have to shout very long. Bashir used to quickly tear himself away from the warmth of his wife's body. The well-shaped hand used to thud on the cold floor as it fell from the bed in a fleshy sound. His eight-year-old son had moved away from the bed. Bashir used to bend himself promptly. He then put his wife's hand back over her neck and brought the child closer. After that he used to come out of the bed cautiously. Taking down the wrapper from the rope hanging in the room, he used to cover himself up completely with it. The scythe shined bright in the darkness and was easy to find. He came out of the room opening the weak door made of mango wood and said, 'Uncle, is it you?'

'Yes, my son, yes. This is me. I have become tired calling you. How deep do you sleep?' Wazddi seemed unhappy. 'Now let's go. It's getting late. Our master Bishe is not a very good man. Don't you understand? The Santal labourers and their wives who have been hired by the master don't even sleep at night. They drink the whole night and come to the field very early in the dawn. We are in trouble for them. It is because of them that we also have to go to the fields on such a cold night. Now, come. Let's move quickly.'

'Okay. Okay.' Bashir is in no hurry. 'Let me smoke a little. Wait a bit'.

'We will get late. You have your smoke. I am leaving.'

'O Uncle, wait a little. Why are you in such a hurry? How late would we be? We will be there very soon.'

'Our master Bishe will mimic you and will take no time to dismiss us.'

'Who cares? There is no dearth of jobs in this month of *Poush*. All the rascals need labourers now. Master Bishe, my foot!'

Bashir said this while he was tearing straw from a plaited pile of straws.

He created a small round ball with the smashed straw. Then slowly, keeping the ball in his palm, he went on rubbing it. He would not be able to go out without having his smoke. He told this once more.

In this terrible cold, hearing so many times about smoking, Wazddi also gradually felt a strong desire to have a puff. He sat at one corner of the veranda and said, 'When you are determined to smoke, let me have a puff or two as well. And be careful. The tobacco is ready. Don't rub it anymore. It will turn into dust.'

Rubbing the tobacco ball, Bashir turned it almost to dust and then putting it at the top of the hookah, slapped it hard twice. From a corner of the veranda, he brought flint stone, steel and cork. In expert hands he put fire first into the cork and then to the lump of straw. Wazddi kept on watching silently as the tobacco was getting ready. He was shivering from the cold. A gust of cold wind came; men from different households woke up and got out of their rooms taking their scythes in hand which were shining at the dark corner of the rooms. Some of them will work at their own fields and some at their masters'.

After getting the tobacco ready, Bashir, in order to puff it, kissed the hookah a few times. Getting satisfied he handed it over to Wazddi and said, 'Now have it'.

Wazddi smoked intently for no less than three minutes and then almost hidden in smoke, said, 'It would have been unwise to go to work without smoking'.

'Isn't it so? Didn't I say the same? You were talking so much of Bishe Master that it almost spoiled the charm of smoking.'

'When will you cut your own crop?' Wazddi asked.

'So little crop. In no time it can be harvested. Paddy produced in only one *bigha* and a half. I can manage only three months with that. These are the early days of the harvesting season. Let me work as a hired hand at others' fields. Don't you understand? I will earn some money by that. Are you done with your harvesting?'

'My crop? Now, take this hookah. Are you asking about my crop? I have cut and put those sickly crops of mine in heaps much earlier. Didn't you see the heap of my paddy?'

Wazddi laughed like a jackal as he continued to speak.

'It is such a huge heap! Do you know one can see the heap of crop of some people even from a sixty-storey building? In my heap of paddy even a goat cannot hide. It's better we don't talk about my crop'.

'I didn't want to hurt you. It is you who has raised the issue. That's why I have asked you.'

'Come on. Let's go. We should not be late anymore.'

'Okay. Let's go'

They departed.

In that pale darkness someone from a different group walking slightly away called out, 'Who is there?'

'Are you Bhakta?'

'O, it's you, Wazddi uncle. Who is with you?'

'Bhakta, it's me'. Bashir answered.

'O, in which field would you work today?'

'The field at Jamtala. Where will you work?'

'At Verendagara. In whose field would you work?'

'Our master Bishe. Bhakta, have you cut the paddy of your own field?'

'Yes. That's done. From day after tomorrow, I will carry them home. Come one day and help me thresh.'

'Sure. Sure. Why not?'

Bashir and Wazddi moved ahead. It was yet to be morning. A light fog had descended over the earth. The black soil was slightly moist and hard as rock. Smoke coming out of the cow-shed was mingling with the fog. A heavy curtain was coming down over the village. They reached the fields piercing that curtain. Heavy moist ears of paddy lying on the ground hit hard at the calf of the feet. The wind whispered; there was a rustling sound as bundles of paddy brushed against each other. Other than this faint sound, there was no sound in this wide open field. These men were seen walking hurriedly amid the darkness. Then suddenly, tearing the veil of fog, the immense red light of the sun fell on the fields, and one could see that the fields were full of people. Then a sound could be heard, a vast solemn humming that circled around the land and the sky of the field. This does not have any other name; it can be called the humming of life. It is the murmuring of living—warm, intense and eternal.

When he, crouching in the canal, was watching these pictures, it came to his mind that he might die. He did not know how people die. But he felt that a man, at the verge of his death, glimpses all the pictures of his life in one go. He also believed that a man, while dying, cannot think anything, cannot feel happiness and sorrow, can only see. He also could think of nothing. Like his body, his mind had also frozen into numbness in this cold. He seemed to have gone beyond all the happiness and sorrow as he had lost the ability to feel pain. At present he was not even trying to save himself from the cold. But keeping the eyes closed, looking intently at his mind, he could see in a resigned and helpless manner one picture after another. The pictures were coloured in bold hues and whatever were there in those pictures, men or field, sky or tree, were brushing past his body.

Mingled with that wonderful humming of the morning, came sounds of scythe, of dry, dead snails and crabs being crushed under the feet, of a rat suddenly scurrying away, of abrupt yelling and folk tunes rising over that humming. Cutting of the crop, putting them in bundles, arranging heaps of paddy, the slow movement of the bullock carts carrying the crop, the shrill screaming from the wheels of those carts lacking oil, sound of threshing done in a mood of competition—these trifling details from the soil of his land and many events from his own life got reflected on the opposite wall of his heart. As the day advanced, the red sunlight turned into a harsh white. The work of the second phase of the day began. The humming sound got enveloped in the silence of the field. Innumerable scythes shone simultaneously in the bright light of midday.

The last picture, which closely huddled together with all these images, came and got stuck in his mind. He shivered from his head to toe. Tried to shake off the picture. He tried to smear it with darkness. But the picture kept still and hung in his mind.

That day almost everyone from the field had gone back. Sitting around the fire, Santal men and women were carefully burning and skinning a rat or a squirrel. The farmers and the householders were calculating the day's harvest. That day Bashir and Wazddi were late in coming back home. Covering the ears and wrapping the heads, they were coming back quickly. They were not talking to each other. The ground beneath their feet was bitingly cold. After the silence of some time, Bashir said, 'O Uncle'.

'Yes,' Wazddi appeared somewhat absent-minded.

'O Uncle, can't you hear me?'

'Yes. Tell me.'

'Can you explain what we have been hearing?'

'Why? What have you heard?'

'Didn't you hear anything?'

'Why don't you just say what you have heard?'

'Once again there would be trouble.'

'Where?'

'You haven't heard anything?'

'No. I have heard nothing.'

'You are really incorrigible. The whole day there was whispering. Have you heard none of these? Hindus of Pakistan are being butchered en masse. And on the other hand, Muslims of Calcutta are being executed.'

'Who told you all this rubbish?' Wazddi almost growled at Bashir.

'People are talking about it.'

'Let them. You just go home. Have your dinner and sleep'.

'But tonight, if they do something to our village…'

Wazddi said 'Just see! This is what we call an idiot. Do you think idiots grow on trees? Tell me, what would they do to our village tonight?'

'They will come.'

'Which scoundrels will come?'

'The Hindus from Lababpur, Chistidharpur will come after offering puja to their goddess, Kali'.

'Just go home'. Wazddi got so irritated that he couldn't speak anymore.

'Have heard it and therefore told you.'

'Couldn't you chop off the head of that man who said this with your scythe?'

'But everyone is saying this.'

'Now, keep quiet a bit. I am feeling very cold.'

Both of them remained silent. But a little later Bashir again said, 'I think everything will resume once more.'

'You are really a good-for-nothing. I am telling you to go home for such a long time and yet, here you are, blabbering on and on.'

Bashir didn't pay heed to these rude words. He whispered almost to himself, 'After all Pakistan is the land of the Muslims; Muslims rule over there.'

'Then, why didn't you go to Pakistan?'

'Can people like us muster the courage to go to some other land uprooting the home and the hearth? Still the country is…'

Suddenly Wazddi turned and looked angrily at Bashir, as if he might silently burn Bashir alive with his eyes. Bashir stood like a fool. Wazddi went on staring at him in the same manner and then asked him, 'How many fathers do you have? And how many mothers? Just one. Isn't it? Similarly, you can have only one motherland. Do you understand? Now go home.' Saying this Wazddi himself walked away hurriedly.

But finally they really came. From far-off villages, leaving the warmth of their small clay huts, smearing vermilion all over their foreheads, they came to kill people they never knew. Before they reached the village, Bashir and his people, sitting on their beds arranged over the cold floor, heard the sounds of *dhaak, kansor* and conches for no less than three hours. Crossing the silent fields, piercing the fog of the winter, came the rumblings of *dhaak*. The sky of the month of *Magha* shuddered at the ringing of *kansor*. The night, like a gigantic eagle, got hold of the village with its ugly talons.

The feeble arrangements of resistance crumbled easily. The bullock carts placed diagonally over the road were broken. Then first to be attacked, as Bashir witnessed, was Wazddi. Fire flamed around the straw-thatched clay huts. It brightened up the faces of the unknown murderers, the vermilions smeared on their foreheads. Wazddi's fresh blood gushed out; fire began to play on the dead, surprised face of his.

'Bachir, hey Bachir—they have gone towards your home.'

'Is it so? When?'

'There, there. They are going to your place. My house is also—'

'Hey Rakib—there are those bastards.'

Bashir left the group and ran as fast as he could. The house has already been gutted to nothingness. They are gone. Bashir's seven-year-old son, pierced and stuck to the earth by a spear and the body of a twenty-six-year-old woman, looking like a black, burnt piece of wood, were there in the ruined gutted house. The air was heavy with the foul smell of raw flesh burning.

'Oh Allah, if you stay within the body of human beings,' Bashir screamed his soul out, 'then tell me where do you stay, in which part of the human body.'

He stood erect. Till then he was lying crouched in the canal; all his limbs have gone numb in the cold. Going beyond all the fears, worries and distress, beyond all the physical pains, he, lying motionless and staring at the fog, was watching those images.

While watching this last picture, he stood up as firm as steel. The veins in his throat swelled up. His two hands with the prominent veins became as hard as an iron rod. He could not see any more picture. Suddenly he became completely blind. He has come far away from his homeland in the last few nights, blind, haunted and insane as he has been watching this terrible picture. He has hidden himself in shrubs and bushes during the daytime. He has not gone close to any human being, did not pray for any help. Not even to God. He said to himself, 'I am not Bachir anymore. Bachir is no more. Bachir is done for. He doesn't have any country any more. I will be born in another country.'

This is how he has spent today. Hiding in a bush, he has heard the great varieties of the sounds of the earth. Those sounds have got tangled with his meaningless thoughts. Throughout the day, a strong northern wind has been blowing. The wind has stopped the moment evening has descended on earth. But by that time the earth has frozen. A heavy curtain of fog has come down. He has not noticed when the world has become silent. When he noticed that silence, he tried to listen to something. But he could hear nothing. Just then he realised that he had reached the border of another country. Unknowingly, at any moment, he would step into the country to which he was fleeing. He had to be very careful lest he would be seen by someone.

He didn't want to be noticed by men or even by animals. He has also heard that just as one is not allowed to leave one's own country, one is also not allowed to enter another either. Every moment now, he is thinking that torchlight would flash over his face, then there would be a terrible sound and his dead body would stumble and fall.

Then came a strong wave of chill. The chill pierced through his bone and reached the marrow. Like a sharp knife, it cut through his flesh, his bone and his marrow. A sharp pain spiralled through the cells of his brain. After one point of time, he became unconscious. Even then he was moving forward; at least that is what it looked like.

Actually, he was taking his steps like a machine. The numb feet have become separate organs, unrelated to his body, and were shaking and falling here and there at their own will. Suddenly, he tripped over and fell on a piece of hard, firm land. Against his own will, his body rolled on to find shelter in a canal. This time he was certain that he would die.

Perhaps he was dying indeed. There was not a single sign of life around to encourage him. Life was completely missing from the fields, the waterbodies, the canals, bushes and the sky. The canal in which he was lying had such a high embankment that nothing could be seen from it. The earth became very small to his eyes. As he was dying in that very narrow world, he started once again to see the pictures.

At that moment, a very disgusting yellow moon, almost one fourth of its full size, rose in the sky. In that light, one could see a man, crossing the fields from the east, has reached the high embankment of the canal in tentative steps. He was wearing a soiled, coarse dhoti tucked around the knees and had a thick wrapper around him. He had a bamboo pole on his shoulder. On the two ends of that bamboo pole there were wicker baskets. The various items in the baskets and a big axe, all were shining in the moonlight.

Standing still, Bashir lifted his head. But almost instantly it dropped. He was watching those pictures with great attention. He could see his whole life in an instant. He was looking at a vast flat country. That country, with all its minute details, was hanging in front of his eyes in a tiny form. Then everything started to change with the pace of a shooting star. He saw the fresh blood of Wazddi, his dead stunned face, warm blood, redder than the dazzling fire, his seven-year-old son speared to death, a woman of twenty-six burnt black as coal.

All of a sudden, the canal seemed to explode with a horrifying sound. Bashir came up as a squirrel. He stood in front of the silent man with a bamboo pole on his shoulder. In the light of the moon, under the sky that was raining dew over the fields, two complete strangers stood at the high embankment of the canal facing each other. There was a burning sensation in his ears. Someone screamed at him, 'Bachir. Hey Bachir.' Warm blood from his son gored by the spear spilled on him. The eyes of Wazddi, as white as those of a dead fish, stared at him.

Looking angrily at the man, Bashir suddenly picked up the axe and hit hard at his head. There was a loud thundering sound. The man with the bamboo pole, shocked and surprised, cried an ear-splitting death cry and rolled on to the canal.

'You bastard, you were running away from this country.' Even in the dim moonlight the big white teeth, like those of a gorilla, shone bright.

Two torch lights flashed. One on the face of Bashir and the other on that dumbfounded one facing the pain of death. When the light moved away, Bashir noticed that the face of the other man was like that of Wazddi. Blood-smeared, horrifying and surprised. As if the foggy curtain got removed from the eyes. The tears streaming out of his eyes turned the two worlds grey—one that he left and the one to which he was going.

ଓଃ

Translated by Tajuddin Ahmed

Tajuddin Ahmed is an Associate Professor of English at Aliah University, Kolkata. His area of intrest includes Latin American fiction, Dalit poetry, Partition Literature and early writings of Indian Muslim women.

Hearth and Home

Jiban Sarkar

This time, on 21 February, I got a chance to visit my birthplace. Agniva is my grandson. He works in Dhaka; stays at Banani. One day he said to me, 'Would you like to see your place of birth? I'll take you there.' Without giving him any time to reply I said, 'Yes, I'll go'. We left the country many years ago during the troubled times of Partition. *Ma* sent me to Hindustan along with my elder brother. Our parents decided thus, as they thought our studies might be hampered due to tension and turmoil. Back then our likes and dislikes were of no account to them. That was the age for communion with the earth—a time when we were always supposed to bow our heads down to the soil.

A crow cawed that morning from the branches of a mango tree. I heard a *shalik* tweet in the clean courtyard where *Ma* spread the paddy to dry. She would make rice with the husking pedal. She used to do everything by herself. Her eyes were brimming with tears. She said to me, 'Jiban, just take a plunge in the pond and come back.' Her voice sounded heavy. She could not gather her words properly. She was sobbing. She knew, it was for the last time she uttered that.

I was struggling continuously against every drop of my tears. I could not tell *Ma* that I won't go and I would like to stay with them all. I was not that mature then. Actually, we siblings were not used to contradicting our seniors. I was not at all happy with the idea of going to Hindustan. I felt my eyes were full of tears.

The pond was clean with only a few hyacinths near its border. It rained a couple of days ago. Hence the water was crystal clear. Chhentu and I were swimming from one end to the other. Even Chhentu didn't know that we're leaving that very day. A ferryman named Bisha had been asked to arrange for a big boat. He would ferry us over to Goaland. Some others would be there in a different boat and they would protect us from dacoits. *Ma* repeatedly forbade me to tell anybody about this lest some untoward incident takes place. Chhentu was my bosom friend. Even from him I hid the whole plan. I felt sad for that. At the core of my heart, I asked for forgiveness. We also heard that they would go to Tanti Bajar in Dhaka. And from there to Calcutta. Chhentu did not disclose anything either. Neither I asked him anything. How could one utter that terrible thing! Everyone was secretly planning to leave. This place was no more secure. Only Muslims would be allowed to stay in this Islamic nation and not the Hindus.

Oh! My dear Bengal! My motherland! Were we cursed with this fate? Did we want this *Independence*? We had to come here empty-handed leaving parents, home, hearth, everything behind. Why? Who will give us an answer? We want an answer.

Thousands of rootless people streamed across the roads of villages, mofussils and towns bewilderedly, in a flux of uncertainty looming large over their heads. Relatives and neighbours were torn asunder. Someone's father was lost and someone else's mother. Someone's brother drowned in the Surama river and someone's sister in the Meghna. Some others were carried away by Dhaleswari or Brahmaputra. The cry of near and dear ones faded out.

The tumult of screaming was all around. Beware! Danger was always ahead. People were whispering that the houses of Hasa Roy and Kanu Saha were set on fire. Someone kidnapped the daughter of Megha Kale of Kuchiamore. The ferryman named Bishu stood in protest. He was a young man, tall and stoutly built. His chest resembled the stem of a *hijal* tree. They cut his throat and threw the dead body down the Ichhamati river.

One gets afraid when the sun sets. Perhaps the plunderers will burst in upon us. They may hack at our throats. Where are the young men? Vidya Thakur, who used to sing whole night out of trepidation, was not heard anymore. Has his head been hacked off then? Where is Sudhir Doctor? Who shouts '*Allah Ho Akbar*'? The Hindu lads timidly answer back—'Vande Mataram'.

Ma stands along with my younger sister in the pond among hyacinths with just their noses raised above the water. Leeches and mosquitoes are all around. My elder nephew is calling out, '*Baba*, where are you? No time for rest. The thugs have arrived at Kalibhita. Give me my spear. I'm bringing another.' Father is shouting, 'Where are you, Buri's mother? Don't get afraid. I'm here. You women, blow the conch. Give *uludhwani*.'

This was the place of forefathers. *Baba* won't leave this land. That meant *Ma* would've to stay here too. Being stricken with terror we came to this country. It occurred many years back. *Ma* and *Baba* stayed back. They breathed their last there.

Kaula Sheikh's sons still take care of the tulsi plants. They spontaneously said, 'We have bought this house. Will you take it back again?'

'No, we won't take anything. Just give a bit of soil from my parents' grave. You need not feel afraid. I have come on the occasion of 21 February this time. I'm staying at my grandson's place in Dhaka.'

'Will you take tea?'

'No, thanks.'

'Tea is available in our village these days.'

'Wonderful. Is everything available here?'

'Every house has electric and gas connection and TV sets. Look at the roads. We have made all these things. Everything familiar to you is past, even the *hijal* tree and its shade.'

I sighed.

'My parents are at their eternal rest in this house. No bad things will happen to you here.'

'We know. *Kartabaap* was a gentle soul. I heard it from *Abba*. He bade us to see to it that your father's cemetery remained intact. I'm keeping my father's word, although I know not how long I'll be able to do that. The situation amounts to a quarrel between two women. It's a nuisance of a different kind. Each demands absolute attention. We are crushed by the rivalry between the two. We are on the horns of a dilemma. If we support one, the other will kill us; and if we support the other, it's no better. I believe you don't have this sort of crisis there. You were at peace when you lived here. But those are bygone days.'

Without delving much into any political quibble I asked, 'Wasn't there a plum tree at this place?'

'Right. But they had cut it down.'

Days of yore! One does not recognise familiar things. Everything has changed. The whole village where we used to have the *Rasa* festival has vanished. People set it on fire.

'Do you remember Kalachand Doctor?'

'Yes, I do.'

'They ruined the whole village. And evicted everybody. None could prevent the disaster.'

I was watching the places where *Ma* used to wash utensils and make *muri* and plant vegetables like cucumber, green pepper, okra and others. We didn't have to buy those vegetables. Alas! Where have those days gone? Who ruined them? Our countrymen couldn't capture those fellows.

After a long while the bearded man said, 'Come again. We'd thatch your cottage. We promise.' The upper portion of his body was bare. He wore *lungi* and his cheeks were unshaven. But his eyes had a different shine. I thought aloud— 'Well said. Perhaps he is sincere. But his father doesn't want that.' However, this is not the right moment to talk about this. He definitely had the conviction to utter that because it is he who planted the tulsi sapling in my parents' graveyard. I parted with no other words with the man.

Chhentu lives in Dhaka. He used to teach at a college. Being a local, his experience is different. Kalibhita has been turned into an empty space through which runs a concrete road. People used to worship Goddess Kali during the winter. *Ma* took a leading role in decorating the *mandap* and in all the rituals of puja including *dhunuchinaach*.

Foreign-made cars are plying by my side. Who knows if *Ma* is aboard those expensive cars to catch those who made the Partition and shed blood? Will she be able to catch them one day? I believe she will.

Time is up. Agnibha is insisting on our return. Chaos is all around. Strike is on. Cars are being blasted with petrol bombs. The fundamentalists have assassinated the liberal-minded writer Abhijit Roy. The town is filled with dreadful uncertainty. We will have to return before evening settles down. Chhentu is a local resident; he must have known these things. Our house was close to his. I have brought him along with us.

Look, that's our paddy field. The flashing paddy plants are bidding us adieu. We often played the game of hide and seek behind that field. Fishes used to stream down the Dhaleswari river in the monsoon. Jogesh da had the habit of catching fishes with *tota* and I used to stand knee deep in the water with a creel.

The anguish of Chhentu is of a different kind. He still stays in this country and is a citizen of Bangladesh. But he nurtures a sense of belonging to Hindustan. When would he be able to reach Hindustan with a passport and visa! He has three daughters and they are all studying in college. They are good-looking. Chhentu is always worried about them. He has no peace of mind. He always lives in dread. They watch the programmes of Calcutta on the TV screen. And they are keen on coming to this country. Perhaps Chhentu is brooding on that.

I, however, have a different thought. Where would I be able to see Ma? I haven't seen her for years. Till today I believed that *Ma* was in this country. The myth is shattered now. Is *Ma* buried here in Bangladesh or does she hide herself somewhere else? Sometimes I feel that she is lying just beneath the tulsi plant. The present owners of this place take care of my parents. Otherwise, they would have uprooted this plant long ago. There were so many among them who did not want Partition. Even today they are against it. But they are obviously fewer in number. Most of them have flourished at the expense of the property of the Hindus and they don't want the country to be united again. They have become rich with the assets left by the Hindus.

The car is moving toward the Sadarghat. None utters a word. Chhentu shouts, 'Look, that's Dhaleswari river. It has shrunk to a canal. You'll find no hilsa now in the river.'

The local fishermen say that all the fish have left for Hindustan along with the Hindus. Perhaps they are true. These villages have lost their past glow with the Partition. This thought agonises them. They have no tears in their eyes. It's not clear whether Chhentu is crying. But my eyes are brimming with tears. I can't sit erect. Dhaka is on strike. But cars are plying and the shops are open. I am not sure, what kind of strike is this. The strike in Calcutta is absolutely different. Although these two countries are parts of Bengal and although the mother tongue is the same, there is almost an unbridgeable difference in customs and practices. There is indeed no comparison between the two.

Everybody remains silent. One may see a signboard in the paddy field: *The Great Dhaka Will March Forward*. The signboard in the Residential Office reads: Villages will not remain villages any more. The present-day technology will swallow them up. The rural Bengal, the Bengal of bountiful crops, will cease to exist. River Padma will dry up. Horrid! Nature has turned her face in disgust from us.

Chhentu, like me, is five feet tall. His round face resembles a bottle-gourd leaf. He can't be called dark but he is not fair either. His eyes are small in comparison with his facial features. They tend to shrink while he speaks. He speaks quietly. I met him almost after forty years. He says to me, 'Fruits, fish, vegetables—everything has left with the Hindus after the Partition. We are only left with the refuse. Even the *shapla* and *kalmishaak* have become sparse. Do you get it, Jiban?'

I didn't understand why he said that all of a sudden. Satya is a reserved man. He used to work at the Reserve Bank with responsibility. He is reticent. He has adequate hair even at this age. His face is flat. With a gaze of wonder he is staring at the paddy fields all around. They are all green. The ears of corn are not yet out. Shanta belongs to Calcutta. She likes villages. She is a good match for Satya. She is completely silent.

Agnibha is fair and handsome. He is six-feet tall. Salma is also very beautiful. She had her place at Chandpur. She holds a high position in the office of Agnibha. She has a broad, beautiful face. Her eyes are big and liquid. She is pretty smart and articulate. But neither she nor Agnibha responds to the words of Chhentu.

I respond, 'It's true. That's the market of Kuchiamora. It's a launch station. But is the banyan tree no more?'

'No. That's dead for long. I told you the sign of poverty is in every nook and cranny. Neither there is prosperity nor happiness anywhere. Everything has vanished with the Partition. There is a sense of barrenness everywhere. The river is devoid of water and the field of corn. Vegetables don't taste the same as they used to. Those things have left along with you. Only the skeleton remains. There are signs of emptiness all around with the departure of the Hindus. The atmosphere of the village was once filled with sport and merriment. Villages used to hum with life. But those days are past.'

What Chhentu says is true. He continues, 'When you left the country, it made us sad. But we are in another kind of predicament now. We remain always worried. We know not what will happen to us. Grown-up girls at home. No suitable groom. We are not at peace. The golden Bengal is no more.'

Suddenly Salma says, 'You're absolutely right. We now live in a village dilapidated in its heart and soul. Isn't there sadness in our minds? In our childhood days, we had seen that people of two different communities lived in harmony with each other whether be it the Durga Puja or Eid. But now it seems, an air of melacholy pervades everywhere. We feel it. Can you believe that *Ma* still misses her *Sai* ? What an outburst of tears when the two pals parted from each other! We're not well. We merely pass our days. When the mango tree is laden with fruits, *Ma* calls her friend, "Rani, please come and see. So many fruits to your tree! So sweet! How are you, Rani? What about Ranaghat? Is there any river like Meghna or Jamuna? I'll certainly go once. Hope you're well. You don't write letters anymore. Telephone has come in. But I don't know the number. Please come once. You'll see, the coconut tree that you planted has become tall. Who'll watch over your house? Thieves and dacoits are all around. They even terrify me. Please come back. The house and property remain all intact. When will you come? My days are numbered. The kids of this place won't recognise you. Even I won't recognise your children." People will forget the story of these two friends. The memory of those who have parted will fade away—will turn to history. This is the way of the world. Only nostalgia brings tears to the eyes of those who have become old.'

Chhentu remains silent. It seems that his eyes are wet. It is after a long while that we meet. Yet we are so close to each other. Whether it is Chhentu or myself or whoever on earth, none will forget their place of birth. The casket of one's memory that contains visions of open sky, tree or water, remains locked. Nobody has a key to open that.

We've come to this side of Bengal by flooding our birthplace with tears. Memory haunts us. *Ma*'s image flashes upon me as she suns paddy or uproots herbs and creepers in the pond. Rice will be made from paddy with the husking pedal. Boiled rice in an earthen pot, chilli paste and a slice of lemon along with mango pickle—ah, what a dish! Delicious. Mouth-watering. Why don't I get that taste now? I miss it even when I go to Dhupguri, despite all the efforts by my elder sister-in-law. She set up a husking pedal at home. She used to make *muri*. She made all these arrangements for *Ma*, yet somehow she never reached there. The fact goes, my elder brother heartily wished, *Ma* were here in this part of Bengal. But she harped on the same string—she won't leave her ancestral place.

I heard that towards the end she had struggled a lot to make ends meet. The share-croppers refused to give her the due. She started selling household goods one by one—even the huge trees that grew in our place. *Borda* used to send her 50 *supari*, equivalent to 50 rupees, at regular intervals, and *Ma* also acknowledged the receipt. At the same time, she let him know that her resources were exhausted to meet the medical expenses of our father. She used to make *muri* along with Dipni *Pisi*, and Bucha *Kaka* sold that in the market of Imamganj and Mohanganj.

It won't have been possible for me to come here if my grandson hadn't accompanied me. I got a chance to meet my childhood friend Chhentu. All my relations were there with me— Satya and Shanta, the parents of Agnibha, and Salma, Agnibha's colleague.

After reaching there I got to know that whatever I heard earlier was partly true. *Ma* had to sell *muri* for quite some time after the demise of *Baba*. Most important of all, Kaula Sheikh, who used to serve our family and who called my mother *Bouthan*, performed the last rites. He attended *Ma* for a few days after my father passed away. It was the rainy season. He couldn't bring the dead body to the burning ghat. He made an altar on the burial ground and planted a tulsi seedling there. His sons didn't damage the altar ever.

Bucha *Kaka*'s sons had gone to Hind Motor. They don't enquire as to our whereabouts. The elder brother of Dipni *Pisi* lives in Dhaka. Dipni *Pisi* had gone blind. Smallpox impaired her vision. She used to say that it was the mercy of Goddess Shitala. She accompanied *Ma* at all times and used to chat with her. She died later.

Nobody saw *Ma* after *Baba*'s demise. Dipni *Pisi* inquired about her in places like Kamarchar and Shikarpur. But she got no news. The air was thick with the rumour that she had been seen in the burning ghat of Langalbanda. Others said that she was seen in the *akhraa* of Serajdigha. We the brothers were struggling hard to keep our families alive. By that time passports had been introduced. One would need a passport to cross the border. Who would arrange all these? It was an awful task to meet the ends. *Borda* went to Dhupguri and *Mejda* to Alipurduar. They had really no time to inquire about the whereabouts of their parents. What a catastrophe! Just to survive on herbs and creepers. *Sejda* started selling conch bangles at Dhupguri. After a long while we came to know from a letter that our parents breathed their last at home. We were relieved. At least their dead bodies were not devoured by dogs and foxes. The Muslims residing there did the funeral rites.

We, particularly myself, had no inclination to fathom the truth. I was a vagrant—spending days and nights here and there. I found my stay in a shop of the marketplace at Dhupguri for a while. I used to sing for the shopkeepers in return. One day I saw a woman selling *muri* in the marketplace. She exactly resembled my mother. I advanced and called her '*Ma*'. The woman made a scream. I cried, 'You're my *Ma*'. She got really terrified. I awkwardly slipped out of the place.

Another episode happened in a tea garden of New Dooars. I got a job as a compounder in the dispensary. I saw *Ma* plucking tea leaves with a small basket around her shoulder. But the garden was sold. And my job was over. After that I got a service in the office of Social Welfare at Calcutta. By that time, Agnibha, the youngest son of my eldest niece, had got a job in Dhaka. One day he said to me, '*Dadu*, let's go to your birthplace. I'll show you all.' I at once agreed.

That was why I came here. I had a craving for seeing my birthplace. I wanted to see where my parents breathed their last. I saw the house. The *hijal* tree is still there and the pond as well. Only our rooms are no more. A new construction is over there.

While returning to Dhaka with Chhentu, it felt like someone was crying out—'Jiban, take care. Worry not. I'm always with you'. The car was running over the Dhaleswari bridge. A word was ringing in my ears—'Always, always'.

ଌ

Translated by Joyjit Ghosh

Joyjit Ghosh is the co-editor of this anthology.

The Lady and the Red Rose
Sadhan Chattopadhyay

Very recently the daughter of Lord Mountbatten, the last Viceroy of India, has confessed in London that there was a platonic love affair between her mother and our Jahawarlal. There was of course nothing illicit or physical about it. Today when Arunprasad came to know of this, he is more than seventy-three years old—quite an old fellow.

And when Jahawarlal was secretly presenting rose to the accomplished English lady and was kissing her soft fingers, then Arunprasad was known as Bilu, who was two and a half or three years old back then. In those days there was no custom of recording the exact dates of birth and death in remote villages full of rivers, ponds and small water bodies! Hospitals or maternity wards, as we find them today, could not be dreamt of at that time. Back then, arrangements for delivery of babies were made in shanties thatched with hay and leaves of betel nut and coconut trees. Those were called *anturghar*. There were quack nurses in the villages. Even the aged aunts in joint families trained themselves to do the job.

The day Bilu was born, his mother was almost fainting due to labour pain in the delivery room. Sundari *Pisi* performed the role of a nurse with a big bowl of hot water heated by the fire made from tinder dry woods and sharpened bamboo flakes, she had made everything ready the previous noon for detaching the umbilical cord.

After the partition when Bilu became Arunprasad in course of time, he came to know that his aunt in her childhood was exceptionally beautiful. The colour of her skin, her sharp nose and her large eyes—all contributed to her beauty. Even before she could proceed with her education, she was given away in marriage at the age of six. By then she was just beginning to get her primary lessons. She became a widow at ten and came back to her parental house to live there for the rest of her life. She became old at the age of forty, losing one or two of her teeth. With her black and white hair cut short, she ultimately turned out to be the controlling power in the huge family of her brothers and their wives. Be it boiling of paddy, or grinding of rice, or keeping the food grains in big cane containers, or distribution of fish haul from ponds owned by many shareholders—Sundari *Pisi* had the final say.

In the big family there were at least four widows of whom she was the chief. She seldom used the usual Bengali word *bidhoba* for a widow, rather chose to use the disrespectful Bengali alternative *ranri* for the purpose. The widows had many superstitious reservations about what they could or could not touch. And for these very reasons, they had to dip in the pond innumerable times in a day, be it monsoon or winter. There were separate thatched sheds for them to cook, separate utensils, separate ovens with only firewood and thousands of such discriminatory arrangements—everything dictated by Sundari *Pisi*. The widows were forbidden to eat sponge gourd since it had ten ribs quite like Ravana's ten heads. The grip of superstitions on their dietary practices did not end there. It extended, for example, to eating egg plant and pumpkin—these were not allowed on some particular lunar days. In this world they were the most neglected, cursed and wretched yet indispensable. Apparently without practising austerities there would be no redemption of their sins. They were required to practise strict control over their senses. In fact, there was a popular saying: 'Only when a woman is burnt and her ashes are carried away by the wind, will her praises be sung'. Or else the lack of morals in these women would open the doors of hell for many. All they got in a year were a couple of coarse white cotton clothes for daily wear.Purifying themselves every now and then was something that became part and parcel of their daily life. Only in the late afternoon could they have a meal of meagre portions of sun-dried rice along with curries cooked with just a drop of oil. The curries were made from wild edible leaves, stems, seeds collected from forest and bushes, and there was a certain tangy concoction, *ambal*, at the end of the meal. It was believed, the spice and oil could entice their libido.

Arunprasad no longer remembers where Sundari *Pisi* was on the day of Gandhi's death. Given his blurred memory he cannot recollect today if Sundari *Pisi* was among the members of the Chatterjee family who, against the backdrop of riots in Calcutta, Noakhali and Bihar, had migrated to this part of the country to save their lives and honour. Within a month of the Partition, Bilu's panic-stricken father, Ramaniprasad, sailed off in the middle of the night in the waters of Kaljira river to save his family. Since the tiny boat could not accommodate every member of the joint family, the people who were with Bilu on the boat that night were his brothers and sisters, his father, Ramaniprasad, his mother, his father's elder brother Atulprasad's eldest son, Shyamaprasad, and his newly wedded wife. Bilu's father and his uncle Atulprasad were very close to each other. Bilu was not aware that his uncle was not among the people on the boat that night. He only got to know this when he grew up to be Arunprasad. But then again how could he be on the boat? He was the only government employee in the family. In those days he was the pension officer of the Public Works Department and lived in Calcutta with his wife. She was a dumb lady—unable to speak. Back in those days Atulprasad was duped into marrying her. The woman who was made to meet him as a prospective bride was covertly replaced by his current wife during the event of marriage. Still his uncle, for the sake of humanity, did not dump her in her parental home and remarry, forsaking his newly wedded wife. In fact, he did not even make any plan to marry a second time while making the first wife work as a servant in the household. He, instead, accepted his fate.

Atulprasad used to visit his ancestral home only during the long holidays of either Durga Puja or Christmas—a gift of the British, given the long history of their rule in India. His visit was a cause of celebration for the whole family. He used to come in the boat and along with him he would usually bring the sacrificial goat for Durga Puja, a small box of Capstan cigarette and ovaltin. During winter he brought either yellow oranges or a box of sweet-smelling cake. He had three children by his dumb wife, all of whom lived together in their ancestral home as a joint family.

Arunprasad secretly came to know that his uncle, who was a grave, dutiful person, spent a lot of money betting in the race course. Some Saturdays he used to be very jovial and happy making small impulsive purchases whereas on others one could find him crestfallen and sitting silently with his back hunched in a dark room. That Bilu was around three or four years old on the day of Gandhi's assassination might be a guess work as almanac was not available in every household of the village in those days, the calendar being merely a useless luxury—in that case how could Sundari *Pisi* determine the exact date and time of Bilu's birth? After delivery when Bilu's mother was almost in a state of unconsciousness in the *anturghar*, Sundari *Pisi* was the only witness present there. In those days nobody cared for the exact time of birth and death—there was no such custom. All that was required was a Brahmin astrologer to make the horoscope of the child, and the premises for making this were merely based on guess work. Even Arunprasad's current date of birth had its own brief history attached to it. Once Ramaniprasad reached this side of Bengal, he, after multiple trials and errors, could manage to get Bilu successfully through the scholarship examination for admission to a school. And all of these finally led to the moment where a fat and bald-headed clerk wanted to know the age of Bilu. At this very moment, he finally took the task of calculating his son's age. While Ramaniprasad was busy in his calculation, the clerk continued to stare at him through his glasses hanging loosely over his nose. Finally, as a consequence of such a concocted and complicated calculation by his father, Arunprasad now is a senior citizen—seventy-three plus.

Back again to the boat episode, Atulprasad, as concluded already, could not have been in the boat that night. But today, when assuming himself as Bilu, he tries to reminisce with his eyes closed, can he recollect the image of the Kaljira river on that night or the movement of the tides or the changing contours on the face of the sailor Siddique in the darkness or the thick air of love and hate that hovered over the boat that night?

Even today when Arunprasad goes back to the self of Bilu, his memory serves him with some indistinct flashes, not in much detail, for obvious reasons. Who was Gandhi, why was he killed, who were behind the killing, what was its significance—could he understand any of these at such a tender age?

Tucked away in the small town of Barisal was a house even smaller with floors damaged, inviting barely any light even in daytime. In front of the house was an unknown river flowing, but as far as Arunprasad could guess, it was

Kirtankhola. In the small house overlooking the river stayed his elder cousin, Shyamaprasad, also called Gonu *Da* by the younger members of the family, along with his newly wedded wife—*Natun Boudi*. They were on the boat that night.

Bringing a faint smile on her fair yet slightly shrivelled face, *Boudi* announced one day that there would be no cooking in the house, since *Gandhiji was shot dead*. Even that faint smile of *Boudi* would produce unknown feelings in Bilu's young heart. It was hard to remember if any boat sailed on Kirtankhola on that day. But one could remember the coils of smoke on the other side of the river. They emerged slowly from *Marakkhola*—a local name for the burning ghat. Bilu was always fascinated with the colloquial words but that's a story for another time.

Gandhiji was shot dead, but these words did not mean anything to Bilu that day, nor could one expect him to understand the significance of the words at such a tender age.

The flash of beauty on *Boudi's* face appeared as a mystery to Bilu. It was a smiling face, shining even though it looked shrivelled. A starving face usually wears a sad look. Often such a face draws attention. Her fair face was shaped like a beetle leaf, broad, and at the corner of her eyes could one see a faint sadness. She seldom spoke without a smile on her face, her hands and feet looked a bit yellowish white and a thick black lock of curly hair covered her forehead. Even at such an early age, Bilu was aware of the mystery and coyness that marked the relationship of the newly wedded couple. One day he would also have a beautiful wife like *Boudi*.

Before Gandhiji's assassination Bilu was not acquainted with the word 'dead'. He did not quite understand what it meant to be 'dead'. Maybe the elders of the family did not discuss the subject in front of the children. Bilu was not aware of the mystery of 'birth' and 'death'. Today Arunprasad, even when he tries to imagine himself as Bilu, can't call to mind if he had seen someone dying. That was perhaps the reason why the impact of Gandhiji's death failed to have any impression on Bilu's mind, swayed by the beauty of *Boudi*'s face. Today after so many decades, Arunprasad cannot remember how long his family lived in Barisal after being evicted from their own land. He can only faintly recall some fragmented pictures, some discontinuous conversation, some sound or some smell that might have impressed him in those early days of his childhood. 'Gandhiji was shot dead'— even today if he mutters these words to himself, the face of *Boudi* emerges in his mind as if it were a moving picture in celluloid. Suddenly the blurry images of two persons— Gonu *Da* and *Boudi*—appear in his mind only to disappear and then again reappear talking to each other with smiles on their faces. It was like some scene from a bioscope. But he cannot remember the spectators or the cinema hall or its surroundings. It might be that Gonu *Da*, prompted by a romantic urge, went secretly without Ramaniprasad's knowledge to watch a movie with his newly wedded wife after a few days of Gandhiji's death. Bilu was with them as a pawn in a game of chess. Today Arunprasad can recollect that the cinema was *Chandrasekhar* by Bankimchandra. In that film Asok Kumar and Kanan Devi jointly sang the song: 'We are the two souls in the tide of eternity'. Today both those popular film stars are dead. By delving into the self of Bilu, Arunprasad can recollect some such flashes from the past. Turning the reel backward he can see some indistinct images of those days long gone by. Even he can momentarily summon up some fragmentary pictures of the days before Gandhiji's assassination. Images like some patches of muddy road, the dark water of some pond in the midst of trees with stairs on its bank turned slippery, the water lily, the reed bush, the big myrobalan tree—all these appear in his mind's eye.

Another image of a wooden first floor resurfaces from the past. He could visualise Bilu holding the window, his gaze fixed at something far away. The faint image of a huge pond appears in the sight. Evening is gradually settling. With a towel tied around his head, Bilu could see his father sitting with a fishing rod. Suddenly he hurried into the water. The vision got snapped with this.

Again there is a flashback. His father, a plump man, stood in the courtyard, his wet dhoti tied round his waist, with the fishing rod in his hand to which was hooked a giant murrel (channa marulius) fish. It was still alive. A musty smell came from his father's wet clothes. Sundari *Pisi*, standing on the raised veranda, was issuing commands to her younger brother, 'Hey Ramna, stay in the courtyard and don't come inside. Call somebody from the Majhi locality'. It was a *shol* fish with its body decked with variegated spots.

Hindus did not eat the fish. It was usually distributed among poor Muslims. That day a Muslim, lean and thin with little beard on his chin and wearing a *lungi*, took away the fish with great joy and expressed his gratitude to Sundari *Pisi*. Arunprasad assumes that the man was Siddiqui in whose boat their family travelled to save their lives. How old was Bilu then? He must have been very young not to identify the man. Sundari *Pisi* was still a member of their joint family. Else how could she accept the gratitude of Siddiqui?

Today Arunprasad can distinctly remember the day his father, Ramaniprasad, along with the members of his family, was compelled under a difficult situation to take shelter in Sundari *Pisi*'s house; his mother told him that his father had previously taken a vow due to some past incident that he would never see the face of Sundari *Pisi*. But why was such a decision taken? It may be discussed later. But this much can be said at present that Bilu's father had to break his vow under an economic compulsion and uncertainty.

Sundari *Pisi*'s house, surrounded by hillocks and a forest of *sal* trees, was somewhere far in the west. It was actually a typical old-model railway quarter painted red for the assistant station master of a not-so-major railway station. It was only after coming here that Bilu heard for the first time words like 'murder', 'revenge', 'slaughter' and the like. It was then that he realised that natural death was not the only option for a man's life to come to an end, the above words could also put an end to a man's life. He was exposed to a whole variety of new words. Arunprasad can recall today that it was here that

Bilu got acquainted with the name of Nathuram Godsey and the phrase, 'Assassination of Gandhi.'

Today Arunprasad cannot remember clearly how and with whom he travelled to Calcutta to his uncle's residence from their home at Kirtonkhola. Along with him came *Gonu Da* and *Boudi*, his mother and his elder sister Chhalana. Arunprasad feels that in him the self of Bilu still remembers these characters of that time. Even now as he closes his eyes, he can clearly see the old Calcutta which was just like a locality where in the afternoon a man with a ladder on his shoulder used to come regularly to light the gas lamps on the lamp posts. The residence was on the first floor of a building on the main road in the old Mirjapur area. In that residence there was a spacious balcony fenced with chest-high rot iron railings cast with designs of creepers on them. Child Bilu did not have the height to lean over the railings. It became rather an obsession with him to view either side of the road from the balcony through the gaps in the railings. He used to grieve over the fact that because of the railings he could not seize the free-floating kites as they got detached from the flier's thread. They escaped his grasp and landed on some other spot. In Bilu's imagination those kites were like gods of heaven. During noontime when everybody used to take rest, Bilu, standing stealthily on the balcony, watched the kites flying in the vast sky of Calcutta. At times the kites cut from their thread floated for sometime in the sky and then at a point, disappeared from his sight. Bilu earnestly prayed so that at least one such kite might drop inside their balcony.

There were no ventilators in the rooms, kitchen or the washing area. All the rooms were dimly lit and very stuffy. Bilu could remember that even during daytime the rooms were lit by electric bulbs.

Arunprasad's father did not stay with the family in that house. Leaving the responsibility on his uncle his father moved from one place to another in search of livelihood. The entire responsibility of the household chores had to be shouldered by his mother. In front of her elder brother-in-law she had to always cover her face with the veil of her sari. She had to do all the tasks from cooking, cleaning the utensils, to cutting fishes and vegetables. His aunt, though dumb, chided his mother even for minor lapses in a peculiar nasal tone. She, however, never protested. She could figure out the meaning of those nasal sounds. Which piece of fried fish his uncle would eat, which particular piece of fish in the fish curry he would prefer, which fried items he would like to have with pulses every day, what would be the proportion of potato and pumpkin in the vegetable curry—everything Bilu's mother had to understand from the commands of his dumb aunt.

It was in this house at Mirjapur that Bilu saw a wall clock with a pendulum for the first time. It was within a small wooden box a small section of which could be opened for winding the watch. Every time the clock chimed with a musical sound, two birds from either side of the clock came out to swing and then disappeared as the chime ended. Bilu came to know from his uncle that it was a wall clock.

Uncle was very affectionate to him. Habitually he was a late riser. With a smile on his face he sometimes asked Bilu the difference between his native home in the village and the residence in Calcutta. He himself gave the answer saying that while in Calcutta the practice was to go to bed late and wake up late in the morning, in their village home it was just the opposite.

In the morning, Bilu responded readily the moment his uncle shouted his name from upstairs. Quickly coming down the stairs he was out on the road with his uncle holding his hand. They went to a particular tea shop and got back with a big enamelled glass filled with tea. It was here that Bilu got the taste of tea. He could still remember the nearly saffron colour of the tea and its strange smell. Aruprasad thinks that such a strange smell which attracted him very much at that time has disappeared from his present life. It was through this morning habit that Bilu first stepped onto the footpath of Calcutta.

The Saturdays on which his uncle lost his bet in horse racing, he did not come downstairs the next morning. After he got up from sleep, he sat crestfallen for some time, leaning his head against the wall. Then summoning Bilu he gave him money to bring the tea. He, however, didn't forget to caution Bilu to mind the stairs. This was, in fact, Bilu's maiden experience of buying something by paying money. Arunprasad, even today, could clearly recall the reddish colour and shapes of coins of different denominations— *anni* (four paise), *duanni* (eight paise) and the copper coin with a hole in it. Today he thinks at times that, given the numberless times the coin sizes changed after the issuance of the *naya paisa* (new coin currency) in 1957, it is not possible for anybody to remember such little changes.

Despite his uncle's cautionary words one day Bilu stumbled on the staircase and some hot tea spilled on his soft thumb. What a burning sensation it was! In fear and shame he could not let anybody know about this. The whole day he thought himself guilty. Although the pain gradually subsided, there emerged a small brown spot on the finger. Even today at this age when Arunprasad sees his thumb, he can see the old house at Mirjapur in Calcutta.

One day when *Natun Boudi* gave Bilu an orange from Darjeeling he consumed it in a trice with great delight. He swallowed the carpels so quickly that *Natun Boudi*, with a broad smile on her face, asked in surprise, 'Where are the seeds?' 'I have eaten them up'—Bilu said with a smile that denoted an achievement and then pointed his fingers to his stomach to make it clear. At this *Boudi* with a mock gravity said, 'Now you will face the consequence—you will not be able to eat anything, you will not be able to talk anymore.' Bilu became serious and looked at *Boudi*'s face in astonishment. *Boudi* continued saying, 'Are the seeds really inside your stomach? Now the orange tree will take its root inside your stomach. Then the tree will grow bigger. One day you will see the tree will spread its branches through your oral cavity. You will not be able to close your mouth, will not be able to eat or call anybody.' The fear created by *Boudi*'s words haunted

Bilu's mind for many days. Every morning, he used to think if there was a tree germinating in his stomach. In the corner of the dimly lit, damp veranda, adjacent to the washing area, there hung a few broken buckets full of clay. During noontime when the loud cries of the street hawkers selling clay was heard on the lonely road, *Boudi* used to come down with Bilu on someday and bargained with the hawkers on the price of the clay. That even clay could be sold at a price, incited the little Bilu to think of some mysterious world. He also thought that when he would grow up, he would carry some clay from his home on the boat to sell in the city. He would thus become rich.

Whenever Bilu got the opportunity to stand under the hanging buckets he stared at the two plants—tulsi and the thorny bougainvillea with its slender branches—which were nurtured by *Natun Boudi*. He felt a strange and fearful sensation if by chance the tree would germinate inside his stomach and its zigzag branches come out through his mouth in the open air. In his imagination Bilu could see the green leaves, a ripe orange hanging from a small branch in front of his nose. He thought even if he could tear it off with his hand how he could eat that!

The thoughts of Bilu make Aruprasad think of phenyl which has a pungent smell of lemon. Those imaginary thoughts of the remote past evoke laughter today. Those old thoughts now disappear yielding place to new ones in his mind. He thinks that people throughout their life remain engrossed in some kind of fanciful thoughts. Today he realises that even the people sitting at the helm of affairs in our country are also affected by some kind of fantastic thoughts. Arunprasad can still recall some such thoughts of child Bilu.

He still remembers those days at the residence in Mirjapur when Bilu could never be sent to the washing area alone even by force. It was always wet, with scattered remnants of leftover rice. The place was rather dark and there were few rats moving around. Even though one electric bulb continued to burn in the room throughout the day, it did not have enough light.

His dumb aunt seldom went to the washroom. She always had the apprehension that she might fall in the washroom because of the wet, slippery floor. If by chance her leg got fractured, she would not be able to walk throughout her life. This thought made her extremely afraid. His uncle was of the opinion that this kind of fear might occur in a person suffering from deficiency of calcium in the body. As per his order, one 'Hindustani' used to come regularly with his big goat straight to upstairs and milked it in front of the bystanders to fill a glass with frothy milk. The *duty* of Bilu's mother was to boil it and then send it to his aunt in the hands of *Natun Boudi*. Someday his uncle went out to office on time and on some other days he was a bit late. Before that Bilu's mother had to go to his uncle's room, covering her face with the veil of her sari, to take orders from him about the daily chores. Sometimes he expressed his sympathy for his mother and lamented the partition of the country. One day he said,

'Several times I told Ramani to buy a house in Calcutta...had he adhered to my advice then you would not have been in this state today...once your cooking is over, clean the washroom properly...today I skidded in the washroom.'

A few months later Ramaniprasad, with permission from his elder brother, brought two girls, two sisters, with him and put them under his elder brother's care in the residence at Mirjapur. These girls were among those members of the joint family who could not sail on the boat on that dark night, those who were absent on the bank of Kirtankhola the day Gandhiji was assassinated. They were compelled to stay back in their native home in panic and fear at the mercy of Siddiqui. Arunprasad cannot remember today the particular loop of the joint family to which these two girls belonged but he can still remember the name of one of the girls whom he called *Kutti Di*. She was twelve or thirteen years old. Her menstruation cycle had started by that time. Therefore, Ramaniprasad risked himself to personally go to their native place to escort them to Calcutta. That was the last time he visited their native place. Siddiqui met him and requested him to come again and assured him that he would properly maintain their ancestral house mostly made of wood. Arunprasad can understand today that history does not repeat itself in the same manner. About a couple of years back he met a professor in Calcutta whose ancestral house was in the same village. He along with a number of other male and female professors from a university, close to their ancestral village, visited Calcutta. He informed Arunprasad that the wooden first floor of their house was not occupied by anybody. It was in a dilapidated condition. He also informed that the descendants of Siddiqui were now living in Sweden. This forms the experience of senior Arunprasad.

Kutti Di was very talkative and frivolous. She always laughed loudly, talked at full volume like people in the villages. For her it was fun to make Bilu afraid every now and then. Uncle at times pretended to be angry with her—'Indira, this is Calcutta...this is not your native home... do not speak so loudly'. After the arrival of *Kutti Di* and her sister in the family, *Natun Boudi* looked more serious. A few new rules were enforced in the household—Bilu's mother would only take care of the kitchen, *Kutti Di* would not be allowed to laugh so uproariously. She would take care of the leftovers in the unwashed utensils after the meals at night, washing of clothes and the washroom. In that house water was not free-flowing unlike in their village, here the water supply was time bound. The taste of the water was somewhat strange, smelling of some kind of soap, as it were. *Kutti Di* did not particularly dislike managing things in the kitchen. It used to be unclean with leftovers of food scattered everywhere—fish bones, squeezed lemon slices, even the unwashed utensils were kept in a disorderly manner. But one thing was there, the moment you open the tap, the water would flow continuously. It seemed magical for her. Although initially *Kutti Di* was afraid of cockroaches in the washroom, now she could kill them quickly with the stub of a broom. *Natun Boudi* liked this skill in her as she also was really scared of cockroaches. At times when she found cockroaches walking on the walls of her bedroom, she went on shouting the name 'Indira' in an awkwardly fine voice until she came. In a mood of fun, *Kutti Di* stealthily walked into her room like a hunter with the broom-stub in her hand. Bilu followed her holding the fringe of her sari.

Arunprasad, even today, gets a particular whiff—the smell of that room of *Natun Boudi*. The moment one entered the room, one could find it dimly lit with neatly arranged bedstead, dress-hanger, drawer, bracket, and could get a faint pleasant smell. The smell would not make one feel excited. Today while analysing his ruminations, Arunprasad remembers that the moment the smell entered Bilu's nostrils, it made him feel as if he had lost someone.

Kutti Di used to call Bilu along with other kids of the neighbouring house to play together an indoor game, *Baghbandi*. The kids were incorporated only to give them a sense of participation. One day in the corner of the washroom *Kutti Di* was breaking coal with an iron hammer. As Bilu peeped in, she called him. Bilu said, 'I am afraid to go there. What are you breaking with the hammer?'

'Why are you afraid? Look, how I am breaking the coal.' Bilu did not have much idea about coal. He had an idea of fire in the *unun*—it burned with great flames and spread sparks. The logs of wood made cracking sounds; they needed to be poked from time to time. In the village *Ma* called the oven 'ahal'. And in the house at Mirjapur *Ma* used to ask his aunt, '*Didi*, should I put fire into the oven?'

Responding to *Kutti Di*'s call as soon as he entered the washroom, she lifted Bilu with her hands and put him into a shallow square water reservoir. Bilu felt as if he was in an infernal region, he was terrified to think that possibly he would never again be able to run to the balcony to have a look at the kites cut off from the threads. He started shouting in fear. He could not remember anything after that. Later on, he came to know from *Natun Boudi* that after that incident his mother silently wiped the tears from his eyes as he was crying in panic, his spasms were hard to bring under control. She did not scold *Kutti Di* but his aunt possibly pretended to beat her with the handle of a hand fan. When everything became normal, *Natun Boudi* said, 'Aren't you a hero? Should a hero weep like that?' At this Bilu's face reflected a strange fascination. In *Boudi*'s face there was a touch of dreaminess. But even after this incident *Kutti Di* was not bothered. She went on laughing as if it was something very funny. For her the incident was an inferior substitute for what she did in her native home—randomly wandering in the groves and gardens, swimming in the river and plucking water-lily. All these activities had been stalled for a long time after she came to Calcutta. Afterwards Bilu did realise that there was nothing to panic about the reservoir.

One day *Kutti Di* told Bilu with her eyes rolling, 'Listen, Bilu, there is a ghost in the washroom.'

'Really?'

'I swear by touching my eyes.... if I am lying then I should die.' Bilu, on hearing this, indulged in imaginary fears. He felt that ghosts could be a reality not only in the darkness of the villages or his native place, but even in the houses in Calcutta.

Uncle used to dine late at night. After dinner he took his last cup of tea at 10 p.m. The dining room was a small one. Spreading a beautiful printed mattress for Atulprasad to sit in, *Ma* served his dinner. In the first batch Bilu and his uncle were served the dinner, and almost immediately after that, his aunt and her distantly related brother sat to dine. Arunprasad could still remember today that he used to address him as *Khokamama*. He did not stay at night in that house. He was a ruffian. In those days the word 'mastan' (rowdy) was not in use. Arunprasad could still recall indistinctly that he was rather fat and plump with curly hair, his face slightly pockmarked. His habit was to tie the watch on his right wrist. Secretly he used to steal from uncle's stock of capstan cigarettes and incited Bilu for various acts of mischief. One day there was a black Austin car parked just below the balcony. *Khokamama* drew Bilu's attention to an empty coconut shell and told him to drop it on the car with the words, 'See, what a fun it would be.' For Bilu, doing mischief was fun. The moment he dropped it there was a thud and immediately somebody shouted, 'Who is that?' On hearing this both of them rushed inside.

One day *Khokamama* gave Bilu a treat with fries and cutlet. He still remembers the name of the eatery— 'Firpo.' What a strange delicious smell! His mind was filled with delight. The smell appeared very familiar to him and it reminded him of an occasion when he went with Gonu *Da* and *Boudi* to a cinema hall and watched on the screen a male and a female dipping in the water and then floating on the surface singing songs. This was a few days after Gandhiji was shot dead. Coming out of the cinema hall Gonu *Da* and *Boudi* ate cutlets.

The memory of the cinema hall brought back in Bilu's mind another incident. After the dinner, Kuttidi's task was to clean the pile of utensils in the bathroom, and while doing so, she used to hum a song '... *Anadi kaler srote...*' (In the flow of eternity) while cleaning the utensils. One night she suddenly came rushing with great hue and cry to Bilu's mother and holding her in her arms shouted 'Aunty! Ghost!' and almost broke down in tears. Half of the unwashed utensils were still lying scattered. She was panic-stricken and Bilu's mother pacified her. *Natun Boudi* and Gonu *Da* did not come out as they had already gone to sleep.

The store room with its red floor was a little spacious and was used to keep *boti*, vegetable baskets, the containers of rice and pulses and jars. At night *Kutti Di* cleaned the room with a wet mop and made a large bed which accommodated Bilu, his mother, *Kutti Di* herself and her sister. If somebody came to visit them without prior intimation, they also slept in that room. Arunprasad cannot remember the details today. In those days there was no mosquito in Calcutta and mosquito nets were not used in beds. During daytime the room, however, was infested with flies.

On that night as *Kutti Di* was panicking, Bilu's mother had to clean the rest of the utensils. She did not say anything. At night in bed when *Kutti Di* whispered her experience into Bilu's ears it made Bilu's hair stand on end. After attaining maturity Arunprasad realised that fear was also kind of imaginary, either personal or pertaining to community. That day *Kutti Di* was humming a song with her face downwards but as she looked up she saw a shadow swinging with noose around its neck on the wall adjacent to the reservoir.

It is commonly believed that ghosts are only found in villages—in cops and bushes, in the clump of bamboo, in some lonely spot under a banyan tree on the fringes of the village. Bilu, who regularly heard stories of ghosts from Sundari *Pisi*, had started believing such stories. When Arunprasad reflects on such stories he still feels excited. Even today he narrates a particular story to his grandchild but fails to evoke that interest. The grandchild asks him, 'Do you know Goblins?'

Sundari *Pisi* once narrated the story of her father, Ramaniprasad's real life experience—'Once your father was returning home quite late at night. It was a dimly moonlit night. In those days there was the fear of thieves and dacoits on the way. Your father was walking with trepidation. Suddenly as he looked back, he could see a person at a distance walking up to him unfalteringly. Ramani thought he would get a companion. In the village pathways one does not find many pedestrians at such late hours of night. He thought that possibly the steamer in which the person was travelling arrived late. *Who could be the person?* In those days people living in the neighbouring villages more or less knew each other. Ramani asked him his identity but there was no reply. Again, he asked him about his place of residence but there came no reply. Ramani then stopped and looked back. The man had come to a halt. He did not step forward. Ramani thought that the man was not a thief or dacoit, rather he was possibly afraid of him. Your father assured him not to feel afraid and asked him to accompany him. Still the man did not stir. Suddenly Ramani could feel that the man was gradually becoming taller and taller and outgrew the palm tree only to melt in the moonlit night. All around him nobody was there. Your father has always been a brave man but his whole body was sweaty and his heart palpitated. Ultimately he could come back home chanting the name of Lord Rama. Immediately on entering the front room he called me and told me everything. I took off his clothes, touched his body with a piece of iron, sprinkled holy water on his head to save him from the evil influence of the ghost. That night he was given a small quantity of milk and parched rice to eat.' Arunprasad has reflected on this incident recently and felt that such strange people, male and female, can be found on the way and then suddenly they prove to be ghosts or apparitions. After this incident Sundari *Pisi* kept the windows on the northern side of her room shut for a couple of days.

Coming back to Bilu's story, he could not shut his eyes for sleep in fear since he heard from *Kutti Di* about the shadow-ghost with the noose around its neck. Even during the noon when it was lonely, he dared not go to the washroom. He chanted the name of Lord Rama silently and prayed sincerely so that he might not have to attend nature's call in the evening. The loo was a little further of the washroom.

Uncle did not attach any importance to that incident. Closing his eyes, he was possibly thinking of the horse race and praying to the Goddess Kali for her blessings for the coming Saturday. But otherwise, he was eager to answer Bilu's curious questions on various matters. He used to call him in various names and in different tones—Bilu, Bilai, Mr Bilu and the like. Bilu in his childhood was really very inquisitive. He thought about so many things—his aunt's dumbness, what was speech mechanism, what was larynx, how could a seed, when swallowed by a human, germinate inside the stomach, what was the meaning of employment for which his uncle went out every day. He had a strange notion about employment—for him to polish the floor continuously with a pair of cymbals in both hands was called employment. What was an office? It was a place where men squat on the floor and continuously polish the floor with a pair of cymbals.

There were two specific incidents that generated guilt consciousness and a feeling of sensuality in Bilu. Later the incident of dropping the empty cell of coconut on the car made him realise that it was not merely a fun. Several times after the incident he harboured the idea that possibly one day the police with red turbans would come upstairs blowing their whistle to nab him. Bilu's notion of police was like this—they were persons with red turbans on their heads, wearing Khaki half pant and stockings, their feet shod and standing on big empty drums of tar they blew their whistles and moved their hands and feet at different directions to control the traffic. On many a night lying on the bed he brooded over the possibility of the police coming to the room blowing their whistle to catch him for that offence. One day as he could not bear the anxiety anymore, he confessed his thought to his mother. She fearfully whispered to his ears, 'Take care! Never drop it again. *Khokamama* is a goon. Don't be intimate with him.' Bilu heard the word 'goon' for the first time. They are bad and wicked people.

Bilu, however, could not gather courage to disclose his second experience to his mother. He by that time had become mature enough to realise that there are certain things one cannot share with elders. In the tenanted house of Mirjapur, Bilu with all his curiosity, his fears about the unknown and the mysterious, enjoyed the affectionate shelter of uncle and *Natun Boudi*. One day, a kite detached from its thread somehow came inside the balcony through the latticed design of the railings. For Bilu it was a fantastic thing to get the kite in hand. He hung it on the clothes line inside the room. It was square shaped, part green and part white. At times he ran into the room in the afternoon just to have a look at the kite but especially in the wee hours of the day so that nobody would notice him. The road below usually was empty during such early hours. The coils of smoke confirmed that somebody had lit the earthen oven somewhere. Someday he could find a person washing the road sprinkling water from a leather bag on his back. Afterward he came to know from his uncle that they were known as *Bhistiwala* (water-carriers). In the early morning, the newspaper, rolled like a stick, used to be dropped inside the balcony. The newspaper vendor, who threw it from below, was a hero in Bilu's eyes for his perfect aim. One day the kite got torn as *Chhotomama* was trying to pull it from the clothes line and Bilu broke into tears in front of his uncle. It was possibly a Sunday. The previous Saturday his uncle, for some happy reason, brought a packet of *Sandesh*. Bilu was so upset that he refused to eat the sweets even though *Natun Boudi* insisted him. Such was his emotional nature in childhood. On one rain-soaked afternoon, Bilu, in the hope of listening to stories from *Natun Boudi*, went into her room abruptly opening the unlocked door. She was perhaps in a sluggish mood wearing her clothes in a relaxed way. She became conscious suddenly and catching Bilu by the ear dragged him outside the room saying, 'Children should not enter the rooms of elders whenever they like.' Her face looked serious, as if she was a different person. Gonu *Da* was lying on one side of the bed. He did not even say a word in favour of Bilu, but rather asked her to lock the door saying, 'Bilu is crossing the limits.'

Today, as Arunprasad looks back, the days spent in the tenanted house of Mirjapur do not appear that significant to him. He can remember that before going out to office his uncle regularly rubbed oil on Bilu. Coming downstairs if one took the road and walked a little on the footpath, he would reach the *Goldighi* (a round-shaped pond), though it was actually a huge square-shaped pond. Everybody came to this pond with a swimming costume to learn swimming. All four sides of the pond were cemented and there were benches on all sides to sit. Uncle took Bilu to the pond every day and holding his hand tightly, made him dip into the water. He enjoys recollecting those things today. He could remember the sky where the kites floating loosely, detached from their threads, could be seen from the portico, the houses in the slum roofed with tiles, the water-carriers washing the roads, and so on. It was in some remote past that Goldighi, though square-shaped, derived its name from some fan palms planted by a few people around it. He could remember the pond with its clear water. It was not like other ponds usually found in villages which are full of water lily, hyacinths or water weeds. Bilu quickly overcame the fears of dipping in the pond and then he realised that as he dipped in the water, his uncle's grip on his hand became stronger. Even then one day he slipped on the bathing ghat and slid into a step well within the water. He was there for a few seconds. In such an early age the meaning of death was beyond his understanding. He heard the word for the first time from *Natun Boudi*. That was on a day when they were beside the Kirtankhola river and there was no cooking at home because of Gandhiji's assassination.

    Arunprasad can recollect today that on that day Bilu saw the colour of the water for a few seconds. Behind the light green there was the luminosity of indistinct light, but on the surface of the water one could see no colour. Uncle rescued him within seconds and after wiping his head, he made Bilu walk home with a wet towel around his waist.

On a particular Saturday Bilu expected his uncle to bring flavoured foreign biscuits on his way back home from office but contrary to his expectation, he spent the evening sitting in the room with his head against the wall with lights switched off. This was a different uncle.

Bilu bathed in the Goldighi regularly. All around the pond he could see many funny sights, costumes of various colours and could hear different sounds. One day Bilu saw a group of well-dressed boys and girls walking to the tune of big brass trumpets and drums. A flag was flying on the bank of Goldighi. Pointing to the flag Bilu asked his uncle, 'What is it?'

'It is our national flag...don't you know?'

Bilu heard the word 'national' for the first time. He had no idea what it meant, just like the time he encountered the word 'employment'. So Bilu again asked his uncle about the meaning of 'national.' Atulprasad could not give any definite answer to Bilu's query, rather he wanted Bilu to hurry up as they were already late. Bilu's inquisitive mind formed a definition of its own—that day when he slipped into the water in the pond, he saw the light green colour mingled with luminosity and for him 'national' meant that colour. As in case of the meaning of the word 'employment', his inference was 'rubbing cymbals on the floor.'

Gradually Bilu got occasional permission to come downstairs and move out on the road independently. On one afternoon during vacation, he went out to buy a tin of cigarettes for his uncle following the sudden depletion of his stock from the shop which sold things on loan. He saw that a store house just beside the shop was being reopened after a long time. Some people, being inquisitive, gathered around. The floor was being washed and cleaned. To satisfy the curiosity of Bilu, the betel leaf and cigarette seller, who was affected with leukoderma, told him that it was a warehouse of cotton. Then what the person said is still imprinted in Arunprasad's memory. He said that during the riot in Calcutta the Muslim owner of the warehouse was killed by goons who broke his skull to pieces with iron rods. Since then, it has remained closed. It was reopened almost after two years.

Bilu took an opportunity to peep inside the warehouse. He saw some people, in order to give the wall a fresh look, were continuously rubbing it to wipe the stains of blood on it. Bilu heard the word 'riot' also for the first time. Like the other two words 'employment' and 'national', he could not quickly form any idea about the word out of his imagination. Climbing the stairs cautiously with cigarettes for his uncle, he thought that perhaps 'riot' meant either the warehouse of cotton or any old stain on a wall. Should he ask his uncle the meaning of 'riot'? But he forgot. Just in front of the door *Natun Boudi* with a smile told him that he had now learnt to go downstairs independently all by himself. The sense of pride in child Bilu felt amply contented.

Within a few days after this, Bilu's father came home one night, his mother wept in secret. Today Arunprasad cannot remember what his father finally decided about the family. He cannot recall today if there was any altercation with uncle. His aunt, Gonu *Da* and *Natun Boudi* would shift to a quarter near the Lord's residence. Uncle was then employed in the Public Works Department and was attending office in the residence of the Lord. He can recollect today that many years after this incident he came to that quarter after the sudden demise of his uncle. He met Gonu *Da* with his tonsured head, and *Boudi*'s face looked sombre. She had a cute baby. Everybody called her 'Bulu'. *Boudi*, by pointing to Bilu, told her that he was her uncle.

A faint smile appears on Arunprasad's lips as he recalls those things today. At that time Gonu *Da* was an employee at the Lord's House. He joined the job when his uncle was still working there. He also saw *Khokamama*. He looked after the garden in the Lord's House. Though he had become obese, the smile on his face was same, and his habit of tying the watch on the right wrist had not changed either. He asked Bilu in which class he was. Bilu replied 'Class V'. Then addressing *Boudi*, *Khokamama* said that Bilu was a cute little plump baby in the house at Mirjapur. Bilu stayed there for seven days on the occasion of the Shradhha ceremony. Gonu *Da* took him for a round for a couple of days. Bilu still felt a sense of amazement whenever he stood in front of big buildings. He could, by the time, read English on the sign boards. On one such building he saw the words, 'Dead Letter

Office' and thought that the names and addresses of all dead persons were recorded in that building. He thought that the names of his uncle and Gandhiji, must have been recorded in that building. But this time he did not express his curiosity about the meaning to Gonu *Da* with his tonsured head.

2

Today it appears to Arunprasad like a puzzle as to where his father, after leaving the house at Mirjapur, settled with the members of his family. The good name of Bilu's Sundari *Pisi* was Tarubala. The family to which she was given away in marriage at a very early age had some landed property. The distance between her parental house and the village of her in-laws was 24 kilometers. There were canals and rivers on the way. When *Pisi* went to her in-laws' house, she was only six years old. And when she came back to her parents' family as a widow, she had just stepped into her tenth year. At such an early age she had no understanding about the meanings of marriage, husband or family. But even at such a tender age she became the butt of attack by the distant relations of Baradaprasad. According to 'scriptures', a girl should be given away in marriage within the age of four. Another girl, named Khirodabala, was married at the age of two in the family of a distant relative. When she was just eleven, she came back to her parental house, widowed. She had just started menstruating, which the village folk used to describe as 'ready to bear fruit.' In the case of Tarubala, when she became a widow, she was not even menstruating. Without being 'ready to bear fruit', without attaining womanhood, she returned to her parental family after losing her husband.

Among the brothers and sisters in the family, Tarubala was the immediate senior of Ramaniprasad; they were almost of the same age. Their father Baradaprasad was a trader in tobacco. He had the experience of travelling to many places. In comparison to his time his outlook was rather modern. In the court of the king of Cooch Behar he also developed a small acquaintance. The queen of that place had, by that time, earned a name across the states for her modern outlook. Baradaprasad wanted his daughter to remarry. When he expressed his desire, it literally created a commotion among his neighbours and relatives. His wish remained unfulfilled.

Tarubala and Khirod, the two widowed girls, were close companions. They called each other 'Bel' and 'Bokul'—the names of the two fragrant white flowers. After their daily grind in the family as soon as it was afternoon, they went to fetch water from the pond in brass pitchers. In those days houses in villages were not thickly set, the roads were unmetalled, narrow pathways interspersed with dense bushes and some abundant houses here and there. There were snakes, malaria, and people who were infected with malaria had their spleens enlarged. Sitting side by side on the lonely and dilapidated stairs of the cemented bank of the pond, the two companions enjoyed a little free time from their daily drudgery. That was the only time when they could exchange their minds, talk about their wishes and desires. Tarubala resorted to worshipping Lord Krishna while Khiroda didn't. In a dreamy state of mind, they both cherished the idea that they would be able to meet their husbands in the life hereafter. Such a thought helped them calm their sexual urge. Bilu, when he grew up, heard about these episodes from one of his elderly relatives who became a revolutionary in his early life. Khiroda was rather dark-complexioned, not like Tarubala whose skin had the colour of green turmeric. Tarubala, at times, wilfully forgot the expectation that they cherished about their afterlife. At this Khiroda used to protest by cursing her, 'Why don't you die, Bel?'

Once a freedom fighter came to their village from the town in the guise of a saint. He was probably an internee. He was accompanied by two persons. They secretly visited the houses of fishermen and peasants to inspire them. Khiroda eloped with one of these persons following which the police and men from the CID came to the village. It created a real commotion in the village. When the police specially interrogated Tarubala she was so tight-lipped that they failed to extort any information about her friend. Lying on the bed she sighed and wept for her Bokul. But the police didn't give up the investigation so easily. They suspected some connection with the Swadeshi movement. More than the elopement they tried to find out if the leaders of the Swadeshi movement were secretly organising the young widows by providing them with pistol or similar firearms.

After the death of Baradaprasad, Sundari *Pisi* gradually became the driving force of the joint family. Arunprasad, when he grew up, came to know from his mother that ever since she came to her in-laws' family she could not move out independently of her house, even if it was in her own locality, without the permission of Sundari *Pisi*. Before Birajabala, Arunprasad's mother, came to her in-laws' house, her father-in-law had passed away.

Sundari *Pisi* had her eye on every tit bit of the family. Almost immediately after the birth of Bilu, his mother suffered a postpartum infection. Up to two years Bilu was under the maternal care of Sundari *Pisi*; even she secretly gave Bilu a feigned experience of breastfeeding. Arunprasad came to know from his mother in private that one day Sundari *Pisi* left the family in tears against the opinion of everybody. Tarubala, by that time, had become quite a known figure in the locality. Displeased and grieved at her departure, his father and uncle did not eat anything for two days.

One day an unknown person came to visit them. He was robustly built with a square face and back-brushed hair. He had with him a trunk made of tin. Everybody in the family was surprised at his appearance. His face was covered by a black beard and he had a touch of aristocracy about him. On the day of his arrival, Ramaniprasad and his immediate elder brother, Sudhaprasad, were present in the house. From the ferry ghat the man found his way home by asking people whom he met on his way. The moment he stepped into the courtyard of the house there was curiosity writ large on the faces of other relatives living in adjoining portions of the premises. This is how in remote villages curiosity spreads its wings immediately on the arrival of a stranger.

The great famine was over; the bitterness in the relationship between the League and Congress was on the increase; from time to time, police visited the villages—against such a backdrop the arrival of any new visitor was looked upon with misgivings. Besides, the elopement of Khiroda with a Swadeshi youth in the past had already become a 'myth' in the village. Ramaniprasad called his Ranga da. Sudhaprasad was rather surprised to get such a call but Ramaniprasad insisted him to come out of his room. The stranger by the time had come under the shade and was standing before the front room. Sudhaprasad with folded hands greeted him and asked his identity. He wanted to know from the man whose house he intended to visit. The man reciprocated the gesture and told him that he was coming from the family of Talukdars of Lakhutia. The words of the man suddenly sounded like a whistle in the ears of Sundari *Pisi* taking her back in an instant to a remote past and evoked in her a host of other memories following the death of her husband. Alas! If she could remember the face! Only the sound of frequent cough and the indistinct picture of an old man with wrinkled skin asking for a dose of opium came up to her mind. It was considered a sin for a woman to utter the name of her husband—late Mahendra Mukherjee.

Sudhaprasad now asked Ramaniprasad to join him. The entire family, especially the widows, were looking through their veils, through the chinks in the windows and fences,

Sundari *Pisi* being no exception. Suddenly as the veil of a past life which had long been forgotten was gradually lifted to make things visible to her imagination, Sundari *Pisi* ran into a room to lock herself in and did not come out. The room was infested with rats and was filled with stacks of paddy, husk and various other articles.

She heard from the whispers that the person who stood at the door today was a relative of her in-laws—that very family where she got married and left behind at the tender age of ten. It is the blood of the Talukdar family that was running in his veins. The man was the grandchild of one of Sundari *Pisi*'s brother-in-laws who was very close to her dead husband. How much share of the landed property of the Talukdars was still enjoyed by him was difficult to guess. Yet what was important to her was that he was the representative of her in-laws' family. His name was Bireswar Mukhopadhyay. He had recently joined the Bengal–Nagpur Railway Company as office staff after passing the first examination. His place of work was a remote one. He had just started living a family life.

Bireswar had suddenly felt the urge to enquire about his *Ranga thakuma* (grandmother) because he wanted his grandmother to live with dignity and respect for the rest of her life, thereby absolving himself of the sin of his noble family which subjected its widows to some cursed customs. The two brothers, Sudhaprasad and Ramaniprasad, were initially confused as to what to do. Such things hardly happen even in dreams. But there should not be any lapse in welcoming the guest. The two brothers discussed the matter confidentially. They were not sure about the identity of the man—was the young man really an heir of the Talukdars or a petty member of some political party? Was he a Swadeshi dacoit or a communist working as a spy of the Russians who talked about liberation of women, social progress and did not believe in religion?

The drawing room was cleaned to make it ready for Bireswar who was their guest. He was accorded the care and attention due to a guest. For two days there was an undercurrent of excitement among the relatives and the old headmen of the locality. They discussed the matter again and again with the two brothers. Only the aunt silently shed tears for the couple of days. She had no memory of the ten-year-old girl's husband but perhaps the reaction was a mark of *duty* and respect for the departed soul of her husband. There was great commotion among the other widows in the family. They asked her why she didn't say anything and if she could recognise her grandson, what she would do next. Sundari *Pisi* replied with a sense of exasperation that she would hang herself.

Finally after discussion with the male members, some aged ladies and the headmen of the Chandimandap, Sudhaprasad and Ramaniprasad decided that Sundari *Pisi* could not be allowed to leave the family. The eldest brother, Atulprasad, was in Calcutta and in those days there was no means to contact him and get his opinion on the matter within a couple of days. The historic honour and dignity of the Chatterjee family of Sholna village could in no way stoop to the aristocracy of the Talukdar family of Lakhutia. But man thinks something and something else happens in real life. Bireswar stayed back for a third day in their family and Bilu's Ranga Thakuma left with him to the amazement of everyone. Ramaniprasad, terribly shocked at her decision, went running to her and implored her to come back saying that if she did not come back, she would never meet him alive. But she did not reply. Even she maintained her silence when he told her that as long they were alive they would never see her face. Sudhaprasad shed tears in private. After their boat left, one relative told Ramaniprasad that let alone humans, even gods fail to understand the nature of women. This incident triggered the memories of remote past which became the subject of discussion in every household of the village. People referred to the episode of Khiroda. They pointed out that it was in this way that the history of faithlessness of women got repeated.

The relatives in the village were unaware about things happening in the world outside—the failure of the Cabinet Mission, how Radcliff's 'knife' demarcated the boundaries of our motherland, thereby smearing her with blood and how it finally made the way for Lady Mountbatten to be greeted with the rose by Nehru. After many decades, history would try to prove that the love was asexual. But other than that, was there any other impact? For Bilu, Partition surely meant something more. He was born under the supervision of Sundari *Pisi* and during one night in a rented house beside the Kirtankhola river where they were living as a fragmented family, Bilu heard from *Natun Boudi*, with melancholy writ large on her face, that there would be no cooking in the house as Gandhiji was shot dead.

3

It was an irony of fate. When the rented house at Mirjapur ceased to be a shelter for him, Ramaniprasad, swallowing all his earlier vows, was compelled to approach his Taru *Didi* to allow him stay in her house along with his son Bilu, his daughter Chhalana and his wife. He wrote a letter to Sundari *Pisi* imploring her to provide food and shelter to his family, else he and Bilu would have to beg on the streets. Finally, one day Ramaniprasad along with his family set out on his journey to the unknown. Bilu could only faintly remember that during the journey he could not remove his eyes from the jungle outside that he was looking at through the window. The quarters in the new place were not as small as the house at Mirjapur street. The vision did not get obstructed by the narrowness of the place. Living in the midst of wide expanse, Bilu here enjoyed unlimited freedom. The soil here was dry laterite and the horizons on all sides seemed ever-expanding. There were only a few quarters of red amidst dark huge trees. The railway line was at some distance. Standing on the veranda one could see the trains. Even one could see the station. It was a small one and looked peaceful with small laterite stone chips strewn over the platform.

This was where the conscious self of Bilu first saw Sundari *Pisi* from close quarters—she was plump with her closely shaved milk-white hair and was sitting on a cot in a reclining posture with her swollen feet stretched out. Her eye bags were puffed up and her nose was very sharp. Looking at her eyes one could understand that she was a beauty in her youth. Bilu could smell the odour of medicine from her body. Her face was full of wrinkles. With a smile on her toothless mouth, she told Ramani that his son had grown big. And then she called Bilu close to her to tell him that it was she who took him out from his mother's womb. She also said how she breastfed Bilu in his babyhood. The child Bilu felt embarrassed to hear this. But this feeling of embarrassment was not something new to him—be it getting an earful from *Natun Boudi* for entering her room with no prior notice or throwing coconut cell on the car. But this time the feeling was somewhat of a different sort.

Bilu suddenly asked her pointing to her swollen feet, 'What has happened to your feet?'

'Yamaraj, the king of death, has made my body his abode,' she replied.

In Bilu's imagination the two words 'Yama' and 'king' assumed two different dimensions. Who is 'Yama'? Is he also the 'king'?

Suddenly *Pisi* kissed Bilu on the chin. The smell of medicine hit his nose strongly. Bireswar regularly bought hemp for his grandmother. Then she said to Bilu, 'You please go out now. The elders will have their talk.'

Arunprasad can no longer recollect how his father, following his exit from the room, admitted his past wrong to Sundari *Pisi* and expressed his emotions. Arunprasad's eyes moisten with tears as he could remember how his father, the otherwise stubborn man, broke down after the Partition and literally had to beg for shelter from his elder brother and sister. The day his father died of liver cirrhosis in the house Arunprasad was married by then. The blood in his body became blackish, it was not red like the rose in the hand of the Lady.

Standing on the veranda, Bilu looked at the railway track and saw how the red-coloured wooden compartments were moving at great speed on the rails with smoke coming out of the engine. It was not his maiden experience to see a moving train. He himself with his father travelled in a crowded compartment of a train while coming to his *Pisi*'s place. Arunprasad could see in his imagination that men in this country travelled in overcrowded compartments often hanging outside. Hordes of them sat on the roof of the coaches. Where were they going? Almost all of them had turban on their heads. Some of them wore short dhoti, some wore pyjamas. These trains did not stop at small stations. These were known as mail trains. The people in those crowded compartments were shouting in strange language. But Bilu could not guess where they were going.

At night Sundari *Pisi* called Biru and told him that Bilu was his uncle by relation. With a smile on his face the old man said, 'Okay, I will call you Bilu *Kaka*.' Bilu felt a little awkward but nevertheless enjoyed the fun part of it. As if after coming from Mirjapur he had suddenly become much bigger here. Then *Pisi* laughed away the idea and said, 'I was just kidding. Rather I will ask Bilu to call you Biru *Kaku*.' The man immediately started laughing. Then quickly taking a shower and finishing his food he went to the station through the field full of spear grass. Many new thoughts thronged his imagination while many memories of Mirjapur faded out from his mind. Now he could understand that a seed, if swallowed, would never germinate inside the abdomen and rubbished the childhood thought. His mother told him laughing, 'Such things like seed do not remain in the stomach. Is the stomach something like soil that a seed would germinate there?'

Here in Sundari *Pisi*'s place there are thrills of many kinds. Bilu learnt from his uncle that the iron pillars with arms standing beside the railway track were called signals. If the arms were in a drooping position, then it was an indication of a train coming on the tracks. But if the arm is straight that meant the train could not proceed. Biru *Kaka* was in charge of the signals. When Biru *Kaka* received a message for the signal he instructed a man to operate the handle, he either lowered it or made it straight. A few days after watching this, Bilu secretly set up a signalling system of his own by planting two sticks near the fence that marked the boundary of the garden. Whenever he got the sound of a mail train coming, be it day or night, he rushed through the veranda to lower the arm and again made it straight after the sound faded away. He felt a real thrill in this. He thought that it was under his command that the train could pass, else it would have stopped there. To ascertain the veracity of his impression, he asked his uncle for corroboration. With a serious face Biru *Kaku* replied, 'Yes, Bilu, the drivers have told me about you.' Bilu eagerly asked, 'What do they say?' 'Biru *Kaku* replied, 'Without the signal from Mukherjees' house the mail train cannot move.'

Coming over to this country Bilu learnt many new words. For example, the word 'murum' meant red shingles of large size made of laterite soil. The word 'bhainsa' meant huge buffalos on which rode the shepherd boys. One day as he was running by the side of the slum area, Bilu saw a few people had gathered in front of an old two-storey house. As he peeped into the room, he could see a man lying on the floor bundled in a white cloth soaked with blood. A white-haired woman, lean and thin, was sitting with her knee folded in front of the body. She was beating her heart and venting out her anger in an incomprehensible language. Bilu had never heard such language before.

Danuj, a boy senior to Bilu and bigger in size, lived in an adjacent house and with whom Bilu developed a friendly relationship. The boy whispered to Bilu's ears that Bilu was really stupid not to understand what had happened. Still Bilu looked vacantly at him. He then made him understand that Arjun Seth, who was the owner of the house, was murdered by Sagar Seth of another locality. The police would come now. The old lady who was the mother of the slain man was ordering her other sons for a retaliatory murder of any of Sagar's brothers. She would not hand over the body of her son to the police until the murder was avenged. Bilu's inside suddenly became hollow. Why did he come here! For the first time in his life, he heard the words 'manslaughter' or 'murder'. He saw the dead body and realised that man does not always die naturally, he could as well be slaughtered or murdered. When Sundari *Pisi* heard everything she severely upbraided Bilu. She wanted to know why Bilu went there. This can lead to riot between the two groups of the Seths because the murder was committed by the Seths of the lower social status.

The new place was remote and not quite populated. Most of the children were uneducated and as they grew up a little, they either resorted to crimes or worked as shepherds for the rich people of the area. In the very next month after this incident under the instruction of Sundari *Pisi*, Batu *Da*, Biru *Kaku*'s eldest son, got Bilu admitted to a nearby pathshala run by a Panditji. The idea was that Bilu should learn the language of the place and also some elementary mathematics. Bilu's father, Ramaniprasad, on the other hand, was running from pillar to post to somehow earn something. He visited Sundari *Pisi* by fits and starts to give her some money. Ramaniprasad was sick at heart to see that Biru alone had to bear the financial burden for so many heads in the family. He, however, did not say anything. Bilu's mother and Chhalana di agreed to the decision of sending Bilu to the pathshala. In fact, Bilu's mother opined that it was good to learn the language of the place.

Arunprasad can no longer remember the face of Panditji. But after a lot of efforts, he can faintly form an impression of the face. One could smell bad breath as he spoke. He regularly chewed myrobalan which transformed the bad breath into a smell similar to that of the soil. Bilu, whose senses were very strong since his childhood, could get the smell even when he sat furthest from him. Even today when Arunprasad gets a whiff of the wet soil he can imagine a picture of the teacher wearing a soiled dhoti and loose-fitting pyjamas. His tonsured head looked fair and there was a thick tuft of hair at the back of his head. On a special day Panditji used to offer each student a sweet, one slate and a black stone pencil with which one could write the letters in white. Bilu's delight knew no bounds on that day. A shepherd boy came to the school at times but the moment the word 'bhonsri' was uttered Panditji flew into a rage and caned the boy twice. Holding his ears, he was made to look straight at the sun as punishment. Another boy whispered to Bilu that to utter the word was like calling names. As soon as Bilu rubbed the slate with some teuri leaves, the slate again became clean, again he felt like writing something on it. It turned out to be a new game for Bilu. He went on rubbing the slate and writing something new on it. It was like opening the door of some mystery with a key.

The teacher then offered a sweet to each of them and then pointing to the national flag, asked the children to salute the same. The moment Bilu heard the words, he could see in his imagination the lake of his childhood days. For a few seconds he plunged into the storehouse of his memory and could call to mind the green colour of the water, the dimly lit surface of the placid lake and could hear the voice of his uncle uttering the words 'national flag' to the rhythm of the band when Bilu was coming back from the pond wearing his towel. In those early days of childhood, the word 'national' prompted him to find a resemblance between the green colour of the flag and the water. But now that he was in his *pathshala*, the meaning of the word suggested a different connotation. Now the word 'national' meant for him rubbing the slate with teuri leaves to clean it and then writing on it again.

Back at home Biru *Kaka* was a very jovial person. After his duty, while taking rest at home whenever the sound of some train was heard, he, with a sense of seriousness, asked Bilu to lower the signal for the train. Bilu accordingly lowered the arm of the signal and put it straight once the train passed by. How he had grown up—he thought about himself. That he could now carry out so many responsibilities successfully made the world around him colourful. Bireswar Mukherjee, who liked Bilu a lot, was popularly known in the neighbourhood as Mukherjee *Babu*. Nobody here called a person by his first name. There was no fixed time of duty in the railways then. One had to attend the duties at the station whenever a message was sent through the 'callman.' During his leisure time Bireswar enjoyed telling stories to Bilu. These were exciting stories about ghosts, dacoits and apparitions. Bilu was greatly interested in the stories of the ghosts who were disembodied characters. But after listening to the stories, he could not gather courage to go to the veranda alone, be it noontime or night.

Biru *Kaku*'s job was a transferable one. He had to move from one station to another. The present station was rather a small one. The stations before and after this one were even smaller. They were known as 'flag stations.' Arunprasad can remember the names even today—Sitnathganj and Dadapara. Once Biru *Kaka*, after finishing his duty at Dadapara, was coming back late at night walking beside the railway track. There was no quarter at Dadapara. With a torch in hand as he was crossing the sleepers, he suddenly realised those small pebbles were being pelted from somewhere and were falling at his feet. Surprisingly the stones, on hitting the ground, were not rebounding or moving in any other direction. It was pitch dark and on either side of the track there were barren lands with some bushy growth here and there. The stones as they fell were emitting a burnt smell. The very description was spine-chilling for Bilu. Suddenly Biru *Kaku* stopped narrating the story and asked Bilu in a sombre tone to bring his match box from the veranda. Immediately Bilu clasped Biru *Kaka* in panic. Biru *Kaka* thoroughly enjoyed Bilu's plight.

Occasionally he used to take Bilu through a shorter route to his office at the station. The stone floor of the station was overgrown with grass. There were some huge trees at the base of which were strewn laterite pebbles. Not many trains stopped at the station. When some unimportant overcrowded passenger train stopped at the station one could see the passengers were hanging from the roof, foot rest and window of the compartments. Mostly they were bare-footed rustic people, their feet daubed with dust and heads decked with various types of turbans. The women covered their faces with long veil and wore heavy silver or brass ornaments. Looking at the crowd Bilu wondered about the destination of these people—were they going for some pilgrimage or some fair? He heard from his mother in his childhood that in their erstwhile country there was a temple of Lord Shiva, where during the annual festival a huge crowd used to gather. Bilu, as he grew up, realised that the people usually go to a fair or pilgrimage in a group. The passenger train whistled out of the station emitting black smoke. A man with his head covered with a cloth was feeding coal into the boiler as the train chugged out of the station. And Biru *Kaka*, while doing his duty, told Bilu that this crowd was going to witness the prosecution of Nathuram Godse for whom the verdict could be capital punishment.

Bilu looked at him vacantly. He asked Bilu if he knew that Gandhiji was killed by Nathuram Godse. Did he not hear this during his stay at Mirjapur? The question immediately evoked in Bilu's mind the 'murder' of Arjun Seth, whose old mother uttered the word. Now that he heard the word again, it brought back to his mind the picture of the house at Barisal beside the River Kirtankhola and the pale face of *Natun Boudi* on the day of Gandhiji's assassination.

His imagination faded into insignificance. He was brought back to reality by the sound of the 'bell' which resembled that of the bells tied to the neck of the buffalos. It was produced by hitting a forked iron beam by a turbaned man. He stood with a green flag in his hand. A little later, a mail train passed at great speed. Bilu feared that the train might stop at a little distance as he had not lowered the arm of his signal in the garden. His anxiety was increasing, which in his imagination reminded him of the guilt he experienced after dropping the empty coconut shell on the roof of the car. When Biru *Kaka* came back to the quarter at night, Bilu came to know from him that there was no problem. He felt much relieved, but at the same time the name of Nathuram Godse continued to haunt him. He was wondering about the meaning of the word 'prosecution.' But how could prosecution or trial of a person 'go on'? He was also pondering over the meaning of the word 'execution.' Was Gandhiji murdered or executed? He thought that execution might be a synonym for murder—such strange thoughts preoccupied his young mind.

4

When Ramaniprasad could not succeed in any of the jobs he was trying his hand on and was becoming a burden in his sister's house, he was rather compelled to leave that house and was forced to live with some other relative along with his family. Though Arunprasad today does not remember anything of Bilu, those fragmented and indistinct pictures of the past came back to his mind. He can now realise the mystery of the red rose in the hand of the lady. Today it is not Bilu but Arunprasad who laments how love of an individual could play with the fate of millions of people. Otherwise if the Cabinet Mission was allowed to work, Bilu would not have lost his childhood, or Gita, the daughter of their relative, Saroj *Kaka*, would not have to leave this house in tears leaving a message to her family to forget her, to assume that she had died. After that Gita walked away with Sagiruddin, the son of Samser *Miyan*. By the time the Indo-China war broke out, Bilu had fully transformed into Arunprasad.

One day his father Ramaniprasad came home without any prior intimation. Arunprasad was about to leave for his college but he dropped his plan as he saw his father. His father was then employed as an accountant in a brick kiln at a remote place. Some months he visited home to give some money to his family, in some other months Arunprasad had to go to collect the same. He was surprised to see his father for this unscheduled visit and on enquiry, came to know that his father would have to go to the Governor's House. His uncle Atulprasad, his cousin brother, Gonu *Da* and even *Khokamama* (nickname 'Gunda') were engaged in the Governor's House with various jobs. His father told him that his employer, Nagen Mazumder, the owner of the brick kiln, would donate some gold ornaments to the National Fund as a token of his love for the country. Ramaniprasad was a trusted employer, and hence was entrusted with the duty. Arunprasad who disrespectfully addressed his father's employer as 'Nagen', wondered how his father could work under such a person who was corrupt, self-seeking and a drunkard. He felt like laughing aloud to think that even such a person could be a 'patriot'. At this the old Ramaniprasad became angry and said that he would have given him a sound beating if he were in his childhood days.

As his anger subsided, he told Bilu that this was a 'national duty'. He said, 'The country has been invaded... however corrupt my employer may be, he trusts only me... other employees are drunkards and coolies...so who else would go to the Governor's House? I will have to go but I feel nervous these days to go to Calcutta alone'. Arunprasad could understand that his old father wanted him to accompany him as a security guard to go to the Governor's House. He had become much weaker physically. Arunprasad, who had the obstinacy of his youth, did not show any concern and just ignored the matter. He was wondering that even after so many years the word 'national' did not acquire a definite meaning. Like a jellyfish, its meaning was still wobbly—ever-changing. Though for him the world of childhood imagination had long been a thing of the past, such instances of donating gold and the self-sacrifice of common people for the national cause flashed in a 'fantasy' in Arunprasad's mind.

Arunprasad's elder sister, Chhalana, passed away a couple of days before the day his father was scheduled to go to the Governor's place. In the back side of their house, in the corner of a dilapidated veranda, Chhalana was lying bedridden and was gradually pining away infected by some incurable disease. Nobody, not even Arunprasad, was aware of the exact name of the disease. Ramaniprasad's economic condition then was almost beggarly. He did not have the money to get her admitted to a hospital. She used to lie on the bed day and night. All the cures that Ramaniprasad knew by virtue of his travel far and wide, were applied on Chhalana. Arunprasad also thought in his fantasy that his sister would be cured one day.

Today at seventy-three, Arunprasad feels like laughing. Simultaneously his eyes get moistened, unaware. He considers himself a part of this sin of the family. At that time, he was no longer a child. Why couldn't he appeal to everybody to save his sister! Why couldn't he clamour to the world to show mercy to his sister! Why couldn't he say that the quality of mercy is the best quality! He was not home in the afternoon his sister breathed her last. He went out with his friend secretly to have the first experience of smoking cigarettes on the banks of the Ganges. He got the news on his return. During the final moments of her life, she was desperately trying to bite the old pillows and bed sheets. Today as Arunprasad looks back, he can't be sure if that was in pain or a desperate attempt to come back to life.

The neighbours who were afraid of the unknown disease peeped in from a distance, that too covering their mouth and nose. Only three persons volunteered to take her to the burning ghat. But only three cannot carry the bier and Arunprasad's father, with his dry, emotionless eyes asked him if he would go. Arunprasad stubbornly said a 'no' to his father. Swallowing the heavy burden of sorrow, Ramaniprasad ultimately lent the fourth shoulder to the bier and walked steadily to the burning ghat. It was with the same steadiness that his father performed his duty at the Governor's House the next day. Standing on the veranda as he looked at the corner, he found the bed had been removed and heaved a sigh. In man's life death comes in many ways but he was not sure whether his sister died a natural death. These were memories of the remote past. It has been a long time since he is not in touch with *Natun Boudi*. He has heard that Gonu *Da* passed away a few months before his retirement. His daughter may get a job as her father died in harness. The day after the funeral, Ramaniprasad went out in the afternoon through the main door of the house, putting the packet of the gold in a jute bag. He did not ask his son to accompany him to Calcutta anymore. Arunprasad could see from hiding that his father was silently rubbing the tears with the back of his palm. He pondered, 'Does the meaning of "national" connote a different meaning like secretly wiping the tears?' These are memories of more than fifty years ago. It has been forty-nine years since Ramaniprasad passed away. Arunprasad's mother breathed her last twelve–fourteen years after his father died. She always covered her face with the veil of her sari and looked after everything in the family of his father's elder brother. In the year of his mother's death the burning ghat was gifted with the electric furnace. In Arunprasad's mind a sudden flash occurs—someone lifted an iron lid and her mother's body was pushed inside a hole that was burning bright with a golden glow.

Now Arunprasad's imagination has become weak. When in the morning he tried to narrate the description of Lady Mountbatten's daughter, people like Probodh, Sanatan, Sudhababu or Muktinath reacted with a smile rubbishing the 'newness' of the episode.

'We all know this already.'

'Do you?'

'Yes'. Sudhababu continued, 'Are you talking about the famous love affair—his offering a red rose to the lady and kissing her hand?' At this Muktinath mildly expressed his disapproval, 'Don't use such language.'

Sudhababu retorted, 'Why shouldn't I? Do you mean to say that individuals have minor roles to play in the history of a nation?'

'What has that to do with this?'

'Otherwise, how could the Cabinet Mission fail? Was it not related to the red rose in the hand of the Lady?'

Sudhababu could hardly finish his words when Arunprasad started feeling a commotion within. He could see in his mind's eye rose petals sprinkled on the shoulders of Chhalana's bier-bearers, his father Ramaniprasad roaming in the rose garden. He sees in a vision, as it were, that Aminuddin, along with Siddiqui, is standing in the field amidst a good harvest due to a sufficient irrigation with the water of Kaljira river. He is saying to Arunprasad's father, 'Katta, we want power tiller... And from now on three fourths of the yield will be mine and one fourth will be your share'. Someone from the depth of history suddenly appears and addresses Arunprasad as 'Bilu'—the forgotten name of his childhood.

ଔ

Translated by Goutam Buddha Sural

Goutam Buddha Sural, Professor, Dept. of English, Bankura University, has been in teaching since 1990. His area of interest includes Victorian Poetry, Indian English Literature, and Tribal and Dalit Studies.

Ends of a Broken Bridge
Jatin Bala

Getting acquainted with fellow passengers on a journey is my unfailing habit. When my daughter accompanies me, she vehemently reproaches. She says: '*Baba*, can't you stay quiet? Do you have to talk to anyone who is in front of you? What's their name? Where are they from? Where to go? Bringing up stories of the bygone times. What's the use of knowing everything about a stranger?'

I joyously laugh at her words and dismiss her point. I say: 'We are not here to stay forever. Knowing a person has its benefits. This might be the last time I am meeting one. The person will then be lost in the crowd forever and I might never get a chance to talk to them again. Nature has bestowed man with language, has created within him a storehouse for memories. Language, coupled with memories, helps one in finding out those who are close to heart—in reconciling with the lost ones.'

So any new person in my vicinity awakens within me a storm of curiosity. That desire is like a stubborn tortoise-bite, would not leave until all is known, all is revealed. Neither the daughter's reproach, nor the wife's rebuke can alter my habit.

Bongaon railway station. The train was waiting at the platform to run to Sealdah in the next moment. The platform displayed usual signs of business all round. Quite unknowingly, breaking my self-made norm, I dodged the overbridge, risked my life and jumped on the railway tracks, crossed over to the platform and jumped on to the train. Witnessing me racing towards the train, a strong young hand pulled me on to it. The young man ushered me into the compartment and heartily said: 'Please come, please sit here'. He arranged a seat for me, and with contentment, occupied the opposite seat.

At the right end of the compartment sat a young lady, closely wrapping her arms around an old woman. At a glance one could say that the old woman was quite unwell. To protect the sickly lady from the rush of passengers, the young man made me sit by their side and was content by his feat. This contentment showed bright and clear on his face.

Either from a feeling of gratitude from his help, or may be compelled by my incorrigible habit, I asked him: 'O boy, where are you going?'

'We are going to Calcutta for my ailing grandmother's treatment.'

Pain was audible in his voice as he raised his hand to point at his grandmother; his empathy for his ailing grandmother was so vivid in his demeanour.

Age and ailment had made the old lady raddled. She sat bundled up in the corner of the seat, her eyes unmoved by the scenes passing by. As the young, healthy, good-looking young lady was stooping over the older lady, her face was not visible.

The younger ones had similar faces. As he saw me looking with scrutinising eyes, he straightforwardly said: 'She is Mithu, my own sister'.

I tried to sound earnest: 'So, boy, where do you come from?' In a voice warmed by the wish to offer all of himself, the young man replied: 'We are coming from Bangladesh.'

'Where in Bangladesh do you stay?'—Curiosity had, by then, won over me.

'The old name is Jessore district,' the man said, looking at me, and waiting with eagerness to answer more.

But I silently started sifting through my memories. My facial expression must have changed with that. The young man intently looked at me and added, 'Our home is in the Madhupur village under Manirampur police station. We crossed the border only today.' He seemed impatient to listen to me, hear my thoughts.

Madhupur. *Ma…dhu…pur.* I repeated the name to myself. I am an uprooted man who keeps memories within his heart like wounds of yesteryears. A soft pinch can ooze that dark blood out from those wounds of Partition anytime. Distinct are those memories of woe and bloodshed, of torture and trauma. Their sounds still ring in my ears.

As I close my eyes, I can still recall that along with Madhupur there is another village close to my heart, Machhna. These names make me anxious even today Emotion had overwhelmed me, my voice turning almost alien to myself. With all my heart's desire to know more I asked: 'You live in Madhupur?'

'Yes, yes. We live in that village. Did you ever stay there? Do you know anyone from there?' His voice resounded with the excitement of someone who has found a kin in foreign lands. His eyes were fixed on me as he asked, as if his heart was enfolded by the warmth of the land.

Unmindfully, I heaved a deep sigh. I had to try hard to breathe freely. I shoved aside the burnt-out dreams, the dried-out desires; I buried the cries deep within my heart. The aeons-ago-deserted village! With the rekindled excitement of hearing a call from the roots, with the compassion of the left-away ties, the spilled-over memories, I said: 'We lived in Machhna village once upon a time. That is my birthplace. Both these villages—Machhna and Madhupur—lived side by side in close communion. Perhaps, even today, they are locally referred to as "Machhna-Madhupur".'

'Are you from that village? Is that your birthplace?' It seemed, as if, a rudderless sailor had finally found land. The young man looked at me curiously and asked anxiously: 'Do you remember names of any villagers from your days?'

'*Chacha*, just try to remember,' he began scrutinising me with inquisitive eyes.

It has been about forty–forty-five years since I left the village. Even if Partition is comprehensible by reason, within the core of the heart it is unacceptable. So when I reckon Madhupur, the ones who come foremost to my mind are

Fatema *Amma*, her husband Tofazel *Chacha*, that is, Tofazel Choudhury. Although in two different lanes, we lived close by. Memories of an ancient and huge tamarind tree that stood between two villages rushed to me—Tofazel Choudhury—and memories of the bygone days whisked me away to dear times left behind, in a land forsaken. I can see clearly with my eyes closed—the courtyard, two *shiuli* trees around the tulsi-*mancha*; how the courtyard would be covered with flowers fallen from the tree in the mornings. I can still smell its fragrance within my soul. My heart cuddles up to the warmth of my birthplace.

I must have been five–six years old back then. Half-naked, naked feet, amulet on my right arm, I would be playing, running around with friends under the tamarind tree. A perfect crystal-clear picture. How it shines bright even after so many days! The call of the roots is irresistible. Another face rises up from the faded pages of memory. I am torn within by bouts of doubt. Unmindfully I said, 'How many times I have eaten in that house!' Then a little louder—'I knew Tofazel Choudhury'.

'To-fa-zel Chou-dhu-ry! My grandfather. I am his son's son. I am Aakash Choudhury.'

I couldn't control my excitement then. I cut him short: 'You are Mahidul's son?' I couldn't believe my eyes. My subdued heart bloomed again. My body shivered with emotions and excitement. With goose pimples I called out impatiently: 'Fatema *Amma*, Fatema *Amma*, I am Khokon, Abinash Biswas's son, Ratan. I am Ratan, *Amma*.'

Mahidul's son and I were so enrapt in the conversation that we took no cognizance of the people around intently listening to us. Fatema *Amma* had already turned her face away from the window and was looking at me absorbedly. It was, as if, she was being able to see the past through me and was touching every chord that throbbed with love for her.

The thin, rugged face drained by pain, sickness and age, brightened up that very moment. She stooped down as if in more pain; a deep sigh cut across her heart. Her soft lips trembled in compassion: '*Hai Allah*! Can all of this happen on earth? Kokhon, my heart's love! Is it you?' Her voice got choked. The heart seemed to break open the bodily cage. Fatema *Amma* was beside herself in a moment. I have no power to describe that truth, that appeal of the heart. I stood numb.

The world running with me on the train faded from my consciousness. I touched her feet. Love and affection weighed heavy inside my heart. It could find no way out. That pain, exuberance, excitement hit against the tough walls of memory and bled.

She extended her heavily veined hands to cushion my head which she then pulled close to her heart, as if I was a child. She forgot all around her. She wailed and said, 'O dear, never did I think that I would meet you here. O God! Where will I go? Where will I keep him, my Ratan? *Hai Allah*...' Fatema *Amma* became breathless. She took deep breaths amidst kissing my face. She was all ruffled up, as if the wound of the soul was breaking the heart to pieces. Her tears washed her heart...

Mithu was not able to control Fatema *Amma*. Yet she tried with all her might and looked at me intently, without blinking. I too was transformed by the changing circumstances. Forgotten memories seem to have loosened me up within. Was I really seeing Fatema *Amma* before me? Seated there was a haggard old lady, wearing spotless white cotton sari. Her hair was white as a crane's wings. Her complexion was fair. Lines of experience criss-crossed her face. Half of her face was veiled. She was almost a broken being. While tears made the vision dim, memories like scattered storm clouds rushed off and darkened the mind.

Washed by complex emotions, I did not notice when I had surrendered myself to the warmth of compassion that lay buried within her bosom.

Just as a seed sprouts after the shower, my thoughts also effortlessly sprouted and bloomed at the touch of a mother's love. The heart shone with starry words. A shiver flowed down my spine, eyes met a dawn, brows quivered and opened up to the brightness of memories as they thronged before me. All these burnt my consciousness, and the wounds made me trip over every time I tried to walk past.

The train was running fast; it had already crossed four stations. But I still found myself taking dips in the troubled waters of remembrance and forgetfulness. I tried to reach the bank. But alas!

Fatema *Amma* seemed to have laid aside all pain and troubles. She brightened up and asked, 'Khokon, dear, where do you live? How many children do you have?'

Only the almighty knows the magic by which all her pain seemed to get relieved in an instant. She spoke normally, as a healthy person. She seemed to have opened up her heart, her life force seemed to have transformed her for a moment. Tears, stranded in the folds of her rugged face, were still trembling, yet there seemed some ray of life, bright and shining.

I became conscious: '*Amma*, I have a son and a daughter. The next station is Ashok Nagar. All of you must come and stay at my place today.' I said with a lot of confidence and looked at *Amma*. She too was staring at me without blinking, as if she wanted to capture thousands of events, all slipping away.

Akash was anxious: 'We have an appointment with the doctor, *Chacha*. The appointment is this evening at 4 p.m. Abba's friend has fixed this appointment with Dr Bose. It might not be appropriate to shift this appointment, *Chacha*. And grandma's condition is too bad to cancel the appointment'. Aakash's voice seemed wet with tears. He said after taking a breath: 'My sister Mithu will understand this better. She is a prospective doctor, a final year student of M.B.B.S. She had her exams last month. She left no stone unturned to bring grandma over here'. The worry was writ large on his face.

Mithu left Fatema *Amma*, came forward, paid her respects, and said, 'We have to consult the doctor today itself, *Chacha*. You know that without dire necessity no one comes to a foreign land to consult a doctor. We won't be able to go back today. Allah has been kind to make us meet. You will be our support in this country. You can see how grandma has already improved just by your touch. We won't leave you now'. Her words were charged with immeasurable earnestness.

Mithu had a genuine compassion in her voice, a compassion that could rekindle many lost feelings. She seemed relaxed having been able to convey the urgency of the situation with the warmth intact.

I started collecting myself after brooding on the thoughts for a while. But the heart was full of wavering emotions. I said, 'I will definitely be with you. We will all go together. Akash, Mithu, I cannot, perhaps, tell you in words how dear *Amma* is to me! Come, we will go together. Once we reach Sealdah, I can call up home and inform them.'

They both cried aloud: 'That would be perfect, *Chacha*. That we got you, nothing more could be desired.' Akash emphatically added, 'We must also call *Abba* and let him know about you.'

Fatema *Amma* was alert to all that we spoke and she silently, greedily devoured our words. Her heart seemed to be overwhelmed with pure love for all around her. And that started transforming her, it transformed me as well.

The train rushed on. Ashok Nagar station passed away, unnoticed.

2

Fifty years have passed, yet it seems as if they happened yesterday. Reliving those memories is almost like rebirth. The events seemed to flash before my eyes. My heart is filled with words and I can hear their footsteps from a distance.

Machhna and Madhupur were two neighbouring villages. Machhna was a village of Hindu dwellers whereas Madhupur of Muslims. A huge tamarind tree marked the border between the villages. But we, kids, played under the shade of that tamarind tree, putting aside all the differences—of caste and creed. We were playmates, dear to each other, one mind, one soul.

Mahidul was perhaps a couple of months younger to me. Yet, he was my heart's mate; my childhood was largely spent with him. Our mothers shared their stories with each other and would also spend time at each other's homes. Mahidul and I would run around to catch colourful grasshoppers, or collect birds' eggs from the banks of the dead river, or play hide and seek. All these remained as hazy pictures. But I remember that evening—nothing is more vivid in my memory than the happenings of that evening.

The days were running past frantically. We were pretty young but could sense that the air was heavy with two mortally fearsome words—'Independence' and 'Partition'. And clubbed with these words came another word which spread like wildfire—'riot'. And riot meant Hindu and

Muslim were to be separated. Distrust spread among the two communities within a blink of an eye. And it resulted in the partition of the land. But among the two villages there was nothing like hatred, or distrust. But once the air spreads poison, one inescapably inhales it. Humans become inhuman, there are bloodhounds all around. The fire is contagious.

The Muslims were celebrating some festival. After the play under the tamarind tree was over, Mahidul said: 'Khokon, come, *Amma* has called you over. Come, let's go to my house'. Mahidul pulled my hands and we made our way to their house in each other's arms.

Crossing the tamarind tree, we left a couple of houses behind to reach Mahidul's house. We saw that at the corner of the courtyard a date log was buried in the ground. In that semi-boundary space of the courtyard, Fatema *Amma* was baking *pitha* in a mud oven using an earthen pot. By the time we reached, she had finished baking quite a few. Mahidul rushed to me with a hot *pitha* in his hand and insisted on eating it.

I kept moving away, refraining myself from taking it. While retracing my steps from Mahidul, I went rather close to Fatema *Amma*'s back but I did not take the *pitha* from him. Although he tried heart and soul to make me have one, I didn't. His sincerity made me feel utterly helpless. I grew impatient, sullen and unable to resist his advances of love by any other means, I blurted out: 'No, no I won't eat from you. How can I! You are a Muslim!' This new consciousness of identity had found its grip within me. I didn't have time to think over it.

Having said that I looked at Fatema *Amma*. I found her staring at me. What a life-changing look that was! A helpless look, pitiful—a look that could tear the soul apart.

The colours of the earth changed all of a sudden. Blood started oozing out from the veins of my heart. I felt as if the heart-rending cries were all pent up within Fatema *Amma*. Subduing all her pain, she said: 'Kokhon dear, today you don't want to eat this *pitha* because we are Muslims. But one day you survived by my milk.' Fatema *Amma* couldn't speak any more. Her voice got choked. Her inside was shattered into pieces. Tears started welling up in her eyes. I was washed away by the salty water.

I couldn't look at Fatema *Amma* anymore. Self-reproach wearied me down. My heart was burning within. I could think of nothing else. I ran home hastily. I didn't stop nor did my tears. Shame and disgust did not allow me to look back. Yet I could hear Fatema *Amma*'s desperate calls—'Khokon, come back. You won't be able to go home alone. Let Mahidul make you cross Tapo's bamboo grove. Come back Khokon! Don't go alone!'

I could hear her call from a distance. The words were following me like sparks of fire. They were drawing me like a magnet from behind. The feelings of self-reproach were constantly lashing at my back. I had no power to turn back. So I kept running—running through the darkness—running through ages.

I could feel Fatema *Amma* had come behind me near the bamboo grove. Yet, I could not turn back, I just ran on and on.

3

I have spent my childhood mostly in East Bengal. On the east side of Sri river lay the village of Machhna. After dusk we would all sit around grandma in the huge courtyard on a mat and listen to her stories. As the stars would come up to the sky one by one, grandma would be engrossed in her storytelling by and by.

Right after my birth, *Ma* was affected by acute anaemia that reduced her to a skeleton. She couldn't breastfeed me. I heard this from grandma and also *Ma* herself. Those stories clearly surface on my mind once again; they come up in a flood of memory.

Ma and Fatema *Amma* had been soul sisters. Mahidul was born just a month after my birth. Fatema *Amma* would rush to our house at any opportune moment to help *Ma* with her work and child care. During such visits she would pick me up with loving warmth and feed me with milk from her breasts.

The short and stout Fatema *Amma* would be wearied with the weight of milk in her breasts. Mahidul couldn't suck all of it. So she would come over to my house to feed me too. I would drink the precious milk to my heart's content. And while sucking, I would often cuddle up in the warmth of her breasts and fall asleep.

When I could walk a step or two and Fatema *Amma* would appear at the corner of our big courtyard, *Ma* would say: 'There comes your Fatema *Amma*. Go dear, run to her and bring her in!'

And I would toddle with enthusiasm to reach her. Then unable to balance myself with new-found gait, I would almost fall to the ground. But before I could touch the ground, Fatema *Amma* would sweep me off the feet. She would drown me with her kisses and hug me dearly. That love, that happiness is beyond all earthly expressions.

The train bound for Sealdah was crossing station after station. And every moment I was being transported to the bygone days of East Bengal. Although I have been uprooted from my country, its love encompasses me—I feel it running in my veins—I feel it in the pores of my skin. Those ties would never be severed. Life has traversed through many different twists and turns. Yet the river of life has always been flowing towards its source, perhaps unnoticed. Even if the river dies, the trace of the riverbed never disappears.

The will to live is not always enough. My mother wanted to live. But during the riot a three-day fever took her life. The city by then had succumbed to riots. Hindus were running away to Hindustan with their lives in their hands. The air was heavy with the odour of all that was burning—houses and humans. Hindus were being looted of their wealth, their lives, their homes, their women, children, all. The beautiful Hindu women were being forcefully married off to the Muslim youths. The Hindu students were being forced to eat forbidden meat. Dead bodies of Hindus were left scattered here and there.

My father believed riots would not touch our village. But with a bunch of selfish people, the Muslims who were fleeing from Hindustan and seeking shelter in Pakistan, brought the deadly riots to our village as well. These rioters killed Tofazel *Chacha*'s brother Moinuddin *Chacha* just because he was trying to save two Hindu women from abuse.

Overnight the ambience of our village changed. Tofazel *Chacha* came running to our house. My father and he had a closed-door meeting, we never came to know of it. But that very night Tofazel *Chacha* and his friends assisted us to cross the border. All of this happened in the blink of an eye. We left behind our land, our home, our trees, our animals, all that made us, our forefather's mark, our past, and smuggled ourselves to Hindustan with a small pack of clothes and an uncertain future. It happened fifty years back, yet I can see it all vividly—how the fear of death was making people run for life. Dishevelled hair, eyes reflecting the fire burning all around, looking for some solace, some shelter, people were running helter-skelter. I can still hear those death groans, those murderous howls.

The wounds of Partition have not yet been healed. There are episodes of bloodshed everywhere. Blood still oozes out of the wounds caused to the roots that have been hacked off. While blood dripped from the poisonous wounds, the homeless heaved deep sighs and crawled towards the future, even stood up as times passed. They shoved aside the debris, made new homes and dreamt new dreams.

When the storm ceased, everyone realised that both the Hindus and Muslims had lost equally at the hands of riot-mongers. They wished at the core of their hearts that this should never recur. The kin should know the kin. Brothers should never be brutal towards each other. May the broken ends of the bridge be conjoined to become one again! As soon as the selfish dark clouds disappear, one will realise how pure the flow of blood is! One will feel the self-devastating pain. One race, one life, one language will all bloom from deep within. It will sprout like a sapling from the seed.

4

We did not face much trouble to admit Fatema *Amma* in the nursing home. After examining her, the doctor said, 'Surgery is the only cure to the disease. We must do it in the next twenty-four hours. Or else we won't be able to save her. And at her age operation means that we would require blood for her. So be prepared.'

While we were preparing to go with her blood samples, the nurse came running. She told us: 'Please come quickly, your patient is dying. Come fast.' We at once rushed with the nurse and entered a room dimly lit. Encumbered with anxiety and stress, our lips were unable to articulate words. When we looked at the patient with restlessness, the doctor informed, the operation was to be done right now. Blood is needed. 'Anyone of you three may donate blood.'

Akash came forward to donate his blood immediately. But his blood group did not match with hers. Akash came back, and Mithu approached to donate. Again, her blood group showed a mismatch. What a strange mockery of fate! Inevitably I went forward to donate my blood. And surprisingly, the blood group matched. While transfusing the required amount of blood into the patient's body, the doctor said, 'The old lady is saved for now. Wait for forty-eight hours. Then let's see what happens.'

I returned home with Akash and Mithu in the morning—as if a family got back its own members. Within a moment, everyone in the home treated them as parts of the family. Even Akash and Mithu got intimate with them without hesitation—as if they knew each other for a long time.

The next day as usual. I went to the nursing home and saw Fatema *Amma* sitting on the bed, awakened from sleep. She was breathing with gasps, putting her hands on the chest. Though she was about to die, a line of sweet smiles appeared on her face, seeing me. Like a person in full spirit, she said comfortably, 'Now you have come, my child, I know, I am out of danger. How could I die when I have found you, Khokon! I am now more than better. Khokon, my son, come here. I am back to life—for you only. Come, dear, come....' She called me closer, spreading her arms with pure affection. The pupils of her eyes were thrilled with vitality in endearment—as if a sweet fragrance came out of her to encompass me.

'Are you feeling ill, grandma?' Akash shifted near to *Amma*. I also moved close with him. Hugging me with her two arms, Fatema *Amma* said to me: 'You people are my sons, what pain is there for me? Death was knocking at the door for the last two days. And then all these happened! No, never worry my dear, what gibberish I am uttering! I am hale and hearty now. It happens sometimes in old age,' Fatema *Amma* said many things in a mild voice putting a sweet little smile in the corner of her lips.

For five more days, Fatema *Amma* was kept in the nursing home for a complete recovery. Akash, Mithu and myself used to visit her every day. While discharging her, the doctor said on the last day, 'The patient has survived for this time. But the danger is not rooted out, one more surgery is needed for a better treatment. But considering the age of the patient, another risk could not be taken. Serve the patient with utmost care. If you can, bring the patient once again after six months. She will take only those medicines that I have prescribed, and she won't be in trouble. She will be fine.'

The doctor bade us goodbye with a smile. We were returning home along with Fatema *Amma*. We felt that a new horizon had been opened up in the core of our heart with no boundaries and no barbed wires. We were like glistering stars, each shining brightly, bound together by a bridge of humanity—in the sky that knows no border. We were walking along the path with a knowledge that spreads the light of pure hearts.

The visa of three months expired in a blink. In the early morning, I went to the border outpost to bid them farewell. Fatema *Amma*, at the last moment, cried aloud like a little girl embracing me affectionately. She said crying, 'Oh Khokon, Allah has not given me the words to describe how I feel at this moment leaving you. How will I show you what you are to me, my son. Dear Khokon, come to visit your Fatema *Amma* for at least once'. *Amma* could not complete her words, and broke down in profuse tears. She was shivering, as she held her breasts tightly. I bowed to her, touched her feet and said standing up: 'I will come to visit you *Amma*, I will'. I could say nothing more. My heart was torn in pain and grief—eyes brimmed with tears. Biding her goodbye, I looked at her in silence. Time passed by, leaving the blankness in my eyes for long.

Fatema *Amma* was crossing the no man's land. She was walking, supported by Akash and Mithu, and was turning around again and again. Like a gigantic conflagration, her heart wavered with boundless thoughts. An immeasurable agony was ripping and tearing her heart into pieces. But how could she express those feelings? She was gazing at me, waving her hands silently, in an acute anguish. She was going forever, it seemed, leaving behind her treasure—torn away from her umbilical cord.

At that moment, I thought—there was perhaps no difference between Fatema *Amma* and my motherland. Two mothers became one and identical. And I am beholding on, towards that direction for my entire life...

ଔ

Translated by Pritha Kundu

Pritha Kundu is Assistant Professor of English at HMM College for Women, Kolkata. Her area of interest includes Classical Literature, 19th Century studies, Art and Culture, Music and Comparative Literature.

Homecoming

Sailen Sarkar

It was something like an aquatic plant. Its silent stirring was like a tree standing still with its branches spread out, like a moonlit night. The fog covered the paddy fields and the houses. Like an astonished fish, Anupam stared at the window. The unruly wind carrying drops of water had made the glass wet. Some of the bodies seemed to be just bodies—nothing else, as if they were just hands, or legs, or waists or bellies. Anupam was alone, as if it was midnight. It seemed, his father's sleeping body was just beside him and he could smell his sweat. He thought that he was again a little boy in half-pants, hearing a faraway 'ho-ho' noise. Afraid, he would call 'father', and all would vanish—the wet glass, the drops of water, that darkness, fog, shadows and that procession.

Anupam saw those people throughout last night. Those people—their hands, legs, bellies, bodies spread out like branches of a tree—were like shadows. Perhaps it was not a dream. The tension, fear and intoxication of the last few days must be the cause behind such a vision. Abinash had said, 'If you want to live, you have to cross the border, Anu.' He had given it a lot of thought and talked with a middleman.

Anupam had spent two days by just sleeping and dreaming in the decrepit house in the Gangulys' garden. According to Abinash, he might be murdered by his own men. By 'his own men' he meant the men of the party. The fact that he was alive would prick the party as a thorn now. When he boarded the train today as some 'Dilip *Da*', it was 5:30 a.m. The sun of the dawn looked like a pink dish glued to the sky. Abinash said that there was no other way then. By 'way' he meant 'taking steps'. According to him, it would have been better if the murder was not done so openly, or Anupam did not get identified for the charge of that. At this moment it was impossible for Sujit *Da* to shield Anupam. Even he had to promise the party that Anupam would surrender within forty-eight hours. Then...then the law would follow its own course. And the law was what the party wanted. Crossing the border was a better option for him. He had been asked, 'Don't you have anyone in your country?'

'Where else is my country? This is my—'

'Why, man? You used to say that your country was Jessore, and the village was Darimagura.'

'Nah, it was just the stories my father told—'

'That's fine. Can't you find anybody there where your father or grandfather used to stay?'

As some people jostled into the train, Anupam realised that they had crossed a number of stations. Turning the head, he tried to read the name of the station. Thinking of asking somebody, he turned to his left and saw the dark-skinned, thin, married woman with a little boy of around four years. He had seen this woman as a member of Dilip *Da*'s party in Dumdum station. Abinash had reminded him repeatedly not to talk much with anybody and to listen only to Dilip *Da*, as he was a faithful middleman of this line with many years' experience.

Anupam had never travelled before in the Bongaon line. Through the window he saw the arable land almost touching the railway tracks and the people walking on those fields. A little girl, open-mouthed with wonder, waved to him, as if to say, 'See you again', and Anupam, too, waved back to her. The train had moved quite a distance already, yet he bent his neck to look at her for the last time.

They crossed a station and Anupam heard the cry of the tea vendor. He looked around him, but could not find the man named 'Dilip *Da*', so he ordered just a cup of tea for himself. He found that the little boy, sitting with his mother's hand in his own, had been staring at him, as if with an intent to say something. What could he say? Should Anupam ask his name? Or should he ask where he was going? Or, where his home was? Should he speak to his mother? He recalled Abinash's words. If you ask somebody something, be prepared to tell something about yourself as well. And that could lead to revealing some unwanted secret. Abinash had repeatedly reminded him, 'Everybody recognises your name and photo from the newspapers.'

The train was reducing its speed when Dilip *Da* suddenly appeared. The man looked at the thin, dark-skinned married woman sitting beside Anupam and said, 'Will get down here'. Then he glanced at Anupam as if to ensure whether everything was fine.

Father used to talk about Darimagura village, Jessore district; and thus the tales began—tales of escape. Anupam's father wore a Hawaii shirt, *chappals* made from tyre, and pyjamas. Then Anupam had to listen to the story of how his father was in the habit of taking bread and tea in the early morning and then selling his portions of peppers right on the streets. '*Lalakunja*'. The word brought a smile to his face. '*Kunja*'—what a strange word! It meant 'garden'. He had seen this 'Lalakunja' a lot of times. He had visited the place and spent nights there. It had a dozen houses, like a slum. It was perhaps made for the workers of the paint-mill on the opposite side. To its right was the crude-mill. Both of the mills had ceased to exist by now. Anupam had spent a lot of nights in this Lalakunja with women like Sandhya from Kakinara or Shikha from Sodepur. Father said that on their first arrival in India, they took shelter in the room on the right in the backside of Lalakunja. Among them were father, mother, two uncles, aunt, grandfather and grandmother. And then came the episodes of land occupation, police invasion and the sleepless nights of precaution. Someone from India had written a letter to Grandmother, saying, 'All of you will survive if you can come here. Just cross the border somehow—'.

A mild breeze caressed Anupam. He had to sit here for some time. 'To sit' meant 'to wait'. He read the name of the station: 'Machlandpur'. The platform had a cemented bench, but nobody would have a place to sit until a down-train passed. A lot of people used to go to Calcutta from here. It seemed that the thin woman with the child wanted to stay near Anupam. Perhaps Dilip *Da* had shown him to her and instructed her to do something like that. In a shop, *luchis* were being fried. 'Are you hungry?' Anupam asked himself. How strangely had Abinash told him that Anupam would get killed within a couple of days if he stayed here! Anupam was not much surprised at first. He knew that he could be the victim. Why would Biswanath Banerjee's group spare him? Perhaps they had arranged for someone after Naren *Da*'s murder. Perhaps it was Pinta, or Bapi.

'Not them'.

'Then?'

'It was none but your Sujit *Da*. He may even use the police—.'

Dilip *Da* came after two Bongaon local trains touched Machlandpur and went towards Sealdah. The married woman and her son got a seat long ago; they had untangled the bundle of *muri* and ate it with the water of the tube well. Sipping the tea, Anupam noticed the woman carefully. She did not have *sindoor* on her forehead. Was she a Muslim? Perhaps she came to India for some purpose; now she was returning to her country.

'Let's go, catch a bus—'

Anupam saw that there were three more people with them—an elderly man with a woman and a little girl. The woman wore a bindi. Before boarding the bus Dilip *Da* came closer to Anupam and told him an important thing for the first time. Pointing to the married woman with the boy on the train, he said, 'Take care of them, please.'

Anupam wanted to buy a newspaper in Dumdum, or even in Machlandpur station, if possible. Who knew what they had written today? Biswanath Banerjee's men must have instigated them; or why would they write so much? They had published the same news for seven days in a row—with sketches and diagrams, with every bit of information about Anupam, even the year of his father's coming to India as a refugee from Pakistan.

As far as he could see through the window, there were patches of empty land. Empty, but not barren; sometimes the green stuck with the land, and sometimes it was raised just a little above the land. Who knew what trees were those? Had the police really been doing nothing, just like the newspaper reported? Was it due to the pressure created by Sujit *Da* ? The minister had given his word that nobody would be spared, regardless of which party he belonged to. He had said that the police would roll up the net within a week. It meant that the net had already been laid, just like those of the fishermen—laid silently, before the coming of the tide.

'Hey Bilu, what happened?'

Anupam woke up almost in a shock. He could see through the window that empty field and one or two faraway houses and mango trees.

Yes, it was meant for him. It meant that he had to get down now. He looked at his left and was shocked as he could not see the woman, who stood by clutching upon the rod, and her boy. Before Abinash handed Anupam over to Dilip *Da* at Dumdum station, he repeatedly mentioned the name 'Bilu' or 'Bimal Mondal': that was his new identity to Dilip *Da*. Dilip *Da* had been informed that Anupam would go back to his country and it would be enough to drop him at Satkhira bus stand. Abinash had asked Anupam, 'You would be able to go anywhere if you reach a bus stand, won't you?'

As soon as the bus had left, Anupam realised that this was not a proper stoppage. They had dropped him in the middle of the road. Perhaps Dilip *Da* instructed the driver to do so. Just as the bus left, the man scolded them—'All of you, get down from the road, go to the garden side; the white sahib is on patrol now.' A drain-like construction, full of clammy mud, was there just by the road. While crossing the drain, Anupam noticed that there were at least twenty people with them, not just the six from Dilip *Da*'s party. And there were two more middlemen like Dilip *Da* with them.

Father left the country long back. When his father finally left his house and came to the road, and looked back once with teary eyes at the house, the straw-roof, the veranda, the curled-up dog, the guava tree, the middleman asked, 'Why are you crying? That is your real country. One should never cry while going back to their own country.'

It was a big garden. Anupam saw that there were at least a hundred people. That meant they had gathered here before he came. The sunrays came down over their heads. Seeing these people under the trees, it seemed like a picnic to him. Dilip *Da* again spoke of the white sahib who was on patrol.

'Who's this white sahib?'

'One from the BSF. Eat something and take rest. Don't worry, he won't come here.'

The woman who came with him in the same train had been leering at him. Her son slept on the ground. Anupam was not hungry, yet he had to eat. Some men appeared with bread and bananas. It meant that this gathering was a regular thing. It was like a station on the way to the country. His father, too, had to halt at places. From his childhood, Anupam had heard the same story for a thousand times from his father and memorised it—the great escape at the last hour of the night through the road, the walk through the main road from Darimagura village to town, the turn at Vaina and then the trip by bus, and then the unknown Churamonkathi.

Anupam had fallen asleep on the ground. When he lay upon the grass and started dreaming that dream again, he could not remember—those shadowy bodies, that last hour of the night, the fog. *One should not cry while going to one's own country.* Why would India be father's country? Why did the middleman say that? And why didn't father reply to the middleman? Later he had wept his whole life for that straw-roof, for the veranda, for the betel nut tree, for the bat-eaten guavas, for a river named Nabaganga. Abinash asked why

Jessore won't be Anupam's country. Anupam smiled. Right. Whenever anyone had asked him where his country was, he answered 'Jessore'. Why did he say so? Why did he want to cry now? One should not cry while going back to one's own country.

Amongst the twitter of the birds, Anupam saw that the day was waning. Shadows were descending, and it seemed like there would be a little dew. The garden was almost empty. There were hardly twenty people including Anupam. Who knew where and when the others had gone? Dilip *Da* was speaking with someone beside a banana tree. A van-rickshaw appeared and Dilip *Da* raised his hand and said, 'Get in, all of you.' Nobody asked it, yet the man cried aloud the name of the destination, 'Baltikhali.'

What a strange name, 'Baltikhali'! Father had to get down from the bus at Churamonkathi. He could clearly remember the names. Whenever father got a chance, he started to speak about it like a tape recorder at night in bed or at lunch. For many a time Anupam had scolded him, but father never listened to him. Father said that they had to board the bus from the turn of Vaina and go to Churamonkathi. There they hid all day long till it was dark. Outside their hiding place, EPR, or East Pakistan Rifles, patrolled. Father said that EPR was like the BSF of India. Whenever the bus stopped, or whenever they stopped the bus on the road, they began their searching by opening the bundles, fumbling inside the pockets and squeezing the pillows.

'Here, stop here—'

Suddenly someone ordered the van-rickshaw to stop. At the left were the green creepers and the yellow mustard flowers. After that yellow patch, green had started again. The road on the left had bushes adjacent to it with a few huts and bamboo groves. Somehow Anupam guessed that it was not Baltikhali; either they were instructed to get down before Baltikhali, or the man had intentionally lied before the journey.

Earlier the rate for crossing the border was Rs 100 per head. That middleman would hand over one to an Indian middleman in the land of India for that Rs 100. Then one was free to take either a bus or a train. The people had been searched in that house in Churamonkathi where father and his companions hid. How did EPR get the news? Perhaps the middlemen themselves had informed them. They received Rs 10 per head and all the belongings of the refugees—gold, jewellery, and money. The central message was: 'You are free to go, but you can't take anything with you from this country.'

'Police, police!'—Somebody shouted from behind. Some people began to run frantically.

All of them had started walking through the road—Dilip *Da*, Anupam, that married woman and her son, the middle-aged man with a woman. Seeing the reddish glow on the sky on the left, Anupam was sure that it was the west. It meant that they had to turn to the right at any cost.

'To your left, to your left. You'll be shot down if you go to the right,'—the man, uttering the words without a pause, got down from the road and began to run. Someone shouted by calling some other's name. A faraway flock of ducks quacked suddenly. They heard the sound of branches breaking. 'To the house. There's the straw-roof—'

'Get out, get out—not here, the police will catch us—'

Somebody scolded Anupam as he broke into an open space under the straw-roof. It was someone speaking from one of the dark rooms. The sky over his head was covered. He could hear a twittering sound. It was like a tunnel with its mouth far away from him. There was just a little tint of light there.

'What happened?'

Anupam was not afraid of the scolding from the dark. He just wanted a little rest and a chance to stand still for a bit. He heard Dilip *Da*'s voice. 'Here! Here!' It was cautious like the breath of a snake. As his eyes got adjusted to the darkness, he could sense slight movements on his left. 'Everybody there?' The man called all of them by name one by one—Safiul and Amina *Bibi* from Birati, Naran Pal from Dumdum, and so on. 'Everything okay?' And then, as if to make things easier by joking a little, he kept his eyes on Anupam's and said, 'Bilu, Bimal Mondal from Belgharia'.

Naren *Da* would have lived if he did not cross the limit. He became a member of the group of Biswanath Banerjee in the area that belonged to Sujit *Da*, and he even challenged him. He advertised himself as an honest man, found fault with the municipal tender and every other thing and even spoke ill about Anupam's relationship with Sujit *Da* in the party meetings. It could not be tolerated anymore.

'But why did you do it so openly on the platform?'

It was hard for Anupam to explain. He had followed Naren *Da* from Bidhan Nagar but did not get the slightest chance to do it and then he was compelled, perhaps by mistake, provoked by Somu, to do it. They had a plan: after Naren *Da* would get down to the station, they would take him to the factory shed. It was planned that Bulbul would be ready with the car. But somehow Naren *Da* sensed it as soon as the train had entered Belgharia, and jumped from the train, shouting, 'Save me, save me!'

They had to move to their right on Dilip *Da*'s order. They came down from the road to the arable land. Fog gathered at a distance from them. One or two crackers went off somewhere, perhaps for some religious festival.

'Dilip, I presume?'

Someone called from the field. The man suddenly came out of the dark. He wore a *lungi* and a shirt with long sleeves. He said, 'Out of danger now'.

Another cracker. It was a signal. The man said, 'If you need to run, always keep to the left. But no trouble for you anymore. No, you don't have to walk from now on. There will be a helicopter.' *Helicopter*? Seeing Anupam surprised, the man said again, 'Helicopter means bicycle. The carrier will be large enough to sit. Two can sit comfortably on that.'

Frogs croaked somewhere. Some birds flew flapping wings over their heads. Bamboo leaves touched upon their bodies and heads. Once his father along with the companions came out from that room in Churamonkathi after dark then they had walked through the darkness of the paddy fields, the footpath and the thorns of acacia trees. According to father, they had lost the measure of time. They only sat once to have a little *chira*, bananas and water, and then walked again. *This cold of the late winter could overwhelm even a tiger*—father used to say. In such a cold, father only had a cheap wrapper, bought for him once by an uncle. Was Anupam feeling the cold? Or the others? The woman and her son who were with him from Dumdum—were they feeling cold? After a long time, he thought of them. Should he call them? But how could he recognise them among those bodies under the sheets sitting on the back seats of the bicycles?

It was planned that Somu would thrust the muzzle against Naren *Da*. His job was to follow Naren *Da* closely. Anupam was not supposed to come to the front. His task was to remain close to them after getting down to the platform and to save the situation if Somu and Paltu got into any trouble. But sometimes even well-devised plans did not work. Did father ever think of leaving the country? They indeed regarded Darimagura as their home, and their family flourished there with all the agricultural lands. But how did Naren *Da* get wind of it before the train entered Belgharia station? He should not have sensed it anyhow. Probably Somu lost his cool because of the heavy crowd.

The bicycles halted one by one all of a sudden.

'What happened?'

Two men, covered with sheets, stood there. 'It's still clear,' they said and asked for money. Anupam should not have asked it, yet he got a little impatient and said, 'How far from here?' He was not sure whether the man heard him; he just turned his head and had a look at him.

The bicycle jerked violently at times as it moved through the holes and the occasional uphills. Sometimes a torchlight flashed before them. Sometimes there were sounds of rustling dry leaves, and sometimes one or two birds woke up, perturbed. Except for these things, sleep prevailed over things. They could see sudden houses, almost ground-touching straw-roofs and hear distant sounds abruptly coming to life. Anupam felt that he had been floating with those sounds. What hour of the night it was, who knew? He heard Dilip *Da*'s hushed voice, just like the foggy moon— 'Go down to your left from the road. No, don't run. The river is just ahead of you.' *River*? Anupam realised that the land was descending into a slope. Dilip *Da* said that it was River Ichhamati.

His father had to cross the Kapotaksha river. He, too, had been surprised after coming through so many bushes and agricultural lands. The middleman told them, 'You need to cross the river. The boat will be near the bank—a *tabure-boat*.'

'What's a *tabure-boat*?' Anupam asked. He came to know that it was a boat with a roof-like cover, used for carrying passengers. It was the Masila border, the last point of Pakistan at the village Masila. The Kapotaksha river was just beyond that village, and India was at the other side of the river. But they did not cross the river horizontally, rather went north from Masila to the village Kalipur. From the *tabure-boat* father had noticed for the first time that the moon in the sky moved just like a boat—the more one wanted to go far away beyond the border, the more it would accompany one with splashing sounds.

Anupam came down a little through the river bank and was surprised to see the boat. *Just this one for so many people?* He noticed the two men in uniform and realised that they were from BSF. They were counting the heads—one, two, three, four. There were a few others like Dilip *Da*, and it meant that there were several parties. One of them suddenly started quarrelling with a BSF soldier. The soldier raised his gun. 'Get down, get down—!'

Anupam felt a little tremor inside his chest. He got angry with that middleman who had taken Rs 700 per head and now acted as if he had got not a single penny.

Anupam saw Dilip *Da* standing at a little distance from the gun-yielding soldier and realised that this was a daily ritual. From the other side came the noise of a cracker accompanied by the flash of torchlight. Anupam already knew the meaning of this. It meant that the line was clear and they might proceed. This was their chance. As soon as Dilip *Da* saw the light, he moved to solve the problem. He scolded the middleman and tried to reason with the soldier by saying that it was really a relative, but the demand for a discount on two people was a bit unreasonable from the middleman's point. He requested, 'Please let one of them go,' and then he started using filthy words to the middleman, which, Anupam realised, was an attempt to soften the heart of the BSF soldier and to get the permission to leave with the boat as early as possible.

As the boat left the western bank of the Ichhamati and started moving towards the east, Anupam turned back. He saw that the descending fog was covering everything from the river to the bushes at the back, the houses, the arable fields and the garden. He asked, as if to himself, 'Where shall we land then?' Nobody knew if anyone heard his words. There was only one sound—the splashing of a never-ending water.

Father also came to India by a boat. The *tabure-boat* stopped near a cremation ground in the village Kalipur where a dead body was still burning. There was a lot of smoke, and the BSF watchtower stood tall over that smoke. They came to the hand of the Indian middleman from the Pakistani middleman. The Indian middleman wanted to know, 'Could you bring something from your country?' Then they left the mango garden to the footpath and then to the mango garden again and to the arable lands. The Kapotaksha river, *tabure-boat*, the border, Churamonkathi beyond the border, the journey by bus from Magura, the turning at Vaina—all were left behind. Left behind were the village Darimagura, the houses, the yard, the verandas, the guava and betel nut trees, the straw-roofed buildings, the floor, the broken ovens. The yellow sun was rising from the side of Darimagura they had left yesterday. Slowly the fog was clearing up. When father thought of turning his head to have a look for the last time at the river and the cremation ground, the Indian middleman uttered, 'There, that's the bus, that's the Boyra bus stand. Take bus number 92; it will take you to Bongaon station. You'll get the train to reach Calcutta from there.' Someone had written in a letter to Grandmother: 'All of you will survive if you can come here. Just cross the border somehow—'.

Anupam noticed that the night had its own sounds, or perhaps a unique soundlessness, as he was experiencing now. He could hear some distant conversations amidst the continuous sound of the crickets and the blinking of the fireflies. He seemed to hear the sound of a train, of the whistle, of the whirring of the wheels and see eyes filled with wonder upon the window.

As the boat dropped them upon the eastern bank of the Ichhamati, again they had to ride bicycles, their private 'helicopters'. Again, the same experiences—the bamboo groves descending from both sides, holes on the ground, dried leaves, sudden flashing of torchlights, the shadowy figures and whispers. All the bicycles would stop sometime; Anupam would spend so many months, so many years. It was, as if, he was in that village Darimagura, that little crossing at Vaina, Churamonkathi, in the shadowy darkness, and Dilip *Da* would say, 'We've reached there, nothing to worry anymore. We shall go to Satkhira bus stand after the night, and from there you can go wherever you want.'

It was not an agricultural land but a garden where they had to land. The bicycles stopped one by one. There were some mango, jamun and other trees, and two or three empty rooms. Dilip *Da* said, 'You may sit or lie down a bit if you like till dawn. There is a pond, you may wash your hands and feet if you feel like.' That immediately reminded Anupam of his *chappal*. It still had the stain of blood even after washing so many times. Blood. Though it was hard to identify if someone was not already aware of. Anupam wanted to throw it away when the stain did not go. But for Abinash, it was a bad idea, for it might remain as a clue—a proof against him. Who knows, perhaps the police dogs or something like that. There should be no evidence.

Anupam had no doubt that the stories he had heard from his father in childhood came to his dreams. These were the dark bodies, the shadows, the people seen through the wet glass window. He could see only their movements, the procession of the silent shadowy forms.

When Anupam shook off the drowsiness and stood up, he found that there was a slight rain with a light drizzling sound. He suddenly woke up to reality in the darkness of the afternoon. Dilip *Da* said, 'The Satkhira bus stand is nearby. My duty will be over once you reach there—'.

'Are you from India?' Asked a dark-skinned, round-eyed man in *lungi* and rubber shoes.

'Why do you ask?'

Dilip *Da* had left long ago after dropping him at the bus stand. He had shown him the buses for going to Jessore and Magura. The luxury buses stood in a row and inside them tape recorders were played even at these early hours.

'It's clear that you are from India. Please come here.'

A smoke rose from the left side. At his front and back, a couple of buses roared. Anupam saw the woman with her son, who came with him from Dumdum, standing in front of a bus and speaking to someone. She turned to this direction once, and then the son too followed her. Before entering the bus, she turned her head again to look at Anupam. Did she say something? Or smiled a bit? Someone shouted, 'Magura town –.'

'Who sent you? Abinash from Belgharia, isn't it? You worked for Sujit *Babu*, didn't you?'

'No, I mean—I—'

'Your real name is Anu—Anupam Mondal, isn't it? Don't you have the stain of blood in your *chappal*?'

Who wrote that letter? Father used to speak about it a lot. It was written: 'All of you will survive if you can come here. Just cross the border somehow. 'It was written: This is your own country—.'

There was, as if, a little bend in the darkness. The night was thinly moonlit. The fog spread over the paddy fields and the houses. It was, as if, Anupam was looking through the window. There was an unruly wind with water droplets, wetting the glass. There was only a tender darkness, assuming the shadowy forms of some hands, some feet, waists, bellies... There was only walking—walking from a small road to a bigger one, to bus stand, to station. The green patch was outside the window. They moved from one ground to another, from one paddy field to another, from one house to another and from one country to another. And border! Kapotaksha, Ichhamati. They moved from one river to another...

☙

Translated by Soumya Sundar Mukherjee

A school teacher of English, Soumya Sundar Mukherjee has done his M.A. from Vidyasagar University and is now pursuing his PhD at the same institution. He is particularly interested in tales of dystopia and high fantasy, of supernatural horror and Lovecraftian monsters.

Border

Devi Prasad Sinha

No sooner had the whistles of the BSF and the barking of the street dogs evaporated in the thin air around the peepal tree, than Haroun whispered, 'Run, you scoundrel, run'. Cowering under the long grasses and thorny shrubs, their veins were stretched to the limits, just as the sprinters waiting for the sound of the rifle shot. In their hearts the weaving machine went up and down, up and down—up in the sky the lit-up piece of pumpkin floated and gradually entered inside the open sack in the clouds—fog-like darkness covered the paddy fields in front. This is the time, this moment, run scoundrel, run, otherwise it will be late forever. Inside the torn *lungi* Rajab Ali's phallus is swelling up like the sail of a boat, partially from fear, partially from anxiety and the rest from the perennial protest of sexuality confronting death—run, run, clear the border in a single attempt. Rajab and his companions spring from the forests and started to run through the middle of the paddy fields.

The paddy field was not too big; along the middle of the field within every few hundred metres were dug concrete posts—that is the border. In daylight, people on either side can talk loudly to that of the other, but now when darkness has smeared itself on Rajab's body like a layer of cow dung, so impossibly long, impenetrable has become this little path—as if someone is pulling a piece of rubber continuously from both the ends—no matter how much he runs, the path goes for eternity. Rajab's knees are giving away in an effort to run, under the huge raindrops, sweat flowed down his whole body, inside his chest the train is running over the Saraighat bridge and deafened his ears, the eyeballs will pop out of the sockets this moment. *Oh Allah! How far is it?* Yet the pole of the border pulled by destiny keeps on receding to the distance. The mud sprayed above with the pressure of the limbs. Blades of paddy cut through Rajab's body in stripes. Suddenly he remembers that he had *maka* fish curry in the afternoon; now those fish danced in his stomach with a bliss of vengeance, he felt an intense urge to shit. *Scoundrel! Is this the time to shit?* Nearby, somewhere an infant cried out. *Shut up! shut up! throttle that bastard*! Up there was a thin film of white clouds over the light of the stars, and finding the right moment, from the darkness of the sack, jumped out the slice of the moon. That light, that light like a shrill cry, tore apart and penetrated Rajab Ali's body running along the paddy field. Did one hear the sound of a whistle somewhere? Some people are running towards this direction from the other side, Rajab can not decide whether to go forward or retreat by taking to the heels. Not being able to decide, he stands immobile in the middle of the paddy fields, droplets of sweat shinning on the tip of his nose. Where are you running away, you *behenchod*? The cold iron of the rifle reared up its hood as a snake. The hood of the snake swung looking at the torch and so at that time, the moon, stars, clouds and the sheaf of the paddy became motionless for a moment. Stopping, they were waiting for the sound of the bullets.

Thereafter, that slice of moon swam and crossed over from this side to that side of the sky, and Rajab Ali's corpse lay down on the spongy mud throughout the night under the subdued light of the stars.

At dawn, after the moon set, tired of swimming, when the stars were falling like the stale flower petals, and there was a tinge of blue in the pallor of the sky and the earth filled up with peaceful and calm light like that of an aged *ghee*, Rajab Ali sat up on the mud. A few birds were flying in the sky, the sheaves of paddy were swinging lightly in the breeze and the world was still noiseless in sleep.

On leaving behind the partition post and walking ahead along the ridges one will come across a pond. The colour of the pond water is moss green; in the centre, a couple of water lilies have bloomed. In this auspicious moment, nobody is there at the bank of the pond. Rajab's vest and *lungi* are smeared with blood and mire. A morsel of puffed rice and a little money is there in the knot of his *lungi*, Rajab collects leaves and keeps the puffed rice and money on the heap carefully. He undresses himself, washes the clothes he wore in the pond water and leaves them to dry on the grass. Then he jumped into the pond, immerses himself up to his head and takes a bath by scrubbing himself repeatedly till the black blood congealed right under his chest got washed off completely. Rajab readies himself for a new day and comes out of the pond, the eastern horizon brimming with the blood washed off from his body. Rajab Ali spread out his legs and sitting beside his drying *lungi*, chewing *muri* noisily, is looking all around him. The ridged pathway comes and merges itself with a higher concrete road. Village Habibpur stands at the long end of the dusty and gravelly road with coconut trees, betel nut trees and straw roofs amid bamboo groves—with small huts with mud-plastered courtyards. The only minaret of the mosque in the village can faintly be seen from here. There is no habitation in these parts. Some grassy land for the grazing of cow and goats and some marshy land. Haroun will come here around dusk. He has to keep waiting here for him. Unless Haroun comes, nothing will happen.

Where the concrete road has gone and merged with the horizon, just above that, inside the guts of the hanging, glowing sun, did something move? Rajab is looking with sharp eyes. His naked body has gradually dried up by that time, a drop or two of water from his hair still flowing down to his shoulders and back. When the shadows gradually separate themselves from the body of the sun, Rajab understands, not one but two shadows. And the two shadows are coming this way following the concrete road. Rajab puts his hand on his wet *lungi* lying on the road. A bird flew above his head and towards the horizon emitting a shrill cry. The shadows are gradually taking the shape of human figures. Now it is clearly understood that one is a male and another female. The male is carrying and bringing something on his head and there is an infant in the arms of the woman. Rajab stands up and wraps the wet *lungi* around his waist. The couple was leaving the concrete road and was coming down towards the pond. The nagging cry of the infant indicated that it was hungry. In an exact opposite corner to Rajab, the man reached the other side of the pond and kept his shoulder's burden down on the grass. The woman squatted on the grass, removed the sari on her chest and started giving her breast to the infant. Rajab could not take away his eyes from the pair of breasts looking like ripe coconuts. The woman looked at Rajab from top to bottom still giving her breasts to the infant and turned away to sit in an oblique way. The infant stopped crying. The man went down to the pond, washed his hands and feet well, sprinkled water on his face and shoulders, took a fistful of water inside his mouth, gargled it and threw it back to the pond. Rajab lits a bidi after so long. The man came up from the pond and while drying his hand and feet with the gamchha, told the woman something. It seemed that the woman turned her face and showed him Rajab. But by then, Rajab Ali lost his interest in the family.

Apart from the occasional ripples in the pond created by the fish, and the erratic flights of the birds from one branch to another, there was no event on the earth, neither was there any enthusiasm , right now at this moment. Rajab sits on the grass snugly and starts to smoke a bidi with deep pleasure. It is shadowy and the breeze is blowing gently, his eyes should have shut in comfort, maybe he would have also slept, but there is a discomfort in wearing wet *lungi*; more than that a burning sensation in his scrotum due to an ant bite kept him awake. He loosens his *lungi* and maddeningly searched the ant, and found it too, trying to escape by crossing the forest-like hair growth on his legs. In the bliss of vengeance, Rajab grips the ant between his two fingers and brings it in front of his eyes. While seeing the restlessness of the imprisoned ant, he utters—*bastard*—thereafter presses it between his fingers and threw it into the air. The burning sensation did not allay till then, yet he made an effort to lie down on the grass. He still has to spend a lot of time here. Just as he was getting ready to disarm and relax, right at that moment, on hearing someone clear his throat very close to him, looked up.

Gopen Nama calls in a modest voice—*Miyan Bhai, O Miyan Bhai!*

Whatever Gopen may seem from afar, now from close proximity one identifies him as a very modest, courteous, ever affrighted and ever anxious individual. Rajab retorts with irritation—'Why, what do you want? Why are you unnecessarily nagging *Miyan Bhai-Miyan Bhai?*'

Gopen's sooty set of teeth along with gums revealed itself in a condescending smile.

'Won't I get a bidi, *Miyan Bhai?*'

Whatever was there in stock has been exhausted, also there was no shop nearby. Rajab had a very limited stock, that could just sustain him till the next morning when he reaches a shop on the other side. Whatever it be, if anyone asks for a bidi—to say no was not in his habit. He shelled out a bidi with a sulky face.

Matchsticks were already there in his pocket. He lit the bidi, inhaled it deep for a couple of times, again flashed out his gums to say—'Where is *Miyan Bhai*'s home? Is it here?'

Without waiting for an answer Gopen answered back, 'I happen to be Gopen Nama, my home was in Itkhola, five miles away from Habibpur station'. 'There is,' he points out with his finger, 'my family'.

Rajab exchanged a glance with the family. But that did not create a ripple on the waterbed of the pond. Rajab, on the other hand, started yawning. He said in an irritated voice, 'Yes understood. Your name is Gopen Nama, you stayed at Itkhola. If you do not have anything more to say, then you go and sit with your family, let me have some sleep'.

Gopen is never an easy nut to crack. He badly needed someone to speak with, he had a long night ahead. He did not take Rajab's annoyance to any consideration. Gopen talks fast; when he talks, the veins of his cheeks throb. Repeating a sentence twice is his bad habit. Gopen kept his gums pronounced and asked, 'Are you angry *Miyan*? Tell me, with whom shall I share my tales of grief? Have left the ancestral house behind, will cross the border, will cross the border'.

Gopen paused a bit, tried to understand Rajab's reaction, then, as if a little relieved, continued further, 'My younger brother has left the country six months ago, he says, "You fool, you still sit fixedly applying glue to your ass, run while it's still time". Parul says the right thing to me, "You will get neither food nor honour here. You will die yourself and you will kill my Ganesh too!"'

Gopen now spoke in a slightly lower voice. 'You seem to be a good man, that is why I tell this to you. O *Miyan*, the people of your community did not allow us to stay anymore.'

'The Muslims…'

'Damn the Muslims!'

Gopen halted. He did not expect this. He kept quiet for some time and again resumed, 'We Hindus…'

'Damn the Hindus'!

'In Bangladesh…'

'Damn my Bangladesh!'

'To go to India…'

'Damn India!'

Gopen thereafter had to stop. He kept on looking at Rajab with a frown and tried to understand his thought but failed. Rajab was looking at the sky resting his head on the folded arm. The sun had managed to complete one fourth of its diurnal course today. Does the piercing blue light of the day shelter the eyes of Rajab? Like the stick of the blind man? Gopen tried for the last time—'You didn't tell anything about yourself *Miyan*. Are you too going to cross the border? Cross the border?'

'Fuck the border!'

Had Rajab Ali wanted to prolong the conversation with Gopen, or had he wanted to tell the matter differently, then what would he have said?

He would have told that he was Rajab Ali, the Rajab Ali of Guwahati, who pulled the rickshaw day-long, then late at night kept the rickshaw back at his master's house and had toddy at Kanchi's inn. He would then totter back to his broken home, lit dimly with a lamp, above the mound where his two sons Moidul and Motin and his wife Sakina sat waiting for him, keeping the rice bowl in front of them.

Maybe they are still waiting for him, or maybe they aren't, Sakina might have eloped with some other rickshaw puller to wait in front of a different lamp for another night, Moidul and Motin might be washing cars in some garage and sleeping in the same place. Once considered as an outsider, he was thrown inside a truck like cattle at the border on the basis of suspicion, and from there he was pushed into this side of the border. What could he do other than damning the border, could a few poles in the middle of the paddy fields turn his intense desire of homecoming into a lie? Were these few stumps a greater truth than Sakina, Moidul, Motin and the half-illuminated lamp-lit, dilapidated room? That the border is there, and therefore, he has to cross it. For how many more years would the legs of a nationless man be stuck at the border?

Not uttering a single word, Rajab Ali turns over and closes his eyes. Gopen went back to his family frustrated. Shadows and gentle breeze, the chirping of birds and humming of crickets gradually became indistinct in Rajab's ears till they merged into silence.

Rajab's sleep got suddenly interrupted with an unknown irritation. His body did not move at all. He lay down still and riveted his eyes in all directions to see all around. His sixth sense alerted him to a possible danger nearby. But so near. He spotted five or six shadowy figures coming down his way from the concrete road. They had guns and *lathis* in their hands. Fuck the B.D.R buggers. Rajab rolls his body noiselessly and takes refuge in the dense, thorny bushes, not even bothering the thorns piercing his hands, chest and back. He narrowed his eyes and saw Parul, with the baby at her waist, get up and move backwards to the margins of the pond. Gopen with folded hands was trying to tell something to those shadowy figures, and fell down on the ground with a violent slap on his cheeks; laathi and kicks were showering on his cowered, womb-like body. Parul, along with her baby, was as if floating away, up into the concrete road by a few jerky pulls. Upon her hands, shoulders, waist and *anchal* of her sari, the victory flag of the B.D.Rs fluttered. Her womanhood was bordered with lathis, guns and violent lust. When the infant at her lap cried again, it was thrown away towards Gopen, who by then was following like a dog, and gradually this bizarre caravan disappeared towards the horizon, throwing up dust. The sun was then exactly above the pond, the fishes as if were no longer moving, there was murmuring sound of wind in the trees, the birds were drowsily resting on the branches.

When Gopen came back alone, the sun was about to set. Rajab was sitting on the bank of the pond. Gopen could see Rajab, but was not looking at him. He put his head between his knees and sat still on the other bank, till all the stars appeared in the sky, till the slice of moon covered in the shroud of clouds laughed at him lilting in the pond water, and Haroun came wrapped in a thick quilt smoking a bidi. By that time, eight or ten more shadowy figures had congregated at the bank of the pond.

Haroun came, counted the heads silently and then asked, 'Is everyone present? Right now sit silently, you fuckers, we shall cross over exactly at twelve at night. Today is an ideal day, there are clouds in the sky.'

No sooner had the whistles of the BSF and the barking of the street dogs evaporated in the thin air around the peepal tree, than Haroun whispered, 'Run, you scoundrel, run'. Cowering under the long grasses and thorny shrubs, their veins were stretched to the limits, just as the sprinters waiting for the sound of the rifle shot. This is the time, this moment, run scoundrel, run, otherwise it will be late forever, run, run, clear the border in a single attempt. Rajab and his companions sprung from the forests and started to run through the middle of the paddy fields.

Along the middle of the field within every few hundred metres were dug concrete posts—that is the border. So impossibly long, impenetrable has become this little path— as if someone is pulling a piece of rubber continuously from both the ends—no matter how much he runs, the path goes for eternity. Rajab's knees were giving away in an effort to run, under the huge raindrops, sweat flowed down his whole body, inside his chest the train was running over the Saraighat bridge and deafened his ears, the eyeballs would pop out of the sockets this moment. Oh Allah! How far is it? Yet the pole of the border pulled by destiny kept on receding to the distance. The mud sprayed above with the pressure of his feet. Blades of paddy cut through Rajab's body in stripes, up there was a thin film of white clouds over the light of the stars, and finding an opportunity from the darkness of the sack, jumped out a slice of the moon. That light, that light like a shrill cry tears apart and penetrates Rajab Ali's body. Did one hear the sound of a whistle somewhere? The cold steel of the gun reared up its head like the hood of a snake and started swinging, looking at the drop of sweat shining on the lip of Rajab's nose. Again, time–moon–stars–clouds– the sheaf of paddy stopped for a moment. They stopped and waited for the sound of the bullet.

Thereafter, that slice of moon swam and crossed over from this side to that side of the sky throughout the night, and Rajab Ali's corpse lay down on the spongy mud under the subdued light of the stars. At dawn after the moon set, tired of swimming, when the stars were falling like the stale flower petals and there was a tinge of blue in the pallor of the sky and the earth filled up with tranquil light like that of aged ghee, Rajab Ali sat up on the mud. The world was still noiseless in sleep.

Beyond the pathway is the pond. Parul sat motionless by the bank, the infant on her lap. When Rajab had picked up his body smeared in blood and mire and had come to stand by the periphery of the pond, Parul had looked up. But was she seeing? Rajab was not in a condition to see all that, to understand or pay attention to those, he opened his vest and *lungi*, washed them with care and put them to dry on the grass. Then he dived into the pond and he immersed himself in the pond water upto his head, bathed by rubbing himself thoroughly till the congealed black blood right under his chest was completely washed away. Rajab prepared himself for a new day and came out of the pond, the eastern horizon was then splashed with the blood washed away from his body.

Rajab had tied the same wet *lungi* around his waist and had started munching *muri*. Suddenly on hearing an infant wail, he turned to see Parul sitting in the same manner for a long time. Rajab took some time to think. Yesterday, almost the entire day there was nothing to eat. Today, right at this moment, if this bit of *muri* is shared, how will the day go on? Yet in front of these pairs of hungry gaze, food would refuse to go down his throat. Damn it, all sorts of problems have to be with me! Irritated, Rajab gets up and walks towards Parul.

The wild shrubbery behind Parul had taken a bright yellow look; it's swinging in the breeze, where the grasshoppers and butterflies fly around. The road had gradually come down to a low gradient covered with grasses and thorns, where the twilight of the morning was busy playing a crisscross game. Parul's sari, torn into shreds, was trying hard to somehow cover her young fleshly body. The nipple of her left breast was inside the mouth of the supine infant. The infant was frequently crying out, removing its mouth from its mother's breast shorn of milk.

Standing in front of her, Rajab passed on the *muri* and said—'Hold! Eat, feed your son too. The way he is yelling, o my God!'

There was not much change in her unaffected eyes, her hand, too, was not thrust in front. The infant stopped crying, turned its head and saw Rajab with awe. And Rajab saw maps drawn on Parul's lips, on her face, created by an intersection of countless straight lines with blood as a result of harrying. Rajab mellowed down his tone and said, 'Take. You cannot stay without eating your whole life. Take'.

It was the infant who first thrust its hands towards the morsel. A little later, Parul. Mother and son munched on *muri*, Rajab sat beside and lit a bidi. The pond water was slightly trembling in the wind, the water lilies were bending a little and enjoying the caress of the sun. One kingfisher swooped down and flew away upwards, a silver fish twisting inside its beaks. This morning was not yet familiar with sin.

Parul went up to the pond. The infant's wailing had stopped; it was gesturing wildly and talking to its mother. Parul dispersed the water with her hands and took a mouthful. She made her baby drink and wiped its mouth, hands and feet. Thereafter, she splashed water on her face and eyes. Drawing patterns of water on grass with her feet, she came up to sit in her own old place. Rajab saw that Parul was no longer looking at him, she had riveted her eyes and kept them in the other direction. The infant was busy crawling and catching butterflies in the grass.

Rajab broke the silence. 'What, will you cross the border today?'

Parul still kept her face turned away.

Rajab again said, 'With this infant? Will you be able to?'

Parul stared blankly at some other direction and did not say anything.

Rajab threw away the bidi into the pond and said, 'Your husband, that hermaphrodite bastard had escaped yesterday by crossing the border at an opportune moment'.

Parul turned and looked this way, sunlight shone in her eyes brightly.

'What is it to you? Why are you troubled?'

Then after a short pause she added, 'He will wait for me on the other side of the border. I know'.

Within Parul's words were hidden a lot of tears, much anger, desperation and fear. She had come across a long dark way, perhaps had more to tread on. He sees in the implication of her words, the horrible guffaw of darkness, sees in Parul's eyes the reflection of his own gloom.

Rajab said slowly, 'When did the bloody fuckers leave you? Today morning?'

Parul again turned away her face. Her face was burning like the corpse at funeral pyre. In order to remove himself from the burning heat of that face Rajab turned away his eyes. Inside the belly of the soft crispy sun hanging above the dam road one or two things started moving. When the shadows gradually separated themselves from the body of the sun, Rajab understood that three individuals were coming this way along the concrete road. Rajab stood up. Those three people came to the edge of the road and were coming down this way. A middle-aged man, a woman past her youth and an adolescent girl. The man had a big trunk decorated with leafy patterns on his head, in the hands of the women were big jute bags. They kept their burden on the other side of the pond and were looking all around, panting with surprised eyes. They saw Rajab and Parul too, discussed among themselves God knows what, laughed aloud. The lady past her youth, opened her bag, took out a sheet of cloth and spread it on the grass, then she sat on the sheet cross-legged, beside her the adolescent girl. The man went down into the pond and washed his hands and legs properly, applied water on his face and shoulders, gargled his mouth with a fistful of water and threw it into the pond. When the man came out from the pond and was patting dry his body with a *gamcha*, the aged woman past her youth had by that time taken out foods from her bag and arranged them on the sheet.

When you are hungry, you should not look at others eating, it only increases one's own hunger. Rajab removed his eyes and stretched himself on the grass. Sometimes the fishes were jumping out of the pond and there was the indecisive flights of the birds—except this in the world there was no event, no excitement at this moment. There was a faint murmuring breeze—his eyes almost close in comfort.

In the shadowy space just before sleeping, he was watching Parul spoiling her baby in love.

Rajab's sleep got suddenly interrupted with an unknown irritation. His body did not move at all. He lay down still and riveted his eyes in all directions to see all around. His sixth sense alerted him to a possible danger nearby. But so near. He spotted five or six shadowy figures coming down his way from the concrete road. They had guns and *lathis* in their hands, erect as the male organ. He sat up with the support of his hands, and saw Parul sing songs in low voice to put the infant to sleep. He jumped in front of Parul without a noise and dragged her shocked into the bushes at the back. The *children of the whore* have come. The suddenness of the event shocked Parul so much that she could not even resist. She tried to say something, Rajab slapped her, he whispered, ' Shut up! Want to die?'

Behind the bushes they lay down side by side, their bodies touching each other and saw the two girls go backwards and backwards till they reached the margin of the bank. The man folded his hands and was trying to plead with the shadowy figures, and then suddenly fell down on the ground with a violent slap on his cheeks; laathi and kicks were showering on his cowered, womb-like body. The girls were as if floating away, up into the concrete road by a few jerky pulls. Upon their hands, shoulders, waists and *anchal*, the victory flag of the B.D.Rs fluttered. Their womanhood was bordered with laathis, guns and violent lust. The man kept on following the group like a dog and gradually this strange moving scene blended into the horizon. The sun was exactly above the pond, the fishes were no longer jumping above the waters, there was the murmuring sound of the breeze on the trees.

Suddenly an air of thrill blew down Rajab's spine once he realised that Parul was densely latched to his body. Parul looked at him, looked down but did not make any effort to remove herself. Rajab put his lips on the tips of Parul's breasts. She turned red. The infant put a finger inside its mouth and looked surprised at the intense, pathetic coitus of a primitive couple inside the bushes.

Then they both sat on the bank of the pond side by side, silently, until all the stars twinkled in the sky, the slice of the sun covered itself with a cloth of clouds and smiled at the faces swinging in the pond water and Haroun came puffing a bidi. By that time, another eight or ten shadowy figures had gathered round the bank of the pond.

Haroun said, 'Now sit silently you bastards, right at midnight we shall cross over. This day is a good one—there are clouds in the sky'.

No sooner had the whistles of the BSF and the barking of the street dogs evaporated in the thin air around the peepal tree, than Haroun whispered, 'Run, you fool, run'. Cowering under the long grasses and thorny shrubs, their veins were stretched to the limits, just as the sprinters waiting for the sound of the rifle shot up in the sky. The lit-up piece of pumpkin floated and gradually entered inside the open sack in the clouds—fog-like darkness had covered the paddy fields in front. This is the time, this moment, run scoundrel, run, otherwise it will be late forever, run, run, clear the border in a single attempt. Rajab and his companions sprung from the forests and started to run through the middle of the paddy fields.

So long, so impossibly long is this border, as if a slice of rubber is being pulled by someone continuously from both ends. Rajab's knees were giving away in an effort to run, under the huge raindrops, sweat flowed down his whole body, inside his chest the train was running over the Saraighat bridge. Oh Allah! How far is it? The mud sprayed above with the pressure of the feet. Blades of paddy cut through Rajab's body in stripes, and his body and the stump of the border gradually moved backward and backward with the pull of destiny. Just at that time the slice of a moon came out of the sack of darkness in one jump—that light, like a sharp cry tore Rajab into two parts. Somewhere the whistle blew and the gun's cold steel looked at the bright drop of sweat at the tip of Rajab's nose and reared its hood. Rajab Ali stood still like a stupefied person, a child wailed out loudly, somewhere very near him. The hood turned away and the cloud above became a horrible huge jackal and again gobbled up the moon.

Rajab, at that moment, had sprung into the paddy fields and therefore heard the sound of the bullets. Right in front of him in the dark paddy fields, something very heavy fell with a tremendous thud and the infant cried out horribly, too loudly, and kept on crying. Rajab tried to scramble and stand up and tried to run ahead, and with an extreme fear discovered, that wail, that scream had clung to his feet. From corners there came sounds of whistle blowing, torches lit up here and there, there were more sounds of bullets, in the paddy fields one or two more bodies dropped down. Rajab tried all his life to pull free his leg but could not. How is it that there is so much force in a thin, emaciated tiny body? The stump of the border bares all its teeth and laughs in front of his eyes in the pale moonlight. The sound of the whistles comes nearer. Finding no way out, Rajab kicked the small bundle of darkness, kicked and removed it lying above his feet. And ran forward, kept on running.

The moon, tired of swimming, sets at one point of time. The stars drop like the petals of stale flowers, gently. The dull grey of the sky is smeared with a tinge of blue and the world fills up with a peaceful solitary light like that of an old ghee. Dawn comes into this side of the border.

ങ

Translated by Sharmistha Chatterjee

An Associate Professor of English at Aliah University, Kolkata, Sharmistha Chatterjee's area of interest includes, South Asian Literature, Translation studies, Post colonialism, Partition Literature, Eco criticism, Gender Studies, Modern Linguistics and English Language Teaching.

Photograph

Adhir Biswas

I was looking desperately for an important piece of paper under the bed. Suddenly, I came across the bill from Chabbighar. This was not what I had been looking for. Yet it was no less important. The memory of this bill was gradually being effaced from my mind. Whenever I had thought of the amount of money, I would have to spend for binding the photographs, I thought I would take the delivery next month on receiving my salary. Now I saw under the bed in a corner the bill in a yellow paper.

Last night I had thought I would retrieve the paper I was searching for. I had told *Khuku* about it, and she immediately said that there was no point in looking for it elsewhere since I had this habit of tucking every bit of paper down there.

I didn't make a fuss of it. The loan I had taken from the Co-operative, according to my calculation, was repaid in full the last month. But even this month the amount, Rs 337, was deducted, as I saw while receiving my salary. I shuttled between the cashier and the clerk of the Co-operative. There were quite a few gentlemen around, and so I exercised control over my mind for the time being.

Photograph

Since then, I have been searching for the pay-slips of the last twelve months. The search has been quite exhausting. Still, I am searching in suffocating earnest.

Inside the house all the women are laughing over something. I cannot pay attention to that now. Amid the roaring laughter, the mattress, the quilt and the pillows are scattered all over the bed, while I am on this never-ending search mission. The side pillow falls on the floor through the gap between the bed and the wall. But I refuse to give up. I am determined to go to the office today with a concrete proof. If my assumption is right, then...

I am feeling a rise in temperature in my ears as I search assiduously. I feel like bringing Khuku over here to this room, dragging her by the end of her sari and saying, 'Dig out my payslips, wherever they are.' I even moved a few steps towards her. On the table are the bundle of bidis and a matchbox. They catch my attention, but I ignore them. My all-out search has taken me down to the mat under the bed. And there is the yellow paper. I know this is not the thing I am looking for. I will go through it hurriedly and keep it back. But oh! What is it?

I, as a matter of fact, am actually sweating this winter morning. My hand is rough and dirty. With the 'bill' in my hand, I fall silent. My sisters-in-law have stopped laughing outside. I saw through my window Khuku shouting away a crow from the kitchen. I gulp down the sound of swallowing spit and get to think of my mother's photo-binding.

It was a long time back when this happened. It was I who offered to take four photographs of my mother taken at the time of her death from my elder brothers and get them enlarged and bound in beautiful frames. I thought of surprising everybody by doing this. I distinctly remember how Nabakumar took the snaps. My brothers had sent for a photographer from the town—a photographer of renown like Nabakumar. At that time mother had been ailing for a long time.

I very clearly remember: *Ma* was seated in a chair in front of the space where the husking-pedal was kept. She wore a *Katki* sari and had a deep red vermilion dot on her forehead. The mild winter sun made her blink. *Chhorda* and I were holding a cloth hiding bundles of jute-plant stalks, sacks containing cow dung cakes and heaps of leaves of bamboo plants and jackfruit trees. Nabakumar kept his camera on a stand and shouted 'one, two, three' from under a cloth-cover.

The date of delivery of the photograph was near. But we didn't care to take delivery and days went by. In course of time, we forgot all about it.

Mother's health condition deteriorated. Even after the lapse of the year, it did not occur to any of us that her photographs had to be brought from the studio. When we were leaving our country, it was my father who asked my eldest brother one day: 'Kalidas, did you bring your mother's photo?' *Dada* could not give a ready answer. 'Why should you bring it? You didn't care to hang her photo even when she was alive! It's all for the good!' father said.

That was the first time I saw *Dada* behave very uncomfortably. I had never seen a more helpless and guilty face of his. And he left home then and there on his bicycle without telling anybody anything. On his return, he said, 'I had been to the studio. Nabakumar said casually that he had thrown away the photograph long back. I told him I would pay him a lot of money, as much as he wanted.' While saying these words he was almost losing control over himself. I understood *Dada* was not exaggerating at all. He had implored Nabakumar to try to remember. He even reminded him that he took the snap a few days prior to Ayub Khan's distribution of handbills from an aeroplane after his promulgation of the martial law: the handbills contained the instruction to clean the jungle. Nabakumar could then remember. He said even if we came to his studio only a few days earlier, then...

Bhadro is the month of my birth. Mother passed away in *Poush*. *Ma*'s memory haunts me the most in the month before the Durga Puja. At this time our clothes, after a whole year, are spread in the sun. Oh, a large number of old clothes are spread on the floor in the sun: shirts, English pants and the monkey-caps of our childhood days. Mother would hold these clothes aloft and say, 'Look, this shirt is perfectly fine. Let Kanai grow up, your shirts and pants will fit him perfectly.' These dresses would smell nicely since they were taken out of an earthen vat.

Boudi spreads, even now, mother's *katkisari*, chemiz and the clothes meant for Goddess Laxmi, on the trunk or the mat to let those get warmth of the sun. It is, as if, the sun comes out only once in the month of *Bhadro*. And we feel it is not the sun but *Ma* herself comes back on this day, to fulfil the never-met desires of the members of our family.

Ma would often appear in our dreams. At night, during our dinner, we would mention those dreams. One night, *Boro Boudi* told us that in her dream mother came to the place around the tulsi plant, clad in her sari with the red fringes. She said, in the dream, 'The evening was passing by, unnoticed. So I myself came to light the lamp and the incense stick.'

Two months after my mother's demise, our niece was born. I heard *Kajal khurima* say: 'Ah, it's a pity (that *Ratan*'s mother did not live to see the child). She was not fortunate at all. She had the craving for a girl child.'

What *Kajal khurima* said, was indeed true. We are four brothers and we don't have a sister. We don't even have an aunt (father's sister). At Basana's birth almost every one of the locality said, 'Look, your mother is reborn.' Since then, we four brothers have been calling Basana '*Ma*'. Oh, how long I haven't called someone '*Ma*'!

The only memory we have of her of the last two–three months is: *Ma* is sitting in a chair. An earthen basin filled with burning material is at her feet. She is wearing the *Bhutani* coat that father had bought for her and sleeping with her head slanted to one side.

Ma could not even lie down properly during her last days. She was drowsy and couldn't sleep at all. Her tummy was like that of a tortoise. Her feet were swollen and had a shining look. If one pressed her feet with a finger, the place would sink, giving it the look of a hole.

Father gathered at the village market that *Ma* would become alright if we could get hold of a *Kaviraaj*. Since that day a bitter broth would be prepared by boiling various herbs. *Ma* was compelled to drink that concoction in empty stomach. At noon she would be given the arum porridge.

The *Kaviraaj* would prescribe many such recipes. When her medicine started having a large variety of new ingredients, we all thought that the accumulated water in her stomach would dry up. On our courtyard, slices of arum would be spread all over for drying. We had to go to the kitchen for our meals, dribbling through these slices on wicker-baskets.

Ma would sit on the veranda in front of our big room. Hanging her feet, she would sit on its edge. A black stone-made dinner plate would be kept there by her side. *Boudi* would come and pour on it the arum-porridge which contained no oil, salt or even sugar. I saw through the opening of the kitchen fence how *Ma* was swallowing her afternoon diet, keeping the fingers on her neck. It would go beyond the level of her tolerance; she would beg for a little tamarind from her daughter-in-law. She wanted it to get rid of the unbearable itching in her throat.

When I went to the village market with my father, I would approach the shops selling mixtures, *kadma* or the *tiley-khaja* from Radhanagar, but retreated with the paisa in my palms without buying a thing. It was as though I could buy these items at will, but would not, since *Ma* loved these delicacies.

Once *Ma* got an ear full of scolding from my father when she was about to buy *hawai mithai* from Pocha *Kaka* and then *Baba* sternly ordered all of us not to give her any money. I didn't get angry at his command, since we all wanted *Ma* to come round.

The *Kaviraaj* from Kundeswari felt *Ma*'s pulse and examined the inside of her lower eyelid and declared that after two more weeks of medication, *Ma* would be able to walk freely. On hearing this, I ran to my mother at once. I said I would not go to school that day. She didn't say anything much, but ran her fingers through my hair for quite some time. As I drew close to her body, I got the odour of her dead skin; her sari gave out foul smell. But that did not prevent me from hugging her tight.

'Oh, you boy, release me', *Ma* said smiling, 'I am feeling suffocated.' But I did not take any note of these protests. I had not touched her for so long! 'Do you remember, *Ma*, once when coming back from maternal grandpa's house, we were waiting at the Launch-ghat of Rajpur, our suitcase kept down on the ground, and you wept like a child?', I asked. Mother's eyeballs were raised like those of a blind person, and she was searching for her answer by touching my head, my eyes and ears, nose and fingers.

The earlier snap which Nabakumar had taken in front of the husking pedal room was anyway lost, but even the photos we brothers took of our dead mother by standing beside her body are not at home. The photos came with us in the box when we came away from that ancestral house and I myself took them to the binder.

Photograph

Our room is nicely furnished. There is a calendar hanging on the wall. The colour photo of Khuku and myself is within sight. Not the photograph alone, many other things of sweet memory are now within our reach.

I thought last month I would bring over mother's laminated photographs. Today is the first day of this month, but after paying up the loans and meeting other expenses, I have almost no money in hand. I know where Khuku keeps the keys of her almirah. I have the wedding ring and I have my wristwatch, too. I would pawn the watch, but keeping that a secret, I would tell them at home that it fell on the road and I took it to the watch-repairing shop.

Now I have the ring in my pocket. The watch is on my wrist. On my way to the office, I shall go to the studio. I didn't tell anyone. To find and match the address, I am scrutinising the some-years-old bill. On Thursday the shop remains closed. Today is the day of closure.

At night I don't feel like going back home. On alighting from the train, I am feeling a little cold. My eyes are burning. I am walking straight ahead like a forgetful man. I have a shoulder bag. I am feeling very cold now, although I have a wrapper on my body. In order to feel warm, I have hidden my nose under the wrapper and am breathing hot on my palms. The jungle is on either side of the muddy road. There is more jungle ahead. There is not a soul seen anywhere, neither in front of me nor behind. The electric lights I have left far behind. The fog and dense darkness have combined to make me press with hands both sides of my bosom. My body, after a time, feels quite heavy. If only my house were close, right here!

I was said to be weeping in a dream while asleep that night. Khuku pushed me repeatedly, but I didn't know. Then, when she cried loudly and shook me by the head, I opened my eyes. Tears came rolling down from her eyes. Within me were waves of cry. I kept looking at her for quite sometime. Khuku's face betrayed sympathy. 'What did I see, oh Khuku,' I said. Turning panicky, she asked, 'What was it?'

'I saw mother. This is the first time I got a glimpse of Ma; she was dying, keeping her hand on my head.'

The next morning, I told the story to all in detail. I then asked *Borda*, my eldest elder brother, 'What is the date today, *Dada*?'

Eldest sister-in-law said, '12 *Poush*.'

I don't know how bitterly I had wept in my dream. And I understand that I can't cry now, but in the region of my eyes I feel a kind of solidified, accumulated pain, which is rotating there.

This date we remember very well: 12 *Poush* 1368. It was a Friday. Twenty-five minutes past four in the morning.

Borda is looking forward absent-mindedly. Without lifting his eyes he says to me, 'Go, take your bath. And then send for a *Vaishnob* and give him a *sidhe*.'

The sun peeps through the blackberry tree. We are shifting our sitting positions to bask in the sun. *Chhorda*, my youngest elder brother, says, 'It's all fated. Our new house, your securing a job—*Ma* would have been overjoyed to see all this.'

Photograph

In front of me is sitting my second nephew. I stare at his figure. He was born three days after mother's death. He is Prosanto, and he would say in his childhood, 'I missed seeing granny by a whisker.'

All the members of our family come to the courtyard. It is thus, talking to one another, we stay close. I am looking at everybody's eyes and facial expressions. And I am watching my brothers with particular attention. If one of them tells me, 'Hey, Ratan, you took mother's photograph to the studio long back, has the man lost it, or what?' But nobody touches on the subject.

For a long while, *Ma* and our long-gone ancestral house have come back and been staying with us. I can visualise, by shutting my eyes, the *uttorponta*, the room of the husking-pedal, the dump, the wild parrot sitting on a branch of the Kashi-guava tree. I can also envisage the scene where my sister-in-law is arranging cow dung cakes and husks in the earthen pot containing fire for our mother. I also see in my mind's eye *Baba* putting charcoal cakes in the chillum and constantly blowing into it.

Chhorda tells me, 'Go, do as *Borda* has asked you. Keep this in mind, whenever you have a dream like this, you have to give a *Vaishnob* service, and only after that you can eat something.'

Khuku has a napkin in her hand and a clean cloth. She has drawn a veil on her head and followed me to the bank of the pond. I am going down to the ghat. It's very early in the morning. The fog is still floating in a random fashion on the surface of the pond. I am sitting on a stair, staring at the stretch of the water.

The bathing on that day at the river ghat comes back to my mind. Kajal auntie was standing up on the bank. I was wearing a pair of pants and a bunch of keys. That was my piece of a loin cloth. A branch of the *aash-seorah* tree came in sight. Sitting on the brink of the river, I kept my feet on the glittering sand and looked at the frisking of the tiny silvery fish. I was also watching the jute-laden boat proceed along the bank drawn by the boatmen. I sat at the ghat and played 'crossing the boxes' on the mud-mixed sand. I was drawing the face of goddess Kaali. Auntie was asking me urgently, 'Oh, Ratan, my son, take a quick dip.'

These calls are so full of affection! It is, as if, I knew instinctively that she would not scold me today even if I went on doing a series of mischiefs. She would not complain to father, either. Because a little while ago, treading along the path trodden by the sellers in the haat, *Baba* and *Dada* had taken *Ma* to the crematorium at Satdoa, accompanied by the locals. The pen meant for Kanai was dismantled and the carrying platform was prepared with bamboo. *Ma* was lying down on the platform wearing her *Bhutaani* coat. Her forehead had marks of sandalwood paste.

I was not allowed to go.

On the way, when the carriers proceeded a little after crossing the Battola, *Borda* told me, 'You aren't to go.'

I did not cry, but simply asked, 'Where are you taking *Ma*?'

'Taking her to a doctor.' Then, shedding his eyes, he told me, 'Go back, *Dada*.'

Whenever *Borda* addressed me endearingly, he would call me '*Dada*', and did not call my name. But at that moment I felt some kind of a pain. And just when this happened, Kajal auntie touched me. She had brought me along by hiding me under her apron string.

Today, sitting on the bank of the pond, I keep throwing brickbats, aiming at the hyacinth in the water. It produces a plop. On the surface of the water, shadows are quivering. Khuku, standing up on the bank of the pond, is repeatedly pestering me: 'Please hurry. Why have you been sitting, like a child, all this while?'

ଔ

Translated by Tapan Jyoti Bandyopadhyay

Tapan Jyoti Bandyopadhyay is retired professor of English, Vidyasagar University, West Bengal.

The Other Jews

Kapil Krishna Thakur

Right at the centre of platform no. 3 was this flowering *kamini* tree. Though not huge in stature, its top spread out like an umbrella, and in its shade was Brajabasi's seasonal fruit shop.

It was a hot, arid afternoon that made people feel parched and thirsty, and the dogs lay sprawled with their tongues lolling out. Having successfully sold three batches of cucumber since morning, Braja was hoping for some rest when Chenno's granny Harimati arrived.

'O Bejo, has the news reached you?'

'No, *Jethi*. What news?'

'People have come over from Boultali.'

'Really? Who?'

'Bishtu Pandit.'

'Bishtu *Khuro*!' Braja stared in amazement for some time at Harimati. 'Alone?'

'No, no. All of them have come together. They're sitting in front of your house. He told me, "Can you give this news to Bejo?" I thought, now who do I send this afternoon? So, I came myself.'

'Thank you, *Jethi*. Have a cucumber and sit here awhile?'

'Na, *Baba*, I have no teeth.' Harimati smiled a gap-toothed smile, the few remaining tobacco-stained teeth sitting like milestones of her age.'

'Then just sit here awhile, *Jethi*. There may come a few customers for these few remaining cucumbers. One for eight annas, two for a rupee. Will you be able to manage?'

Harimati gave a toothless grin again. 'You think your *Jethi* is the same as earlier! I can recognise the coins well now!'

Assured, Braja stood up. He called the neighbouring shop boy.

'Keep an eye, Moti, will you? *Jethi* will be here.'

The railway tracks were lined with the rows of huts. All people who had come over the border, were chased out of Bangladesh. Anyone who walks from Sealdah station along the Eastern Railway lines will be able to see thousands of such little shanties. Those who had arrived earlier had been able to grab the more convenient areas nearer the railway station. Among these lucky few was Brajabashi.

The road to his hut lay across the railway tracks. Repeated footfalls had worn down the defiant hardness of the cobblestones to a more amiable smoothness. Braja's hut was after about a dozen one along this route.

The huts were not very high, resembling in structure the igloos of the Eskimos. To enter, one had to bend down and crawl in. Most of the huts were roofed with leaves and wood, though a few had tiled the roofs or spread hay over them. Those who had not been able to manage even that had spread a cheap polythene sheet over the walls to shelter their heads. Brajabashi's house had a tiled roof though. In this world of hapless paupers, his tiled roof gave, as if, a hint of some sort of an aristocracy.

Bishtucharan sat on a mat spread in front of Braja's house with his legs stretched in front of him. His earlier robust health was gone, the bald patch on his head had grown bigger and his complexion had changed. It was only six or seven years since Braja had last seen him, yet he felt that he was seeing Bishtucharan after a lifetime.

'Look, look! My *Khuro*'s come!' exclaimed Braja in joy and sat down close to Bishtu on the mat.

'Tell me, *Khuro*, how are things?'

Though preoccupied with despondent thoughts and anxieties, Bishtucharan's eyes now shone with joy.

'Bejo, you! After so many years!'

The two gazed at each other with silent eyes, misted over, for some time before the endless words broke through. So many words that the two scarce had time to speak coherently. Till finally Braja asked, '*Khuro*, you too had to come away?'

'Yes, I had to,' answered Bishtu. 'Was not possible to live there any longer.'

'But you had said that you would rather give your life than leave the land of your forefathers!'

'Yes, I had,' said Bishtucharan. 'I had not known then that one day... I taught at the pathshala. The villagers respected me. And I had thought this is how it was going to be. Why leave our ancestral land?'

'What respect, *Khuro*! A land where you have no right to speak, where you have no freedom to be, where your little wishes have no value...'

They were interrupted by a young girl who came over to bend down and touch Brajabashi's feet.

Tall, fair-skinned and with a heart-shaped face, she had a sweetness that charmed the heart. But the exhaustion of the past few days of travel had dulled her glow somewhat. Like a fine veil of cloud across the autumn moonshine.

'Jhunu, right?' said Braja with a smile.

The girl went back into the house with hurried steps without a word.

Stifling a sigh, Bishtucharan said, 'No, she is Runu.'

'Runu! My God! She has grown up! I mistook her for Jhunu! But then, of course, they were very close in age. So Jhunu has grown up even more! Where is she? Is she feeling shy to come in front of me? Jhunu! O my dear sister Jhunu! Come, come. I am your Bejo *Dada*, remember?'

Without warning, Bishtucharan covered his face with his palms and broke into sobs. And almost immediately was heard the sound of Runu's sobs from inside the hut. Braja stood shocked for a while, before clasping Bishtucharan by both his arms and demanding, 'What, *Khuro*? What? What has happened? Why do you cry! I cannot understand!'

It took Bishtu Pandit some time to control his sudden burst of weeping. The sobs from within the house also grew quieter. Wiping his eyes with the end of his dhoti, Bishtucharan said, 'O Bejo, Jhunu is no more!'

'No more? What do you mean, she is no more?'

'No, not just dead. Killed. My little innocent beautiful girl....'

'Who killed her, *Khuro*?'

Braja noticed the pallor of Bishtucharan's face had changed to a flaming red.

'That bastard swine Pheru *Miyan*! They picked Jhunu up from the jetty as she was returning from college. They said Pheru had wanted to marry her and make her his bibi. But she did not agree, and so they tortured her all together for the whole night. My little flower! And then when it was light...'

Brajabashi's face too had changed colour.

'I had told you! This is why I left my land! You did not listen to me. Now you say what I had said! Now! After paying a very heavy price! It is not Pheru *Miyan*! I say it is. . . !'

Teetering on the verge of vulgarity, Braja pulled himself up short. He looked at the man seated in front of him. This man had been given the highest position of respect by them in the village. He did not want his language to deny that respect. Bishtu Pandit looked at Braja with helpless eyes, reached out and clasped his hand.

'You boys would call me Pandit, Braja. In reality, I turned out to be the most ignorant,' said Bishtucharan. 'And that is why I have finally come to you. Let me stay with you, Braja. Where can I go with Runu? I cannot rest till I have settled her somehow.'

Braja heaved a sigh and fell silent.

Bishtucharan and Braja's father were first cousins. He had grown up in the care of Braja's family since his childhood. Later, he had gone back to his own village and opened a school there. The relations between them had always been affectionate and warm. Where could he go wandering in the streets now with his young daughter? And with such a heavy burden on his soul? Bishtucharan and Runu remained with Braja's family. He had earlier lost his wife, and now his darling daughter had been devoured by Pheru *Miyan*. His memories-identity-future—all were now focussed on this one girl. He could not rest in peace till he ensured her safety somehow. The loss of Jhunu had so alarmed Bishtucharan that he had fled Boultali with Runu the very next day. Seeing the wan, pale face of his daughter would send tremors of fear through his heart.

Brajabashi said, 'Let some time pass, *Khuro*. Then we can find a suitable boy for her.'

This was the only worry of Bishtucharan. He must, in some way, settle her in this land. He would not ever return to that accursed land with Runu. But a marriage was easier said than done. Especially for the people who had no firm land beneath their feet, no familiar sky over their heads. To the people of this land, they were unwanted, contemptible, people to be pitied.

The keenness of this contempt was felt by Bishtucharan within a few days. That day he had managed the shop well past dusk with Brajabashi. Then, after shutting down, he bought a packet of bidis and two kilos of wheat flour before setting out for the huts. Just beyond the platform, to the right and nestled close to the railway tracks, was a hooch shop. Raucous laughter and the sharp smell of cheap liquor usually pervaded this place. Though nobody had warned him, Bishtucharan would always pass this place cautiously and quietly, gingerly stepping across the area. That was what he had been about to do that day too, but suddenly a beam of torchlight was flashed onto his face. A thinnish youth lurched a few steps up to him and asked, 'Going where?'

The pungent smell of country liquor almost immediately hit Bishtucharan's nostrils. He half-turned his head to a side to evade the nauseous smell and mumbled, 'There—just ahead.'

'Oh! The shanties! *Banglu*! Hah hah…!'

The two words 'shanties' and '*Banglu*' almost pierced through Bishtucharan's heart. His 'pandit's pride' reared its head up for a moment and his palms tingled to teach the ruffian a proper lesson. How many times had he disciplined such boors in his school? Memories came flooding back. But he didn't do anything this time. He could not find the courage in his heart to protest and invite more trouble. A youth sitting to the side said in a low voice, '*Arre yaar*, I think this is that new *mynah*'s father!'

'Which one?'

'That new chick!'

'Oh!'

Bishtucharan escaped that day, but the vulgar whistle that followed, hit him like a burning iron rod.

That night Bishtucharan told Braja of the incident.

'Nothing to fear, *Khuro*,' said Brajabashi. 'They do behave like that when they're a little drunk, but they will not trouble us. After all, they are not *neres*, they are from decent families.'

Brajabashi's logic did not entirely satisfy Bishtucharan. He was like a cow driven out of its burning shed, now terrified even by a cloud with a pinch of crimson hue. Above all, those whose very existence was threatened by uncertainty, who were without country, without home, without roots, how could such people feel assured? The mystery eluded Bishtucharan. He felt his helplessness increase when he glanced at Runu's face. A lifeless form who moved around, sat down, stood up. She did not chatter on as before; she did not rouse the home with her joy-filled laughter. She had even thrown away the tinkling anklets on her feet in some unbearable agony.

As evening was nearing, the girls would gather together in the open space in front of the hutments. Stretching their legs in front of them, they would relax and chat, pick out lice from each other's hair, with teasing and banter. Like an indifferent princess, Runu too would go and sit with them. Braja's wife would comb Runu's hair with her fingers, burying her pale fingers in the long black hair and weaving in and out like swans. The crowded trains that passed by would have passengers who gazed at this scene in charmed wonder. Some male passengers would sometimes throw a light-hearted comment at the girls which they ignored. But

Bishtucharan's soul would rebel even at such trivialities. Having lived his entire life in a quiet rural spot, his soul had difficulty getting accustomed to this rather noisy, crowded life here. How far away was his dear scrubbed courtyard, clean, pure white, and how different was this open, shameless world, beside the rail tracks!

Yet it was quite possible that he would get habituated to all this. But Bishtucharan failed to find an immediate solution to another pressing question which has already made him thoroughly worried. In the land which they had left, a group of people now referred to them as Indian spies. And in this land where they had come to, they were either '*Banglus*' or refugees. Most of these simple, unlettered people with him did not understand the intricacies of nation and government, of citizenship or its implications. And therefore, they did not worry their heads over it. They had accepted the fact that there would be no help from the government, no help for rehabilitation. They had no stakes and therefore no rights in any governmental system of the world. Despite knowing all these, how did these people muster up the courage and hope to live on beside the rail tracks was something beyond Bishtucharan's all logical senses.

That morning, a leader-like man came to Braja's hut. 'Braja, you here?'

Braja was preparing to leave for his shop, running a comb through his wet hair. He hurried out of the hut, flustered. 'Yes, yes, please sit down.'

But the leader seemed to be in a hurry. 'No time to sit. Have many people to look up. Listen, there will be a lorry coming this Sunday in the afternoon. There's to be a meeting in Calcutta. About a hundred men must be there.'

Braja hesitated a little and murmured, 'So many people… during working hours…'

'Don't go telling me about work and all,' answered that man harshly. 'Remember—a hundred needed.'

Chenno's granny was passing by. She heard the man's voice and came up.

'God is great!' she said. 'It is you I have had in my mind these past few days. What happened to our ration cards? We do not get any kerosene at all! What can I say about our miseries!'

The leader gave Chenno's granny, Harimati, a sharp look. 'Ration card! Forget all that, old woman! If I get ration cards for people beside the lines, I will be in jail!'

Bishtu Pandit was about to say something, but Braja stopped him short and said, 'Please don't take offence at *Jethi*'s words, *Dada*! Please, just make arrangement of our voter cards, see that our names get into the voters' list soon in future.'

'Will see to all that later! First the meeting on Sunday! Don't forget.' He walked away hurriedly.

Chenno's granny heaved a sigh and turned to Bishtucharan, 'We are illiterates, Pandit. But you are an educated man. You could have said a few words to make them understand.'

Bishtu Pandit lifted his eyes to the sky with an incredible despair and said, 'Whom do I tell? Who is listening! They scarce treat us as human beings!'

A few evenings later, Bishtucharan was sitting with Braja in front of a fruit shop when a group of young boys began going round the shops on the platform, handing each shopkeeper a receipt of some sort. Within a few minutes, Brajabashi too had a receipt in his hand. Bishtucharan looked up at the boys, all those who sat at the hooch shop. Braja glanced at the receipt and stiffened.

'What is it?' said Bishtucharan, and took the receipt from his hand. It was a receipt for the Durga Puja donation. Beside Braja's name was written the amount 'Rs 500.'

'Five hundred!' Bishtucharan felt, as if the soil beneath his feet got a tremor.

'O Moti! What have they given you?'

Moti lifted up three fingers silently. Three hundred.

An enraged Bishtucharan said, 'What do they think this is? Their fiefdom! Don't give a paisa!'

Braja glanced around furtively and said, 'Keep quiet, *Khuro*. If anybody hears you, there will be hell to pay! You want to live in water and pick a quarrel with the crocodile!'

From the other side Moti said, keeping his voice as low as possible, 'This is the tax we have to pay to carry on our business on the rail platform. More, less, whatever—but you will have to pay. There is no way out. I am thinking I will take Rs 50 and go fall at their feet. That is what I did the last time too. It will not help to lose your temper.'

Bishtucharan listened in amazement. He said, 'If you are going to kowtow to such unfair demands, why did you leave your land?'

At these words, something in Braja roused itself. Searching for strength within himself, he said to Moti, 'How can poor people like us give even Rs 50, Moti! If only we could stand up to them together!'

Moti smiled wanly and said, 'From where do you get this courage? No land, no home, nobody to support you.'

But even that support appeared to present itself one day. At least that was what it had seemed to Bishtu Pandit on first acquaintance. They were going to drive the Ram-ratha all over the country during the Puja this year. Yes, they would come to this side too. That was why he had come to talk to them. Bishtucharan had been greatly assured by his concern for Hindus all over the world.

Bishtucharan's voice had choked up with emotion as he talked to this man. He had said, 'You are our true friend, *Dada*! We are totally helpless, please save us! If you cannot make arrangements for our citizenship, at least declare us refugees! Let there be camps where we can live. At least there will be some help from around the world. If you do feel for us as Hindus, why will you not do at least this?'

The man perhaps would not have come in this direction had he sensed that he would invite problems by alluding to Ram-ratha. His voice faltered, 'Certainly. But before that, the mandir must be possessed, and after that, to stop the infiltrators…'

That someone could think of their huge problems of survival in such a trivial manner got Bishtucharan somewhat disillusioned. In a heated voice he said, 'No one is serious. Millions of people are dying on the roads like stray dogs and cats, and you say you are busy saving the gods!'

That this sudden ray of hope had paled so quickly depressed Bishtucharan. 'There's no place for us in any country, Bejo! You don't have food to eat, but if you manage to give Rs 50 for the puja donation, that is unacceptable to them. All rascals! Is it for this that we left our homes?'

'Don't get so disheartened, *Khuro*,' said Braja. 'We are staying here now. Nobody is coming to chase us away! The trepidation that constantly haunts—at least that is gone!'

Chenno's granny said, 'Even if we don't get food to eat, at least we can sleep peacefully. Nobody pulls our girls by their hands or begins a riot at the slightest whim. What else can you ask for?'

Bishtucharan shook his head and said, 'I don't know. I am getting confused. What is more precious and needs to be honoured—my honour, or my life?'

Braja said with some mockery in his voice, 'Maybe you better not think about that *Khuro*. Go back to your land and sign yourself in bondage to Pheru *Miyan*. Even if you lose your honour, your life will be saved!'

Unable to find a resolution to this debate, Bishtucharan fell silent. He had well understood that he and his people were unwelcome everywhere in this world now. Though nurtured in the same air and water, by reason of some religious divide, the world would now be one of endless sorrow for them. To some they were untouchables, to the others they were born enemies.

About five or six months had passed since then. Earning enough to keep body and soul together was proving extremely difficult for Bishtucharan. On Braja's advice, he had begun selling *chanachur* on the local trains. Runu too did not sit idle. She had begun working with Braja's sister, Shiuli, stitching sleeves on blouses. Nobody in this slum, in fact, sat idle.

A voice that has been used to teaching students for so many years, sounded a little ill-at-ease when selling his ware in the train compartments. 'Cha-na, hot cha-na!' But Bishtucharan could not stay home. If he sat idle for a few minutes, the ravaged body of Jhunu came up before his eyes. He felt driven to tear his hair out at those moments. Immersing himself in the fast-moving life around the railways, Bishtucharan hawked his wares till late into the night on the speeding trains, seeking to forget his past in his newly found job. By the time he returned, the Orion had already begun their descent into the western skies. The bustle of the hutments beside the tracks had also quietened down. Runu alone would be waiting up for her father with sleepy eyes, guarding his plate of rice, and sometimes falling asleep beside it.

The day after the Kali puja, Bishtucharan received some wonderful news from Gobinda of Paschimpada. Somebody had shot dead Pheru *Miyan*, and some of his accomplices too. The information cheered Bishtucharan's heart and he moved towards his home, yearning to tell Runu the news. There was God's justice after all! Perhaps this would be a good time to make a trip back home once. To see if he could settle his lands formally.

Walking home immersed in such thoughts, Bishtucharan got the sudden feeling that he had taken a wrong turn after crossing the platform. The place seemed unfamiliar. It took him a moment to understand what had happened. The familiar sight of the glowing fire, ever burning like Ravana's pyre, at the hooch shop was not there. The shop was covered in silence and darkness. Though the pungent smell of liquor hung heavy in the air, Bishtucharan heaved a sigh of relief.

Every day they sat here with illegal liquor, openly defying the law of the land. Nobody said a word to them. Was all the rage of society reserved for the refugees? But what had happened today? Did the police chase them out? Bishtucharan laughed at his own foolish thoughts. What am I thinking? They are not hapless like us!

He crossed a few houses in a daze. And then had to pull up short. Four youths had emerged out of the darkness to block his way.

'Not a step further. *Khabardaar!*'

The voice was familiar. He had heard it before at the hooch shop. But why did the voice sound like Pheru *Miyan*'s today? A cold chill went down Bishtucharan's spine.

'Who are you?' he said in a trembling voice. 'What do you want?'

'You will see soon!'

One of the youths came forward and pressed the barrel of a pipe gun to Bishtucharan's chest. He became speechless with fright.

And then within a few minutes took place an unbelievable event.

Those intoxicated brutish 'gentle' fellows barged into the huts and dragged out all the young girls of Runu, Shiuli, Chenno's age. They picked them up with the strength of giants and disappeared into the darkness across the lines. Though gagged by their own clothes, the groaning and the scuffle of the girls could be heard clearly.

Bishtucharan gave the boy with the pipe gun a hefty shove and threatened:

'Wait, you scoundrels!'

But he could not make it. Something heavy came down on his head and he fell to the ground, unconscious. Braja, too, lay near him, hit by the buttstock of the pipe gun for his inability to stay quiet. But Bishtucharan did not know that. After a while, the voice of Chenno's granny cursing some unknown people reached his consciousness faintly. His eyes saw helpless, shocked faces surrounding him. With all faith destroyed, they were sinking into the depths of a despair too deep for any words of consolation. Bishtucharan stared at the faces for some time before breaking into violent sobs.

'Bejo, O Bejo! Why did you leave your land, Bejo?'

This simple question could not find any answer today. But Bishtucharan would not be silenced today. He jumped up. 'Tell me, tell me! Which really is my land, my country?'

Finding no answer from anyone, he began beating his chest with his fists. Then a sudden change came over him, and seeing the last train moving towards Bongaon, he rushed towards it over the lines.

'Runu... Runu...'

At one time, his agonised cry was drowned out by the rushing, roaring sound of the engine which, much like Bishtucharan, went speeding into the darkness towards a destination unknown.

ॐ

Translated by Sipra Mukherjee

Sipra Mukherjee is a Professor at the Department of English, West Bengal State University. Her research interests are religion, caste, and power. Her work, *Interrogating My Chandal Life: Autobiography of a Dalit* (translation of Manoranjan Byapari's autobiography) won The Hindu Non-fiction Award in 2019.

Soil

Anil Ghosh

It is an unusual summer midday—instead of the scorching heat of the bright burning sun, grey cloudlets have hovered across the sky with gusty winds blowing north-eastward. It is a peculiar summer noon with threat of an imminent storm or rain, along with whizzing sounds. Darkness descended in the middle of the day with the dust storm of brass-red sand particles. The roads are bereft of human clatter. Sitting in the government quarter of the suburb, Manorama feels within herself a dejected emptiness. The bus-road is nearby, beyond which is the River Ichhamati. The muddy waves of Ichhamati are tossing around—the prison bell strikes one and the sound has thinned into the sound of the stormy wind. The normal suburban noon that moves at a snail's pace at this hour is threatened by a storm that seems to burn out and sweep away everything in its stride. In such an unusual midday, Manorama's vision experiences a cold surprise. She is motionless like a piece of stone in front of the swaying image developed in the light and shade. Hiren, Manorama's husband, now sits face to face with an aged stranger—swaying between the extremes of familiarity and remoteness like a pendulum. A faint line of recognition winks from behind the veil of amnesia. Who is this man? *Do I know him? Can I remember? Perhaps...perhaps not. Who is this man?*

The stranger came sometime ago and was trying to attract Manorama's attention from outside the door, kept ajar. He was looking like a storm-tossed crow. The figure of an elderly man was out despite being all covered in dust: the shining bald head now had only a narrow lining of grey hair around; a slightly cracked face with stubbly beard and moustache, saffron kurta over a knee-length dhoti and grey cambyss shoes, now dusty. A white cotton bag in the right hand and a thick cane stick in the left, he asked Manorama anxiously, '*Ma*, is this Hiren Bose's residence?'

Manorama softly replied, 'Yes.'

'Is he in?'

'Yes, but you...!'

'I'm coming from Hajrakati.'

Hajrakati! The moment the name entered Manorama's ears, the aroma of damp straw overwhelmed her and she got startled—the intimate surprise was exclusively hers. For the next few moments, she was beside herself with the clouds of memory rumbling in her heart. The old stagnant pool of memory of half a century has all of a sudden been stirred by a stone from the past. Hajrakati...Hajrakati...oh...like a gusty wind it shook her entire being. Her senses, the pores of her being, were being overflooded by the waves of emotions. And in a series of kaleidoscopic motion pictures, the frames began to surge up in her mind—Hajrakati, Talar Ghat, the metal road of Satkhira, Kapotaksha river, beyond that the dusty road, green pastures, a village, a country, a world… and…a hand—white conch-bangled—repeatedly pulling her back, '*Seija Bou… hey, Seija Bou…*' like a cinematic flashback, the images presented themselves in front of her trembling eyes that forgot to blink. A surge of emotions came down like a pool of blood to the seat of her consciousness. Almost instinctively, she raised her hand on her forehead to pull the veil over her head, and in a tone of deep kinship, welcomed the elderly man, 'Please, come in'.

Hiren was busy with his midday meal in the inner porch but probably overheard the conversation. Curious, he came into the room without washing his hand and stood face to face with the stranger. They were looking at each other—unblinking, surprised. Thus time flew moment by moment, like the running stream, like unending, torrential rain. Manorama is a mute spectator to this spectacle. Only dust was falling off from the yellow and worn-out leaves of memory, put to slumber for thirty-five years. *Do I know him*?

The old man spoke first, with a sparkle of amusement writ large on his face, 'I recognised you the moment I saw you, Hire'.

The quivering dark letters in his blurred vision gradually stopped the ripple to become a poetry: *Darao, pathik bor, Jonmo jodi tobo / Bonge! Tishtho khonokal! E Samadhisthole* (Stop a while, traveller!/ Should Mother Bengal claim thee for her son./…here in the Long Home) The image of a river, with a great current, full to the brim, almost immediately flashed onto his mind—Kapotaksha river with its blue waves—one at the steer, supported by perhaps two others with the oars—moving upstream against the current flowing southward—sailing against the cascading silver-head waves—*heave ho... heave ho...* the boat was moving on to Jessore, Sagardanri—the birthplace of the poet of the Dutts—as though in one pull of the oar, the cloud of amnesia got cleared and the past brightened up and like waves, came surging up to his mind and he heard a call—*Ohhh... Hire*—the familiar call, as though coming from the banks of Kapotaksha. It shook Hiren completely like the coconut leaves stirring with the strong wind. Hiren was trembling and clasped the hand of the old man, 'You...you are Nagen *Da*, right!'

The old man smiled and shook his head in agreement. Opening the door of memory, a small marbleball started rolling in Hiren's eyes. Hiren was smiling too and said, 'How can I recognise you! Our familiar Nagen *Da* has changed so much!

'Same for you. Remember I am five years older than you—now seventy-seven'.

'Oh, after so many years! Do you remember that trip to Sagardanri? You, me and Tarikul, the boatman."

'How can I forget that!'

'We met for the last time probably at Khulna station, perhaps the year after Independence. You were returning to Hajrakati and me... leaving for good!'

Then descended a deep long sigh and a hush; only strolling across the isolated, secluded dunes on the shore of memory while time takes its flight on the wings of silence. Manorama's vision was floating across the past—sailing upstream—no port anywhere—no definite destination—just sailing—moving here and there with the waves of memory and conjuring up fragmented shades from the past—the house at Bhomra, the maternal uncle's house at Hoddili, rivers, villages, green pastures...all. All of a sudden flashed the image of a hand—a white conch-bangled hand, a gentle, soft, affectionate hand, and a world brightened up by the sunrays with a tint of land-lily—that hand pulls Manorama even now. She can still hear the fervent appeal, ' Hey, *Seija Bou*...why will you go? This is your home too, your land, your *desh*. This is our root, this is where we belong. Once uprooted you can never replant yourself anywhere. You are worried about your daughter, right! But there is fear everywhere. Do you think leaving the country would allay fears? Just ask yourself, is there any place in the world where women are safe? Hey, *Seija Bou*, please don't leave the country...' No, I could not respond, Manorama thinks. What was it? A fit of pique? Maybe. Those agonising memories seem to come to her back again after so many years—she does not remember what was there in that hand but somehow, she could not gather up enough courage. It was a phase of darkness. Cold, deep darkness. The house was full with brothers- and sisters-in-law, children, grandchildren—a full house, packed with all the near ones, yet I couldn't be assured. There was fear even in broad daylight and that trebled during night. We could never go outside—we were so traumatised that we had to finish our chores early, and then get inside the stuffy room—a claustrophobic feeling—full of stress and discomfiture. *Why, why should one live in one's own land like an offender?* Questions raised their heads, but who will answer? There was chaos all around with dread and anxiety looming large. The mood, in general, was of migrating—escaping. Discussion continued in a hushed tone in the household: the Dey family of Nakshapur have left. The Duttas of Rayhati are packing to leave. The route through Satkshira is inaccessible, so they will reach Jessore by boat and then take a train to Bongaon. Such was the atmosphere. The call '*Naraye Takdir*' would create tremors in hearts. An ambience of trepidation prevailed. Different kinds of rumours from Talar Hat were doing the rounds. Each would create a chilling sensation of fear. News came that Satkshira was burning; in Hoddili, girls have been abducted in broad daylight; the market at Fingure has been burnt down in broad daylight. All such news acted like explosives; people just believed in what they heard. Nobody had the courage to go out and verify those. With every piece of news, the faces of the inmates of the house turned pale. The house looked like a lifeless deserted place and all wanted to escape. Things would be packed. Then with daylight, some ray of assurance would creep in. Such was the time then. In this uneasy atmosphere, the greatest worry was with the daughter. Some secretly informed us, 'Tell Seija *Babu* to be careful of his daughter—there was a whisper in the market'. After this, can the parents rely on anything or anyone? We were as though waiting for the worst in the dark corner of that huge house. Every night would come with a cold chilling fear. We had no moment of respite. After that, we made a surrender to an uncertain, dark future. Leaving our homestead, our village, our country, we began our journey towards another land, an unknown territory. The journey was mixed with dark fear and apprehension. But at the end of a day, we crossed over the border and heaved a sigh of relief. But, did crossing over ensure safety and liberty? The same concern about the daughter persisted here as well. On this side of the border, the apprehension of being tempted, trapped and abducted continued to haunt us. In Hajrakati we had only rumours—here there were real abuses, threats bringing in waves of fear. As if a refugee girl does not have any dignity! We had to survive this, preserve the dignity amidst this. Nowadays, my daughter occasionally asks, 'Mother, why did we come here? To save what?' I have no answer. Only I am reminded of those words, 'Just ask yourself, is there any country in the world where women are safe?' And that caring hand still tries to pull me back. Why, I don't know yet. I didn't know back then either. A collage of indistinct, fragmented images is evoked before the eyes; they are all dim snaps now. I cannot distinctly recollect. Human mind is quite wayward, always busy to fill in the void. The candle of grief dwindles. Now we are just going through the routine drudgery. Time moves like a river with strong current. I can feel now that I am aging both physically and psychologically. The daughter has been married off. The elder son is a government employee and has got this quarter. The younger one is still unemployed, that is the real concern. Don't know what is in future. Actually, after leaving our ancestral house, village and *desh*, we could not manage to either have a house of our own or a piece of land to settle down. If somebody asks how we are, I don't know what to answer—don't even know whether there is any answer at all.

Manorama's internal monologue was broken when she heard the two talking.

'Nagen *Da*, when have you crossed the border?'

'This morning itself,' Nagen said.

'Have you come legally, with a passport?'

'No, through secret path'

'How much did you pay?'

'They demanded one thousand but at last it was negotiated at seven hundred rupees.'

Nagen now turned to Manorama, '*Bouma*, I don't see your sons and daughters.'

Manorama replied, 'The elder son is in office and the younger one has gone to Calcutta. The daughter was married soon after we crossed over. She has four children now.'

As the conversation was on, Manorama could feel the midday heat as the sun had reappeared removing the dark stormy cloud. She went inside to make arrangements for lunch. Hiren left his meal unfinished. He would not eat again and took a quick wash. Manorama invited Nagen to lunch but he loudly protested, 'No, No, *Bouma*. I have already taken my meal at the house of my wife's sister at Itinda.'

Manoroma then offered, 'At least have some snacks and tea!'

Nagen again refused, 'No. I take just a self-cooked meal once a day and nothing else.'

Hiren did not press further. The dark room was getting darker. Manorama invited Nagen into the inner porch.

Hiren led him there. This bright inner porch was much better than the shadowy room. Nagen looked all around and appreciated the little greenery, the small garden in one corner of the courtyard.

Nagen said, 'Hiren, you have not left the hobby of gardening yet, I see.'

Hiren shook his head in agreement, 'That sustains my life. As they say, do a bit of gardening if you want peace.'

Nagen laughed loudly. Hiren joined in and Manorama too, silently. Hiren noted with surprise that Nagen's laughter lacked the passionate outburst of the tidal waves of the River Kapotaksha. A note of trouble and pain permeated his laughter. Equally surprising was Nagen's sudden visit after so many years. Hiren thought to himself: Shall I ask Nagen *Da*, why he has come after so many years—you were the one who told me under the thick cloud of mourning of the hapless mass at Khulna station, 'Hire, you are making a mistake. Rootless people cannot settle anywhere'—and with what confidence did you say that! I was not ready to listen to anything—like a frenzied person, I left my home, my village, my country. Was it merely a craze of the time? I did not know then. You said, 'Is this country alien to me?'— those were your last words. You returned home alone—in the dark, sailing upstream. And we moved, empty-handed, towards an unknown land, with hope, with confidence. Now I look back and ponder on your words. That self of yours has now become so broken, so miserable. Shall I tell him, ask him?

'How is Sundor di?' Manorama asked.

'She is no more,' Nagen sighed.

'And your children?'

'All have settled on this side.' Nagen sighed again.

And then a dip into the stagnant pool of grief. These questions are immaterial. Nagen is visibly irritated. *Why do people ask these questions?* Relations are like isolated islands segregated by channels. All very temporary.

The wind started blowing in gusts and seemed to uproot the plants in the garden. However, the furious wind subsided after sometime, and things got back to their normal places. The centre of this suburban town was then awakening from a peculiar slumber. The prison bell sounded thrice to indicate it was 3 p.m. The normal clatter outside was audible—the movement of vehicles, the horns of rickshaw—all familiar sounds and they crept into the conversations of these three. They were no longer alone, isolated.

'What is the condition of our house, Nagen *Da*?', Hiren asked.

Nagen lifted his eyes. It seemed that the intervening years had been too long. Nagen's eyes burned with anguish. Sadly he said, 'It stands somehow. Such a huge house. Now covered all over with bushes and weeds.'

'Why, my two brothers live there with their families. They are enjoying the entire property.'

'Yes, they are—but that matters little.'

'Didn't get you.'

'Your brothers are definitely there. Their daughters have been married off to this side; the sons are busy with their job or business in Khulna, Satkshira, Dhaka. They have almost forgotten their house.'

Hiren as though could get the aroma of ripe mangoes, and he was lost in the past. 'Oh, I can still visualise the huge mango orchard in the midst of which the palatial building of Hajrakati bustled with life. Cart-loads of vegetables came from the field and we would rush to that. And on auspicious days we competed with each other for the *sola* flower. The entire terrace would be blood-stained after the sacrifice on the occasion of Kojagori Lakshmipuja. The scar is still there on my thigh. The goat could not be sacrificed in one blow. The falchion rebounded and hit my thigh. I can visualise everything. Ah, if once I could touch that!'

Hiren heaved a sigh, 'We don't get any news from them.'

Nagen laughed, 'On your part, you too don't try enough.'

'What can we do? They don't provide us any news.'

'This problem is everywhere. We are keen on collecting news about the world, but don't know how our neighbours, relatives are. They have become so alien to us. Does the partition of land bring in partition between hearts as well?'

'Really, what we were and what we have become! This is not what we desired,' said Manorama.

'Did you at all know what you wanted?', Nagen asked.

Manorama kept mum.

Nagen again said, '*Bouma*, you see, earlier, villages used to be known through certain families—the Ghosh family of Hajrakati, the Mitras of Dhurole, Palits of Bhomra. You just had to mention the villages, and the names of families would come out. Even today, these things become important especially in case of a marriage. Relationships are finalised on the basis of the names of the villages.'

Hiren sadly said, 'The partition threw everything into disarray'.

'Look brother, I don't understand politics or diplomacy. But one thing I know, the land was ours. If we could have stuck together, we could have stopped things from going away. If you allow, others will take the opportunity, inevitably. That is the truth and has to be accepted.'

'Nagen *Da*, I feel a deep desire to go there.'

'Well, you can go there any time. Where's the problem?'

'But how to arrange a passport?'

'Who is going to check?'

'But how can you go in this physical condition?', Manoraman now interrupted.

'I will go,' Hiren said, irritated. 'I don't want to stay in your family'.

'Whose family? Who is staying? But I can't understand what you'll do there.'

'Why, I'll look after my property there. That is still very much there.'

'Of what use is that property? The sons are never going to go back. Who will enjoy that?'

'Does it mean that I should give up my rights!'

'Now you remember your rights? Where was this thought when you threw away everything and left the country?'

'Why did you come?'

Manorama now looked towards Nagen as an ally, 'Did we know anything at that time? And what was the benefit of coming here? Your friend used to earn eighty-ninety rupees a month then. Only I know how I managed to run the family. And now there is nothing—neither could we manage a piece of land nor a house. I don't know where we shall take shelter if we have to leave this government quarters. And now he is lamenting over lost homeland. Why did you come here then? We were not the only ones to suffer there.'

Manorama's words fell like lashes on Hiren's mind. There was an unfathomable grief and pain. There was no escape from it. *Fear*? Fear in one's own homeland—in one's own being? Quite ridiculous. Politics? Why could he not feel safe when Imanul Haq Chaudhuri told him at Talar Hat in a reassuring tone: '*Seija Babu*, you talk of our rights—why can't you see your own rights?'. Hiren is at a loss of words. Why did you leave? Hiren has no answer. Why did you separate from your own family? Why have you become alien in your own family? Hiren shook his head in desperation. Something shook him from within. The intervening years began to expand like an elastic band. The logic which appeared valid at that time now seems stale, useless. Hiren becomes restless as if prompted by some inner urge. He could not tolerate it any further and looked towards Nagen as an ally, 'Nagen *Da*, can't I have a desire to go back to my roots? Is it so unacceptable?'

Manorama smiled, 'It's not easy to go back.'

Hiren paid no heed to Manorama. He addressed Nagen, 'You know, *Borda* was almost crazy about going back at the fag end of his life. At last, he went through the Bhomra border, leaving everything here. Do you remember Biresh Dutta of Magro, the one who used to come to Talar Hat on horseback? I have seen him too here, like a pauper. Every time we met, he would say, 'I'm returning'. He could never return.

Another spell of deep sighs. Everything looked sombre. The pale lights of the afternoon seemed to announce the imminent arrival of the evening. Hiren is listless. He said, 'The word "*desh*" still creates ripples in the heart. When we were in Calcutta, on holidays the Sealdah Station would be crowded with people returning to home. The word used to create a turmoil in the mind. Look at the present generation— they don't realise what 'soil' means—they've forgot the roots, they've forgot "*desh*".'

Nagen broke the silence, 'Why blame them? Have we allowed them to realise what *desh* is?' His voice was clogged with. The eyes looked heavy, he felt like laughing out. All of a sudden Hiren was reminded of his homeland. As if he was going back to Hajrakati in reality! Does Manorama also think that way? Is *desh* their love or are they attempting to retrieve the property left behind in the homeland? Is homeland a mere property? Alas! He spoke out, 'Actually we had covered up everything. Neither did we understand the meaning of *desh*, nor did we allow others to understand. So when a blow descended from above, the base crumbled into dust. Everyone thought that probably escaping would ensure security. But do you really understand what happy living is? Can anyone be really happy running away from one's own rights? Nowadays, all have become isolated—none is bothered about the other. Hire, try to consider, if families can be divided, why not a country? After all, a country is a large family. The Germans finally acknowledged it, so they could not be kept separate for long, they have become one again.'

Nagen paused and there was silence. He spoke again, 'There is no point in showing your love and affection for your homeland now. You understand it full well, that the country you left is no longer yours. It may be that you have become emotional with my arrival but that does not alter the truth. It is a reality that now you do not belong to that country.'

With head down, Hiren said, 'Yes I know. You are right. Your arrival has stirred some deep chords within us. We have become emotional. It is also true that with your departure it will subside. That homeland will remain only in our memory. The mistake cannot be undone now'.

The atmosphere in the room became tense. Just to lighten it, Manorama asked, 'Where will you go now?'

Nagen replied, 'I'll visit my sons. I have various other engagements. And then I'll return.'

Hiren asked, 'Does it not pain you that you are left there all alone?'

'Yes. It's very painful. At times the lonely house becomes too much to bear. I can feel that my days are counted. Probably that is why this desire to see my kin and come close to them. I cannot deny the pain of separation.'

Manoroma intervened. 'Why don't you come to your sons? Why are you staying back?'

'Yes, that is an option. But I can't find any reason for coming over here. That country is my own—I was born there, will die there too. I don't feel tempted by the lure of comfortable life here. I can see what happens when one is uprooted from one's own place. Do you remember Kamal Dutta of Ashaguni? He is sending requests from Calcutta to provide him with a photograph of his homestead. Baren Chaudhuri of Kalarua now stays in Barasat. When he heard that I was coming over, he requested me to bring a branch of the *bhuti bombai* plant. My *Beyai* at Magro last year requested me to bring him soil from his homestead. These wishes are nothing but little tokens of clogged emotions. I'll finish these tasks and then return. Nothing is eternal. But the pain lingers. If they are happy with it, let that be—let them remain in a make-believe world.'

The afternoon glow was almost dying. Slowly evening was approaching. Nagen's eyes became moist with tears. His body was giving in. The two faces in front of him were fast receding along the line of time. He woke up and took out a small packet from his white bag and gave it to Hiren, 'Take this.'

Hiren was surprised, 'What is this?'

'Soil, of your homestead. Your brothers have sent for you.'

Hiren was startled. An old tune wailed up from the inmost core of the heart. He took out a mound of reddish soil in his fair hand and tried to smell it. Does it still have that old familiar smell? The intervening time as if did not quite exist. Only memories of the past crowded Hiren's mind. He visualised that Nagen's small, bending frame ultimately became one with that mound. The smell of the dry soil dampened by rain as if whispered to him, *Hiren, there is no greater god than earth. The country may have been partitioned but earth, air, water and mind—these cannot be partitioned.*

Manorama too took out a mound of soil. Perhaps just another silly mound, but within it lay the finest tintsof a heavenly bliss. This is a mysterious feeling. Soil—they are talking of soil—soil that makes paths, creates villages, countries, the world. It carries on its body the footprints of millions. Once upon a time a group of horse riders settled on the Indus basin with fire and *Somrasa*, and sang the *Samagana* of life. Then came the invaders from Samarkhund-Bukhara and boldly proclaimed, '*This land is ours...*'. Subsequently on the borders of Murshidabad the Badshahi glory was defeated and the Union Jack unfurled to declare the victory of the British force. Those who entered as merchants became our rulers. All this happened on the face of the earth. A small mound of that earth is now in the palms of Manorama. Waves after waves of emotion flooded her heart, and her eyes were filled with spontaneous tears. A damp aroma of the soil, sweet and endearing, seemed to come out of the heart of the man that was gradually turning into dust.

Perhaps there were whispers in Hiren's heart, 'Who are you?'

That mound of damp soil as though answered, 'I am that.'

'Who are you?'

'I am that. You know.'

ॐ

Translated by Snehasis Maiti

Snehasis Maiti is Associate Professor of English, Prabhat Kumar College, West Bengal. His doctoral thesis was on writers of Indian diaspora which was subsequently published by LAP-Lambert, Germany.

Notes:

The quoted text is a part of the epitaph on the grave of Michael Madhusudan Dutt. Interestingly, it was written by the poet himself. The epitaph reads— *Darao, Pothik-bar, Jonmo jadi tobo Bonge! Tishta khanakal! E Shomadisthale (Jananir Kole Shishu Lobhoye Jemti biram) Mohir pothe mohanidrabrito Dattakulodab kobi Shrimadhushudhan!*

That translates into—

'Stop a while, traveller! Should Mother Bengal claim thee for her son. As a child takes repose on his mother's elysian lap, Even so here in the

Long Home, On the bosom of the earth, Enjoys the sweet eternal sleep Poet Madhusudan of the Duttas.'

- *Desh* Normally means country or nation. However, in Bengali parlance, the word is used in a much more liberal sense with a wide range of applications. In colloquial usages, people from Bengal often use the word '*desh*' to refer to one's place of birth, especially in a rural area or small town.

Address

Goutam Aalee

'Allah Meherban! You tell me which one is my country. How could I live in peace in this land you made for me?', the old man cried aloud at the end of his namaz. He was praying under a tree in scorching heat. Nobody can measure his age. His head is bald and his teeth have fallen. The thin man was offering namaz on a tattered piece of cloth.

He has lost his address, something he surely had once long back when he was born in Bengal. That address had neither east nor west. Neither was there any border between the two. He was born in a nondescript marketplace. His father had a small business of sesame and jute. He used to amass many seasonal crops and sell the whole lot at wholesale price whenever he got an opportunity.

He was born after so many elder sisters. And the joy of his *Dada-Dadi* and *Nana-Nani* knew no bounds. In this air of joy and happiness the wedding ceremonies of all his sisters took place one by one. One day his newly wed bibi came to the house amid pomp and grandeur. He soon became a father.

At this point of time everything went topsy-turvy. One fine morning, their country was no longer their own. It had been divided and a line of demarcation had come into being. Their identities too had altered. They were no more Bengali—rather Muslim and Pakistani.

The riot started. People engaged in murder and bloodshed. But his father remained nonchalant. Men and women were fleeing from their places. Even then the father stood rigid. It was his land—it belonged to his father, his forefathers. He won't leave it at any cost. He won't go by the words of others who claimed that it was not his land. His life of toil and hope always revolved around it. Under no circumstances he would abandon this dear land.

Partition took place. Some people left this land and here came a few from the other side. The riot gradually subsided. The old man's father, however, did not leave the land. Then that night came in his life—the experience of which he would never be able to forget. That very night, all by itself, messed up the graph of his entire life.

His father was asleep. The couple was also in bed. Just at that moment some distant clamour reached their ears. That noise got enhanced with every passing second. And suddenly they started banging on the main door. An incessant bang coupled with abusive words. A frightful hubbub of a group of people; but it was different and altogether unfamiliar. The old man shrank in trepidation. His father couldn't stop coughing, and leaving his bed he came out in the verandah. The old man shouted at his father—'Don't open the door, *Abba*'.

But his father didn't respond to that panic-stricken plea. He moved forward and opened the door. Some rowdy men burst in upon them. While using slang words and foul remarks they dictated, 'Get out immediately if you want to save your life'. He stood in front of them. Raising his hands, he shouted, 'Just go away. This house is mine, my father's and my ancestors. I won't leave this land under any circumstances. I won't till I'm alive. Go away.' His father was quivering with rage

But their voices were stronger and they soon overwhelmed his lone voice. Someone shoved my father. He fell down heavily on a pillar of the verandah and uttering the name of Allah, he lost his consciousness. He didn't recover ever. From his place of birth, he went straight to the abode of his beloved Allah.

The old man's address got changed. Along with his wife and son he took his shelter in a relative's house in the village. But he failed to keep up spirits. After losing everything, he started passing his days, dejected. A kind of conflict got accorded with his breath—this is not his country although it's his place of birth, the place of his father.

His son grew up and insisted on going to Pakistan. One day he even went there along with his friends. He came back with a big dream. This time he would bring his parents to Pakistan—a country of dreams—a country for the Muslims alone. He would walk there with his head held high. He won't have to depend on others' mercy.

The old man succumbed to his son's capricious insistence. He wanted to gain back his lost hope. Overcoming his conflict, he asked, 'But my child, where will we stay there and what will we eat?'

His son answered, 'You won't have to worry about that. My friend has agricultural land in plenty.' The old man sighed deeply. Another new address. Another form of dependence.

The old man moved on to his new shelter. He met some new faces. But nothing seemed new to him. However, those new acquaintances have the same tongue. They offer namaz five times a day. But not all of them. As everyone is not a Muslim in the holy land of Pakistan either. The *uludhwani* comes from some dwellings across the village. The bell rings from some Hindu temples and the spire of a church can also be seen at a distance.

Sometimes thoughts of loneliness possess the old man. Temple, church, masjid are also here like that of the land they had left behind. Everyone has not fled from that side and all have not deserted this side either. How the Hindus, who stayed back here, are surviving? Are they in the same state of fear and dejection as he was? If they could hold onto their soil like the ones who stayed back, why can't he? Why has he left his father's place?

Religion does not spare one from thoughts of hunger. Even his son feels that. He struggles a job day and night. Meanwhile, his family has increased and so has his pain of living as a dependent. He wants to free himself from this anguish. Following his son, the old man again crosses the border in the hope of freedom and life. Once again, he steps in his ancestral land which is now his son's as well. While taking a full breath in his birthplace, he becomes a dweller of a hovel in a far-off land—an alien state. Another new address. His offspring grow up with an alienated mother tongue.

Family life goes well. Food is available twice a day. His son works. And so does his daughter-in-law in a rich man's house. His grandson is now grown-up enough to be a libertine. He often loafs around, copying the stars on screen. He also does some kind of work to earn his bread, but of what kind, is unknown to the old man. It seems as if he has forgotten his mother tongue. He has bought a tape recorder. He dances crazily all by himself by playing it in his room. One fine morning he brings home his newly-wed wife.

While brooding on his white beard and bald head the old man has forgot his own identity. He was thinking of a piece of land where he would finally close his eyelids and perhaps, go straight to his parents in some other world.

But his thoughts came to a stop. The hushed-up whisper became loud. He again got marked as a 'Muslim'. Not only as a 'Muslim' but as an 'infiltrator' as well. He was branded as an infiltrator in his own birthplace!

Administration guised as a secular force sat on the bulldozer of oppression and started crushing everything. His beloved grandson has not yet come back from his work. All except him were pushed into the prison van by the police. After three days, changing several vehicles, they came empty-handed along with others to the border of the country which the old man crossed twice earlier.

They had to cross the known border as branded fellows. By shaving off half of their heads, as though they were branded thieves, the administration shoved them over the border. The blankets and wrappers, the last resources of olds and kids alike were set on fire.

Under the butt of a rifle the old man and his companions crossed the border of their land and attempted to enter another. There again they had to stop abruptly after moving a bit. In front of them stood another group of rifle-holders—just like those whom they had left behind—but in a slightly different uniform. They raised their rifles. Even this land was not theirs. They were the unwanted ones.

Thus passed four days. They lay without food and sleep under the bare sky. On the one hand their own country and on the other, the country of their religion. In between lies a small piece of land where mango trees and others grow—a place which the government has labelled as 'no man's land'. On a tattered piece of cloth beneath a tree the old man makes a pitiful prayer—'*Allah Meharban*. You tell me which one is my country. How could I live in peace in a small corner of this land you made for me?'

ఠ

Translated by Mir Ahammad Ali

Mir Ahammad Ali is the co-editor of the anthology.

One Land

Amit Mukhopadhyay

Sagirul got up late at night. Nocturnal animals were still asleep then. It was too early even for the day to rouse to life. The earth reveres the stillness of time at this hour. It gathers energy to create an air of melody. As Sagir wakes up at the call of the body, he can hear the sound of nature. The night's companions get busy amid branches of trees, shrubs, and even grass to complete their tasks. Spreading the liquid and flapping the wings, they declared their territory in the evening. Yet, what does one or two declare? The time for the provision of their food has also passed. Or does it, in unison with silence, want to calculate and measure everything before leaving its gift to the day? Returning to the bed, Sagir gets the answer to his curiosity by listening to a leaf-trickled shriek coupled with the flap of wings. Then, giving a certain chance of shift between the role of change and the change of role, he turns off the light and again enters inside the mosquito net.

Even before he returns to sleep, Sagir realises that the peaceful time of the meditation is not on the list today. The creatures of the dawn don't have the opportunity to shake off the sleep by their chirrup. The sound of the microphone startles them before that. That gentle, sonorous voice of Birendra Krishna! No, it has not been wafted through the radio. The enthusiastic loudspeaker completes its exercise even before that.

Sagir pushes his father to wake him up. Abul loves the mornings of *Mahalaya*. So, with difficulty, he gets up early only on this day of the year. The advent of *Devipaksha* somehow instils a sense of elation in Abul's mind.

Covering their ears and heads with the bedsheets, father and son come to the balcony. Instead of darkness, there is a magical tinge of blue all around. Burning the light of oblation, shops wake up here and there behind the curtain. The glow of unearthly colours casts a spell on both of them. An uncanny smell of mystery meanders through every nook and corner of the alley. Amidst the hazy movement on the road and in the shops, and the hasty preparation across the streets, the radio begins its transmission. They wonder how the mantra of *Mahalaya* has made people spellbound. People at the tea stall forget to even take a sip. Even if the cup touches someone's lip, it moves very slowly, almost with an unfamiliar sense of caution. Even the *papad* ceases to make its customary cracking sound. The man who was frequently spitting out betel, begins to swallow it.

Sagir has never seen so much enchantment. People have been mesmerised all over Durga Choumahani! As if everyone has joined in the psalm. Buds that open up with new light welcome Uma with all submission. Nature is offering her homage with the incense of mist.

The two sides of the road are filled in silence. Abul had heard about the place. He has come here on an official visit. He wants to spend the auspicious moments of *Ma* Durga's arrival here. Parvati will come down from the Himalayas. So, the people of Tripura vividly wait for the arrival of Trinayani. A clear image of a festival of the people begins to take its shape before Abul's eyes.

There is almost sheer bliss at the end of *Mahalaya*. Small waterbodies, filled up to the brink, connect to the river. The flow of the crowd moves towards Akhaura station. Those who were unable to get to the shop in the first attempt, at last chanced to have tea, *papad*, betel and sweet with great fervour now, followed by another group eager to break the morning fast. Children have got permission to play the flute of palmyra leaf.

Abul has heard about the border of the other side from his friend. Akhaura station is across the check-post. In Bangladesh, his birthplace. It's been years since he last visited his hearth and home, kept secret in a chamber of his blurred memory. Though it is far away from here. So what! At least a fringe of it can be seen from this new side. He has been able to go there twice after he had left. Home tantalises Abul still in a dream—so many memories!

Sagir is behind Abul. The road moves on, leaving the shops, houses, and trees behind. Hundreds of people! The pilgrimage becomes a confluence of people, young and old, friends and relatives amidst stories, songs and laughter, where every single turn of the alley becomes a witness of the grand journey. The elderly people make way for the father and son. The old people are being carried upon the shoulders of the youth. Abul feels invigorated by the fresh air. He buys *jilipi* and gives it to Sagir.

Durga Choumahani has discovered its estuary. Abul and Sagir keep their pace. The music is playing far and near. They take the aroma of paddy fields to their hearts' content. The fragments of autumnal clouds are perhaps floating towards the holy sanctuary. Sagir gets mesmerised. A stretch of fields seems to nod with the rhythm of the catkin flowers. They begin to tell their stories. The canals, rivers, and other channels of water seem to splash. The image of a broad clean verandah rises with the smell of burnt coconut. The playmate of his father—a Hindu adolescent girl—has joined hands in the kiln. Sagir must go to that site of the pilgrimage once.

Thousands of people have gathered around the border. Thousand others are also in the queue on the other side. The hidden stream flows in between. Even in front of the eyes, it is not possible to sense how the crowd forms a whirlpool. The rule of the border becomes loose. The police are just spectators today. People are crossing the outpost in a water-like motion. Sagir keeps looking at the spectacle with amazement. Is it delusion? People are shouting and waving hands on both sides. The interaction is proceeding among the familiar faces. They are seeking information about those who are absent. Various messages are communicated through one person. Hope and anxiety are mixed with these greetings. And Sagir could sense the tension, worry and excitement in the exchange of various pieces of news. But above all, this communication seems to be one of love, and there is no feeling of dissonance anywhere. There are similarities in the folds of the faces. The occasional exuberance of the old man thus perfectly fits in the spectacle. So does the elderly woman who is engrossed in prayers with her raised hands.

The woman has come forward on the empty space between two outposts. She puts down the basket of flowers. She picks up flowers and scatters them all around.

As Sagir is about to say something, he notices that Abul has steadily been looking at the gentle yet solemn woman. Again, the eyes have broadened with the mouth small and jaws hung. She looks unfamiliar. As Abul moves forward enchanted, Sagir follows him.

Her white sari spreads like the wings of a crane and comes back lovingly. She bows down to the ground in obeisance. Maybe she is one of Abba's friends, perhaps the neighbouring teenage girl whom father often used to talk about.

Sagir is almost a little baffled—he cannot even understand his own father. The moment many people around have just begun to feel like near and dear ones, his father seems to move away from him. Again, the one he is getting drawn to is no less mysterious. Is it the workings of fairies, *hurs* or genies, O Allah! O *Ma Dashabhujaa*, I am here to make an invocation to you. Save my *Baapjaan*. Thinking of that he laughs to himself. Sagir has been imagining that the wall of Germany has broken down before him. The waves have churned everything into a chaos. The two sides have merged into one. As all the signs of barrier have collapsed, people are picking up its broken pieces as mementos and running and singing in merriment. Just then *Abba* shatters all his daydreams.

For the first time, Sagir feels the touch of melancholy in the voice of the masses. The agony of separation of the whole year hides behind the joy of one morning. Suddenly a terrible sound explodes inside his head—he can almost visualize the rail line scene from Ritwik Ghatak's *Komal Gandhar*, the 'minus' symbol unfolding its meaning in his head. Holding the camera along the lines, he stops with a jolt. The *new* Bangladesh is on the other side. There is no straight and unhindered way to it. Now it seems that people are suppressing their tears only for today, as if with a pretension of ecstasy. Nobody wants to show helplessness. In the broad daylight the scene before him changes dramatically. His eyes, under an illusion, were about to make such a mistake—this is a festival of pain, not of happiness.

The country that got bruised repeatedly after its partition, has kept her pains hidden in the nerve cells of these people. Do only Abul and his contemporaries feel this pain from time to time? Does not the next generation also bear the burden of that injustice and carry that heart-rending pain? Looking at the pieces of distorted language, they sometimes get enraged; the neglect of the mother tongue makes them angry. The legacy that has been snapped away by the fingers of the colonial masters makes people sigh and goads them to desperation. This is an awful anguish!

No, Sagir will not entertain all this frustration today. He will learn how people, by various means, integrate life to the bleeding wounds by giving it the colour of festivity. Festivals beyond the borders will show him the way.

Crossing the groups of scattered people, Abul goes forward with his head held high. Scrimmage and pushing even can't divert his gaze. Tagore's 'Sonar Bangla', Nazrul's 'Bangladesh' and Jibananda's 'Rupashi Bangla'—these songs are playing along with the eloquent address by Sk. Mujib. Sagir listens to the discussion of Water Distribution Agreement—how the water of the Ganges is being distributed. How the relationship is getting easy! How the spheres of movies, songs and writings are harmoniously blending together. One day they will surely merge into one again. We'll not leave it in three-four pieces. One member of the audience comments, 'That's the essence of the speech. The poet says, Nazrul has not been divided. Why didn't we make Amartya Sen our own? When Sourav Ganguly received the trophy of the best player from Sheikh Hasina, didn't the whole stadium burst into rapturous applause! The dividing policy of the British and the riots could not separate us. Now the fundamentalists, too, will step back. They have reached the peak of evil, now it is the time for their downfall.' Another member of the audience says, 'Match my words, now the buses are running and later the trains will too'. Who'll leave such a huge market untouched? At least there should be a benefit for the businessmen; let them merge together in business.

In Sagir's mind, the picture of the *Komal Gandhar* surfaces. The railway line does not end up on a minus sign all of a sudden. The faint 'plus' sign unites the horizontal line. The moving train sounds like the jingle of the anklet-bells.

Abul appears straight before the woman. Sagir does not hear what they say. Surprised, the woman stares at them with mounds of earth in her hands. Sagir tries to hear his father's words. But it is hardly possible. The chirping of birds fills his ears. The creatures of the night have given up. The discriminators have hidden in the cave today.

Sagir does not want to go near them. It is not right to spoil this rare moment of their relationship. What a beautiful smile the woman has! His father seems to melt away. Sagir never got enough of his *mother*. He lost her in childhood long ago. This woman could have been his mother. Perhaps she is. It gives Sagir a shudder. *Mother!*

Once their conversation is over, Sagir will walk forward to that motherly woman. He is so eager to know her. The land which was forcefully segregated has come within his reach today. He has to find a new way.

ఆ

Translated by Ujjwal Jana

Ujjwal Jana is Associate Professor in the Department of English, Pondicherry University, India. His area of interest includes Indian Poetics, Translation Studies and Digital Humanities.

Between the Borders
Sohrab Hossain

The sun seemed to be on an endless walk, without a care or hurry in the world. He was, as if, intoxicated with the rhythm of his own leisurely pace, and could go on walking unhurriedly for eternity. One felt that the sun was simply unable to cross over that slender line of a border.

'Hey master, the dazzling ball of fire, are you too caught up in some invisible pact with the BSF and the BDR, that you're unable to cross over this little stretch? Or have you too come to fear the batons these jawans' wield, now fuming hot and now sleepily cold in their hands! I'm sure you do. Why else would you take so much time to simply cast a foot forward from that side to this, I wonder!'

Such were the words of silent communion that passed between Hayat the *agent* at the border, and the sun, as he kept staring at the ball of golden fire that raged right from the mid-skies. For a change, it seemed to Hayat that the passage of the day had also halted, and he sat with his gaze transfixed on the sun. One could hear him fervently telling the sun, 'Hey ho the Sun God, could you just slip in a tad to this side of the border, so that I get to share a few words with you—the words lying deep down my heart?' Saying so, Hayat, the seasoned agent of this border area, seated himself in the bushy undergrowth by this Icchamati river and began his communion with the sun.

'Hey, Sun God, do you really have a nose, a face and even a pair of eyes like we have?'

'Of course.'

'You lie. How come then you don't see into the ways of this world?'

'I do.'

'You really do? I'll test you, let me try and gauge what it is that you see.'

'I see that along these borders, nights turn days while days are insipid like nights.'

'Wow!!! You got it right. What else do you see?'

'I see how like a chameleon, you people change colours night and day. I see how with an eye for an eye, you people square up revenge—one for one, one for two, for three! You fire bullets from your machines, surreptitiously exchange money. The BSF and BDR folks turn their asses and shut their eyes. The smallest of living creatures gets wind of all that you guys do, but the BSF remains blind and deaf! I see people incessantly crossing borders.'

'Bang on! Tell me one thing more. The BSF and the BDR shut their eyes as you rightly say, and border-crossers operate at large in that while. But why does it take you ages to cross over this thin line of a border?'

'Well, there are reasons.'

'Pray what?'

'Over your borderlands, I get wide-eyed with wonder as I perceive how the borders actually alter the basic nature of people. It strikes me with dismay to see how you people shed all vestiges of conscientiousness, how you confuse day and night. I simply lose track of time as these perceptions get the better of me. So, even though the border is only a narrow stretch, yet it takes me eons to cross over.'

'You mean you see it all? The ethical and the unethical, the legal and the illegal, and even the immoral...all of it?'

'Yes.'

'And everything is run by this same rule everywhere?'

'Yes.'

'Now this is an utter lie. You are one-eyed. You have no knowledge of the mind of Hayat. I acquiesced with the norms of illegality and yielded as was asked of me. Two members of my team got hauled up. Did I exact my revenge? What laws are to be had on the borders? Can you tell me dear Sun God?'

'An eye for an eye, one for one.'

'Well then. I did try my best to appease and adjust. They did away with my best accomplice; I stayed silent. Not a month could pass when they drew my paramour, my beloved Fazila into these bushes by the river. They teamed up with the BSF, went on a killing spree. Hey master, what did I do then? I left my land. Isn't that the truth?'

'Yes it is.'

'What then? After a good six months I have now returned to this lap of the Icchamati. What do I do now?'

How old would Hayat, the agent be? Thirty, thirty-two, or forty, or maybe even forty-two...who knows and who cared! The one thing about Hayat that one could never elude was the searing look in his eyes. With this intense look, he watched the sun go silent. With the same clairvoyant eyes, he saw fishing nets floating in the river. It was, as if, he could perceive the Icchamati unbosom its dirt-stained covers and open up inner recesses for the fishing nets. He observed the muddy waters turn colourful, and in that spectrum of colours, Hayat the agent could feel an upsurge similar to that felt by the waves within him; and in those waves lashed out the vivacious smuggler woman whom he so loved and had to lose to his professional hazards. 'Hei Fazila, where are you? In these waves of the Icchamati? Oh yes, I see.' To quell the upsurge in his bosom, Hayat lit a bidi. The poor tobacco stick gave in to frequent puffs from Hayat, it soon reduced to its butt, but the disturbing train of thoughts still refused to let him be at peace with himself. He then retraced his attention overhead, and found that in this while the sun had finally crossed over the thin speck of the borderline. Hayat resumed his insistent questions:

'Hey Sun God, do tell me in the wink of an eye, what should I do now?'

'Who am I to answer? Blink your eyes time and again, see the world for yourself. Follow the rule of one for one, two for two. When you live by the borders, follow the rules of the borders.'

'You say so?'

'Yes I do. For if you don't, you will simply drown in the depths of the flowing river.'

Hayat, the agent looked on as the sun steadily continued its journey towards the western banks of the River Icchamati. The passing of the sun, however, left in its trail a drift in his blood vessels, and he seemed to stir up. He was besieged with a powerful thought—*So what if it is a six-month-old issue now, there can be no letting go of the perpetrators.*

Well, no one ever really lets go. One for one, two for two—that remains the prevalent norm in these border areas. There are no 'laws' beyond that. If that be so, why then should Hayat even think of violating the norm, the 'law' as it were? Ensconced amidst those very thickets by the Icchamati, where his Fazila had been brutally violated and killed, Hayat cast one long look at the village that lay in front of him. Panitar was a border village between India and Bangladesh. The village embanked the Icchamati whose waters flowed by, though such flow never brought any happiness to the residents of Panitar. All round the year, villagers kept tearing through the bowels of Panitar, crossing borders back and forth, and yet it gave them no peace. Even the weaver birds that built nests on almost every palm tree in the village, brought no joy or peace to the dwellers. It was true that every blossoming young woman of this village would dare the lure of illegal notes and bullets, and shed their coyness to get laid amidst the thickets and shrubbery by the river, and yet joy remained elusive to their lives. While the dreamy-eyed, newly married wives of this village would light the charcoal fires in their homes and hearths, they'd still know no happiness. So it was that in search of elusive joy, all menfolk of the village, beginning with Hayat the agent to all those young and old alike, had taken to the work that made them turn their nights into days. The borders lay in their respective places on both sides, and in the in-between spaces, the agents of the village indulged in their trespassing games with the BSF and BDR jawans. Each of them is a pro in this game of taking and giving bundles of notes, and this way the nights are passed. By day, however, they would turn fishermen on the Ichhamati, weaving opulent patterns with their nets, as their brawny physiques glistened by sunlight. Thus, their nights met their days, and days dissolved into nights, while the agents earned ready cash. With the money, they'd buy saris and bangles for their wives and daughters, and occasionally even shop for bodices on the sly! As borders virtually moved this way and that, one could see the agents gloat over their spoils.

As Hayat the agent, long lost in thought, at last stood up from his squat amidst the shrubbery bushes by the Icchamati, he saw a BSF jawan he knew closely, waving a hand and summoning him. The wave sent a sensation of hatred through Hayat. He could feel a fiery ball of anger rising within his throat forming an unuttered curse, a rapid flow of blood cluttering at his heart, quizzing himself. *What's the motive now?* As Hayat's eyeballs dilated on their own, he thought for a while. Just six months back, it was the treachery of this very man that caused him lose his beloved

Fazila forever in the bushes by the Icchamati. It was because of this traitor that Hayat had to leave the place. What could have led this man to call him today, yet again? Hayat battled against himself over a host of such inexorable questions, yet never let a word out, and soon found himself retracing slow steps towards the border. It was the BSF jawan Rabin Mandal calling out to him with outspread arms. Despite himself, Hayat felt he wanted to reach out to those arms, and involuntarily he again cast a questioning look at the sun as if to seek an answer: 'Hey Master Sun God, what is your command?' As the sun seemed to wink at Hayat the agent, all his dilemma vanished in a jiffy, and he stood facing the BSF jawan Rabin—'Why do you call? What's your motive now?'

'Why do you say *motive*? I have things to talk.'

'Speak out then.'

'When did you return? And how are you?'

Hayat began to scrutinise Rabin. There came upon an intense look in his eyes with which he seemed to be taking in a penetrating glance through the inner recesses of Rabin's very essence. His razor sharp vision was slicing across Rabin through and through. In a repartee as sharp as his vision, Hayat shot back, 'Do you want to see me off this place again?'

'No.'

'Then?'

'I mean, let bygones be bygones. Come, let's be friends anew. Besides…'

'Besides?'

'Naren and the rest of the guys are also eager to make amends and be friends with you yet again. They live in fear. Fear of one for one, two for two, as is the norm here.'

'What does Naren have to fear when he has the benevolence of the ruling party on him?'

'Both yes and no I'd say. There are a whole lot of new people in the party now, in both parties I mean. Naren and his cronies are not in the good books of either party.'

'Is that a fact?'

'It is. I tell you. Naren now wants to give up arms and turn an agent like you. He wants truce. What say? Do you agree?'

Hayat refrained from replying immediately. He stared back at the Sun God, as if expecting *divine guidance*. He then cast one long look at his own village. His gaze outward seemed to open up the doors of his mind from within. He realised once again that along the border, it was always the same old story; the mafia, the BSF, or the agent—all were the same. The male members of their village had only two occupations to choose from—either wield country-made guns, or turn an agent. What else was there to be done, for they were all born out of the womb of poverty, the poverty of a torn time! So it was either smuggling, or encounters of the dark that had to be their lot. Hayat's son or other younger folks of the village were to be apprenticed to such nocturnal activities, in the course of which they would also have these close physical encounters with the women, young and old, who performed the tasks of carriers across borders. It was through such risky endeavours that people of this village earned their daily bread, by the accepted practice of receiving a third of the spoils. The agent had rights over two-thirds while one-third would be shared between the BSF–BDR.

While the borders remain in their own places on either side, deals were struck midway between the BSF and the agents. This enabled people from both sides to have passage, as agents escorted them safely to and fro. Hayat's team was an all-woman one. He had with him Fazila, there was Rauf's *Ammi*, there was Chaolaton, and Latika, and Lajjatara—all sensuously young to middle-aged women, who kept criss-crossing the borders with Hayat. They could, as it were, swallow even the moon in their stomachs, and carry their bundles along this way and that. They would carry rice, lentils, salt, oil, and raisins; and bring back clothing material, bodices, cassettes of blue films, packets of milk powder and soap.

Hayat was trying to fathom what the matter was. Why would Naren want to give up arms and become an agent like him? What motives could he be harbouring? Or was it just a pretext, a brazen lie? Why was he suddenly fallen out of favour with the political leaders whose interests he served? Seeing Hayat unresponsive and lost in thought, Rabin asked, 'Hayat bhai, I hope you agree to the proposal?' 'Yes,' said Hayat, having factored in all such possibilities.

'Should I ask Naren to come over then? So that the two of you can meet up today and work it out.'

'Yes. When?'

'In the evening.'

'Fine. So, can I leave now?'

'Yes. But you will remember the evening plan, right?'

Hayat turned back. He took two steps forward, but felt restless in the depths of his bosom, deep as the Icchamati. He stopped and turned to face the BSF jawan again, and called out, 'Rabin *Da*?'

'What is it?'

'Do you remember Fazila?'

'Yes, I do.'

'All of you took her behind the bushes, and shot your cum deep inside her womb. You did, Naren did. And then you killed her.'

'Let that be. Let bygones be bygones. It pains now to think of all that.'

'Really?'

'Hmm.'

Fazila, who lived across the border, was Hayat's beloved. Everyone in his team knew that. One evening, about six months back, the BSF violated their understanding in a state of inebriation. That evening, as it was, Fazila turned up at the borders with her sack full of stuff quite late; and Hayat was really worried. Across borders, there was a lot of distance to be covered; and well, who doesn't know that with nightfall the borders go crazy? As Fazila finally arrived, Chaolaton and Rauf's *Ammi* literally pounced upon her—'Hey woman, why are you so late? Hey Fazila, were you busy entrapping someone on the way or what?'

The entire team must advance in one file, so Fazila's delay meant that they were all stuck up. That day, Fazila was carrying rice in her bundle, Chaolaton had soap, and Rauf's *Ammi* was laden with raisin. Gradually they started walking behind Hayat. In fact, it was behind Hayat's torch light that they were actually moving. One could almost hear the thumping of their hearts; the dead of night made them pretty worried. Suddenly a volley of lights from the opposite direction swallowed up Hayat and his women. As the blinding lights darted forth, all of them with their bundles aligned themselves with the ground beneath their feet, becoming one with it. Hayat lay over them. But he did not panic. With an arm raised, and with a note held between two fingers, he began to dangle it against the piercing light. With his other arm, Hayat shot back with the light from his torch. Soon the two foci intersected, and then the BSF jawan roared out in a voice that echoed authority, 'Tonight, money won't serve, Hayat bhai'. Hearing this pronouncement, and catching the strong smell of country liquor with all their senses, Fazila and the women got numb in their bosoms. Hayat tried to persuade the drunken guard, 'Rabin *Da*, it's late tonight, please let them go. They are all hapless women in search of a living. Some other day maybe...!'

'By no means. It's gotta be tonight. And I want that one.'

Even before Hayat was done with his entreaties, Rabin's torch light had clung to Fazila's buxom body. Hayat tried his utmost to cajole Rabin out of it, but that night, he was destined to fail. Having taken in the initial anxiety, Fazila saw no sense in cringing with fear; for such things were all part of the game for them. They were all used to yielding now and then to the likes of Hayat, or the BSF, or the BDR for that matter. They had come to accept these professional hazards for the sake of livelihood, and to keep base life afloat for their children. They knew that it was necessary to extend such favours if their bundles were to cross borders. Else the watch and ward would turn vigilant overnight, and that would mean an end of the road for their only means of earning a bread. Rather than piquing these gateways to their destinies, it was pragmatic to get laid in the bushes and endure the ephemeral dance of their machismo with placid indifference.

So Fazila saw no point in procrastinating. She stood up from behind Hayat, and advanced towards the bushes to bear out what was inevitable. As she did so, Rauf's *Ammi* and Chaolaton, who now carried Fazila's bundle too, had an easy passage across the border that night.

Hayat had followed the marauders to the bushes that night, on the sly. As Fazila laid herself behind the thick undergrowth, Hayat saw more shadows gather to have their share of her. One of those was Naren, and in all likelihood, on seeing him Fazila had protested aloud—'Who are you? I will not give myself to you.'

'You will.'

'No, I won't.'

Hayat was observing it all from a distance. Being unarmed, there was nothing he could have done. So he remained a passive witness to the spectacle of dark shadows squabbling for possession over Fazila. Fazila's screams and the lustful shouts of the drunken men together seemed to rend the silent night with a groan that was difficult to live down. And then came the unexpected sound of bullets being fired, at which Hayat could no longer stick to his reserves. Despite himself, he blurted out with a scream, 'How dare you!', and immediately he found himself enmeshed in a ring of blinding lights from numerous torches. Instinctively, Hayat leaped into the bowels of the Icchamati, and as he swam away surreptitiously, he could still catch the sound of gunfire in his ears.

Even as these dark memories vividly seized Hayat's mind now, he still told Rabin, 'Okay, so be it'.

'Yes.'

'So peace it is you say, right? Naren wants to turn an agent and mend his ways?'

'Yes.'

Hayat the agent's hitherto dilating eyeballs were now calm. With a poise, he looked at the sun. The sun seemed to say, 'One for one, two for two. That's the real test of your manhood'. Hayat almost shook his head in affirmation, and said to himself, 'Yes, yes Master Sun, I agree to what you say. And I will abide by your words'.

2

Following the killing of Fazila, Hayat the agent had to go undercover and stay away from the locality for four long months. Such was the unwritten code of the place. Either you square up an offence by one of similar impact or go into hiding elsewhere. If one failed to either avenge or fly to safety, the obvious consequence would be the first blow followed by the second, the second by the third, and so on. This wouldn't stop till the entire gang that an agent had built up had been decimated. On returning home after four months, Hayat had learnt from his son that the passing of Fazila had seen heightened police activity. There were raids, detentions and what not. The police even beat up some of Naren's gang, just as Hayat's own digs were raided. And then, things settled down, just as all that submerges in the Icchamati initially muddies the waters but gradually crystallises, and the flowing waters clean everything once again. It was then that Hayat had returned. He now declared that he could no longer carry on with this work and told his son, 'My dear Bellal, it is time for you to get into the trade. Become an agent, and build up your own gang, give and take notes, and carry on the work of bridging borders the way we agents have always done it. You need to learn to battle the winds, my boy'. At the age of just forty or maybe forty-two, Hayat was ready to abdicate his position to his son, for whom this was the only way of becoming his father's true progeny. Bellal was ready for this, and yet he had a few things to clarify from his father:

'What will you do then?'

'I'll work on the river. I'll spread fishing nets; make friends anew with the Icchamati. I'll set my eyes on her bosom, and frolic with her.'

'So we're gonna interchange our work right? I'll take up yours, and you'll do mine? Is that what you're saying *Abba*?'

'Yes. But...'

'But what?'

'Work on the river needs a helping hand at times. Will you assist me at times, Bellal?'

'Oh yes, I will.'

Since then, Bellal would join Hayat in the task of spreading nets on the river in the evenings. However, that was just so. He would come up from the waters once the nets were spread. Nonetheless, two generations together by the river made for a pleasant sight, as father and son toiled hand in hand spreading nets. The waters of the Icchamati seemed to be welcoming them as the lusty waves smooched and kissed the water hyacinths abounding the shrubbery by the river banks. As the banks would flood when the Icchamati was in spate, Hayat was often seen losing himself in thoughts on life as it had unfolded. In such pensive moments, a deep yearning for Fazila would well up from somewhere deep in his heart, and leave a flaccid look on Hayat's countenance. But today was different. Today, Hayat did not lose himself in the labyrinths of thought; rather his deep eyes seemed to visualise the physical forms of Rabin and Naren. The train of his thoughts abruptly snapped at Bellal's words, '*Abba*, I need to get going a little early today'.

So saying, Bellal unfastened the nets that lay on his shoulders and grounded them on the muddy banks of the river. Without saying a word, Hayat kept observing Bellal and realised that his son was fast growing up. This meant that Bellal was also fast learning the ropes of life as an *agent*. The son once again tried to rouse his father from what seemed a reverie, '*Abba*, I am in a hurry today'.

'Why? Where will you go?'

'Nowhere. Just that there is a huge load of milk powder arriving today.'

'Today?'

'Yes?'

'Who's bringing? I mean, whose party?'

'My people, who else!'

'Rauf's *Ammi* and Chaolaton you mean?'

'Yes.'

The conversation between the father and the son abruptly faded into something more integral to their lives. At a distance on the other side of the Icchamati, there was a flotilla of boats passing by. They had flickering lights on their masts, and in such feeble lights, one could see the flutter of the Indian tricolour against the wind. These boats were definitely carrying a cargo of timber, originating from the Sunderbans and heading towards Basirhat, or maybe somewhere else. The song of the boatmen seemed to be constantly mediated upon the crest of the waves, and this was making both Hayat and Bellal somewhat pensive. And yet, the lyrics wafted into their ears: 'Oh this river of *Maya*.../ How does one set sail across this river of *Maya*/ O boatman of this *rangeela* land, how will you row across this unending stretch of *Maya*/ For the flood of its waters ravish the banks and flood the lands/ How O boatman of this *rangeela* country will you have enough of this river/ O River *Maya...*'

This was life for them. Some days, Bellal too would be taken in by the lyrics of the boatmen of either side, and would begin humming as he'd give himself a shake and embark on his boat with the nets in place. Their dinghy would then race on the surface of the waters, as they would spread out their nets to dig into the womb of the Icchamati. Hayat would get off the boat into the waters and hold on to one end of the net, while Bellal would surge ahead broadening the expanse till he'd reach the middle of the river. His task was to plant the stumps at regular intervals in the riverbed and tie the knots of the net to them. This done, father and son would engage in a long wait, holding on to the sides of their net. And then it would be time to wind up the net. On days when luck favoured, they would even get a catch of the hilsa.

Some time, while waiting, father and son would speak their hearts out to each other. Today, however, Bellal was in a hurry, so he got back to land quickly, and said to his father, 'You know *Abba*, there isn't any fun left in work!'

'Why?'

'With Durga Puja round the corner, rules have become strict in all social spheres. Political leaders and cops are hand in glove, it's the same between leaders and the BSF as well. Their bosses have ordered for mass detentions. They'll let nobody go free.'

'What do you mean?'

'It's simple, *Abba*.'

'Nah my dear boy, nothing is simple any more. It's no longer possible to remain easy going.'

'Exactly! That's just what I'm saying as well.' Bellal seemed to lapse into a kind of indifference. Then, somewhat hesitantly, he began, '*Abba*...'

What's it my dear?

'The politicians and the police are in league. They'll let go of nobody.'

'You mean they'll detain everyone?'

'Yeah, that's why everyone is trying out their own way of getting respite and protection.'

'So what?'

'I mean, you're still a fresh offender. You too should seek protection from some solid quarters.'

'What do you mean?'

'Ufff. It's simple, *Abba*. Run off somewhere before you get caught. Let the festivities get over, and then the sway of these leaders will slacken. The police too will rest in relative ease. You can then come back. Simple.'

As Hayat sat listening to his son, his abdominal muscles seemed to be getting taut like the shrubbery of cactus that surrounded him—'So this is why that bloody Naren wants truce. This is exactly the unwritten code of this place. When leaders and the cops tie up, it is time for all the agents to bury the hatchet and unite. But what did Master Sun say to me then?

'Hey ho, Sun God, it is to you that I turn for advice when it comes to identifying people and befriending them.

Hey, is it your words that are true, or my thoughts?' Hayat began to feel besieged with a spurt of excitement from top to toe. His nerves stiffened up just like the leaves of the *keora*. He could visualise right at that moment the scenes of intimacy between Fazila and Naren, between Fazila and Rabin; and an unknown desire crept into his self. The contours of Hayat's face seemed to flatten out like ripe fruits of the *pithe* plant.

Bellal had by now begun to hum…'O boatman, wherefore do you sail forth with your mast unfurled'. Suddenly, he stopped and called out—'*Abba!*'

'What's it?'

'Did you decide upon anything, *Abba*?'

'Yes.'

'Will you go away from this place then?'

'Yes, but…'

'Why "but" *Abba*?'

'You, your *Ammi*…how will you make ends meet?'

'Come on *Abba*, do such things really matter in these border areas? Nah, they don't. Aren't you the one who keeps saying—borders this side and that side, with a vacuum within. A place for the dance of ghosts it is.'

'Yes, that I do say.'

'What then do you worry about? Come on, just shed your cares. Look at the horizon, '*Abba*.'

'What?'

'Clouds. It's gonna rain.'

'Oh, really?'

'This monsoon, I haven't got even one catch of hilsa.'

'How could you? It is the fault of the times. With politicians and cops being hand in hand, the agents don't stand a chance. For all the money we keep giving them and the blows we are used to swallowing from them, we just don't stand a chance, my dear.'

Abba, I'm sure these are rain clouds. Aaaah, only if there is a shoal of hilsa coming up!

Bellal seemed lost in dreams. And yet, for all his wishful thinking, there was no trace of either happiness or peace in his life. He gathered himself and said, '*Abba*, so can I leave now?'

'Where to?'

'To the border.'

'At what time are they expected?'

'It's almost time, *Abba*, for them to be arriving.'

'Oh my dear Bellal!'

'What's it *Abba*? Bellal was somewhat taken aback by the tone of entreaty in Hayat's voice.'

'Today I'll go.'

'Why on earth?'

'It's simple, my boy. With politicians and policemen being in nexus, they'll definitely detain me on one pretext or another. Rather let me try my luck and see if I can nab someone instead.'

'I didn't get you, *Abba*.'

Hayat said nothing in reply. This took Bellal even more by surprise, and he seemed to lapse into a daze at his father's words, of which he could make no meaning. Hayat, however, was impatient now; he got on to land and rubbed off the water from his body. Then he said to Bellal, 'I'm leaving, my boy.'

3

Once they reached the point marked for them, the feet of Rauf's *Ammi* came to a halt. Chaolaton's too. Beads of sweat began to dot their foreheads. As they thumped their loaded knapsacks on the ground, it was time for a slice of the moon to show up in the sky. As moonlight seemed to pervade her body, Rauf's *Ammi* sank on to the ground beneath her feet. She then undid the material of her sari that hitherto covered her bosoms, letting the bare skin get a feel of the damp air that was around. This was luxury! So she wiped her perspiration and settled to take in the cool breeze. All the same, she could hardly hide her apprehension with Chaolaton—'That guy is still nowhere in sight, what do you think?'

Chaolaton kept silent, as her eyes seemed to be devouring the light and shade of the vast open field. Her body was bathed in sweat, and her bundle was unusually heavy today. She unbuttoned the blouse that clung tightly to her breasts, and said—'True. And that's a worry indeed.'

'Let it be. Sit down and take some rest,' said Rauf's *Ammi*.

'Hu'. Chaolaton seemed to utter absent-mindedly from the depths of thought in which she was immersed.

'What are you thinking about? That guy, is it?'

'Yes. He seems a good fellow.'

'Are you taken in?'

These were the women for whom neither their nations, nor their husbands cared. Nations or nationalities never ever recognised them, just as their husbands refused to shoulder even the most basic of their needs. So they kept traversing borders—their lives tied to comings and goings in between those borders. They only longed for belongings and human ties on any side whichsoever. Yet that remained elusive to them. So it was only to themselves that they could divulge the sorrows of their hearts:

'I'm sure the guy won't turn up drunk tonight,' said Rauf's *Ammi*.

'Booze undoes him, and he becomes a totally different man then.'

'Like father, like son, I wonder why he doesn't get the guy married.'

'Even if he does, will that get rid you of trouble, Chaolaton?'

'Ah to talk of riddance ! Whoever comes, you well know I have to get laid in the hiding of the shrubbery bushes.'

'Disgusting. Can't we have even a semblance of respectability?'

'Hai hai hai—Respectability!!! How then will you spread your snare, without which it'll be so difficult to keep life afloat?'

'That's the root of all pain, a veritable curse it is. Keep coming and going from this side to that. And keep getting laid in the shrubbery bushes. Huh, life!'

'Five big fat bullies dangling their organs at a time as if in a monkey dance, and you gotta take in all of it patiently!'

'Aren't we then human beings at all?'

Is there an answer to this question? No. That's why everybody kept mum. The night kept thickening with an eerie silence. The two women again engaged in conversing, trying to sound human:

'What are you pondering over so deeply?'

'Nah, nothing as such.'

'Are you infatuated with the guy?'

'He tries to sound amorous.'

'So what?'

'Do you recall Fazila?'

'Oh yes, I do. It's six months now that she's been missing.'

'Hayat bhai was in love with Fazila.'

'Yes, that's the reason why he's giving up the trade.'

'Ohhh…such deep feelings, is it?'

'God alone knows.'

'Does my body have to be consumed like this all my life—like a prostitute ?'

'God alone knows.'

An intense torch light from suddenly encircled them. Chaolaton could hardly have time to conceal the womanhood that lay between her bare thighs. Rauf's *Ammi* too seemed to have forgotten to pull up the ends of her sari on her breast. Everyone was unguarded. And nobody dared to utter a word. As time passed in silence they were all on tenterhooks: Who could it be?

'Hey, who are you out there? Is that young Bellal?'

'I'm not Bellal, Hayatbhai.'

Hayat re-centred the focus of the high beam from the torch and focussed upon himself. Rauf's *Ammi*'s heart skipped a beat as her breasts trembled; Chaolaton could feel a rumble between her pubes. *What could have brought him back here after so many days?* they wondered. The cool breeze now seemed to be heavy over their heads, as they asked:

'You?'

'Yes, it's me. Come, let's move.'

'But why you?'

'Yes, because the Sun God has so divined. Political leaders and police people are closely tied up these days, keep that in mind. Come on, let's move.'

As before, Hayat began to lead his women. With practised ease he took currency notes, divided up the ransom into a third as was the norm, and kept walking on. The women from across the border following him in close proximity, it looked as if it were their heavily loaded knapsacks that were walking. Unable to contain her dismay, Rauf's *Ammi* began:

'Hayatbhai, can I say something?'

'Sure.'

'What brings you back on this trail after so many days?'

'Nothing much. As I just said, politicians and cops are closely tied up in a pact between themselves, and they will let go of none.'

'What are you saying? You mean the border will be sealed?'

'Yes and no at the same time.'

'Now what on earth does that mean?'

'We agents will keep the otherwise sealed borders open. What are we worth our salt else!'

Amidst such conversation, a light beamed from the other side of the border. Immediately, Hayat responded with his flash of light. The lights from both sides of the border came face to face with each other—Hayat on this side, and Rabin on the other, with Naren in tow. On this side, Hayat determinedly placed his hands on his shoulder, where a machine with six bullets rested in composure. This sight sent a shiver down the spines of the two women. Rauf's *Ammi* couldn't help blurting out—'Why do you carry the weapon, Hayat bhai?'

Hayat did not utter a word. He spread out his other hand towards Rabin and Naren, the hand that held the notes—their share of the usual ransom. He said, 'This is my truce. Accept this.'

Rabin too stretched out his arms, and received his share of the money. He went on to say 'So today onwards, Naren is your friend, right?'

'Yes.'

'Is that your word for it?'

'Yes. Hei Naren, Take them. Escort them safely to your side of the border. Remember, you and I are both agents. Do keep up the faith of an agent. You will, right?'

'Yes, I will,' Naren acquiesced.

'Go then. Leave straight away.'

Naren turned back to leave. Rabin too turned back. Naren then said to the two women, 'You two follow me'. Chaolaton and Rauf's *Ammi* were about to take the first step towards the other border, when Hayat forbade them with a gesture. By then Rabin had commenced his walk, and Naren too. And right then came the sound of two shots being fired one after the other. The six calibre pistol in Hayat's grip shook for once and then went silent. Right in front of their eyes, the two figures that were walking away, now lay on the ground with their faces hitting the dust. Chaolaton felt a violent shiver in her crotch. Rauf's *Ammi* could only mutter, 'What did you do Hayat bhai?'

'I dispatched them across the border. Now they are with Fazila.'

In a whiff, Hayat threw away his six-bore weapon to the ground, and then said, 'Come on, let's move off. This border ain't a safe place to be now. They'll let nobody go scot free. Come on. Hei ho sunny *Baba* see I've gone by your word. Now I'll be off across the border on that side. You stay snug in your kingdom'.

And then in piercing darkness, Hayat trudged towards the border on the other side, his gait steady and increasingly gathering a pace.

ଔ

Translated by Srideep Mukherjee

Srideep Mukherjee is Associate Professor of English at Netaji Subhas Open University, Kolkata. His area of interest includes Postcolonial Literature, Performance Studies, Cultural Studies and Literary Theory.

Therefore, a Border Tale

Niharul Islam

There was a clear indication from the linesmen. A green ensign was fluttering in the village on the sandy river bed. People were moving about on the line keeping it as a mark. After enquiring those people, Ahammad stepped on the sandy river bed to cross the border to come back to his own land. But in the middle he got caught.

Two BSF personnel were on duty on the border then. They were sitting inside a solitary hut on the river bed that the *linesmen* have built for their rest. Ahammad paid no attention to anything. He was walking straight through the very slender road by that hut. He paid heed to nothing because his entrails were twisting in hunger. Then suddenly he heard someone calling him in Hindi—

'Hey brother, wait a bit.'

Ahammad stopped suddenly. He turned to see, two BSF personnel were coming out of the hut while adjusting the rifles on their shoulders. Their faces and eyes were blazing red hot.

'Where are you coming from, brother?'

Ahammad wanted to reply. But no word passed his mouth. A chilling cold fear spread over his body and mind.

'Where are you coming from? Speak out.'

'Do you have a passport with you?'

Two BSF personnel had two different questions. Ahmmad was trying hard to answer. But how could he?

'What have you got with you?'

In Ahammad's hand there were a few books wrapped in a black polythene packet. Those few books gave him some courage. He somehow managed to free his tongue. He said, 'I got nothing. These are books, only books'.

'Books!' The guards were surprised. 'What books? Show us.'

Ahammad's courage was already boosted, now coupled with a sense of interest. They were asking to see the books. Definitely he would show them. Then at least they would understand that even if he hadn't got a passport he was not a smuggler. Besides, the books he got with him were given by a noted short story writer of Bengali. He lives on the other side of Bengal. He teaches in a university. After reading one of his stories, a few questions cropped up in Ahammad's mind. He went to meet him with those questions. He could not but go. How could a writer from another country write a story about this country? And that too in the context of *Rarh Bangla*? It is not possible to paint such an impeccable picture of *Rarh Bangla* while sitting in the *Barendra* region of Bengal, on the other side of the border, unless one has some practical experiences, or some direct references, for that matter. The storyteller must then have had a close relation with *Rarh Bangla* sometime.

Exactly so. The storyteller was born in *Rarh Bangla*. There his childhood and youth were spent. Afterwards during partition he, with his family, shifted to the then East Pakistan, the Bengal on the other side of the border.

All this was a long before Ahammad's birth.

'Where are you coming from?' One BSF personnel asked while turning the pages of the books they got from Ahammad.

'From Rajshahi! Rajshahi! The university there, the university...'

'What?'

'University! University!'

'That's alright, go on.'

'A professor at Rajshahi University, a very big writer, I went to meet him.' Ahammad answered in his own brand of Hindi. See, see, it's him who has gifted me all these books. He has signed on the book see, see.

With a keen interest Ahammad ventured to show them the signature. But the BSF people cut him short.

'It's okay, leave it.'

Ahammad noticed how strangely there was a change on their faces and in their eyes. As if the iron-strong face was transforming into red colour by the rays of the sun already leaning over to the west. Ahammad again felt afraid. So he looked here and there. Some linesmen sitting inside the hut were busy collecting their 'duties'. There was no break in the coming and going of people on the very slender road across the sandy river bed. And there was no counting how many people were carrying how many sundry things! But it was him whom they were dragging still.

'What will you do with this book?'

A strange question! Ahammad got very pissed off on hearing this. But it was not the time to react, he realised. He was grumbling within. What is *meant* by what I will do with this book? What is done with books? A book is meant for reading. Is it an edible thing ? If so, he would have done that already. He was feeling terribly hungry. He thought that he would eat peacefully after reaching home. But he had to wait for a long time after reaching *Godagari*. There that *linesman* was supposed to be present. He was the one whom Ahammad gave two hundred and fifty rupees for crossing the border without hassles. Although finally he didn't see any sign of that person. Left with no alternative, he crossed the river alone and started walking on the road in the sandy river bed.

'Listen brother, we think you have to come with us to the camp.'

'Camp! Why do I have to go to camp?'

'See, we don't have any answer to it. Whatever you have to say you can say after coming to the camp. The company commander is stationed there.'

While listening to the BSF people, Ahammad noticed the trident on top of the water tank by their house. He first noticed the trident while sitting in a tea stall at *Godagari*. But it seemed to be so close then. And now it looks very far!

At that point of time, someone's voice came from the hut: 'Look Sir, the chicken owner is not paying his *duty*.'

Having heard the voice, Ahammad, along with the two BSF personnel, looked towards the hut. At the back of the bicycle there was a cage full of chickens, all poultry-bred. The person standing with his hand on the handlebar must be the chicken owner. He was talking to the person standing before the bicycle. 'Hey brother, please let it go, I don't have money with me now. Tomorrow I promise to pay your *duty*. Now please don't make a fuss over it.'

Hearing this, one BSF rushed at him, 'Why tomorrow? Why not today? Will we sit here waiting for you to come tomorrow? You motherfucker. Will give you a tight slap and then you will understand.'

The chicken owner was holding the bicycle with a cage full of chickens and hence could not fold his hands to beg for forgiveness. Probably because of this, a slap from a BSF landed on his cheek. The man could not hold his balance and fell over with the cycle with the cage on the back. And all the chickens inside started fluttering their wings in bewilderment. But while lying on the ground the man was crying and addressing the *linesmen* in the hut: 'Tell me brother, when I do not pay you *duty*? I am speaking the truth; I have not a single penny with me today. As the market for chickens was high I could not save anything. I have said that I will pay my *duty* when I will come tomorrow. Why haven't you listened to me? You got me thrashed by calling the BSF instead.'

The man kept on speaking, but no one was listening to his words. Another BSF said as if addressing the linesmen: 'Hey Kalua, take out five chickens and get this idiot off.'

Ahammad saw the order of the BSF being carried out instantly.

Meanwhile, the two BSFs, after giving order to Kalua, came to Ahammad again. They asked: 'Tell us what it is to be done with you now?'

What was meant by that? Ahammad was startled. Just now they said that he would have to go to the camp. Then what should he understand by 'what is to be done'?

The linesman named Kalu alias Kalua was taking out the chickens one by one from the cage. This caused in the cage a shudder of fluttering wings. The same shuddering was also in the mind of Ahammad. The only difference between the chickens and him was that unlike the chickens, he didn't have wings to flutter to show his perplexity. Although there was unrest in his eyes, he was watching the group of farmers busy in the field of the sandy river bed. He was watching the flight of different birds. He was watching the coming and going of many people. None of them had any problem. How free, how independent all were. He alone was bound, along with those chickens.

But how long he would stay bound like this? Ahammad thought some arrangement should be made.

While thinking over he felt Kalu to be a man close to his heart. Maybe Kalu could get him freedom from the camp. So he called Kalu. 'Kalu, hey Kalu, listen for a bit brother.'

Kalu was holding the fifth chicken he got out of the cage. Listening to Ahammad's call, he approached towards him, holding the chicken in his hand. He asked; 'What happened?'

The two BSF personnel were standing beside Ahammad. How could he talk about bribing in front of them? Perforce he took Kalu to the cover of the hut. The two BSF personnel did not say anything.

'O brother Kalu, please save me brother! After spotting these books with me they are telling me that I have to go to the camp. I am feeling very afraid, brother.'

'Why did you have to bring books? Don't you know the case of books is very serious? Your life may get shattered.'

Ahammad felt that this urchin is a little too precocious. In a different situation if he had talked like this he would perhaps have given him a slap, but now neither the condition is conducive, nor the situation. Without seeing any help he started entreating the urchin earnestly, 'Please brother see to it. Please manage something.'

Kalu said, 'Give me the money you have in your pockets. Let me try.'

Life came back to Ahammad. Quickly he put his hands inside the pockets. He had in his pockets one ten-rupee note, one five rupee and one two rupee; seventeen rupees in total. Taking those out, he handed them to Kalu. Seeing those Kalu said, 'All are Bangladeshi notes. Why didn't you exchange these for Indian notes at *Godagari*? Do you know that for these notes only you can get screwed ? In the first place, you have books, and on top of everything, there are Bangladeshi notes. Both are absolutely dangerous at this border. You bring along gold biscuits, carry along heroin and still may be saved if you get caught, but these books of yours and foreign currency...'

Ahammad was listening to Kalua's words! These were the *rules and regulations* of the border! Listening to all this he was truly stricken with fear. What if the urchin's words were true! Were they? But really a few days back Mansur Ali of Bhatu Ramnagar was returning from his daughter's house in Bangladesh to his home across the border. His daughter and son-in-law gifted him a lot of articles and helped him mount a boat from a jetty of the River Padma. A lot of articles mean a *lungi, a panjabi,* two bunches of banana, a seer of ground maize and a *Quran Sharif.* Of course, he asked his daughter for the *Quran Sharif* himself. He was getting old only and started to realise that only lately. Any day he would enter the grave. But his worldly affairs have not yet come to an end. From such a feeling of grief he asked for the *Quran Sharif* from his daughter so that in the last phase of his life he could worship and do his duties to God at least a little. While having these thoughts in mind, Mansur Ali was returning home. But alas, the luck of Mansur Ali! The BSF held him up at the border. They searched him. And getting hold of the *Quran Sharif* they thought that this old man was perhaps a secret agent. And then what distress Mansur Ali suffered!

Ahammad was thinking if his luck had similar distress in store!

'Where is the rest? Give me more', Kalu said.

From where will Ahammad get more money to hand over? Necessarily he had to say, 'I don't have any more, brother. I only had that much money in my pocket'.

'How can any arrangement be made with this money? With this paltry amount of money their mind would not be softened.'

'Then brother Kalu, please do one thing. Send someone to my place. How much will it take? I am writing a letter. Bring along whatever amount is needed.'

'Writing a letter!' Kalu told Ahammad with a grimace. 'Do you know if the BSF gets hold of that letter, you are fucked up again? Go and sit quietly under that *Babla* tree. Let me see what can be done.'

So Ahammad was sitting at the bottom of a *Babla* tree in front of the hut. The sun was setting. Bottles of beer and country liquor were pouring in inside the hut. By the side Kalu was cooking meat. Its smell was in the air. Possibly it was the meat of those five chickens. Soon the prostitutes of the fields would arrive at the sandy river bed. The line of black-marketing would open up. So many things would be smuggled through the border: cows, gold biscuits, heroin. Even marked criminals.

Ahammad was watching the group of farmers returning home. A flight of different birds were spreading their wings from the river bed. Stars started coming out one by one in the sky. That trident on top of the water tank was also getting lost gradually in the darkness. Still he remained seated, wondering how the red hot face of the BSF personnel underwent a transformation.

He was not able to understand if this was his misery or experience.

ଓ

Translated by Saikat Sarkar

Saikat Sarkar is an Assistant Professor in the Department of English, Midnapore College. He has extensively written on Black American Literature, Black British Literature, Popular Culture, Indian Partition writing and Indian English Drama.

A Mother Divided

Ahana Biswas

My father-in-law chose me as the bride of his only son. Though not something very rare, I liked to nourish the idea that there was nobody as lucky and privileged as me. In fact, I was prouder of my father-in-law, a widely famous trade union leader, than my husband. Whereas all the leading managers of reputed companies used to look upon him with awe and admiration, only I myself knew how much affection and importance I got from him inside the house.

Frankly speaking, I was a very simple girl brought up in an equally simple and ordinary family. But to me, I was quite different from others of my age. At a time when most other girls' only aim was to somehow get married, I was scared of entering into wedlock. From my childhood I had a flair and passion for painting. My mother was my greatest support in our family. She fought against all the odds inside the household and succeeded in getting me admitted in art college. This paved my way to this family today I live in.

Back then, a painting exhibition of final submission was being held in Govt. Art Gallery. It was there where my father-in-law saw me for the first time. In his eyes there was nobody more graceful than me. He purchased one of my paintings at a very high price for his office room. After returning home he started spreading his kind words of praise for me to his son, persuading him to marry me and bring me to their house as soon as possible. How embarrassed I felt when, after my marriage, I came to know from my husband that my father-in-law had praised me for my gentle nature, my physical appearance and for few other qualities of mine, I myself was unaware of. I have seen myself in the mirror. Among my friends I was most ordinary to look at. And for that, I did not like to deck myself up to look more attractive. Rather I liked to increase my importance through my work. I continued with my painting slowly but steadily. My husband was very understanding, down to earth. I was relieved to see that my father-in-law did not have any objection to my pursuing a career in painting. I had constructed a studio in the attic of my house. I have already mentioned that my father-in-law was an influential person. He used to arrange exhibitions of my paintings at little intervals, in different art galleries. My husband had to remain busy with his business. But my father-in-law, being a trade union leader, could manage leave from his office now and then. He would always accompany me to my exhibitions. I had no complaint against him in this matter. My friends used to feel jealous. They could not arrange exhibitions like me to display their paintings. So they would just pass their time by roaming here and there, watching movies and gossiping among themselves.

I had no mother-in-law. The aunt who brought my husband up went abroad to look after her own granddaughter, and never returned to India thereafter. During daytime, staying alone was not a problem for me. In fact, I loved to be by myself to a certain extent. But loneliness of this degree sometimes seemed too much to bear with. My mother had confided in me that she had suffered greatly by the women at her in-laws. Maybe that was the reason why she had gladly given her consent to this marriage. In my childhood, I had grown up in the close, loving company of my mother with whom I used to share my thoughts and feelings. Maybe that was the reason why I felt the absence of a 'mother figure' in this household. My maternal relatives, however, used to tease me saying that I should consider myself lucky for not having to cope with a mother-in-law, or else I would have surely regretted it.

When my husband was just four years old, his mother passed away. There was not even a single photograph of her in the house. When I used to ask my husband whether he remembered his mother at all, he used to shake his head silently. Since he was brought up by his grandmother and aunt, he said that he never missed his mother's presence in his childhood. He could not even recollect his mother's face. In my mind's eye, I used to subconsciously search for my unseen mother-in-law, by looking at my husband's face. There was a very little similarity between my husband's face and that of my father-in-law. Compared to me, my husband was very handsome. He had a fair complexion, sharp nose and deep black eyes. 'You look like your mother,' I used to tell him.

He would often tease that I had an obsession with 'mother-in-law'. If his mother were there, what more would I have got? I could not make him understand the need and value of a woman for another woman.

I would have felt honoured in receiving the responsibility of the entire household from my mother-in-law. I was not fortunate to enjoy the company of my husband's aunt either. With what care and affection a mother establishes her daughter-in-law in her household, this knowledge I could never gather. I had been permanently deprived of this precious experience.

Since he had no memory of his mother, I could, without hesitation, tell all those things to my husband that I could never utter in front of my father-in-law. I knew the latter had a deep wound regarding this matter. In the fifth year of his marriage, I was told, my mother-in-law died, not because of any illness, but due to a horribly repulsive incident. She was murdered during the riots that broke out during the India–Bangladesh partition. During those dreadful days in Noakhali in Bangladesh, my father-in-law's house was set on fire. Somehow, he managed to escape from that terrible ordeal with his four-year-old son clasped to his chest. But my mother-in-law could not do so. She was supposedly burnt alive in that fire and died thereafter. My father-in-law could not return to Noakhali any more. My husband's mother was not cremated, and the last rites were not performed. Reviving those memories would be too cruel and merciless for me. I would just be calm and get a touch of his sorrow. Whenever he got some free time, he would sit alone on the terrace in darkness, and I could guess who was in his agonising mind.

No, my father-in-law did not go for a second marriage. He not only lost his wife when he was young, but all his material possessions too. He took shelter in his brother's house and started life from a scratch, undergoing great struggle and sacrifice. But even then he didn't think of marrying again. I am a single child. I wish my father-in-law went for a second marriage. Then I would at least have got a brother-in-law or a sister-in-law who would have been quite younger to me.

I could have brought them up in my own way.

My husband was very grateful to his father for keeping him away from the panic of a stepmother in his life. But he had told me that my father-in-law had a relationship with an elderly unmarried woman. Her life also was very pathetic. While escaping from East Pakistan, she lost both her parents. Thereafter, when she had to live her life depending on the mercy of others, serving and attending to her relatives, my father-in-law came into her life. He took her responsibility and gave a new meaning to her life. But thinking about his son, he did not marry her or bring her into his house. After hearing this, my respect for him got coupled. I wanted to meet her. I wished that my father-in-law himself would take me to her, introduce me as his daughter-in-law and I would return home with her blessings.

My husband did not fully understand all these things. Actually, I failed to make him understand the point. He would only tease me saying that perhaps the worm in my brain would stir occasionally and provoke me to ask such questions.

I was fully aware of the inquisitive worm in my brain. After giving birth to my child, I was keen on meeting this woman. I was very much eager that at least once she would sit on my bed carrying my daughter in her lap, and I would take a photo of her in that pose. One day when I mustered enough courage and told my father-in-law about my desire, he stared at me in a strange manner. Then he went inside the room and must have told my husband such serious things that henceforth my husband abstained from sharing with me any information about the family's internal matters. That was the first time I found that my father-in-law, whom I considered more affectionate and loving than my own father, was annoyed with me. I was so hurt that I cried a lot, and the tears dropped on my newly born daughter.

Somehow my life changed after the birth of my daughter. To speak the truth, whenever I read in the newspapers about the torture, insult and harassment that girls had to face in our society, I used to feel scared. I wondered if the same thing would happen in my daughter's life. Whenever I got time, I used to paint. But somehow, unknowingly, the themes used to center on the problems of women. For the first time I realised that perhaps for the sake of my daughter, I wanted to come out of the close-knit boundary of my home.

I should step out of my house without the company of either my husband or father-in-law. I did not even want to take my husband's car. I could no longer tolerate the driver to be my constant body guard. Those things, which in the beginning had thrilled me and gave me a lot of comfort and happiness, began to look like a burden on me and seemed to curtail my independence. In fact, it was for the sake of my daughter that I was getting acquainted with the world in newer ways. I held myself responsible for the knowledge and security of the world in which my daughter would be leading her life. I could no longer remain the same shy, soft-spoken, polite wife and daughter-in-law I had once been.

For a long time, I had been trying to locate the address of my father-in-law's female companion. After many hurdles, I somehow managed to procure it from the driver, thanks to one prolonged conversation. One afternoon, when my father-in-law was asleep, I tiptoed out of the house and arrived at her place. After I introduced myself to her, she was very surprised, and so I was. So ugly! As soon as this thought came to my mind, I felt ashamed and repentant. I myself wasn't very beautiful either. Soon after my marriage, I used to feel embarrassed walking beside my handsome husband. My daughter also resembled me physically. After restraining my thoughts and putting a check on my feelings, I showed my reverence by touching her feet.

She felt apprehensive and asked me the reason for my visit. She wanted to know whether my father-in-law or husband knew about it. She didn't trust me when I told her the truth. She sat in front of me, all shrunken and shrivelled up. I tried to put her at ease by talking about trifling matters. Then at one moment I asked her why she never came to our house.

'How could I go, what would everybody say?'

'Why would anybody say anything? For so many years, you have comforted my father-in-law by your consolation. His wife had died long ago. If you were not there as a refuge, my father-in-law would not have been able to uplift himself and remain active.'

Her eyes suddenly shone up. Her grief-stricken face became pale. For a moment she became unmindful. Then touching my chin with her hands, she said in her motherly affectionate voice, 'You have come. Today my heart is filled to the brim with joy.' Once or twice, she had seen my husband from a distance. She didn't have the courage to go near him.

I could not say, 'So what! You could go near him. After all he was like a son to her'.

I just bent down and felt the touch of her hand on my chin.

But soon after, she became impatient to bid farewell to me. She told me that it was not proper for me to stay any longer in her house, and that I should return home immediately.

I requested her to allow me to stay there a little longer. I wanted to hear so many stories from her, her own life history, my father-in-law's story and so on. These days I was getting fed up with the silence at home. Look how close we have already become in just the first meeting. Then why should I leave now?

She became impatient and worried. She reminded me that my father-in-law pays for her living. It was better I left her place, she said. Being a hot-tempered person, he might get angry knowing that his daughter-in-law had gone to visit her and that she had disclosed many things to me. She was scared of him.

I decided to take my leave, not because she was getting anxious, but because she was gradually feeling uncomfortable in my presence. While leaving, I invited her to my house and pleaded her to come this time.

She said that I was a simple and open-minded girl. That is why I could easily make such a request. 'Perhaps you don't know that your father-in-law has not married me. Does a mistress have the same right as a wife? Why would everybody accept her for what she was?'

Hastily I returned home and took my daughter in my arms and hugged her. My father-in-law was still asleep. He would get up soon, dress up perfectly, have tea and leave for his party office. Perhaps later that day he would go to his mistress. He used to enjoy both independence and reverence.

As I was feeding my tender daughter, so many thoughts came crowding my mind. What if my daughter fell in love with a married man or an inhuman cruel person? After all, love knows no rule. If she had to introduce herself as somebody's mistress too!

At long last, when I could no longer keep it a secret, I disclosed the whole incident to my husband. He instantly became very angry. He even said that if I incurred the wrath of his father, we might even have to go without food. This was because my husband's business used to run because of my father-in-law and his personal contacts.

I almost dismissed that chance then and there by simply laughing it off. My husband countered, 'My father is used to dealing with people of many kinds. He has purposefully selected a simple ordinary girl like you to be the wife of this house so that the latter could never raise her voice against her husband and father-in-law. Otherwise, many marriage proposals had come from highly educated, beautiful girls from rich, cultured families. If you try to cross your limits and act crazy, all your privileges might stop. This will only increase the problems between us.'

I was hurt and angry at the same time. For a second it seemed to me that my life had become futile. If my daughter were not there, I would have run away somewhere, or perhaps would have tried to kill myself that day. But since I had to bring up my daughter, I started living with hopes in my eyes and a renewed energy. Just as my mother had attained her independence bit by bit for my sake, I too tried to loosen the shackles at home, solely for my daughter's cause.

I became fearless. I discovered that now my husband and father-in-law were looking upon me with awe since they could not dominate me any longer. Actually, in the meantime, two very important incidents happened in our family. My father-in-law was gradually being marginalised by his party members. In the end he suffered a stroke. For quite some time, he was bedridden. My husband's business also suffered a setback as a consequence.

Strangely enough, all these incidents, instead of having an adverse effect on me, increased my mental strength and helped me gain more freedom. I continued my painting as usual, but there was no scope of participation in exhibitions. My father-in-law no longer took any interest in those matters. As he did not allow me to mix with the outside world, I could not make contacts on my own either. Neither was I financially solvent. Previously, whatever money I earned by selling my paintings, used to go into my father-in-law's hands. I could not ask him to give me the money back, since he used to bear all the financial expenses of the household himself, even beyond the bare necessities. However, one daring thing I did. During his illness, I forcibly brought his mistress to our house once.

My commanding father-in-law had turned into a helpless, bedridden person when I left him with his mistress and went out for work. She did not stay for long in our house, and she never came again. But my husband did not talk with me for a long time after this incident. He thought that his father might have had a heart attack out of the sheer shock. In other words, I would have been responsible for his *murder*.

My husband could not remain stiff towards me for very long as his business was at a low ebb. His confidence was shattered. It was, as if, his backbone had broken. One day, almost helplessly, he asked if another exhibition could be arranged. There were so many of my paintings lying around in the house. Some money could come selling them.

I said, 'Now everybody has forgotten my name as an artist. Why would anybody buy my paintings?'

He praised my paintings and said that they were very beautiful. Often in this house, I myself have been complemented as beautiful. But getting compliments for my paintings?—I broke into laughter. 'Do not laugh. Your painting is Goddess Lakshmi herself in disguise. I should have paid attention to this fact long ago. If proper marketing of these paintings can be done in future, then it will earn both money and fame for us.'

After many emotions, I picked up my old paintings with renewed energy and started dusting them. While looking at them, an intense passion and desire of painting arose within me. I kept awake at night, and madly started working on my paintings, one after the other. My husband praised my work and supported me in my enterprise. He prepared the frames, started contacting the art galleries, news reporters and other artists. An art exhibition of my paintings was also held. I dressed up for the occasion and attended the exhibition, strolling here and there. My father-in-law could not come. Though my husband organised the whole exhibition and gave his full support to me, he remained in the background.

Since my husband was connected with business for a long time, he had developed excellent marketing skills. I became famous. Good reviews of my exhibition along with my photographs appeared in the newspapers. Four to five of my paintings got sold at a very high price. I made contacts with many people. To be frank, this exhibition was like a rebirth to me. Memories of my mother came gathering at this moment. I thought about my mother-in-law too, whom I had never seen before. There was not a single sign of her in the house, even in the form of a sari, a bangle, or a hairpin. In spite of that, I was all the time trying to project her image in my painting. This urge had become like an obsession to me. In fact, this particular painting earned a lot of reputation too. I could not decide whether I should put the title as 'Partition' or 'A Mother Divided'. Finally, I named it as 'A Letter to a Missing Person'. This painting was sold at a very high price. An industrialist had booked it beforehand for himself. My father-in-law had not seen this painting. But my husband remarked that he was happy to see that my *'mother-in-law mania'* had been well rewarded. It had fetched a good price. I should paint more pictures on the same theme, he said.

Yes, I continued to paint on the same subject. The tortures faced by women as a result of Partition used to be the subject of my paintings. My ailing father-in-law used to see these paintings sometimes, but in between he used to remark, 'Is there no other theme apart from these?' One day he called me to give me a little advice. 'Nobody likes to dig sorrow out of one's heart. It cannot be denied that a lot of tragedy has occurred in our lives. But if you see around, you will find that people have forgotten their trauma also. It is not possible to survive without forgetting. On the other hand, riots can break out if people constantly see such themes in the paintings and listen to discussions on the same'.

I did not agree. I said, 'People study history to rectify it and appropriate the future. Moreover, riots are mainly a result of communal hatred. Hindus have done the same thing in Punjab, Uttar Pradesh and Bihar'.

In an indifferent tone he told me, 'Do not always read history the way you've been asked to by the scholars. Reality is different. Those who have to live and coexist with others in a society, cannot depend on theories. One has to be acquainted with the mundane reality. All my life I have been an integral part of the trade union, and have been successful in that too. It would not have been possible if I had blindly followed these dry theories'.

'I am not theorising at all. Honestly, you are getting hurt perhaps because these paintings are reviving your tragic memories. I just cannot forget that gruesome incident—how my mother-in-law was burnt alive. How much she had suffered. I know how it pains when my hands get slightly burnt while cooking. I am really telling you the truth that it's purely a reflection of my feelings ', I asserted.

'*Ma*, you yourself have seen how much respect I got from the Muslim employees of the union. If I had disclosed this incident to everybody or tried to gain sympathy from it, they might have felt scared and avoided me.'

'I got the courage and strength from there only. I have full faith in your nature and personality.'

He did not say anything further, but kept on gazing out of the window for a long while. I put my daughter in his lap, to distract him from his morbid thoughts, and went in to do my own chores.

I always felt that in spite of having everything at home, the joy of life, which was missing, was due to the absence of a mother figure. Since my husband was not brought up by his mother, he seemed to have developed a shy and timid nature. I pitied him for being deprived of the security of his mother's lap. My father-in-law too seemed lifeless. For this reason, perhaps, in spite of trying hard, I could not free myself from this subject. Moreover, this topic brought me reputation, and my paintings were selling well. So it was not possible for me to change the subject now. In this connection I also made an acquaintance with a gentleman from Bangladesh, called Muhammad Shamim, which developed into a friendship.

We became great friends. His behaviour was like that of a small brother. His friend circle also was of like-minded, sensitive people, and they used to work on the theme of communalism. They were very much interested in arranging an exhibition of my paintings in Bangladesh. They became friendly with my husband too and tempted both of us with an offer of taking us to Bangladesh, even to our village in Noakhali. 'Aren't you eager to see your ancestral house in Noakhali?', they said.

My husband had already agreed gladly to their proposal. He hastily made arrangements for us to go to Bangladesh during the exhibition. I was also extremely happy. Only my father-in-law did not give his consent. He feared that his son and daughter-in-law would not be allowed to return alive to India from there.

For the first time, I saw that my husband protested against his father's impractical and irrational worries, and in front of him ordered me to start my packing. That night my father-in-law did not take his meal. As a result, I too had to skip my dinner. When I went to prepare his bed, I was stunned to see him. Tears were flowing down from his eyes. Wiping them, he said, 'When you want to go to Bangladesh so much, do so. I have become old. I know my words will have no value now. Your art exhibition is in Dhaka and Chittagong. Just keep my one word. Do not go to my village in Noakhali. In future I will never give you any further advice, nor try to guide you according to my will'. After saying this, he started wailing loudly like a child.

All my excitement about Bangladesh fizzled out. When I told this to my husband he also flared up. 'Why are you taking my father's words seriously? He is suffering from senility. Throughout his life he has led a respectful life with his head held high. Now at the fag end of his life, he is crying. I have to take him to a psychiatrist for treatment,' he said. I wanted to say that he was not suffering from any mental disease. Suddenly he must have remembered the traumatic experience of that gruesome incident. Moreover, because the themes of my paintings were partition, communalism, position of women, etc., he was feeling tense and anxious for our safety. There was nothing unusual in his behaviour.

My husband became angrier with me and accused me saying that his father's tears had dampened my enthusiasm and spirit of going to Bangladesh. He reminded me about the theme of my paintings, being so much relevant to the people of that region. My paintings will sell most in this area, he said. 'The more deliberations and debates are held on this topic, the more people with flock to the exhibition to see your paintings, and the more famous you will become. Today's political situation is not such that somebody will kill you. If by chance somebody attacks you physically, at that very instant you will gain international attention. I cannot but praise you for selecting such a theme for your paintings.'

My husband was so elated with the idea of going to Bangladesh that he purchased a black Benarasi sari for me, which he wanted me to wear on the day of the inauguration. He was certain that many photographers would come and that I should be an epitome of beauty in their eyes.

I had narrated to my Bangladeshi friends the fate of my exceedingly beautiful mother-in-law. I had perceived that the story had left a deep mark in their hearts. After being a witness to my father-in-law's emotional breakdown, I had no desire to visit my husband's ancestral house. But I had confided in Shamim all the details about my husband's village—name, location, etc. He had assured us that he would visit and see the condition of their house in his own eyes. From his description too we would get almost a semi-perfect idea of the place.

After returning from his visit to our ancestral house in Noakhali, Shamim anxiously phoned us one day. I happened to take the call myself. I was stunned to hear from him that my mother-in-law was still alive. She was now the widow of a rich Muslim gentleman called Rahamat Molla. I couldn't believe him. I said, 'This is not possible.' He said that in that village many people know my father-in-law. He started pouring out such information about our family, that I had never shared with him. My husband took the phone after me. He also heard the details from Shamim, after which he put down the phone in a glum mood and remained silent.

I said, 'There must be some mistake'. My husband said that he also felt the same. At that moment there was nobody except their father in the house. Their grandmother had already come to India with her younger sons. Since his father was employed in Bangladesh, he could not return to India. I was wondering, maybe my mother-in-law's body could not be fully cremated. Perhaps it was found in a half-burnt condition, and she miraculously managed to survive after that. But was it possible for her to be somebody else's wife? My husband said that he had heard from his grandmother that his mother was so beautiful that she used to hide her face often by covering her head with her sari, and as a result, she often used to stumble and fall down.

After a little silence I said, 'Did she really have a choice but to get married? How else could she have survived? It was not possible for her to flee to another country all by herself. In those days education was not so common among girls.

And even if they educated themselves, of what use was it to them? The price of the flesh was always the same.'

At one point my husband wanted to tell all the details to his father over the phone, and discuss with him what to do. But I asked him against it. He was all alone in his house. I could not gauge his possible reaction after hearing all these from his son. Anyway, after listening to all these topsy-turvy pieces of information from Shamim, my husband was determined to visit his birthplace, hear with his own ears the rumour that had spread and investigate the matter himself.

Whether it was due to Shamim's prior information to the villagers about our intended visit, I do not know, but we were received very cordially. Many families wanted to invite us for lunch or dinner. The village was very beautiful, surrounded with coconut trees and betel nut trees everywhere. We were sitting in somebody's drawing room. Soon after, an elderly person came to escort us. He started caressing my husband like a small child by patting his body and head with his hands. He spoke to my husband in his own language, 'Can you recognise me? I worked as a *kamla* in your house. After you had left this village, your burnt house remained vacant for long. What a terrible condition we were in at that time. We repaired your house and started living there. My children have now grown up, they have completed their education and are doing different jobs. Now since you have arrived here, you will stay in your own house. I won't let you stay in anybody else's.'

That man's attitude was so sincere and affectionate that we had to go with him. He carried my daughter on his shoulders, something he used to do with my husband as well, he told.

Yes, I was compelled to enter the interior of the house. The eldest female member of the household embraced me and said, 'You took so long to visit your mother-in-law!'

I almost jumped and took one step behind and looking at her face, thought to myself, 'Was she the person...?'

She laughed and said, 'Are you assuming that I am your mother-in-law? It's not so, my dear. Have your lunch, take rest, then I will take you to her. She has also got the news about your arrival.'

I was living in the ladies' wing of the house. Many women were coming to see me. But this particular issue was weighing on my mind so much that I was unable to talk with them freely. I just kept on staring at them vacantly. That elderly lady must have noticed something unnatural in my behaviour. She took me away from the crowd, and said in an affectionate tone, '*Ma*, I can guess what is going on in your mind. But where is her fault? Your Hindu society did not accept her.'

I said, 'Did she manage to survive on the verge of dying?'

'Yes *Ma*,' she replied. 'Women have to survive even when they are approaching death. During the riots when the terrible incidents took place, men had become monsters. We had to live with those sinners and lustful creatures, and give birth to their children.'

I had arrived exactly in the middle of my subject. But I had no desire to think about it. I had become entangled in a mystery, and till the time I unveiled it, I had no interest in anything else.

'We knew that she was burnt to death.'

'When your house was set on fire, she was not in that house. Your father-in-law, along with his son, had taken shelter in the Haque household, whose members had saved the lives of five people. They were certainly able to do so. Later on, they even helped them cross the Bangladesh border.

'Then where was my mother-in-law?'

'It was the age of the monsters, *Ma*,' she said affectionately. 'Your mother-in-law was very pretty. Everyone in the village knew there was a jewel in your house This makes me think that luck is not totally against ugly and unattractive women. They somehow get spared from the clutches of these monsters.'

'Tell me what happened thereafter?'

'Riots broke out. I was still unmarried at that time,' she said. 'But a lot of discussion used to take place in the house regarding this incident. As you can see, your house is located in a remote corner of the village. Your locality was not so posh and well-populated as it is now. For quite some time, every night, some unknown people used to carry away your mother-in-law and return her back to her house, the next morning. As I am telling you, men had become demons at that time.'

She continued, 'Your mother-in-law was after all a married woman in a Hindu household. There were no other relatives staying in the house at that time. But her husband was there. She did not go with those men out of her own will. But it seems her husband could not accept this fact. Nor could he prevent them from doing so. If he had protested, he would have been murdered. One day when he resisted, they lifted your husband, only a kid then, and were about to fling him on the ground violently. On seeing this, your mother-in-law fell on their feet and cried that she would go with them whenever they wanted to take her. She would do whatever they wanted her to do, but implored that they should release her son. Ironically that turned out to be her greatest fault. When she returned home the next day, her husband did not let her enter. In extreme agony and grief, she jumped into that pond in an attempt to end her life. Rahamat Molla, who was young and sturdy at that time, was standing nearby watching his fields. As soon as he spotted her, he plunged into the water and rescued her by clutching on to her hair. I don't know much about your religion. Your father-in-law was still adamant about not accepting her. Seeing no other way, Rahamat Molla took her to his house. That same night, your house was put on fire by a few unknown people.'

I was swaying between belief and disbelief. My father-in-law, a fair mix of good and bad, seemed a complete stranger to me at that point. I was feeling tempted to go and narrate the whole story to my husband. But he was engrossed in gossiping and eating with others at that time.

I told her, '*Chachi*, I have heard that she never came out of the house. She was a very chaste and devoted wife. How could she marry again?'

'Was she left with any other alternative? Nobody offered to help her to cross the border. I had no idea about where your relatives were staying in India. Nobody came to enquire about her. Today you have come after so many years. She stayed in Rahamat Molla's house. People constantly kept coming and going in his house, and the number was increasing. Moreover, people were coming and asking for women to be returned to them. Who knows where they were being taken? Many stories were floating in the air then. Rahamat Molla already had a wife and three children. No, *Ma*, your mother-in-law did not attempt suicide thereafter. He married her and had two sons and one daughter from her. But his first wife harassed her and gave her a lot of trouble, though she never complained about that to anyone. I have heard that her second husband treated her well and looked after her nicely.'

In the meantime, *Chachi* had brought an array of delicious eatables for me. But I was not happy inside. I told her, before meeting my mother-in-law, I won't be able to put a morsel into my mouth.

Chachi took me inside. I called my husband too. Who knows whether the person I was going to meet was really my mother-in-law or not? Even then I was not eager to see her in this new role. I just wished that everything was false.

Chachi disappeared into a big house surrounded by high walls. This was Rahmat Molla's house. Some people were calling us to go inside. We proceeded, and then stopped in front of a door. *Chachi* told us to sit down and wait, as she was coming.

We took our seats. My heart was beating fast. My husband's face had turned pale and sad. I somehow managed to touch his cold pair of hands.

My mother-in-law entered the room. Both of us stood up. She was in black burkha and kept standing. *How will we see her?*, I thought. She slowly came forward and touched my daughter, who in turn started pulling at her dress in a child-like manner. Her frail white hand appeared to be trembling. She turned towards the door. *Chachi* held her and took her inside the room.

I followed them from behind. My husband came after me helplessly. We hadn't been able to see her fully yet.

As I observed, it was not mandatory to wear burkhas in this place. *Chachi* did not wear a burkha herself. Seeing a young man, I stood still with great surprise. He also kept looking at my husband in great wonder. Two brothers, what similarity between them!

Chachi said that my mother-in-law's health was not good. 'She cannot bear so much excitement. She is trembling terribly. At least she has seen her son. Now she can go to her grave peacefully. It was to save her son's life that she had to pass through all this ordeal.'

I could not resist myself. In the evening I went to her house all by myself. I secretly entered her room. She was not alone. There was a young girl with her. She was not in burkha, and was offering her namaz seated on a piece of cloth spread on the floor. She did not stop even after seeing me.

After completing her prayers, when she stood up, I showed my respect to her by placing my head at her feet. She did not say anything and started doing her work slowly. She was searching for something. Feeling insulted and dishonoured, tears came to my eyes. She seemed familiar to me. I knew her body, her eyes, her nose, the complexion of her body—everything was known to me.

She asked that girl, 'Why has she come? What has she come to see?'

The girl lowered her eyes after a fleeting glance at me. She said to me, 'Come, let us sit in the other room. My *Ammi* is not in the right shape now. She doesn't have mental stability.'

'I have no mental stability? How can you say that?', she almost shouted. 'It would have been better if it were so. When five – six monsters used to take me away with them, at that time my mental condition was abnormal, wasn't it?'

The girl wanted to push me forcibly to the other room. She scolded her mother. 'Your health is not well, *Ammi*. Please keep quiet.'

'Why should I keep quiet?', she said. 'She should know what an inhuman and cruel person's daughter-in-law she is.'

The girl felt ashamed and covered her mother's mouth with her hands. 'What nonsense are you speaking? She is our guest,' she said. Then she turned towards me and said, 'Please don't mind'.

She removed her daughter's hand from her mouth forcibly. As she sat on the bed, trembling continuously she said, 'I always tell the girls not to trust anybody. Never believe the menfolk. As long as you are somebody's wife, they will behave and talk with you nicely. In what a world of falsehood I was living and having faith in my inhuman husband. How stupid I was!' She burst into tears.

The girl clasped her mother. 'Are you feeling sick, *Ammi*?', she said. I kept on standing helplessly, saying nothing.

She went on consoling her mother, '*Bhabi* has not said anything unpleasant to you, *Ammi*.'

'*Bhabi*? Why do you call her "*Bhabi*"? Who are they? How are they related to me? They have snatched my son from my bosom. They have flung me in the face of the inhuman creatures. I did not understand in the beginning. It was later that I realised, that man also was no less a beast than the others.'

The girl looked at me and said, '*Ammi* just cannot forget all her memories related to her elder son.'

I went close to her and wanted to touch her. She pushed me away and said, 'No, no, I have forgotten everything. Why shouldn't I forget? They are not related to me.'

She started to search for something. She pulled out some boxes and trunks from beneath the bed. Then she took out some pieces of jewellery and threw them at me. 'Let her take away all these things,' she said. 'It all belongs to them. Ask her what else I have to give. I have already lost my chastity, prestige and honour. If she wants to peel off the skin from my body, let her do so.' She wanted to take off her sari. Her daughter with all her strength held her tightly and stopped her from doing so.

I do not know why I was crying—whether it was after hearing my mother-in-law's horrifying, tragic, disgraceful experiences or realising my sense of insult and indignity. I was leaning against the door of their house and crying. By this time other ladies of that house and surrounding neighbourhood had gathered there to have a look at me.

The young girl in a sad and distressed voice requested me to go and sit in the other room, otherwise she would not be able to control her mother.

Slowly I came to the adjoining room. The housewives and other women gathered there were telling me that my mother-in-law always suffered from a mental problem. Only rarely she behaved normal. Her children were very nice and took good care. Otherwise, she would be roaming in the streets by now.

The girl had bolted her mother's room from outside and came and stood by my side. Her head was lowered, as if she was greatly ashamed at her mother's behaviour. I was her eldest *Bhabi*. She was my youngest sister-in-law. But it was difficult to establish our relationship in front of so many people.

The intelligent girl looked at the people and said, '*Bhabi* will take a little rest now. You can come later if you want. You know very well that my mother will get furious if she sees so many people here.'

When the dissatisfied crowd dispersed, I told her to open the door. She said that she had pacified her mother and put her to sleep. Now she would not wake up.

Addressing her as sister, I implored her to open the door. There was nobody else there. 'I will stay for only a little while. Let me see her to my heart's content.'

The door was opened. She was lying on the bed calmly. We were standing near the door. In a lowered tone I was talking with the girl about her, and also invited her to come once to India with her mother and stay in our house in Calcutta. The girl admitted that her mother often talked about her eldest son. When her *Abba* was alive he also wanted to take her to India to see her child. But her *Ammi* had not agreed. Now after seeing her son after such a long time how abnormally and emotionally she was behaving.

But *did our voices become louder*? I saw her sitting up on the bed. Did she hear what we were saying? Otherwise, why did our pale and shrunken mother cry out —

'I would have gone. But the child, whom they had snatched away from my bosom, is not the same individual I am seeing now. He is a different person. I feel scared, *Ma*, I am terribly frightened of menfolk.'

ଔ

Translated by Eva Datta

Eva Datta retired as Associate Professor of English from Kharagpur College in 2011. Her area of interest includes Indian English, Diasporic Writing, Modern British drama and Translation studies.

Authors

Bibhutibhusan Bandyopadhyay (1894–1950) is one of the greatest novelists of Bengal. *Pather Panchali, Aranyak, Adarsha Hindu Hotel, Ichhamati, Kinnardal* are some of his most representative novels. He occupies a major place in the realm of young adults' literature. *Bone Pahare, Hiramanik Jale, Chander Pahar*, etc. are classic examples of this kind of literature. He was posthumously awarded 'Rabindra Puraskar' for *Ichhamati* in 1951.

Satinath Bhaduri (1906–1965) was born in the Purnia district of the then Bihar, and completed his higher studies in Patna. He actively participated in the Non-cooperation Movement and Quit India Movement led by Mahatma Gandhi, and was imprisoned from time to time. *Jagari* (1945), his first novel, was written in the Central Jail of Bhagalpur. The novel won Rabindra Puraskar in 1950. *Dhorai Charit Manas,* which is a largely autobiographical novel, is often considered his *magnum opus*.

Syed Waliullah (1922–1971) was born at Sholashahar, Chittagong of Bengal Presidency, and shifted to Dhaka after the Partition, and then to Karachi for his job at the Pakistan Radio. During this period he had travelled in many parts of the world as a press attaché and finally, in 1960, he moved to Paris as the first Secretary to the Pakistan Embassy in Paris. Later on, he was appointed as program specialists at UNESCO, Paris, in 1967, which he had served until his death in 1971. For his debut novel, *Lalsalu* (1948), which got translated into French and English, he received the Bengal Academy Award in 1961. Two of his other novels, *Chander Amabasya* ('*Night of No Moon*', 1964) and *Kando Nadi Kando* ('*Cry,*

River, Cry, 1968) use stream-of-consciousness technique and deal with French Existentialism and Post-war Absurdism.

Satyapriya Ghosh (1924-2003) was born in Banaripara of Barisal, now in Bangladesh. He always had a penchant for anti-elitist literature and culture. His early stories like 'Mayapath', 'Amode' and 'Biye' that deal with the afflictions of refugees and the agony of the Partition. His novels include *Char Deyal, Gandharba, Raater Dheu, Bohu Basanai, Swapner Pheriwala, Manpatra* and *Banitajanam*. In 2003, his collection of stories entitled *Galpasamagra* (Vol.1) was awarded the 'Kathasahitya Puraskar' by the Pashchimbanga Bangla Akademi.

Dinesh Chandra Ray (1930-1978) wrote only four novels (*Sonapadma, Kusher Putul, Leap year er Mrityu, Bibhabori*) and five short stories ('Oiraboter Mrityu', 'Airaj Moniraj', 'Kulapati', 'Orka', 'Anandamoyir Sandhane'). Graduating from Ananda Chandra College, he settled at a tea garden for fourteen years, before joining the Ministry of Labour, Government of India. The themes of his fictions cover a wide spectrum of issues ranging from the Partition of Bengal, Left wing politics of 1960s, Emergency of 1970s to homosexuality, bisexuality, alternative sexuality, etc.

Dipendranath Bandyopadhyay (1933-1979) is one of the greatest fiction writers of Bengal in the second half of the 20th century. His literary career was brief but dense. His published works include nearly fifty short stories, four novels and a significant number of newspaper articles. His stories like 'Ashwamedher Ghora', 'Charjapader Harini', 'Jatayu', 'Shokmichil' and the novels namely *Tritiyo Bhuban,* and *Bibahobarshiki* are among the finest gems in the casket of Bengali fiction. He was a staunch political activist. His reportages were immensely popular with contemporary Bengali readers that rose to the level of literature.

Atin Bandyopadhyay (1934–2019) is a leading novelist in the realm of Bengali literature. After the Partition, he migrated to India and spent the early part of his life as a refugee. After permanently settling at Calcutta. He acted as an adviser of a publishing company and later took up journalism as a profession. *Nilkantha Pakhir Khonje* is his magnum opus. The novel centres around many episodes relating to the joint rural life of the Hindus and Muslims and does not end up with Partition; rather it ends up with the protest of Samu against the declaration of Urdu as the only national language of Pakistan and later culminating with the death of Isham as a language-martyr. He received the Sahitya Akademi Award for *Panchasti Golpo* in 2001.

Jyotsnamoy Ghosh (1936–2008) was born at Jamalpur in the district of Mymensingh in today's Bangladesh. After completing his Master's in Bengali literature at the University of Calcutta, he joined a school as a teacher. He excelled in writing both short stories and one-act plays. His story entitled 'Kaji Saheb' that appeared in *Sahitya Patra* is worth mentioning.

Debesh Ray (1936–2020) was born in Baghmara village of the Pabna district of the present Bangladesh. He came to Jalpaiguri along with his family before the Partition. He taught at Jalpaiguri Anandachandra College from 1959 to 1974. He also worked as a research fellow in the Centre for Studies in Social Sciences, Kolkata. His first story was published in 1952. *Jajati* is his first novel. North Bengal often serves as a background to his fictional works. *Teesta Parer Brittanto i*s his magnum opus in which he created 'the geography of his narrative'. The author received the Sahitya Akademi Award for this novel in 1990.

Ashis Sanyal (1938) was born in Sushong, Durgapur, now in Bangladesh in 1938. The partition of the country brought him to Calcutta where he had his education. As an eminent writer of the 1960s, he has authored more than 150 books both in Bengali and English. His works have been translated into different Indian and foreign languages. He has received many prestigious awards like National Poet (1989), Sahitya Mahopadhyay Award (1991), Bhualka Award (1992), Michael Madhusudan Award (1996), Bangabandhu Award, Tangail (2006).

Hasan Azizul Huq (1939–2021) is one of the finest writers of Bengali fiction from Bangladesh. Though born at Jabargram in the district of Burdwan in West Bengal, after the Partition, he moved to East Bengal. Till 2004, he served the Department of Philosophy of Rajsahi University. Later on, he was appointed in the Bangabandhu Chair of the Department of History, University of Dhaka, and in 2014, he was elected as the President of Bangladesh Pragati Lekhok Sangha. He has to his credit an extensive corpus including short stories, essays, novels, poems, autobiographical works, critical writings and plays. His novel, *Agunpakhi* won him Ananda Puraskar in 2008. He was awarded the *Ekushey Padak*, the second highest civilian award in Bangladesh in 1999.

Jiban Sarkar (1941–2016) was born in Balliyakanda village of Dhaka, Bangladesh, and came to North Bengal and started living in Dhupguri after Partition. After some time, he moved to Calcutta and settled in the city. He taught at a school in Cossipore. The pain of Partition and the agony of refugees and rootless masses are poignantly represented in his writings. He made his debut as a writer in *Nandan Patrika* in 1966. He has to his credit a couple of novels like *Nadir Naame Naam, Boroma Brittanto, Ekjan Manush*, etc.

Sadhan Chattopadhyay (1944) was born in 1944 in Sholna village of the Barishal district in the present Bangladesh. After graduating with Honours in Physics he taught at a Higher Secondary school. Since 1970s he has been engaged in writing fiction and non-fictional prose in Bengali. In total, his works include approximately 600 short stories, 400 essays and 26 novels. He has contributed a significant number of essays and short stories to little magazines as well.

Jatin Bala (1949) is one of the most prominent voices of Bengali Dalit literature. Born in Parhiyali, Manirampur, in the Jessore district of the then East Pakistan, he completed his M.A. in Bengali Literature from the University of Calcutta and later on served the Welfare Department of the Government of West Bengal. He wrote poems, short stories, memoirs, autobiographies and critical books depicting both the inhuman lives of the refugee camps and the deplorable lives of the Dalits of Bengal.

Sailen Sarkar (1952) was forced to leave for East Pakistan, in his mother's lap, just after his birth in India, crossing the border. There she stayed with the child for three years and again came back to India. His father was a Gandhian activist and travelled in different parts of India. His first story was published in the Bengali periodical *Desh* and thereafter in the *Anandabazar Patrika, Sananda, Ei Samay* of Kolkata, and *Kali O Kalam and Ananya* of Dhaka, Bangladesh. He has to his credit six novels. Last but not the least is his book named *Durbhikkher Sakkhi*, which is based on interviews with more than fifty people, living on both sides of the border, who were victims of the famine of 1943.

Devi Prasad Sinha (1954) was born in Assam, as the eldest son of refugee parents who arrived in Assam in the first flush of exodus following India's partition. After majoring in English Literature, he worked in a bank till he retired a few years back. He shuttles between Guwahati and Kolkata now. He has co-edited a Bengali literary magazine, *Eka Ebong Koekjan*, for about thirty years. He is also the author of two slim books of short fiction in Bengali: *Rupkathar Pratyabartan* ('Return of the Fairy Tales'), and *Simanter Opore Thomke Thaka Pa* ('The Suspended Step').The agony and heartbreak of the rootless masses is the theme that obsesses him, and keeps coming back in his stories.

Adhir Biswas (1955) arrived in India as a refugee in 1967 and completed his schooling and graduation in Calcutta. His four-part *Deshbhager Smriti* ('Memories of Partition') was published in 2005. His four-volume collection of stories, novellas and novels for young readers, *Udojahaj* ('The Aeroplane'), was awarded the 'Vidyasagar Memorial Prize' by the Bangla Akademi in 2017.

Kapil Krishna Thakur (1956) the renowned Bengali Dalit activist who has been fighting for the socio-political rights of the Motua community of Bengal, is also an acclaimed writer whose works range from poetry to short stories to critical writings. Born in Satpar village, Faridpur in Bangladesh, he was taken to this side of Bengal by his mother when he was merely five months old. *Ujantalir Upakatha* is one of his most representative works for which he received the Adwaita Malla-Barmal Award by the Government of Tripura.

Anil Ghosh (1956) was born in 1956 in Basirhat, West Bengal. After finishing his schooling and college education in Basirhat, he went to the University of Calcutta to obtain his Master's in

Bengali Literature. Having a brief engagement with journalism, he switched over to the world of publications. He is the member of the editorial board of *Parichaya Patrika*, a Bengali magazine of repute. He has authored no less than twenty-two books ranging from collections of poems, short stories, to novels, plays, essays and reflections. Some of his renowned works are *Ranakshetra, Khoi Jiboner Rupkatha*, etc.

Goutam Aalee (1957) was born in Hatiara village of Faridpur district of the then East Pakistan. He crossed the border and came to this side of Bengal in 1970. Again, he returned to independent Bangladesh in 1971 but after the demise of Sheikh Mujibur Rahman he returned back to West Bengal in 1975. He has actively engaged with the *Bangla Dalit Sahitya Sangstha*. His notable work is *Jotugriher Chhai*.

Amit Mukhopadhyay (1962) spent his childhood in Maithon, now in Jharkhand, and settled in Kolkata after dwelling in several other cities. He did his M.A. in English from the University of Calcutta and serves in the state administrative service. He is primarily a fiction writer in Bengali language. He has a total of nine books so far to his credit—*Vasandingi* (2017) and *Ashwiner Din* (2019), being two of the brightest creations. He also writes in English and Hindi as well and loves to translate.

Sohrab Hossain (1966–2018) was born at Matia, West Bengal, joined the Department of Bengali, Anandomohon College in 1996. He was a versatile writer. His novels include *Maharan, Arshi Manus, Sanga-Bisanga*, among others. He was a recipient of many awards like Sorbobharotia Katha Puroskar, Ila Chanda Puroskar, Sirajul Haq Smriti Sadhana Puraskar, etc.

Niharul Islam (1967) was born in Harahari village in the district of Murshidabad in 1967. He graduated from the University of Calcutta. He began his literary career in the early 1990s. His first story 'Phuli' was published in *Kourab* magazine although he came to prominence with the publication of his poems 'Janmantar Britanto' in *Desh*. He has to his credit over 350 stories. He wrote novels like *Janam Dour, Ichhaputul,* etc.

Ahana Biswas (1970) was born at Asansol, West Bengal. She completed her studies and research at Visva-Bharati, Santiniketan. She teaches at Vivekananda Mahavidyalaya, Bardhaman. She has published her stories, poems, novels and essays in reputed Bengali magazines like *Desh*, *Sananda,* and Bengali dailies like *Bartaman* and *Pratidin*. Her works have been translated into other Indian languages like Hindi and Tamil, and foreign languages like English and German. Man, environment and fine arts constitute her areas of interest.

Glossary

Aamkasundi: A kind of mango pickle.
Aanchal: end of a sari, often used to cover head of women traditionally.
Agrahayon: Eighth month of Bengali calendar when it is early winter in the region.
Akash-pradeep: ('Akash' literally means sky, and 'pradeep' is lantern); a lamp suspended from the top of a bamboo pole, lighted in honour of a god or goddess every evening in the month of Kartik.
Akhraa: A place where the Vaisnavas assemble for religious worship.
Alaap: The slow, long opening section of Indian classical music that elaborates and develops a raga.
Ashwin: The sixth month of the Bengali calendar.
Babla tree: It is a fast-growing evergreen tree with a broad and rounded crown found in the dry lands of Africa and South Asia. The height of the tree can vary between 2.5 meters to 14 meters depending on the soil. It is a multipurpose plant and is the source of food and medicines for the local people.
Babui: The weaver bird (Ploceus philippinus) is commonly found across the Indian subcontinent and Southeast Asia. They are best known for the hanging resort type nests that they weave from leave and twigs on treetops.
Bachir: Originally Bashir, Bachir in rustic tongue.
Baghbandi: A hunting game played on board by two players.
Bainyabari: Cultivation field made fertile by flood-induced alluvium and used for sowing cereals and flowers.
Baltikhali: The name means 'empty bucket' in Bengali.
Banglu: A pejorative term used for the Hindu refugees from East Bengal.
Barendra region: This was a region of North Bengal, now in Bangladesh. An undulated land of high altitude the region is surrounded by various rivers on three sides. On the west the region is bordered by Ganges and Mahananda while the river Karatoya skirts it on the east and Padma on the south.
Bhadra: Genteel.
Bhog: Food offered to the deity.

Bhonsri: It is an offensive Hindi slang.
Bigha: A traditional unit of land measurement in eastern India, Nepal and *Bangladesh*. It is 1/3 of an acre and is equal to 20kathas/cottahs.
Bishe: Originally Bishu, Bishe in rustic tongue.
Bokul, gondhoraj, hasnuhana: These are sweet-smelling flowers of the summer season.
Boroj: The term in Bengali can be interpreted in two ways—(a) a borough or a fortress, (b) betel leaf plantation. Since the term is used as a landmark in the story the first meaning appears to be more appropriate.
Brahmadatti: A Brahmin male after his death becomes a brahmadatti, a ghost who is believed to dwell in stone-apple/ wood-apple tree. In the hierarchy of ghosts, they hold high status.
Bratakatha: Brata is a ritual performed usually by women during the worship of various deities including folk deities. This ritual is accompanied by ballad-like narratives (*katha*) usually sung or narrated by a woman; this narrative describes the misfortunes that befall men and women for their misconduct which displease the deity, and also points to the good conduct that may propitiate the deity who would then shower blessings on those who are performing the brata.
BSF and BDR: The Border Security Force (BSF) guards the Indian borders, while the Bangladesh Rifles (BDR), now redesignated Border Guards Bangladesh (BGB) are in charge of Bangladeshi territory. In common parlance, BSF and BDR are terms that are woven into the lives of people on both sides in territories adjoining the border areas.
BSF: Border Security Force of India.
Burkha: A loose garment that covers the face and body and is worn in public by certain Muslim women.
Chaitra Baisakh: The last and the first month of the Bengali year.
Chanachur: Bombay mix or Indian snack mix (namkeen).
Chand Saodagar: A play composed by Manmatha Roy in 1927 on the basis of the Manasamangal Kavya (a popular eulogistic narrative paying homage to a local Bengali deity called Manasa, the snake-goddess).
Chandimandap: A structure either square shaped or round made of a concrete base and a thatched roof overhead with sides open situated at the central place in a village used by elderly men for evening gossips and meetings.
Dada-Dadi, Nana-Nani: Grandfather and grandmother.

Devadasi: Official name of maidens dedicated to serve the gods in the temple through their dancing and singing as found particularly in Orissa (modern day Odisha) and South India. One may look up Hobson-Jobson: The Anglo-Indian Dictionary for comparison with their probable counterparts in the ancient temples of Corinth or those mentioned in the Old Testament.

Devipaksha: It is the waxing phase of the moon which comes in the month of *Ashwin* as per Hindu calendar. It is believed that Goddess Durga, along with her family of Ganesha, Laxmi, Saraswati and Kartikeya, starts Her journey to Earth on this day.

Dhaak: Dhaak is a huge membranophone instrument of cylindrical or barrel shape used in India during the religious festivals. The hide covering the mouth is beaten with wooden sticks to produce the rhythmic sound.

Dhunuchi Naach: A dance carrying an incense burner during a religious festival.

Dol: A large corn bin made of straw, bamboo slips.

Dol-mancha: A designated area to play with colours on Dol Utsav.

Dr. Jekyll and Mr. Hyde: Robert Louis Stevenson's famous novel *The Strange Case of Dr. Jekyll and Mr. Hyde* (1886) that revolves around the theme of 'doppelganger'.

Dumdum, Ichhapur, Kashipur/Cossipore, Khardaha: Towns in West Bengal, close to Calcutta.

Dwiragaman: The ceremony of a newly wed bride's coming for the second time to her husband's house from her parental abode.

Gamchha: Thinly woven, net-like linen cloth piece to wipe oneself.

Ganjee: A vest, worn by Indian male, under the shirt.

Godagari: Godagari is an 'Upazilla' or an administrative region in Rajshahi District, Bangladesh. Situated on the western borders of Bangladesh, the upazilla is dissected by the River Padma.

Haat: Open-air market.

Harilooth: Refers to the custom of singing hymns and praises of the lord while distributing sweets among the common people.

Hawai mithai: Candyfloss.

Hijal: Popularly known as an Indian oak.

Hilsa: An oil-rich fish, it is much in demand not only in the Indian subcontinent but also among the diaspora. Hilsa is the national fish of Bangladesh, and its exports provide one of the highest revenues for the country. This explains why hilsa is even referred to as the silver crop of water.

Jagrata: Refers to the belief in Hindus that their deities are more active in listening and granting their wishes.

Jamai-Sasthi: (A ritual where the mother-in-law prays for a healthy life of the son-in-law).

Jamat e Islami: Set up in 1941 as an Islamic political organization in colonial India by Abul Ala Maududi, the Jamat e Islami went on to become the largest Islamic political party in Bangladesh, particularly after the Liberation War in 1971.

Janab: Mister, according to common parlance of the Muslims.

Janmastami: The eighth lunar day of the dark fortnight of the month of Bhadra when Krishna was born.

Jharna: A container full of water is kept above the idol with a hole in it, so that the water drips on the idol.

Kachhari Ghar: Office room – a room used for officiating the entire activity of a landowner's estate.

Kadma: A kind of hard sweet made of sugar.

Kamla: A daily labourer.

Kamranga: An edible sour fruit.

Kansor: A crash cymbal like musical instrument often played in religious festivals.

Kantha: Light quilt, generally made of torn clothes.

Kapotaksha, Ichhamati: Well-known rivers of Bangladesh.

Kartabaap: A term of reverence to a senior fellow.

Katha or Cottah: A measure of land having 720 sq. feet; 1/20 of a bigha.

Kathak thakur: Professional narrator of scriptural and mythological stories.

Kaviraaj: A doctor who prescribed herbal medicine for the patients' cure.

Keora: Keora, or Kewda is an extract distilled from the flower of the Pandanus plant, and is used to add flavour to South Asian cuisine. It grows well in coastal areas.

Keya: Pandanus tectorius.

Khir: An Indian dish of sweet rice pudding.

Khokon: In Bengali households, Khokon is a common nickname, denoting a boy. Here the name of the narrator is Ratan, but his nickname is Khokon.

Komal Gandhar: Literally meaning a soft note on a sharp scale. It is a 1961 Bengali film written and directed by legendary filmmaker Ritwik Ghatak from Calcutta, India.

Koyetbel: A shelled fruit with sour pulp, akin to the wood apple.

Kuladevata: House deity. A deity worshipped for generations in the household).

Kush: Kush is a form of grass which has long been used in many traditions as a sacred plant. This was specifically recommended by Lord Krishna in the *Bhagavad Gita* as part of the ideal seat for meditation.

Lathi: A long fat stick, mostly used for self defence.

Lakhsmi: The Hindu goddess of wealth and prosperity.

Lungi: A cloth worn by Indian male, for covering the part of his body, from the waist to the feet.

Magha: Tenth month of Bengali calendar when it is late winter in the region.

Mahalaya: It is an auspicious day for Bengalis, observed seven days before the Durga Puja which is the greatest festival of the Bengali people. Mahalaya is the beginning of Devipaksha, and also the last day of the Pitri Paksha when Hindus offer homage in the remembrance of their deceased ancestors.

Mamdo: The ghost of one who was a Muslim before his death.

Mandap: A pavilion (usually with four sides open) for assembling together for the purpose of worship or meeting adjacent to a temple building.

Matum: Song of lamentation, an integral part of Muharram festival.

Maya: Etymologically, 'Maya' would mean magic or illusion. It is a basic concept of Hindu philosophy, found in the Advaita (Nondualist) school of Vedanta. By extension of connotations however, and in the sense of its present usage, Maya would signify a powerful psychosomatic force that fosters the illusion of the phenomenal world being real. In Sohrab Hossain's use it is not as much a religious concept, as it is a cultural appropriation that signifies the liminality of the human mind poised between the interstices of metaphysical existence.

Miyan Bhai: Etymologically derived from Persian, the word *Miyan* usually denotes a respectable, high-ranking Muslim man. In Bengali the rich and the powerful Muslim men are often addressed as *Miyan*, occasionally being combined with bhai (brother) implying deference, affection or flattery. Occasionally, it is also used satirically or ingratiatingly.

Mukunda Das: Mukunda Das, born as Yajneshwar De (22nd February, 1878 - 18th May, 1934), was a Bengali writer and a ballad poet (charan kabi), who composed the patriotic play (jatra) called Matripuja.

Munim: Rent-collector.

Murdabad: Opposite to Zindndabad. 'Murda' means dead. This slogan is raised to cry down something we do not support. The English equivalent is 'Down with'

Nare takbir: Nara-e-takbir, literally 'loud shout—God (Allah) the Greatest'.

Nere: A slang, pejorative term, often used by the Bengali Hindus for Bengali Muslims.

Paathshala: Rural pre-primary schools.

Panchagabya: Five articles received from a cow i.e. curd, milk, ghee, cow-dung and urine. These were used for rituals related to expiation or purification from sin.

Panjabi: A loose-fitting and long upper garment.

Panwala: Seller of betel leaves, usually one folded cylindrically with small pieces of bêtel-nut and chewing tobacco etc. within folds. This is chewed, for the juice of betel leaves is believed to increase digestive power.

Partition of Bengal and Foreign Goods Boycott Movement: The Banga-bhanga birodhi andolon or the Movement against the Partition of Bengal was organised to oppose tooth and nail the Partition of Bengal proposed by the contemporary Viceroy of India, Lord Curzon, in 1905. And the Foreign Goods-Boycott Movement refers to the act of boycotting foreign, especially, British produce and imports to register protests against that ostensible partition of Bengal. On 16 October, the date from which that division was to be administered, a strike was called throughout the country. Under the leadership of Rabindranath Tagore, a huge bare-foot procession went to the Ganges for a dip and tied *rakhi* in each other's hand irrespective of class, race and religion.

Pateel: A round earthen vessel used chiefly for cooking.
Pitha: A kind of sweet cake made of flour or rice-paste.
Pithe: Pithe or Bonpitha (Chrysophyllum roxburghii) is the fruit of the plant family Sapotaceae. It is brownish to purplish black in colour and ripens to yellow. It is a soft juicy fruit that easily flattens out, and is abundantly found in the Assam valley and parts of Bengal as well.
Poite: Sacred thread in Hinduism. Only Brahmins are allowed to wear this.
Poush: Ninth month in the Bengali calendar spanning from mid-December to mid-January.
Pujo or Eid: Two most important religious ceremonies of Hindus and Muslims respectively.
Quran Sharif: The sacred religious text of Islam.
Rajakar: An anti-Bangladesh paramilitary force during the Bangladesh Liberation War in 1971.
Ranga thakuma: 'Thakuma' means grandmother on the paternal side, while 'Ranga' denotes the fifth position in order of age in case of brothers or sisters.
Rangeela: Drawing upon the cultural connotations of 'Maya', rangeela (literally meaning colourful) here implies the land of immense physical diversity and its commensurate psychological variedness that abounds the land of Bengal. The character is evidently thinking of Bengal and Bengalis as indivisible entities.
Ranri: Widow in a derogatory sense.
Rarh Bangla: A region of plain lands in Bengal. The region spreads to the Chhota Nagpur Plateau on the West and the Ganges Delta on the East.
Rasa: an important Hindu festival.
Sai: Female companion.
Saitan: The monster.
Salgram Stone: A piece of stone, symbolic of Lord Narayana, kept by the Brahmins
Samkhya-Smrititirtha: A title awarded to one who is well-versed in the philosophy of Samkhya and the knowledge of Smriti or the scriptures composed by Manu and others.
Seija Babu: A colloquial variation of Sejo *Babu*—meaning the third son of the family in order of seniority in a generation having more than three sons.

Seija Bou: A colloquial variation of Sejo Bou—meaning the wife of the third son of the family in order of seniority in a generation having more than three sons.
Shala: A common swear word. The nearest English equivalent could be bloody.
Shalik: A kind of small yellow-beaked singing bird of the myna group.
Shapla and kalmishaak: Edible aquatic plants.
Shehnai: A wooden wind instrument with a double reed at one end and a metal or a wooden flared bell at the other end. It is played at rites and rituals.
Shiuli: A tree with small, lovely while and orange flowers blooming in autumn.
Shradhha: Last rites ceremony in memory of a deceased person as per Hindu custom.
Shravana: The fourth month of the Bengali Calendar, one of the months belonging to the Rainy season in Bengal.
Sidhe: A basketful of rice, lentils, oil, and vegetables.
Simon Commission: The British Parliament constituted a Commission (1928) that included seven British Members of the Parliament under the chairmanship of Sir John Simon for framing future constitutional reforms for India. Despite severe nation-wide protests against this 'all white' Commission, it submitted its report in 1930 about governance related issues.
Sitala: A Hindu Goddess who is worshipped as the presiding deity of pox and measles.
Sonar Bangla: Amar Sonar Bangla ("My golden Bengal, I love you"), composed by Rabindranath Tagore is the national anthem of Bangladesh.
Sondhi Puja: Sondhi Puja is one of the most important rituals of worshipping goddess Durga as Chamunda. The last twenty-four minutes of the Asthami and the first twenty-four minutes of the Navami is regarded as Sandhikshan (transition). This is the exact moment when Goddesses Durga played the notorious pair of Chand and Munda, the two allies of Mahishasur.
Supari: Betel nuts were often used as a medium of financial exchange in rural Bengal

Swadeshi: It refers to a political movement in British India that gave a call to use goods produced indigenously and boycott foreign, especially goods produced in Britain. People associated with the movement were also called 'swadeshi.'

Tabure-boat: One type of wooden-boat that had some kind of "chhai" or roof over the head of the passengers. Narail and some other districts of Bangladesh had the tradition of making good boats like this. Once popularly used in Bangladesh, it is now considered to be almost extinct.

Tafon: A knee length gown tied at the waist by a belt.

The Ansar force: A paramilitary force, formed as the 'East Pakistan Ansars' in 1948, it was deployed at the border to stop smuggling and other illegal acts by the emigrants. In 1965 it was used to support the Pakistani army during the Indo-Pakistan War. However, in the Bangladesh Liberation War in 1971 it largely supported the Bangladesh forces.

Tiley-khaja: Sweet made of sesame.

Tota: A reel on a fishing rod.

Uludhwani: A sound used by the Hindu women during a festive occasion.

Unun: Earthen oven, used to be seen in all the rural households in India.

Vaishnob: A man devoted to Lord Vishnu.

Vedantabagish: A title awarded to someone who has mastered the knowledge of the Vedanta or philosophical doctrines of the Upanishads.

Yavana: In pre-modern Bengali the word was used to designate the Muslims and the *mlechhas* or those who were outside the system comprising the four castes of Hindu society; in modern Bengali it refers to the Muslims, the Christians or usually non-Hindus.

Yudhisthira: In the *Mahabharata*, Yudhisthira is the son of Kunti by Dharma (as her husband Pandu was cursed to be impotent). As the son of Dharma (one meaning of the word dharma is truth), Yudhisthira was singularly committed to truth. 'Yudhisthirer baccha' or offspring of Yudhishira is said ironically to describe one who poses to be honest.

Acknowledgements

We express our gratitude to Mr Adhir Biswas and Mrs Anima Biswas of Gangchil publishers for their kind permission to translate and include select stories from the Bengali anthology, *Deshbhager Galpa: Rakta, Bedona o Smritir Alekhya* in the present volume. We are also grateful to Mr Sadhan Chattopadhyay, the editor of the anthology, for facilitating the contact with the authors and their heirs, wherever necessary. We are also indebted to him for his permission to translate his story and include it in the present anthology.

We express our heartfelt thanks to Mr Sushil Saha, the editor of *Dui Banglar Deshbhager Akshan* (2019) published by Sopan, Kolkata, and Joyjit Mukherjee, the publisher, for their kind permission to translate a couple of stories from the volume for this edition.

Our debt to the authors and their heirs runs deep. Without their kind permission and encouragement, it won't have been possible for us to bring out the volume. First of all, we would like to acknowledge our gratefulness to the authors including Late Hasan Azizul Huq, Late Debesh Ray, Ashis Sanyal, Sadhan Chattopadhyay, Adhir Biswas, Sailen Sarkar, Jatin Bala, Kapil Krishna Thakur, Devi Prasad Sinha, Anil Ghosh, Amit Mukhopadhyay, Goutam Aalee, Niharul Islam and Ahana Biswas. At the same time, we are indebted to the heirs of the authors for extending their fullest support to the completion of our project: Gautam Bhaduri, nephew of Late Satinath Bhaduri, Tapasya Ghosh, daughter of Late Satyapriya Ghosh, Meghendra Banerjee, son of Late Dipendranath Bandyopadhyay, Dr Subhasis Bandyopadhyay, son of Late Atin Bandyopadhyay, Munia Bari, wife of Late Soharab Hossain, among others. We are also grateful to Samaresh Ray, Durba Bhattacharya, Dr Maharshi Sarkar and Dr Jayanta Kumar Mondal, among others.

Our gratitude to the translators is inestimable. All of them have busy schedules. Even then they have devoted their precious time to the challenging task of translation and have given their best efforts to do justice to the original texts.

We are indebted to Mr Arkaprabha Biswas, Junior Editor, Niyogi Books, for his meticulous editing of the stories and related matters.

We are grateful to Mr Nirmal Kanti Bhattacharjee, Editorial Director of Niyogi Books, for helping us at every step and guiding us in the right direction to translate our project which we undertook in 2018 into a reality.

And finally, we are immensely grateful to Mrs Tultul Dey Niyogi, Co-Publisher, and all those associated with Niyogi Books, New Delhi, for their help and support to make the book see the daylight.